MAGIC,
MYSTERY,
AND
SCIENCE

MAGIC, MYSTERY, AND SCIENCE

The Occult in Western Civilization

Dan Burton and David Grandy

INDIANA
University Press
Bloomington & Indianapolis

Publication of this book is made possible in part with the assistance of a Challenge Grant from the National Endowment for the Humanities, a federal agency that supports research, education, and public programming in the humanities.

This book is a publication of

Indiana University Press
601 North Morton Street
Bloomington, Indiana 47404-3797 USA

http://iupress.indiana.edu

Telephone orders	800-842-6796
Fax orders	812-855-7931
Orders by e-mail	iuporder@indiana.edu

The paper used in this publication meets the minimum requirements of American National Standard for Information Sciences—Permanence of Paper for Printed Library Materials, ANSI Z39.48-1984.

Manufactured in the United States of America

Library of Congress Cataloging-in-Publication Data

Burton, Dan.
  Magic, mystery, and science : the occult in Western civilization / Dan Burton and David Grandy.
    p. cm.
Includes bibliographical references and index.
  ISBN 978-0-253-34372-7 (alk. paper)
  1. Occultism—History. I. Grandy, David. II. Title.
  BF1411.B885 2004
  133'.09—dc21

                  2003012243

  ISBN 978-0-253-21656-4 (pbk. : alk. paper)
2 3 4 5 6   13 12 11 10 09 08

TO

Edward Grant,

Mentor and Friend

Some of the scholars, whose work contributed to our modern scientific age, found magic, alchemy, and astrology no less stimulating than the new interests in mathematical abstraction, observation, and experiment. Today we find it easy—and necessary—to separate "science" from occult interests, but many could not.

—ALLEN G. DEBUS, *Man and Nature in the Renaissance*

Contents

ACKNOWLEDGMENTS

Many people have helped bring this book to conclusion. Chief among them is Distinguished Professor Edward Grant of Indiana University, who first alerted us to historical connections between science and various occult practices such as astrology, alchemy, and Spiritualism. We also are indebted to Robert Sloan, Sue Havlish, Laurie Lawrie, Kendra Boileau Stokes, and Miki Bird, whose editorial encouragement, insight, and patience added much to both this book and the enjoyment of writing it. We are most grateful to Joel Silver, Sue Presnell, Becky Cape, and Margaret Baube of the Lilly Library (IU's rare book and manuscript library), who assisted with the finding of texts and illustrations. Many other good people at many libraries aided us, including Sue Nazworth, Wayne O'Neal, and Dr. G. Garry Warren of the University of North Alabama Library; Jim Gravois of the RBD Library of Auburn University; Linda McRae of Phil Cambell College Library; and librarians at Indiana University Bloomington's Main Library and the Harold B. Lee Library of Brigham Young University. Thanks also to Carl M. Johnson, Director of the Copyright Licensing Office of the Harold B. Lee Library of Brigham Young University, for his expert advice regarding intellectual property issues.

We also thank the Indiana University School of Continuing Studies for sponsoring an earlier version of this book as an independent studies course learning guide. Paul Bickley, Linda Yeskie, Cheryl Smith, Marty Byro, June

Solomon, and Dr. Frank Disilvestro helped with the development of that guide, and Lisa Bidwell arranged for the loan of illustrations as this book went to press. The professional artistry of IU Photographic Services' Paul Riley was also of immense help.

We also express deep gratitude for those graduate students and faculty in IU's Department of History and Philosophy of Science who aided us, including Alice Dreger, Arthur Field, Spiro Georgakopoulos, Matthew Goodrum, Noretta Koertge, Doug LaBarr, James Mattingley, Tom McMullen, William Newman, Peter Sobol, and Julianne Tuttle. So, too, thanks go to W. David Lewis and Milissa Ellison-Murphree of Auburn University for their help. And, of course, the faculty and many of the students of our respective departments at the University of North Alabama and Brigham Young University have given us tremendous support and encouragement—thank you all.

Special thanks also go to Marc-Charles Ingerson, who indefatigably checked sources, proofread chapters, tracked down and reproduced illustrations, clarified technical issues, improved the text with cogent suggestions, and together with his wife, Sarah, created the book's comprehensive index.

We reserve our greatest thanks for our wives, Donna and Janet, for their unfailing support in this and many other seemingly unending endeavors—they continuously provide both magic and mystery to our lives. *Finitum est—Deo gratias.*

MAGIC,
MYSTERY,
AND
SCIENCE

INTRODUCTION

WONDERFUL SECRETS

The ultimate goal of science is to produce a theory of everything, which has been likened to throwing on the light switch in a dark room.[1] This optimistic simile recalls H. G. Wells's image of science, given more than a hundred years ago. No one ever championed science with greater vigor than Wells, but even as a young man he sensed that science was not a perfect instrument of illumination:

> Science is a match that man has just got alight. He thought he was in a room—in moments of devotion, a temple—and that his light would be reflected from and display walls inscribed with wonderful secrets and pillars carved with philosophical systems wrought in harmony. It is a curious sensation, now that the preliminary sputter is over and the flame burns up clear, to see his hands lit and just a glimpse of himself and the patch he stands on visible, and around him, in place of all that human comfort and beauty he had anticipated—darkness still.[2]

The metaphor is arresting. Perhaps we are not ready for the conclusion. Certainly the characterization of the room in which the match of science burns is odd, for scientists are thought to be impartial observers, not devotees in a temple. Still, the metaphor rings true for anyone who has attended to the human side of science. Walls inscribed with wonderful secrets may call up images of Indiana Jones deciphering sacred Hebrew characters and Egyptian hieroglyphs in order to find the Ark of the Covenant, but under different circumstances the runic markings will take the form of mathematical formulae or seemingly truth-laden expressions like "ontogeny recapitulates phylogeny." Never mind that no secret, once unlocked, seems to remain persuasive forever. Walls of wonderful secrets, whether real or imagined, draw us onward toward the promise of enlightenment.

This book is about some of those wonderful secrets. At various times alchemy, astrology, numerology, Cabala, theosophy, and a host of other understandings have stirred the human imagination. For a while at least, each has carried its devotees to the brink of apparent omniscience, prompting them to wonder, as Dr. Faust did upon studying the sign of the macrocosm, "Am I a god? All grows so clear to me!"[3] But then, it seems, the vision grew dark. In any event, omniscience and undiluted happiness did not follow in its wake.

Where is the key that opens the door to truth? Rejecting the view that nature is partly opaque to the human intellect, the philosopher René Descartes proposed that truth is grasped as the mind proceeds in a logical manner from one "clear and distinct thought" to the next. In an ideal world this might be the case, but in the present world it seems that "clear and distinct thoughts" are hard to come by, or at least hard to sustain for very long. A Romantic such as the poet William Wordsworth would probably say that this is because we are fuzzy thinkers at heart—the heart blurring and softening the sharp, hard-edged thoughts of the head. One might propose as well—and perhaps this is what H. G. Wells had in mind—that our best theories of reality are not so much instruments by which we disperse darkness as means of keeping darkness at bay. Going further, we might even suggest that the match or candle of human understanding casts shadows or is infected with darkness itself; as one thinker put it, we labor "after light with tools of darkness."[4]

In any event, the inevitable fact of darkness in the world projects us into the *occult*, which generally means hidden, secret, darkened, or dark. If that were all it meant, perhaps it would not tug on so many, but it also may mean supernatural and paranormal, and so we find ourselves hoping that some ethereal light will fall upon walls of wonderful secrets. This interplay of light and darkness gives us the shadow world or twilight zone that we normally associate with the occult. But it also reminds us of our true nature and condition: we spend much of our time in darkness, either because the sun has set or because we need the private madness of our nightly dreams to preserve our public sanity. In brief we are amphibians. On the one hand, we like the finite, solid ground of established fact and rule; Henry David Thoreau said he wanted a world he could not "put his foot through."[5] On the other hand, we also often aspire to a realm of larger possibility, wherein life becomes more than fact and rule. This is why, according to Thoreau, there will always be talk of bottomless lakes: people nurse a hope in the infinite.[6]

For these reasons, we feel the occult is a vitally important subject. Scholars increasingly see it as a "third current," no less important to the shaping of Western civilization than Greek rationalism and Judeo-Christianity.[7] Certainly some people will shun it, for it evokes disturbing, even sinister, images. Others will find themselves drawn to the occult in much the same manner a child listens to a fairy tale that is both thrilling and chilling. Our approach is twofold: both to treat the material as interesting in and of itself, and to see it as relevant to contemporary concerns. No occult topic is so obscure or laughable that it cannot be made compelling once the motivating assumptions are understood. Indeed, readers may find their noses tweaked at times upon discovering that some "ridiculous" notion from the past has a contemporary analogue that they rarely if ever question.

This analogical linkage across worldviews suggests that modern culture never quite leaves behind as much of the past as one might suppose. We propose further that what is left behind is more the result of subjective choice than reasoned analysis. Science does not systematically disprove occult theses; as a general rule, it freely elects not to consider them. There are good reasons for this. For one, even the tentative introduction (or re-introduction) of occult entities would infuse the world with vast meaning, and meaning does not yield readily to the reductive methods of science. It is not surprising, then, that Bertrand Russell, a thinker immersed in early-twentieth-century science, concluded that "the whole temple of Man's achievement must inevitably be buried beneath the debris of a universe in ruins."[8] Eliminated from the outset for reasons of objective clarity and group consensus, meaning or cosmic purpose could hardly emerge *ex nihilo* at some higher turn of the deliberative spiral.

For Russell, that higher turn was the second law of thermodynamics or the principle of entropy. To a scientifically conditioned culture, this law—the inevitable degradation of order in the cosmos—seems omnipotent. One might call it the rule of death in a universe where life is the mysterious and temporary exception. But this characterization makes sense within a universe that is deemed lifeless *in the first place*. Yet could the world be reckoned living and intelligent without any loss of plausibility? This, of course, is the occult hypothesis and it is unscientific only in the sense that it resists the assumption of a lifeless cosmos—not because there is no evidence in its favor. An occultist would say there is abundant evidence, chief of which are the life processes that allow people like Russell to affirm the triumph of death. A truly lifeless universe would permit no such utterance.

DEFINITIONS AND SCOPE

As suggested earlier, the occult resists straightforward definition. It denotes darkness and mystery but in the same breath gives promise of light and understanding. Sometimes that light is of a supernatural character, but this is not always the case. Alchemy, alien abductions, and parapsychology, it may be argued, have nothing to do with the supernatural: they do not necessarily bring God into their explanations of reality.

Nor do all occult disciplines adopt a secretive, self-concealing posture. Some have devotees who are happy to share their understanding with others. Their secrets are open. One of the authors recalls his first experience at a UFO meeting. People from all walks of life talked freely and calmly of extraterrestrials controlling earthly media and decision making. No attempt to identify skeptics, no initiation ceremonies, and no inner circles of privileged believers. Just matter-of-fact discussion about how to thwart hostile space aliens while establishing friendly relations with other, more benevolent species. If there was a cloak over the meeting, it was there because of outside indifference, not self-imposed secrecy.

At times, of course, secrecy is a mark of occult systems. A magician, for example, may wish to keep certain ceremonies and formulas from public scrutiny. Why? Often for reasons of power. Certain rites and recipes, it is thought, give one control or influence over the environment and other people. Should mastery of these instruments of power become widespread, the magician loses her advantage. But, again, this alone cannot define the occult, because controlling nature is a goal that the occult shares with Western technology (applied science). Moreover, some believers in visiting life forms seem to find comfort in not having power but, rather, in leaving the ultimate control over humanity in other, seemingly more capable hands.

Even when power is surrendered, as it were, to higher beings, there often remains yet another aspect of the occult experience—precious knowledge or *gnosis*. Knowing that one's destiny is folded into a larger plan or intelligence confers a sense of spiritual buoyancy that seems priceless. The occult believer may be small as to material wealth and worldly status, but he "knows" that he is part of something vast. In this regard, the occult is like religion. Both may offer, or purport to offer, "the pearl of great price."

In brief, it is impossible to define the occult in a way that sets it completely apart from religion, science, and technology. This sharing and overlapping of borders is hardly surprising when the matter is given historical consideration. Take Plato, for example. His celebration of human reason strikes a scientific chord, but he believed that that faculty, if properly exercised, grants one spiritual or otherworldly understanding. Now mix in his story of Atlantis or his story of Er, a soldier whose "near-death experience" details what happens between death and reincarnation. Elements of religion, science, and the occult interblend in Plato's thinking, but not because he is trying to combine distinct categories. Of course, some categories of knowledge existed in his time and some were taking shape, but Plato assumed they were naturally linked together, so there was nothing artificial or "eclectic," as one might say, about bringing them into mutual relation.

Witness Plato's statement that "as the eyes are designed to look up at the stars, so are the ears to hear harmonious motions; and these are sister sciences."[9] What modern person would listen to and study music to enhance her understanding of astronomy? And on what modern basis could such a connection be justified? For Plato, the answer was clear: both music and the motions of the stars are informed by a cosmic harmony, and each expresses that harmony to a different sense.

Much could be said about this view, but let us briefly note that this is the kernel for the idea of the music of the spheres, a very long-lived tradition that persisted into the seventeenth century and fired the imagination of Johannes Kepler, whose three planetary laws marked the beginning of modern astronomy. Today, mention of the music of the spheres elicits blank stares and further explanation only contributes to the initial perplexity: tones issuing forth from planets as they move through their orbits and blending together to produce a divine harmony? What sort of balderdash is this? For better or for worse, it is the sort that often has come to be equated with the occult. Because modern categories of knowledge are often so distinct as to seem independent of each other, we immediately become suspicious when broad connections are made between them. Yet pre-moderns looked for such connections and correspondences almost instinctively, believing that all true stories and insights were, as two noted scholars put it, "functions of a whole" and thus were capable of resonating harmoniously at various levels with other expressions of truth.[10]

In this book, we hope to recapture this older way of knowing and experiencing the world. Our approach is topical and for the most part, chronological. But the reader should not assume from the semi-chronological ordering that we are trying to tell a seamless, progressive story. The idea of incremental continuity is more at home with science, which adheres to the dictum that *natura non facit saltum.* In other words, no miraculous surprises, no bolts from the blue. Going further, the idea of steady uphill advancement—the idea of progress—draws much of its credibility from science, which in recent centuries has often been touted as the one and only engine of human progress. At the very least, science has inspired hope in the future and thereby shifted attention away from the past. By contrast, occult beliefs frequently direct attention back to the past, back to the fabled wisdom of the ancients. This makes it impossible to craft a narrative that has a great deal of intrinsic forward momentum. More likely, one will find interesting variations on familiar motifs, so the factual rehearsal begins to resemble a fugue with its growing succession of given themes.

In other words, the threads of continuity from one chapter to the next are often not of a developmental or causal nature. Rather—and this is consistent with the occult outlook—those threads tend to be resonances. Of course, some historical connections can be made, but what is generally more important from an occult point of view is that a *new age* is dawning. Or, that a new age is re-dawning after a long night of darkness or historical discontinuity. The fabled wisdom or fabled era of the past is returning and not just in the guise of pale historical memories. Watching the sunrise at Stonehenge on Midsummer's

Day, the modern Druid feels an intense kinship with his ancient spiritual progenitors. Never mind that, from a scientific and historical point of view, such people never lived. And never mind that thousands of years now stand between the Druid and the enlightened culture she imagines. At the "cosmic moment" when the sun rises above the heel stone, the obstacles of science and historical distance evaporate. Two moments begin to vibrate in sympathy, as it were.

Suffice it to say, the occult believer is ready to leap into the deep past to find truth, trusting in the dictum that first is best. The very old cultures, such as Stonehenge and Egypt, are felt to be hoary with wisdom. This presents a challenge for a book of this sort, because the people who built Stonehenge and the Great Pyramid may have had motives other than those assigned by modern occultists. With practices such as astrology, alchemy, and theosophy, one can rely on practitioners who self-consciously embrace recognizably occult principles, but is it proper to identify ancient Egypt as an occult culture simply because it attracts modern occultists? The answer, of course, is no. Better to try to understand it on its own terms, insofar as we can grasp them. Surprisingly, however, some of those terms have an occult quality. This is not to agree with modern New Agers who argue, for example, that pyramids focus cosmic energy. The similarities or connections are to be found instead at the assumptive level, which most New Agers miss completely because they little appreciate the broad shifts in thought introduced by modern science. Consequently, even as they resist science, their minds in many ways remain colonized by science.

One does not truly begin to grasp the occult until one learns to peel back the scientific assumptions that overlay the modern experience of nature. Of course, occult wisdom sees the world through its peculiar set of assumptions, but these can hardly be rendered plausible as long as one retains the thinking cap of science. In this book, we try to remove this cap quickly by first examining ancient Egyptian religion. Whether or not that religion expressed occult tenets, it certainly is capable of challenging modern assumptions about nature. Furthermore, as just noted, ancient Egypt is a magnet for many modern occultists. From Egypt we move on to Renaissance magic, a leap that allows us to lay a foundation for much of what follows. Although Renaissance magic comes after the rise of astrology, alchemy, numerology, demonology, and so on, it gathers together the central principles of all these occult practices and thus offers a common framework within which to explain and understand them. Given that framework, we then backtrack to the practices themselves.

After the Renaissance and the Scientific Revolution of the seventeenth century, Western society became increasingly enamored of things scientific. The occult followed this shift, conforming itself in many instances to the discourse and criteria of science to establish its legitimacy. In the nineteenth century, phrenology, hypnotism, and spiritualism adopted a scientific posture. As we move into the twenty-first century, ufology, parapsychology, and near-death experience research similarly claim the mantle of science. This might seem odd, given the differences that separate science and the occult, but, as a first approximation, we offer the following explanation: as a worldview, science for most people has simply become too authoritative to think their way out of. Although they may resist certain scientific "truths," they know of only one way to publicly and unapologetically play the game of truth and that is the scientific way. In this respect, the modern occultist is like the modern creationist who does not trust any mythic or non-scientific interpretation of Genesis. Truth must be packaged scientifically or not at all.

The latter half of the book is devoted to some of these scientifically conditioned expressions of the occult, which, to believers, are still wonderful secrets. Science may dampen the occult in some ways but the occult has the ability to react back on science. Moreover, since 1900, certain classical scientific assumptions of nature have been undermined by science itself, and some people have read this as proof that science is moving—or should be moving—toward Zen-like elaborations of nature. Combine this sentiment with the post-modernist impulse that is gaining momentum in the West and one has all the makings of a new era (if not a New Age) in which the occult will play a major role. We hope this book will help readers prepare for this era.

INTRODUCTION

1

EGYPTIANS
AND THE
OCCULT

Plato and Aristotle considered God as
abstracted or distinct from the natural
world. But the Egyptians considered
God and nature as making one whole,
or all things together as making one
universe. In doing which they did not
exclude the intelligent mind, but considered it as containing all things.

—George Berkeley[1]

Ancient Egypt has been seen as a source of magical wisdom for millennia—
from before the time that Moses battled, miracle for miracle, with Egyptian
magicians, to Aleister Crowley, a modern Englishman who supposedly communed with spiritual powers from within a pyramid. Part of this fascination
with Egyptian wisdom surely must come from its extreme antiquity. By the
time of Moses, the pyramids had stood for over one thousand years. And, by
the time of King David of Israel (circa 1000 B.C.), almost as much time stood
between him and the builders of the pyramids as between us and the life of
Jesus. By the time of the Greeks such as Herodotus and Plato, Egyptian civilization was both very ancient and but a shadow of its former self. The Greeks,
and later the Romans, held ancient Egyptian wisdom in high regard. Even
today its mystique has scarcely diminished, if we can judge by popular culture's
embrace of ankhs, pyramids, and other Egyptian esoterica.

Widespread fascination with a culture, however, need not imply general
understanding. Indeed, Egypt is somewhat sphinx-like in its reluctance to
speak to us across the centuries, and the elusive tones in which it does speak

are not easily grasped by the modern imagination. No doubt this contributes to its popular appeal. A dark, smoky glass is more interesting to look through than a transparent one that leaves the all-too-familiar world unchanged. The trouble with the dark glass, however, is that it allows us to be speculative or creative in the same old way—and thus not be creative at all! Many tend to read their own pet images into the strange play of shadows and all too often end up talking about space aliens and technological wizardry. These things may reflect the hopes and fears of modern civilization, but Egyptian civilization was responding to a different set of concerns.

Our first task, then, is to try to view the world through an Egyptian lens. In brief, we must learn to think like an Egyptian, which means we must unlearn some of our cherished and often unquestioned assumptions about reality. It is not enough simply to present the Egyptian worldview; at the same time, we must take stock of our own worldview. Throughout this chapter (and this book), therefore, we tack back and forth between the familiar model of reality that modern Western culture embraces and earlier models that no longer command our thinking. This allows us to see others vis-à-vis ourselves; we become aware of the crack in our own mirror while trying to decipher imperfect reflections from the past.

A CRACKED MIRROR?

Living as we do at a time when science fixes so many things, one might insist that it can grant us an unbiased (or "uncracked") reflection of the past. The trouble is that science nurtures its own biases. This is not an indictment of science, just a recognition of its human origin and consequent fallibility. If it did not arise from its unique predilections, it would not be the powerful tool that it is. However, it is not free of paradox. It purports to view things objectively or dispassionately, but, ironically, this claim is often *passionately* defended and has now been dismantled in certain quarters of science (notably, quantum physics).

Human passion is the fault line—the potential crack—that runs through any intellectual system, and passion is what turns scientific objectivity into a firmly held myth. Loren Eisley touched on this point when he wrote: "Sir Francis Bacon . . . once spoke of those drawn into some powerful circle of thought as 'dancing in little rings like persons bewitched.' Our scientific models do simulate a sort of fairy ring, which, once it has encircled us, is hard to view objectively."[2]

Here Eisley, under Bacon's inspiration (Bacon, by the way, championed science with great vigor in the seventeenth century), tellingly blurs the traditional distinction between science and magic. Science has the capacity to captivate, to mesmerize, to cast a spell. This is the old, magical way of saying things; today we are inclined to say that science conditions our thinking, and this sounds less portentous. The prudent language of science, however, may dull our sense of science's intellectual sway over modern culture. This, we hope, will be brought out as we talk about the occult vis-à-vis science. The first cannot be fully understood without occasional reference to the latter.

Three interrelated axioms of Egyptian thought which go against the grain of modern thinking will inform our subsequent discussion of Egyptian culture and religion—the round of nature, the organic universe, and the gaze of nature.

THE ROUND OF NATURE

Egyptian life was deeply immersed in the rhythms of nature. The seasons, the annual flooding of the Nile River, and the motions of the starry heavens were more than interesting phenomena to be taken in at one's leisure; they simply had to be attended to if society was to survive and flourish. Much—perhaps nearly everything—depended upon agriculture, and agriculture necessitated the constant watch of nature. Although the Egyptians developed a calendar, it was (by modern standards) rather inaccurate and consequently lost synchrony with the seasons fairly quickly. The better calendar was nature itself, and so the Egyptians attuned themselves to nature in order to know when to plant and harvest their crops. Through observation, for example, they learned that the heliacal rising of Sirius (the first rising of Sirius not obscured by the rising sun) coincided with the flooding of the Nile, and so used that coincidence of river and star to begin the rites that inaugurated their agricultural year.[3]

When we wish to know a date or a time, we look at a calendar or clock hanging on the wall, and it communicates intelligence to us. If someone were to argue against this practice and say, for example, that clock readings lack informational content and cannot be taken as evidence of a designing intelligence, we would probably dismiss that person as a kook. In the same way, the Egyptians might well dismiss us for suggesting that nature—their clock and calendar—is void of intelligence, that, as one Nobel laureate put it, "the universe [is] . . . pointless."[4] Because nature communicated intelligence to the Egyptians, spoke to them just as a clock speaks to us, it perforce had purpose and meaning.

For the ancients, wrote Mircea Eliade, the world " 'means' something, 'wants to say' something, . . . is neither mute nor opaque."[5] It is ironic that the Egyptians—living long before the invention of telecommunications technology, which promises to bring the entire planet into mutual dialogue—felt themselves to be in dialogue with the entire universe. When they looked up at the night sky, they did not see a random scattering of lights having no story value but, rather, a drama of immense significance. Now, most of us cannot play dot-to-dot with the stars very well—cannot make sense of the stars by forming constellations—but the Egyptians (along with other ancient peoples) made the connections almost instinctively and then carried them into their own lives. They were, in modern parlance, "plugged in" in a way we are not.

All this, of course, presupposes some attitudinal differences between Egyptian and modern culture, and these again seem to arise from the Egyptian propensity to take nature at face value rather than relying heavily upon mediating artifacts like clocks and calendars. For one thing, the Egyptians assumed that time was cyclical, that just as there is a round to the seasons, there is also a round to the years and the millennia. Therefore, the past is always participating in the present; the events of yesteryear invariably return as a kind of primordial reality. This strikes an odd note to the modern ear but, having built, to some extent, what Thomas Huxley called "an artificial womb in the cosmos,"[6] we have been able to buffer ourselves from nature successfully enough to forget that nature's most compelling phenomena involve cyclical patterns. Nature presents itself as a great merry-go-round. The seasons and stars go round and round, and when they return to earlier positions, it followed (at least for the Egyptians) that earlier times were being re-invoked.

By way of contrast, moderns entertain the notion of linear time. Time ticks away in a flat, homogenous way, never looping back on itself. One moment is not intrinsically different from any other; each is just numbered differently. An investigation into the origins of linear time would prove digressive, but a little reflection suggests that our modern experience of time is conditioned by the mechanical clock and its capacity to produce a steady succession of identical intervals. Our time experience thus is determined not so much by the ebb and flow of seasons, births, deaths, harvest times, and holy days but, rather, by a mathematically rigorous production of days, hours, minutes, and seconds. Mechanical time, as it is sometimes called, has been a great boon to modern science, because it allows us to quantify the processes of nature. We now have a temporal yardstick with which to measure those processes. The rub is that those processes often circle back on themselves while the yardstick—like the number line—goes on forever in a rectilinear manner. Which movement do we privilege—the endlessly linear tick tock of the mechanical clock or the circular rhythms of nature?

For ancient Egyptians, of course, there was no linear tick tock to inform their time experience. Thus time had a more qualitative, organic feel to it; some moments were intrinsically better or richer than others. The very best moments were those that allowed for the "irruption of the sacred."[7] Sunrise was one such moment, for it was mythically entangled with the creation of the world and the

EGYPTIANS AND THE OCCULT

primordial triumph of light over darkness. Henry and H. A. Frankfort tell us that in ancient Egypt:

> Each morning the sun defeats darkness and chaos, as he did on the day of creation and does, every year, on New Year's Day. These three moments coalesce; they are felt to be essentially the same. Each sunrise, and each New Year's Day, repeats the first sunrise on the day of creation; and for the mythopoeic mind each repetition coalesces with— is practically identical with—the original event.[8]

Again, a certain irony arises when we compare the ancient Egyptian experience with our own. Notwithstanding our prodigious technological achievements, we never talk as if we can return to the past. Time machines are pure fantasy, and the best we can do is to remember the past from our place in the present. But, for the Egyptians, the past was not just accessible: it was constantly breaking into the present in a larger-than-life way. The universe was a time machine (or perhaps we should say a "time organism"), a place where past and present intermingled, since nature's cyclical patterns invariably returned to time zero—the moment of creation. In flat, linear time, however, there is only horizontal advancement, so return to the past is an *a priori* impossibility.

Note that the Creation looms large in the Egyptian imagination. For most of us, the Creation is a remote event having no practical bearing on our everyday activities. It is lost in the distant past and, as far as science can say, the product of mindless forces. But for an Egyptian, the Creation was the keynote of existence and "the only event that really matter[ed] supremely."[9] And because time looped back on itself, the Creation periodically manifested itself in the seasonal renewal of nature. The unceasing miracle of life could not be separated from the creation of the world—the first was sure evidence of the immediacy of the second. Thus, as Eliade has it, ancient cultures "thirst[ed]" for the Creation, since it was a warrant of life and meaning.[10] If the Creation did not come round again every spring or every birthing season, the forces of darkness would overwhelm the world.

This helps us understand why pre-modern cultures seem so preoccupied with the past. The modern inclination is to use the future as a repository of hopes and dreams. Someday we will be there, but the past is gone forever. If, however, we were more attuned to the round of nature, we would yearn for the past (the moment of creation) to erupt into the present. And that eruption would drive home the idea that "first is best." The brand new world of the present—springtime or morning—is animated or lit up by an earlier moment from the past. It borrows its newness from the newly created world. Thus, for an Egyptian, first being (Creation) was new being and, by implication, best or true being.

MAGIC, MYSTERY, AND SCIENCE

This attitude, by the way, emerges in the early books of the Old Testament, in which humans, evidently because of their newly minted existence, live for hundreds of years. George Berkeley wrote that "[m]en in those early days were not overlaid with languages and literature. Their minds seem to have been more exercised, and less burdened, than in later ages; and, as so much nearer the beginning of the world, to have had the advantage of patriarchal lights handed down through a few hands."[11] Closer to the fount of creation, they were free of the spiritual and physical ills that would eventually overtake their descendents.

Different outlooks such as this one issue from different assumptions about reality, and to most moderns the Egyptian assumption of a self-renewing world seems implausible. That would imply an innate vitality and the eventual triumph of life over death. Implausible as this may sound to a modern thinker, it appears to be exactly what ancient Egyptians concluded from their observation of nature. The revolving seasons were nothing less than cosmic biorhythms, and the living, breathing universe was congenial to humankind's perennial hope in life after death.

THE ORGANIC UNIVERSE

Huge pyramids, extravagant burials, and carefully preserved mummies persuade most of us that the ancient Egyptians were preoccupied with death. But this is not so. They were preoccupied with *life*. Today we do not hesitate to spend thousands of dollars on chemotherapy or heart surgery to add a few extra years to our lives. Think of what we would give up for millions of extra years. In either case—whether one is a modern American or an ancient Egyptian—the hope is for a continuation of life. The difference, of course, is that we feel uncertain about life *after* death; therefore, we invest our means in the continuation of life *before* death.

How is it that the Egyptians were able to look with confidence beyond the grave? It is one thing to talk cheerfully about life after death and quite another to back up one's optimism with a sizable economic investment. For most of us, death is expensive enough, what with the embalming, the coffin, the grave marker, and the cost of a funeral service. These things we provide merely out of respect for the deceased, not in order to "launch" him or her into the next world, wherever and whatever that might be. But if we did feel that we were launching the deceased into the next world, and that the launching had to be as carefully executed as the Apollo 11 moon launch, we would be willing to invest considerably more time and money in the enterprise.

The analogy between the moon launch and an Egyptian burial ceremony is more instructive than it seems at first blush. In 1969, when the United States

EGYPTIANS AND THE OCCULT

sent the first spaceship to the moon, the big question was whether the ship would reach the moon. No one questioned whether the moon was really there. Of course, it was there—everyone could see it. An Egyptian would say the same thing about the next world. Of course it is there—everyone can see it.[12] See that milky-white band of stars stretching across the sky? That is the Celestial Nile, the abode of departed Egyptians who successfully negotiate the journey from earth to heaven.

For an Egyptian, "heaven" was not a vague and dubious reality nearly refined out of existence by theological hair-splitting and scientific abstraction. One could sensibly experience it. As Shirley Case Jackson wrote, "[t]he sky hung low in the ancient world."[13] She continues:

> Traffic was heavy on the highway between heaven and earth. Gods and spirits thickly populated the upper air, where they stood in readiness to intervene at any moment in the affairs of mortals. And demonic powers, emerging from the lower world or resident in remote corners of the earth, were a constant menace to human welfare. All nature was alive—alive with supernatural forces.[14]

Moderns of course would disagree. What the Egyptians called a supernatural life force, we in the twenty-first century would call a superstition. Science, we feel, has allowed humankind to dispel this heavy fog of ignorance, to clear the air, as it were, of gods and demons. But this evacuation of spirits, this cosmic exorcism, seems to have come with a price tag. We live in a universe that is mostly lifeless. We can appreciate the beauty of the stars, but they no longer announce themselves as gods or higher human destiny. None of us wants to leave the earth, for the earth is a tiny pocket of life in a cosmos that is mostly cold, dark, and lifeless. No wonder we are unsure about life after death: our antiseptic universe is like a hospital room, well scrubbed but sterile of larger possibility.

Earlier we mentioned that the mechanical clock has replaced the round of nature as the primary determinant of the way we experience time. We can go further with this point by observing that the modern cosmos is often characterized as the mechanical or clockwork universe. Ralph Waldo Emerson once remarked that every scientific idea begins as a poetic perception,[15] and our modern scientific worldview drew much of its inspiration from the clock. Several centuries ago it was a fascinating object, a "smart" machine with a seemingly preternatural faculty for precision, autonomy, and regularity—almost a miniature world unto itself. Given these qualities, the clock struck some thinkers as a scaled-down model of the cosmos, and that association shaped the thinking of Galileo, Kepler, Descartes, Newton, and a host of other figures who collectively transformed our understanding of the world. Whatever its

MAGIC, MYSTERY, AND SCIENCE

merits and contributions to modern society, the concept of a mechanical universe is not a very life-friendly concept. If the universe is really a big machine, or like a big machine, then how do we explain our own existence as living (non-mechanical) beings?

For an Egyptian, there was no incongruity between the world at large and one's own being: both were alive. The universe was organic, even redundant with life. Like other living things, it had been brought into existence through a sexual, reproductive process. Therefore, any particular miracle of life—say, birth or plant growth—condensed out of the greater universal miracle. This is not to say that Egyptians did not fear death. They did, but when it came to calculating the odds, the universe was on their side. It seemed to say that life is the norm and absolute death is the exception. If one was virtuous and conscientious in the observance of religious ceremony, one could expect the round of nature to catch up or exalt one's dead body to a higher life experience. After all, the universe as a living, breathing organism was not about to reject similar lesser organisms as alien objects.

No doubt there are other reasons for the Egyptian confidence in life after death, but this one goes to the heart of the difference between their model of reality and our own. For them, life was the rule and death the temporary exception. The world was bright with the fact and promise of life. Contrast that with modern thinking. To be sure, many people today believe in life after death, but this belief finds little if any encouragement from modern cosmology. Nature, as science talks about it, is not a resurrection drama in which we can invest our faith. We moderns look elsewhere for such assurance.

THE GAZE OF NATURE

In his study of the ancient Egyptians, I. E. S. Edwards wrote that they were like "a people searching in the dark for a key to truth and, having found not one but many keys . . . retaining all lest perchance the appropriate one should be discarded."[16] In brief, the Egyptians were "pack rats" of religious ideas, and this makes their religion seem contradictory and mysterious to the modern thinker who values consistency and logical coherence. The Egyptians kept everything and threw away nothing. If a new and different Creation myth was told, they did not throw away the old Creation myth but kept both. If there was a new idea about how to gain eternal life, they included the new idea with the old ones. Hence, they had what we might call multiple "backup systems" for eternal life.

We might regard this tendency to collect alternative possibilities or "keys" as a sign that, religiously speaking, the Egyptians were unsure of themselves. To a degree, this is true. They were unsure about their keys—their instruments of salvation—but apparently quite sure of salvation itself. It was there in a physically significant way, inviting their interest and challenging their ingenuity. Again, we are reminded of the Apollo 11 moon launch. The moon was there—no one doubted that. But we were not completely sure of our ability to reach the moon. Consequently, various backup systems were incorporated into the design of the spaceship. If one system failed, another would take over.

This backup-system approach to salvation might not make for a neatly organized theology, but theology (at least, formal theology) deliberately aims for neatness and coherence, and this assumes that we can back off from the phenomena under consideration to reason coolly about them. It is doubtful that the Egyptians were able to achieve this kind of distance or objectivity as they contemplated the world. Martin Buber once remarked that he could never become a theologian because he was unable to think about God in the third person.[17] God for him was not an it, he, or she, but a you or thou. Egyptologists have made the same point about the Egyptians: the thou or second-person relationship informed their religious experience.[18] Actively participating in the human drama (not distant spectators), the gods were "in your face" and consequently unable to be objectified as remote figures.

More correctly, perhaps, you were in their face. The German word *Gesicht*, meaning both "face" and "vision," reminds us that there is something revelatory about faces. The same point is communicated by *envisage:* "visage" means face or countenance but here it connotes vision. When the sun god Ra showed his face in the morning, the world lit up. Ra's seeing the world filled it with light or intelligence, and human beings fell within his field of vision. In his own words, "I am the one who openeth his eyes, and there is light."[19] Light, then, "was God seeing,"[20] and mortals felt themselves under the watch of the all-seeing eye of the sun. At night the moon and stars took over; their light was evidence of their watchful gaze. And, besides the celestial deities, there were numerous terrestrial gods who were mindful of one's activities.

For us, perhaps, this is not an appealing picture: the night—and the day—has a thousand eyes. But it seems to go with the territory of an organic universe filled with sentient beings and points up the immense distance that separates our culture from theirs. Conditioned by science, we step back from the world to view it objectively, thereby putting a third-person frame around most of our experience. Trees, rivers, stars, and other natural phenomena never adopt a second-person posture, never interrogate us as we scientifically interrogate them. When and if they do, the spell of objectivity is broken and mystical or occult possibilities open up. As the Egyptians felt themselves in conversation with the world and assumed that nature could return their gaze, they entertained occult beliefs, that is, beliefs not sanctioned by modern science.

MYTH OF OSIRIS

The myth of Osiris was the keystone of the Egyptian quest for eternal life. Just as Christians view Jesus Christ as the central figure of Christianity, so Egyptians viewed Osiris as a central figure of their religion. There are similarities between the two figures: both were models of virtuous behavior and both were savior gods who were raised from the dead. We should note, however, that Osiris may never have existed as an actual person. His reality lacks historical documentation and is fully enshrined in myth.

The principal characters in the Osiris myth are the four children of the earth and sky gods: Osiris and Isis (who are married), and Seth and Nephthys (also married). The fifth major character is the son of Osiris and Isis, Horus. Although they allude to the story frequently, the Egyptians never seem to have written a complete formal account of it. (They probably knew it so well that they saw no need to.) Therefore, our major sources for the myth are the Greeks, and the following is the story they give.

Osiris was a good and just king who ruled over all Egypt. He had taught the Egyptians the art of civilized living and was planning to teach the rest of the world as well. But Seth, his evil brother, became jealous of him and plotted to murder him. Seth secretly had Osiris measured and then made an Osiris-sized box for him, bedecked with beautiful ornaments. Later, he and his minions invited Osiris to a banquet, at which Seth brought out the beautiful box. Acting as a gracious host, Seth told the guests that whoever could fit exactly into the box got to keep it. Each of Seth's followers tried, but none of them fit exactly, so Osiris finally got in. At that moment, Seth and his followers rushed forward, slammed the lid shut on Osiris, and nailed him in.

Taking the box outside, Seth and his lackeys threw it into the Nile River. The good king Osiris drowned and eventually the box floated to the shore of Phoenicia (modern Lebanon), where a beautiful tree grew up and enclosed it. Later, when the local king was about to have this tree cut down for use as a pillar in his palace, he found the box inside. When Isis, wife of Osiris, heard of this, she traveled to Phoenicia to retrieve Osiris's body and brought it back to Egypt.

When Seth learned of Isis's act, he stole Osiris's body and cut it up into fourteen parts and buried them all over Egypt. Isis, ever the dutiful wife, searched for her husband's parts and found all but one—his sex organ, which had been eaten by a fish after Seth threw it into the Nile River. But Isis made up for the loss by fashioning a new sex organ out of clay or wood. Being a woman of great magical power, Isis was not only able to put Osiris back together again (presumably by tight wrappings), but she also hovered over him in the form of a hawk and brought him back to life.

EGYPTIANS AND THE OCCULT

Figure 1. Osiris and Isis

Thereafter, Osiris was seen as both living and dead, and this helps explain the curious manner in which he is depicted in Egyptian art. Most of his body is tightly wrapped in linen like a mummy but his head and arms are free and with the latter he holds the symbols of kingship—the staff and flail. This ambivalence also shows up in accounts of the birth of Horus, who purportedly issued from the union of Isis and Osiris's only partly revived body. Although Osiris was a resurrected king, he never returned to the land of the living (in this case, Egypt) but was always closely identified with death and the underworld, of which he was the ruler. Simply put, he embodied the death and post-death experience. His living son Horus, by contrast, embodied the pre-death (earth) experience. That is why living pharaohs were hailed as Horus but, once dead, they took on the identity of Osiris.

When he came of age, Horus avenged the death of his father by defeating Seth in battle and laying claim to the title of King of Egypt. Isis, his mother, became the supreme example for all Egyptian women. She was a queen, a very devoted wife to Osiris, a caring mother to Horus, and a wise woman with great magical powers—she, after all, had shape-shifted into a hawk and brought Osiris back to life. It was as Isis that Queen Cleopatra dressed on official occasions, thereby partaking of Isis's divine nature—perhaps even believing that she herself had become Isis.

That one could take on another's identity was a standard assumption of Egyptian thought. John Wilson talks of "a free interchange of being" resulting from the Egyptian belief that the world was made of a single substance.[21] Consequently, one thing could become another thing—not just figuratively or symbolically but literally. This was particularly important when a deceased person was launched into the underworld. Recall that Isis had replaced Osiris's sex organ with one of clay or wooden manufacture. Other body parts and even complete living bodies could be summoned into being on the same principle. Eyes painted on a coffin enabled the deceased to see beyond the coffin. Servants and other individuals essential to one's heavenly bliss were reconstituted as miniature wooden likenesses and placed in the tomb of the deceased for transport to the underworld.

If, indeed, everything were composed of the same substance, then this line of thought would not be farfetched. For us, reality and replica are separated by the unbridgeable chasm of material difference. No matter that a wax effigy of Elvis Presley looks something like the original. The effigy is wax and Elvis was flesh and blood and bone. But if we were not predisposed to make this distinction, Elvis and his many likenesses could hardly be kept apart. The blur between reality and replica would not be merely imagistic but substantive as well.

The more pressing question, of course, is how the Egyptians could be so naive as to assume that everything consists of a single substance. Recall that for

EGYPTIANS AND THE OCCULT

them the universe was organic. That is, they did not—as we do—distinguish between living and lifeless substances; everything was caught up in the process of life. Therefore, wax was not fundamentally different from flesh and blood and bone. This outlook is not so different from that of the first Greek philosophers who supposed that all of material reality originated from a single primordial element. The diverse effects of nature were thus traced back to a single substance that changed or "shape-shifted" without losing its essential character.

Commenting on these early Greek philosophers, Martin Heidegger has argued that they were the last Western thinkers for whom the world was still a unitary revelation rather than a puzzling assortment of things. They straddled the divide between myth, which tends to receive the world as a revelatory answer, and science, which puts a third-person frame around the world and treats it as a question to be answered by dint of human genius.[22] Questions generally signify that things are disconnected, at least apparently so, while answers trade in the coin of integration and coherence. Another way of putting this thought is that one good answer can clear up a multitude of questions. Perhaps because the Egyptians seem to have received the world as an answer— it, after all, spoke to them—they were inclined to see it in unitary terms. To follow Heidegger, "Being" was the revelatory substance that constituted the cosmos.

This unitary outlook (sometimes called monism) allowed for a complete or nearly complete blurring of identities. Indeed, the dead were so closely associated with Osiris that his name was attached to theirs. Where we might say "the late Mr. Jones," they would say "Osiris Jones."

THE EGYPTIAN VIEW OF SPIRIT AND THE AFTER-LIFE

The Egyptians had a complex view of what we would call the spirit. For them, the spirit (or soul) had at least three individual entities, which were released at death: the *Ka*, the *Ba*, and the *Akh*.

The *Ka*, represented by two upstretched arms, was a person's vital life force. Because people need to eat to maintain their vitality, it followed that they would need to go on eating after death. One of the purposes of the *Ka* was thus to eat food offerings brought outside the tomb for the dead. (If actual food was not available, it was painted on the walls of the tomb.) Tethered by its food-eating need, the *Ka* was free to move only among the burial chamber, the *Ka* statue (where it lived), and the offering place. While waiting for offerings, it would inhabit the *Ka* statue; when offerings came, it would enter and exit through a door painted on the wall of the tomb, the False Door.

The *Ba*, represented as a human-headed hawk, was the traveling spirit, which could assume any shape it wished (usually a human-headed hawk) and

Figure 2. Ba *flying above a mummy*

revisit the world of the living or travel across the sky in the sun god's boat. But it always returned to the tomb at night. The *Ba* was the personality of the deceased, what had made him or her different from others, and was apparently formed from the uniting of the *Ka* and the preserved physical body. Thus, the *Ba* came into existence when a person died and was not completely independent; it drew vitality from the *Ka*, who drew its own vitality from food offerings. In response to this dependency, the *Ba* returned to the tomb each night, generally through narrow openings purposely left in the burial chamber.

The *Akh*, represented by a crested ibis, was more transcendental. Whereas the world of the *Ba* was in many ways like the land of the living, the world of the *Akh* was almost totally otherworldly. The *Akh* was that part of the dead that could become part of the universe, or immortal. It severed all ties with the body and dwelt among the imperishable stars, revolving forever around the polestar. Thus, the Egyptians could have their cake and eat it, too: after death they could look forward to both an eternal, changeless, ethereal life and a familiar, land-of-the-living existence.

The *Akh* is sometimes referred to as the "transfigured spirit,"[23] and in this case transfiguration means assimilation into the starry circuit of the night sky. But the circuit or round of the sun also appealed to the Egyptian imagination, and this brought the prospect of heaven closer to home. The sun illuminated the land of the living, and so was closely associated with the everyday activities of mortal life. There was, however, a terrifying aspect of the sun's behavior that prompted the idea of a post-death underworld: every evening the sun dropped below the Western horizon and apparently sank into darkness and death. It thus entered the realm of Osiris, a land lower and in its unredeemed state infinitely more dreadful than sun-drenched Egypt. Osiris's victory over death, however, had turned the underworld into an abode of happiness where life could go on in much the same manner as it had in Egypt, but without sorrow and physical decline. The surety of this was the sun's rising in the morning: it had passed through the darkness, had suffered death but had then been reborn to life. Just as Horus had been fathered from the partly revived body of Osiris, so the sun who is associated with Horus emerges from the dark underworld ruled by Osiris.

The idea that unites these different conceptions of heaven is the round of nature. Whether one is moving about the polestar or on the great circuit of the sun and spending time in the underworld, one is integrated into the rhythmic narrative of life. Death occurred when one got out of sync with that narrative and thereby became untuned, as it were, from the great cosmic cycles. Conversely, life meant being picked up by those cycles, which seemed untiring in their regularity. Indeed, the prospect of endless life was so conditioned by the repetitive cycles of nature that the Egyptians spoke of "repeating life."[24] Just as the sun rose every morning, or the moon returned to its new phase at the beginning of every month, so one could expect to "repeat life" again and again.

THE PHYSICAL BODY AND MUMMIFICATION

For the Egyptians, the idea of eternal life without a physical body was unthinkable. We in the modern West, by contrast, can easily dispense with the body when contemplating post-death existence. If anything lives on, it is the spirit or astral energy form or some other ethereal aspect of our being. The body therefore can be "let go" upon death. An elaborate funeral and burial may be in order, but the idea of fending off physical decay until the moment of resurrection strikes us as ludicrous. We might even choose to cremate the body—reduce it to ash. The very thought of cremation would horrify an Egyptian, for the body was the "physical substratum" of one's hope of surviving death.[25] Without the physical body, there was no foundation upon which to build the edifice of eternal life.

We may ask why they were so attached to their bodies, but perhaps we should ask ourselves why we are not. How have we come to disassociate ourselves from what we see in the mirror every morning? This is a question that we will partially answer in the forthcoming chapters. Let us just note here that the Egyptians did not split reality into physical and spiritual categories, as we do, and thereby relegate life to only one pole of a binary opposition (spirit). As should be apparent by now, for them the physical universe was religiously textured, spiritually resonant; it could and very likely would bring off their salvation. Thus, imagining a non-physical (purely spiritual) after-life was like trying to imagine the grin of Lewis Carroll's Cheshire cat without the cat. Simply put, one's salvation cried out for physical mediation.

More to the point in a practical sense, the physical body had to be preserved in a recognizable form if the *Ka, Ba,* and *Akh* were to survive. The *Ba* in particular needed to recognize its own mummy when it flew back home each night. Hence, measures were taken to ensure the preservation of the body. Osiris was, of course, the first to be mummified, according to the Egyptians. Isis, when she had put Osiris's strewn body parts back together, wrapped him very tightly with linen and then raised him from the dead. Always wishing to follow the example of Osiris, the Egyptians requested that they, too, be wrapped or mummified at death so that they might be raised to life as Osiris had been. This necessitated not only an embalming procedure but ritualistic magic as well. The magic—in the form of spells, amulets, statues, and paintings—would protect the body from physical harm, compensate for physical deficiencies, and prepare it for resurrection and its journey to the underworld.

The mummification ceremony was an elaborate affair. First the body was dehydrated. This required that it be packed in natron, a soda-like substance found on the banks of the Nile that drew moisture from the pores of the skin. Most of the wetness of the body, however, collected in the internal organs, and so these had to be dealt with. Generally they were removed, mummified separately, and placed in canopic jars near the coffin, evidently to be re-integrated into the body at the moment of resurrection. The two notable exceptions were the brain and the heart. For the Egyptians, the seat of intelligence was the heart. The blood vessels running to and from the heart struck them as transmitting media for thoughts and feelings. Moreover, the heart was obviously alive and active—one could feel it beating. Given its supreme importance, the heart was left in the body and was considered to be an essential element of the resurrection.

The brain, by contrast, impressed the Egyptian priests in charge of mummification as having little if any value. They consequently discarded it. First, however, they removed it by inserting an iron rod up through one of the nostrils, pushing through the skull and stirring the gray matter into small pieces, which were then spooned or flushed out. The brain cavity was then filled with linen, evidently to absorb moisture and to restore the natural appearance of the head in the event that it had been damaged by the brain removal procedure.

This derogatory attitude toward the brain strikes us as clear evidence that the Egyptians were very backward in their understanding of human physiology. Certainly the priests were, although Egyptian medical practitioners, who were more empirically inclined, regarded the brain as a vital organ and even performed corrective surgery on it.[26] That said, we ought to acknowledge that more is involved here than mere physiology. Contrary to what seems to us to be the very stuff of human experience, one cannot feel one's thoughts moving about in the brain. The brain, although it senses other organs and body parts, does not sense itself. (This is why the brain need not be anesthetized prior to brain surgery.) Even headaches often originate from outside the brain.

The salient point is that where we feel our thoughts flitting about is a matter of cultural conditioning. Even Aristotle viewed the brain as an inert mass of tissue useful in cooling the body. Like the Egyptians, he located the seat of thought in the heart. Jesus often referred to the heart in the same manner, describing it in the New Testament as the seat of our thoughts, feelings, and intentions in phrases such as "Let not your heart be troubled."[27] Although for moderns the brain has displaced the heart as the locus of intelligence, we still talk at times as if our emotions arise from the heart and thereby betray modern culture's dichotomization of thought and feeling, head and heart. For the Egyptians, however, thought and feeling seem to have participated more fully in one another.

Here then is another clue to understanding the Egyptians. Blaise Pascal once remarked that "[t]he heart has its reasons, which reason does not know."[28] To a large degree, Egyptian magic stems from reasons of the heart that a more scientifically minded culture dimly comprehends. This is particularly true as we move into the next stage of the mummification ceremony, which relies heavily on devices that to moderns might seem childish and ineffectual. After the body was dehydrated, the wrapping process began. In the case of royalty, this might require hundreds of yards of cloth. To ensure a tight seal, resin or bitumen—a tar-like material—was applied to the wrappings. Gooey substances, however, could not protect against theft or vandalism. For this, amulets and statues had to be employed.

The Egyptian proclivity for multiple backup systems is nowhere more evident than in their use of amulets and statues. For example, the *Ka* statue, in which the *Ka* lived, could also serve, in a pinch, as a substitute for the mummy itself if the body were stolen or destroyed. But what if only some part of the physical body were damaged? Certain amulets—of which there were several hundred different kinds—could solve that problem.

Amulets were used to ensure the protection of the body through magic, and each amulet had its own special significance and function. These little charms were often wrapped in the linen with the mummy itself, or they could be drawn on the wrappings. Given the free interchange of being that existed among different substances, one could fashion a hand or foot amulet from clay to stand in for a damaged hand or foot. But some amulets were a little more abstractly conceived, and were felt to possess strength, virtue, or some other ideal quality that was inherent in the portrayed body part or object. One such amulet was the *djed*-pillar, which gave the power of stability (perhaps so the deceased could stand up), and almost everyone was buried with one. It is not certain what it represented. Some scholars suggest that it might be the tree Osiris's coffin was caught in; others, that it is Osiris's backbone, since the *Book of the Dead*, chapter 155, states, "Raise thyself, Osiris, you have a backbone [again]."

Unquestionably, the most powerful amulet to the Egyptians was the eye of Horus (or *udjat*-eye of Horus, *udjat* meaning "whole" or "sound"). Inasmuch as Horus, the son of Osiris, had the head of a hawk, the eye of Horus had the distinctive markings of a hawk's eye. Horus lost an eye in his battle with Seth, but Thoth restored the eye, and thus the wearer of this amulet was thought to gain health. It was worn by both the dead and the living, and was used more than any other amulet. If this were not enough, the story that inspired the amulet was dramatically reenacted every month in the night sky as the moon passed through its cycle. The moon waned as Horus's eye was destroyed by Seth but then waxed or grew whole after its restoration by Thoth.

The amulet best known to moderns is the *ankh*. It was the Egyptian symbol for life and living and was associated with the act of giving life. Like the *djed*-pillar, the *ankh* symbol is of uncertain origin; suggestions range from a stylized Egyptian sandal to a single vertebra or even an umbilical cord tied in a knot. Curiously enough, whereas the *ankh* is often seen in paintings within tombs, very few of these symbols of life are ever found as amulets in the mummies themselves.

Two final amulets stand out among the many possibilities: the scarab and the heart scarab amulets. *Scarabeus* is Latin for "beetle," and indeed these scarab amulets are representations of the Egyptian dung beetle. This sounds like a particularly unsavory choice for religious symbolism, but the Egyptians considered the beetles emblems of life. The dung beetle lays its eggs in little bits of manure, which it then rolls into balls. The emergence of the newly hatched beetles from these balls seemed marvelous to the Egyptians, who evidently understood the process as spontaneous generation. In paintings and amulets,

EGYPTIANS AND THE OCCULT

the beetles are sometimes depicted as pushing the sun across the sky, as if it were a huge dung ball. For, just as the dung ball produced new life, so also did the sun whose rebirth every morning miraculously revitalized nature. One who wore the scarab amulet, therefore, absorbed the life-renewing powers of the sun.

Heart scarabs were much larger than ordinary scarab amulets and were worn only by the dead. There is never more than one found per body, but they were essential and nearly every mummified person had one. Perhaps they served as substitutes for the real heart, just in case of vandalism, but their greatest significance lay in the Weighing of the Heart ceremony.

Let us pause here to reiterate that the Egyptians assumed that the world was intelligently designed or interfitted, and so looked for connections that we would not be inclined to look for. The waxing and waning of the moon, or a scarab beetle pushing a dung ball across the sand, could not simply be arbitrary occurrences; they had to fit into a pattern of divine meaning. Indeed, the verb *to divine* indicates what counted as understanding for an Egyptian. To divine is to grasp a wider, frequently supernatural purpose behind events that often seem accidental and unrelated to other events. A beetle pushing a dung ball across the sand, therefore, had to chime into a large harmony of events and meanings if one were to understand it properly. In this case, the keynote of that harmony was the sun god's journey across the sky, and once the beetle's pushing of the dung ball was assimilated to that divine drama, the explanatory process reached a satisfying conclusion.

If, indeed, all events, no matter how commonplace or seemingly trivial, were assimilated upward to divine meanings, then certain distinctions we presently make might be overlooked. Why distinguish carefully between a dung ball and the sun when the reality of the former is subsumed or taken up in the latter? Here we return to the idea of a single universal substance, but now we wish to suggest that the Egyptians were so God-conscious that they tended to spiritualize away material differences that are fixed for us. Played out on the stage of nature in a sensuously splendid way, the divine drama may have been so compelling as to turn "scientific" questions of material difference into mere quibbles. Why make distinctions between clay and human flesh when the supremely important thing is to conform one's life to the cosmic salvation story? Amulets were means of conforming oneself—by whatever material available—to various aspects of that story.

As we noted above, the story also called for an after-life much like the present world, but better in every way, and here *shabtis*—miniature servant statues—played an important role. At first, they were shaped like mummies and placed in tombs to serve as substitute homes for the *Ba*, in case the real

MAGIC, MYSTERY, AND SCIENCE

mummy was stolen or damaged. Eventually, however, they were used to represent servants—a class of people who were essential to one's happiness on the other side. Without servants, who would plant, harvest, and irrigate crops? The miracle of agriculture was so compelling that it extended right into the next world, and yet one could neither achieve nor enjoy the ease and prosperity agriculture offers without field hands. So the hard work fell to the *shabtis*.

Some people were buried with hundreds of *shabtis*, each with its own little hoe or adze or other tool in its hand and sometimes with a seed bag on its back. With this many *shabtis* around, concern arose that there might be slacker *shabtis* or arguments among the group, so overseer *shabtis* were designated and often equipped with whips to keep the others in line. Instructions and spells were also inscribed on the *shabtis* to ensure that they carried out their tasks.

Besides agricultural workers, other key people were frequently represented in Egyptian tombs. Though not strictly *shabtis* (since they were not inscribed with spells or instructions), they served much the same function. Often these wooden models were very life-like, representing figures engaged in tasks such as baking bread, butchering cattle, and brewing beer to produce food for the dead. In time, these activities were painted on the walls instead.

All this representation—whether three-dimensional figurines or two-dimensional paintings—was meant to fill out the heavenly home of the deceased. Flatly rejecting what would become the wisdom of a later age, the Egyptians believed that "you can take it with you"; you just have to work it into the burial ceremony. And, unlike us, they were not hard-pressed to imagine what the after-life would be like. Mark Twain quipped that he would much rather spend his after-life in hell enjoying the company of his friends than ceaselessly playing a harp in heaven. The remark, albeit lighthearted, hits at an important truth: most moderns draw a blank when trying to summon up an interesting picture of heaven. The Egyptians, however, simply projected earth life into the underworld. Life in Egypt was good, and a celestialized version of that goodness would inform the Kingdom of Osiris.

BURIAL AND BEYOND

With the body properly mummified, measures were taken to ensure its safe journey to the underworld. If they could afford it, Egyptians used multiple coffins to safeguard the mummy, one nested inside another, with a sarcophagus as the outer coffin. These were usually painted with protective illustrations and spells, and they might even have included a map of the cosmos so that the deceased could find her way to the underworld more easily. Early on, the coffins were rectangular, but eventually became mummy-shaped with a head and rounded shoulders (anthropoid coffins). This was probably to emulate Osiris, who was put into a box that fit him exactly. A life-like mask was placed on the mummy's face, no doubt so that the *Ba* could recognize the deceased.

In the funeral processions of the wealthy, the mummy was placed in a boat-shaped bier on a sled pulled by oxen and accompanied by priests, family, and mourners. Most of the procession was made up of servants carrying all the tables, food, and belongings to be taken into the tomb (beds, chairs, mirrors, utensils, game boards, etc.). The priest in charge wore a leopard skin over his shoulders; another priest constantly read prayers and spells. Over the sounds of the priest's prayers could be heard the screaming and wailing of the paid professional mourners, all dressed in pale blue, the Egyptian color of mourning. They beat their bare breasts, tore their hair, scratched their cheeks with their fingernails, and threw dust and dirt on themselves, all to show how much the deceased would be missed.

Once the procession arrived at the place of burial, the Opening of the Mouth ceremony was performed. This rite was a performance involving priests as well as family members as actors. Even the deceased participated in the ceremony, for in an act of sympathetic magic, the mummy played the part of Osiris. The object of the ceremony was to open the mouth of the dead—to awaken the senses and thereby enable the deceased to safely negotiate the perilous journey to the underworld.

In a universe alive with both benign and malignant forces, one could expect to encounter opposition while moving through unfamiliar territory. The *Book of the Dead*, placed in or near the coffin, allowed the deceased to successfully thwart that opposition: the text was a collection of spells capable of neutralizing various evils. But if the Opening of the Mouth ceremony did not first awaken one's senses, the spells could not be invoked as protective formulas.

The ceremony itself re-enacted the revenge of hawk-headed Horus on Seth and his minions for killing and dismembering Osiris. At the end of this battle with Horus, Seth's followers changed into animals while trying to flee. But Horus chopped them up. To re-enact this revenge, ceremony officiants ritually killed bulls, gazelles, ducks, and other animals. Quite a bloody mess, no doubt, but it was all magically linked to opening the mouth of the deceased. According to myth, Horus had opened Osiris's mouth by touching it with an adze that had once belonged to Seth.[29] The aim, then, was to touch the mouth of the deceased with various objects, some of them associated with Seth, in the hope of awakening the senses. One such object might be the foreleg of a calf, amputated while the calf was still alive! Illustrations of the procedure show both the three-legged calf and its mother bleating. Other possible objects include an adze, a ram-headed scepter, a metal chisel, and a forked implement. Here

MAGIC, MYSTERY, AND SCIENCE

again, the Egyptians demonstrate their backup system approach to religion: if one object does not open the mouth, perhaps another will.

An open, breathing mouth implies life, of course, but for the Egyptians there were yet wider associations. Osiris was identified with the cooling North Wind that normally began to blow in Egypt just before the annual flooding of the Nile. Legend has it that Horus had brought the North Wind to Osiris and thereby revived him so he could effect the broad re-invigoration of nature that marked the beginning of the growing season. In brief, the breath of life that awakened Osiris thenceforth awakened the earth in spring and the body of the deceased after its season of death.

This wide-angle ecological outlook is critical to a sympathetic understanding of the Opening of the Mouth ceremony. If we regard it as a desperate and misguided attempt to revive the body by re-enacting a story that has no basis in fact, we miss the point completely. The story was part of the cycle of nature, as much empirical fact as the rising of the sun or the growth of crops. Indeed, these were crucial elements of the story, phenomenological witnesses to its cosmic validity. As long as spring had its way, Osiris would draw new breath, the North Wind would blow, the Nile would flood, plants would grow, and mummified bodies would return to life.

After the ceremony, the family held a farewell feast near the gravesite. Usually, the leftovers were placed near the tomb, no doubt for the *Ka* to enjoy. Finally, the mummy and everything accompanying it were sealed within the tomb. Now the mummy was on its own. Wrapped in linen, armed with the *Book of the Dead*, shielded by protective devices and formulas, and awakened by the Opening of the Mouth ceremony, it was prepared to make its lone and dangerous journey to the underworld. The final obstacle of that journey was the Weighing of the Heart. This was the last judgment—to see if the heart was pure and if the deceased had lived a good life.

As the *Ba* helplessly looked on, the heart of the deceased was weighed in the scales against the feather of truth (the symbol of the goddess Maat). Anubis, the jackal-headed god, watched the scales, and Thoth, the ibis-headed god, recorded the verdict. Behind them squatted the fearsome monster Ammit, with the head of a crocodile, the mane of a lion, the forelegs of a cheetah, and the hind part of a hippopotamus. If the heart weighed less than or equal to the feather, the deceased was home free—he or she passed the judgment and was ushered into the Kingdom of Osiris to live in eternal felicity.

If, however, the heart outweighed the feather, Ammit gobbled it down. The deceased was thereby turned away from the underworld and, without a heart, ceased to exist as a fully rounded personality. Perhaps to improve one's chances, the negative confession was often said during the Weighing of the Heart: "I

Figure 3. Weighing of the Heart

have not stolen, I have not committed adultery, I have not . . ." But, frankly, the chances must not have looked good to most Egyptians: after all, most people don't have completely pure hearts. This is where the heart scarab proved its immense worth. Written on the bottom of the scarab was the "heart formula" or spell. It tells the heart to "not testify against me"; that is, "Please don't tell of my misdeeds on earth and thereby cause me to fail the test." With this kind of protection or grace, one can understand why nearly every mummy was buried with a heart scarab.

Judgment ceremonies are common to religious thought, and the Weighing of the Heart is not strikingly unusual. It has some bizarre images, but they make sense within the overall context. What needs to be reiterated, however, is that the Egyptian religion was not felt to be at variance with the cosmos. The feather of Maat represented divine justice, but this was not an ethical standard apart from nature but, rather, the natural order itself. In other words,

MAGIC, MYSTERY, AND SCIENCE

the physical structure of reality doubled as an ethical system against which one had to prove oneself. The present world was sufficiently bright with the promise of eternal life that no one felt the need to pin his hope to an entirely different, unseen world with a "better" moral configuration.

MODERN RESPONSES

The wisdom of the Egyptians is proverbial, and this is partially because of ancient Egypt's relative isolation from other lands. Mesopotamia, the fertile land between the rivers that lay to the east, lacked Egypt's geographical barriers, and so was overrun by many civilizations. As a result, Mesopotamian thought has been knit into the fabric of modern culture, while Egyptian thought is naturally less familiar and therefore exotic. The otherness of Egypt, together with its splendid ruins, attracts moderns who wish to break the all-too-familiar frame of everyday reality. Let us look at two fairly recent attempts to break that frame—the curse of the mummy and the romanticization of the Great Pyramid.

In April 1923, about five months after King Tutankhamen's lavish tomb was discovered by the archaeologist Howard Carter, a letter written to the *New York World* by Marie Corelli sparked the story of the "Curse of Tut." Corelli, a popular romance novelist, advised Carter and other archaeologists to refrain from further disturbing King Tut's tomb lest they be stricken by a "most dire punishment." This warning, she claimed, originated from "a rare book I possess, which is not in the British Museum, entitled *The Egyptian History of the Pyramids.*" Listed in the book were "treasures buried with several of the kings, and among these are named divers secret poisons enclosed in boxes in such wise that they who touch them shall not know how they come to suffer."[30]

Only two weeks after this letter appeared in print, Lord Carnarvon, the wealthy financial supporter of Carter's expedition, died under "mysterious" circumstances. It appears that his barber had nicked a mosquito bite on Carnarvon's neck, which then became infected and so weakened the financier that he died of pneumonia. With Corelli's ominous warning just released, the press went wild. "Death shall come on swift wings to him that toucheth a tomb of the pharaohs," was the oft-quoted curse in the newspapers. The media cited this curse so often that soon it was considered a fact; yet there is no evidence that it existed before its appearance in twentieth-century newspapers. It has certainly never been found among Egyptian artifacts. The Egyptians left warnings that admonished *Ka* priests to continue to bring food for the *Ka*. They also warned off would-be tomb trespassers with the threat that trespassing would incriminate them at the Weighing of the Heart judgment ceremony. But no full-blooded death curse leveled at people for disturbing a mummy has

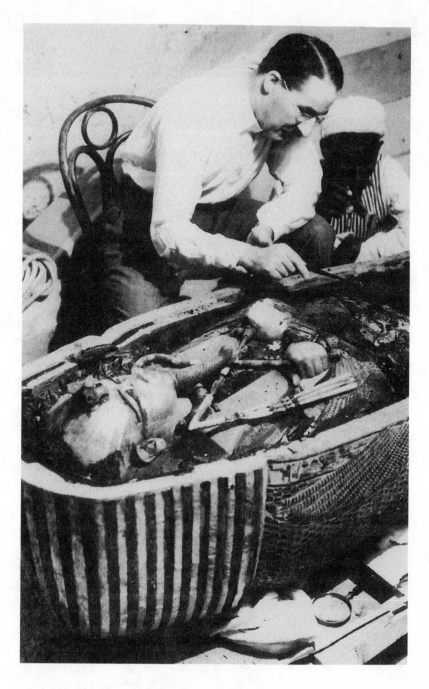

Figure 4. Howard Carter examining the coffin of King Tutankhamen

MAGIC, MYSTERY, AND SCIENCE

ever been found. Nevertheless, over the next ten years, legions of rumors circulated about the mysterious and unsavory deaths of those who had defiled King Tut's eternal rest. By 1934, the curator of the Egyptology department of the Metropolitan Museum in New York decided to find out what really happened to those who had disturbed Tut's mummy. His findings indicated that

• Of the twenty-six people present at the opening of Tut's burial chamber, six had died within ten years; twenty were still alive.

• Of the twenty-two people who had witnessed the opening of the sarcophagus, only two had died.

• Of the ten who, most dangerously, had been present at the unwrapping of Tut himself, all were still alive.

Most telling, however, is the death of the archaeologist Howard Carter himself. Carter had said that any sane person should dismiss the curse with contempt. He should have known. He was the man most closely associated with every single aspect of the disturbance of the tomb, and he did not die until 1939 (seventeen years after the discovery) at the age of sixty-six. And the "swift wings" of death were decidedly slow concerning Carnarvon's daughter, as well. For, although she was present at the tomb's opening, she lived on into her eighties and was present at the fiftieth anniversary of Tut's discovery in 1972.

Why the fuss over the alleged Curse of Tut? After all, this was the 1920s and 1930s, long before indigenous peoples began to dispute science's right to turn their buried ancestors into museum artifacts. No doubt the modern perception that ancient Egypt was a place apart, a land of hidden wisdom, played into the rumors. Moreover, the antique splendor of King Tut's tomb, set against the magnificent and seemingly timeless backdrop of pyramids and temples, endows the physical artifacts with a spiritual luster. The Egyptians were interested in lastingness, and, even if their mummies have not been able to fully resist the ravages of time, it would almost seem that their stone edifices have.

According to an Arab proverb, "Man fears time but time fears the pyramids." The passage of time bespeaks entropy and death, but the enduring nature of the pyramids suggests victory over death. The Great Pyramid, located just south of present-day Cairo, has probably attracted more interest than any other man-made structure in the world. Why was it built? What does it signify? A few of the many modern responses to these questions propose that the Great Pyramid is (1) a prophecy of the world's future in stone; (2) a scale model of the earth or universe; (3) an architectural encoding of sacred mathematical ratios; (4) a mirror for rejuvenating the sun at winter solstice; (5) a gift to humanity from a more advanced extraterrestrial civilization; and (6) an instrument for focusing cosmic energy on the entombed body of the pharaoh.

Although any of these possibilities may engage the imagination for hours on end, they fail to come to grips with issues that were vitally important to the

Egyptians themselves and thereby miss the mark. The Egyptians were not profound mathematicians and their sense of cyclic time did not predispose them to treat the future as a linear string of unique events. Visitors from outer space? Well, that hypothesis may reassure many today who look skyward for technological angels arriving in UFOs, but there is not a shred of evidence to support it. We should recognize also that by giving the credit for the Great Pyramid (or any other human accomplishment) to space aliens, we demean the human race by implication.

There are snatches of truth in some of the proposals, but the proposals themselves are framed to reflect modern rather than Egyptian interests. As a rule, moderns stare past the miracle of agriculture while fixating on the wonders of science and technology. A "scale model of the universe" suggests mathematical rigor to us and we imagine some sort of geometrically esoteric structure, but what the Egyptians had in mind was the primeval hillock pushing up through the waters of creation: the pyramid thus resonated agricultural overtones because it was the mound of creation upon which one could establish oneself and plant crops. If the structure of the Great Pyramid instantiates interesting mathematical ratios, these are merely means to an end.

Similarly, the modern view that pyramids focus "cosmic energy" fails to capture the organic flavor of the Egyptian vision. Conditioned by *Star Wars* and telecommunications technology, moderns imagine electromagnetic forces that operate independently of the round of nature, while the Egyptians hoped that their mummified bodies would gather up life from the spring-producing interplay of earth and sun. As for the pyramid being a mirror to rejuvenate the sun, let us just say that evidence more readily suggests that pyramids were seen as ways of mounting up to the sun. Symbolically, if not also physically, they put one halfway between earth and heaven. The distinctive structure of the pyramid may even have been inspired by the sight of the sun breaking through the clouds, spreading its rays in triangular fashion.

In brief, the Egyptians were neither in advance of modern civilization nor hopelessly lagging behind it. Their path was oblique to our own and that is why it is difficult to understand; we cannot use familiar yardsticks to take their measure but must rather learn new categories of thought. Many of these categories, however, are really very old, but have been discredited in recent centuries. In trying to explain why "Egyptian mythology is so simple, so absurd and sometimes so profound," R. T. Rundle Clark states that it "is dream, metaphysics, and poetry, all at once."[31] The shorthand nomenclature for this strange recipe of thought is magic, the topic of the next chapter.

2

MAGIC AND MIRACLES

Modern science attempts to prove that man is an animal; the teachings of the Adepts show that he may be a god. Modern science invests him with the power to lift his own weight; ancient science invests him with the power to control the destiny of the world.

—*Franz Hartmann*[1]

Again, the mystics of many centuries, independently, yet in perfect harmony with each other (somewhat like the particles in an ideal gas) have described, each of them, the unique experience of his or her life in terms that can be condensed in the phrase: DEUS FACTUS SUM (I have become God).

—*Erwin Schrödinger*[2]

When we hear of people pushing pins into odd-looking dolls to try to harm others, most of us laugh. And yet, imagine that, late one night, you open your front door, and there at your feet lies just such a crude, needle-pierced doll. When you pick it up, you see that it even has a tuft of human hair stuck to it—hair that looks just like your own. Probably even the most rational person would be slightly unnerved.

One should keep this uneasiness in mind while studying magic. If magic can disturb those of us who live in the "rational," non-magical West, imagine the distress—or elation—it might bring to believers. Even if it did not work in a scientifically demonstrable way, mere belief in its efficacy could make it real. Upon receiving the magical blow, the victim might suffer heart failure or slip into depression, and the magician and his patron (the magician's supporter and benefactor) would naturally glory in their success. The patron satisfied, the magician more exalted, and all others more awestruck and fearful—this would be a climate in which magic could flourish.

This is not necessarily to say, however, that magic is mere deception and self-deception. "There are more things in heaven and earth," said Hamlet to Horatio, "than are dreamed of in your philosophy."[3] Magic or the forces of magic may not fit into one's philosophy or worldview, but no worldview can be said to be fully coterminous with reality. Indeed, to some extent, magic trades on the unknown. Esoteric incantations and rituals, recited and performed out of the public eye, are thought to grant the magician secret powers. The skeptic will demand that everything be brought out in the open, so that "neutral" observers can publicly test the efficacy of magic. But a magician might reply that magic cannot flourish in a scientific laboratory: seclusion and confidentiality are central to the practice of magic. So we reach an impasse where magic—if there really is something to it—seems to shrink from the scrutinizing eye of science.

DEFINING "MAGIC"

In modern English, we use the term "magic" in two very different ways. Often it means that enjoyable sleight of hand in which an onstage "magician" does card tricks or appears to saw an assistant in half. This type of conjuring magic now has little to do with the occult view of magic, although sleight-of-hand magicians retain the wonder and mystery surrounding their occult namesakes. (Some modern occultists spell their "magick" with a *k* to differentiate it from the rabbit-out-of-the-hat kind of magic.)

The occult magician lives in a world of forces—forces almost always portrayed as supernatural or spiritual. The magician believes that these forces and powers can be controlled through certain supernatural rituals and incantations. These may vary widely, from a simple curse or evil glance to a highly elaborate rite that none but adepts can follow.

The objective or motive of the magician is *power.* Control over nature, over circumstance, and over other people's lives is the driving force behind all magic. Of course, we all want to have some control over our circumstances; think how much time we spend on finding and keeping a job, or staying healthy, or developing friendships or love relationships. These are the driving interests behind most magic, as well. So the goals of magic are not so strange; what is strange are the means to those goals and how over-inflated those goals sometimes become.

So far everything seems straightforward. But here we have to muddy the waters a bit. As with so many occult subjects, the closer we look at magic, the more difficult it is to define. No sooner do we offer a definition than both ancient and modern practitioners slice off one part and then another until the definition is whittled down to nothing. The definition given above says the following: magicians believe that supernatural or spiritual forces can be controlled through certain rituals and incantations, and thus they can gain power over their circumstances. But the enigmatic Renaissance "magus" Paracelsus (circa 1530) would have disagreed with much of this definition.

Paracelsus was certainly a believer in magic; he even advocated magic over reason, saying that magic is "great hidden wisdom" and reason is "a great folly."[4] But rituals and incantations were not in Paracelsus's definition of magic. In the practice of magic, he insisted, "no external ceremonies and conjurations are required. The making of circles and the burning of incense are all tomfoolery and temptation."[5] They were nothing but outward show with no power to bring off one's magical aims. What mattered were the inner virtues of faith, imagination, and purity of heart.

But what of the "forces" the magician tries to control—are they always seen as supernatural or spiritual? Again, we are greeted by difficulty. Sometimes occult magicians explain these forces as natural rather than supernatural. Of course, they may seem to be supernatural to the rest of us, but that is said to be because they are hidden to all but the adept. Thus, we come up against something that could be called "natural magic" wherein the magician controls nature by using secret or poorly understood natural forces. Here things get fuzzy, for, by that definition, we all become "magicians" whenever we use a car, a plane, or a microwave oven. (Keep in mind Arthur C. Clarke's claim that "any sufficiently developed technology is indistinguishable from magic."[6]) Each time we turn on the ignition and race down the street, climb into a winged metal tube and fly through the air, or press buttons and heat our food by "tiny invisible waves," aren't we controlling nature by using dimly understood *natural* forces? (That is, dimly understood by most of us, although not by "the adepts," whose esoteric knowledge is much in demand.) Then could magic be conceived as a form of technology? Throughout the Middle Ages, it was.

Bert Hansen points out that, in the Middle Ages, magic was seen as a practical technology "because its aim was some useful accomplishment, not mere knowledge or understanding."[7] But what was considered "magical" in ancient and medieval times included things that today we would not consider magical at all. For example, do you regard a tiny mechanical beetle or a huge

MAGIC AND MIRACLES

town-hall clock as *magic?* What of making a rainbow with a prism? Almost everyone before the sixteenth century would have thought so. Why? It's a difference in how we divide the world up, into what categories we drop things and activities.

As Hansen explains, people before the Scientific Revolution classified phenomena into one of three categories: natural, unnatural, and supernatural. Natural phenomena were things that happened normally in nature, *that occurred most of the time*—rocks fell down rather than up, people could not see in total darkness, the sun rose in the east every morning, and so on. Supernatural phenomena occurred when God intervened directly through a miracle; for example, when a person rose from the dead or was miraculously healed. The curious category was the unnatural (or, as Hansen sometimes calls it, the "preternatural"). We would all agree today that a table levitating off the ground is unnatural. So also is an unpropelled rock flying through the air. But a medieval person would have said that it is equally "unnatural" for a rock to fly through the air even if a slingshot was used to fling it, for, after all, flying through the air is not what rocks normally or naturally do, no matter how they get there. Other occurrences would also fall under the unnatural. For example, little wind-up mechanical beetles did not occur in nature; therefore, such devices were "unnatural." Nor were two-headed calves very common; thus, they also were considered unnatural. The category of the unnatural, then, encompassed a great many things we moderns would not group together. Neither natural nor miraculous, "magic" also fell in the category of the unnatural.

This shift in understanding surely has something to do with the way modern science has altered our assumptions about reality. Arthur Imhof has argued persuasively that before about 1800 most people in the West believed their lives would not vary dramatically from those of their parents and grandparents.[8] This is not to say that pre-modern life was highly predictable, for disease, war, famine, and natural disaster could always be counted on to disrupt the status quo. However, because the idea of whole new rounds of life-altering inventions sweeping through society in steady succession had not yet crystallized, pre-modern people did not feel themselves to be on an escalator of rapid technological progress and thus did not feel the "future shock" that accompanies such progress. "The greatest invention of the nineteenth century," wrote A. N. Whitehead, "was the invention of the method of invention." This method, he continued, "[broke] . . . up the foundations of the old civilisation,"[9] one which felt the tug of the past more strongly than our own.

Much less accustomed to invention than we, pre-moderns were capable of being truly surprised—perhaps to the point of awe or dread—upon first seeing something like a mechanical beetle. As noted in chapter 1, the mechanical clock, when first introduced in the fourteenth century, excited the medieval

MAGIC, MYSTERY, AND SCIENCE

imagination in a way we can barely comprehend. J. T. Fraser stated that the clock was once a "quasi-religious object,"[10] and Derek de Solla Price called it "a sort of fallen angel from the world of astronomy."[11] These characterizations bespeak the wonder that the first mechanical clocks inspired. Their turning gears seemed to model the turning heavens, and their regularity and autonomy seemed uncanny or surreal—that is, unnatural.

We should note also that medieval people did not countenance the possibility of nature haphazardly going awry to produce something like a two-headed calf. In other words, they did not embrace the notion of a random genetic mutation. This notion allows moderns to ascribe "freaks of nature" to nature itself, to nature's occasional misfires. But lacking this option and believing that nature's operation was fixed and limited by God, medieval people regarded such anomalies of nature as transgressions or violations of nature. Indeed, they were "monsters" in the old sense of the word—creatures whose existence could be traced to dark, unnatural events.[12]

Magic partook of such events, and was thus an art or technology by which unnatural things were caused through secret or hidden means. Curiously, sleight-of-hand tricks were considered just as unnatural as incantations meant to summon demons. The strong distinctions we make today between the magic of a stage conjurer or illusionist and that of an occult practitioner did not exist before the Scientific Revolution. Case in point: after tearing up a napkin and restoring it before an audience of nobles, a young woman in the early seventeenth century barely escaped the Inquisition with the light sentence of excommunication.[13] Like occult magic, her sleight-of-hand cunning resonated unnatural overtones. Each provoked a sense of unease and wonder because neither seemed sanctioned by God nor part of nature's operation and therefore was felt to exist in a kind of twilight zone between God and His natural creation.

According to Hansen, modern society has done away with the category of the "unnatural" and has reassigned phenomena that once fell into that category to other categories. Today, we call those phenomena either *real* (but uncommon), such as a two-headed calf, or *unreal*, such as a levitating table. Likewise, magical phenomena, all of which used to fall into the single category of the unnatural, we split today into the categories of the real or unreal. A card trick or a mechanical beetle we would call real, classifying it under natural laws (even if we can't explain the trick, the device, or the laws). But a levitating table we would classify as unreal or impossible. Thus, one reason for magic's decline after the Scientific Revolution was that it was simply *classified* out of existence.

Tables can still be made to levitate, of course, but only under carefully arranged circumstances that do not violate nature's laws. We might, for example, design a situation in which a steel table is lifted up once electromagnets hidden

MAGIC AND MIRACLES

in the ceiling are switched on. Then the table would rise quickly to the ceiling, and an observer—if he were thinking in a medieval mode—might ascribe its upward motion to spirits or demons. But the modern thinker, skeptical of demons and spirits, would suspect a trick. For her, magic is not an explanatory key because spirits do not exist. Science, however, is a very good key, because laws of nature most certainly do exist—at least she does not doubt their existence. Furthermore, they must be respected; they cannot be contravened.

Laws of nature make for a rational, orderly, non-magical universe, while spirits and demons touch off a belief in magic because they bespeak mystery, darkness, independence from the rule of nature, and perhaps even anarchy against heavenly powers. These distinctions are implicit in Richard Kieckhefer's discussion of demonic magic,[14] which he claims converged with religion in the Middle Ages. This convergence is not surprising, as medieval Christians, following the New Testament, assumed the reality of spirits, both good and evil. Not all magic, however, was demonic magic, according to Kieckhefer. Some was concerned with nature's "hidden powers" or "occult virtues." Here we return to things like a two-headed calf—strange, freakish things that throw the mind into a spin. Certainly they are abnormal, but are they unnatural—the product of "occult virtues?"

Before the modern era, occult virtues might have been invoked anytime nature seemed to act strangely. Here is just one example, unusually instructive because it bears on a phenomenon that moderns do not regard as strange at all. Is gravity part of nature or somehow unnatural? Most of us would say that gravity is perfectly natural; there is nothing strange or eerie about it. It is merely a force that causes things to fall to the earth. But gravity has not always been so blithely interpreted. Four hundred years ago, when Johannes Kepler proposed that the moon somehow reaches across empty space to tug on the ocean and produce the tides, Galileo dismissed the explanation as astrological or occult.[15] Isaac Newton encountered similar objections when he, about seventy years after Kepler, also theorized that the moon (along with the sun) causes the tides. If science was supposed to be an antidote to magic, how could one, in the name of science, offer an explanation that posits unseen influences traveling without a physical medium through empty space? That came perilously close to suggesting that the moon casts a spell on the earth. Here is how Newton privately summed up his own misgivings about gravity:

> That gravity should be innate, inherent, and essential to matter so that one body may act upon another at a distance through a vacuum without the mediation of any thing else by and through which their action or force may be conveyed from one to another is to me so great

MAGIC, MYSTERY, AND SCIENCE

an absurdity that I believe no man who has in philosophical matters any competent faculty of thinking can ever fall into it.[16]

In responding to his critics, Newton asserted that he was putting forward laws of nature, not reintroducing occult qualities. Note, however, that he had to make careful distinctions between the two:

These principles I consider, not as occult qualities, supposed to result from the specific forms of things, but as general laws of nature, by which the things themselves are formed; their truth appearing to us by phenomena, though their causes be not yet discovered. For these are manifest qualities, and their causes only are occult.[17]

In other words, while laws of nature govern nature's manifestation or phenomena, our knowledge of them does not necessarily provide us with full understanding. Gravity may cause the tides, but what causes gravity? With this query things begin to grow dark or "occult," as Newton says. But for Newton's critics, the issue had already been clouded by the notion of an action-at-a-distance force. Even today, we do not see, in a literal sense, the gravitational connection between earth and moon that is said to produce the tides. It is as "hidden" or "occult" as it has ever been, but, unlike Galileo, few modern people are disturbed by the suggestion that gravity, much like an occult force, allows one thing to touch or make contact with another across apparently empty space. For moderns, gravity is obviously a law of nature and therefore it is, like other laws, unmysterious—never mind that modern science has never quite been able to fully understand it. And so to return to Kieckhefer's line of argument, for medieval truth-seekers nature's operation was often sufficiently ambiguous to permit more than one understanding, and beneath the haze of ambiguity "hidden powers" could be imagined. Magicians thought of them as occult virtues and reveled in their mystery, scientists regarded them as forces of nature and sought to unveil them, and both groups wished to exploit them.

Taken together, Kieckhefer and Hansen's analyses impel one to consider the modern case of psi phenomena, or what are often called paranormal phenomena—telepathy, psychokinesis, precognition, and so on. In recent decades, psi phenomena have attracted the interest of scientists, "mindreaders," spoon-bending magicians, New Age advocates, and people such as Carl Jung and Arthur Koestler who can claim scientific training but whose thinking ranges beyond accepted scientific understandings. Are psi phenomena the stuff of science, pseudo-science, or self-deception and wishful thinking? We will consider this question at length in chapter 10, but for the moment let us note that here again one encounters eerie occurrences of nature and the suggestion of

MAGIC AND MIRACLES

hidden or mysterious powers. Furthermore, these hypothetical powers might be the modern analogue to Hansen's category of "unnatural" phenomena, notwithstanding his insistence that that category no longer exists. Perhaps we now group such phenomena under the heading of "paranormal," a word that literally means "beyond the normal" but does not readily connote the workings of God. Again, in terms of general attitudes we are in a kind of twilight zone, not sure of whether psi phenomena are real, natural, good, or bad.

This is not to propose, however, that things have not changed dramatically. If indeed modern paranormal phenomena roughly approximate medieval unnatural phenomena, the latter played a much larger role in popular culture. For moderns, telepathy and the like are truly fringe phenomena—not central to our thinking, generally just possibilities to ponder in odd moments. But for medieval people, demons, spirits, occult forces, and hidden powers could be very central and even invasive. Moreover, despite the Catholic Church's official opposition, more space existed in medieval society for the pursuit and practice of magic. According to Valerie Flint, medieval authorities allowed magic to survive and even to flourish in limited ways because they viewed it "as a corrective to the excessive rationalism of science."[18] This she finds commendable, insisting that "the early Middle Ages in Europe display a good deal more enlightenment about the emotional need for that magic which sustains devotion and delight than does the post-Reformation Western world in general."[19]

This statement hints at yet another meaning of *magic:* that indefinable quality of things that ensures life and freshness—as in the phrase, "This is a magical moment." Might too little magic, and too little tolerance of magic, cramp the imagination and disenchant the world? We will let readers decide for themselves.

THE MAGICAL WORLDVIEW

We said that the goals or motives of magic—wanting power over circumstances—are not so strange but that it is surprising how over-inflated these goals may become. Some practitioners may use magic to achieve wealth or romantic conquest, but these are mere trifles compared to what the true magician seeks to accomplish. By the time of the Renaissance (and perhaps as early as late antiquity), the object of the great magician was to become omnipotent, a supreme power—to be as God, perhaps even to replace God. This was the Great Work—to become as God. The magician literally wanted to conquer the universe. Of course, actually doing this was (and still is) a little tricky (most of us would say downright difficult), but the magician's view of the world made the Great Work seem possible.

What were the elements of this worldview? Broadly speaking, the doctrines and beliefs of the magical perspective reach into other areas of the occult, and, taken together, these constitute a shared foundation for many of the topics of this book. One tenet, however, readily comes to the fore in any consideration of magic: "As above, so below." This doctrine has a long history, perhaps extending back to ancient Babylon.

"As above, so below" was a shorthand way of saying that all that happens in the realms of the universe above us, such as the doings of the gods or the movements of the stars and planets, is directly reflected in what happens down here on Earth. Astrology was founded on this idea: what happens in the starry heavens affects or influences earthly events. If there is a conjunction of two planets in the heavens, then there is a conjunction of their powers here on Earth. For example, some believed that the conjunction of the "healthy" planet Jupiter with the "malignant, deadly" planets of Mars and Saturn in 1345 brought about the horrible Black Death in Europe, which began in 1348.

In the magical worldview, the opposite of "As above, so below" also had credence. "As below, so above" meant that humble earthly occurrences might reflect or foretell major events in the universe (or at least foreshadow important events in one's life). In Shakespeare's *Macbeth*, for example, an old man, after having watched a "mousing owl" attack and kill a falcon, remarks that something ominous is afoot.[20] That night Macbeth attacked and killed King Duncan. Another example might be cited from Einhard's *Life of Charlemagne*. Einhard, Charlemagne's official biographer, wrote that many omens, some in the heavens and others on earth, portended the great emperor's death: "Eclipses both of the sun and the moon were very frequent during the last three years of his life, and a black spot was visible on the sun for the space of seven days. The gallery between the basilica and the palace, which he had built at great pains and labor, fell in sudden ruin to the ground on the day of the Ascension of our Lord."[21]

The list goes on, detailing, all told, about fifteen omens. But Einhard is looking back after the fact of Charlemagne's death, while magicians looked forward. Their reading of omens or signs presumably allowed them to foretell the future and the health of both nations and individuals. The birth of a "monster," such as a two-headed calf, could portend peril for an entire region. For the Babylonians (and later the Greeks and Romans), a diseased liver found in a sacrificial sheep could be a very bad omen for a whole nation. Even very mundane events were believed to reveal one's future—and for some they still do. Among some people of modern Appalachia, for example, one's future health may be discerned in the way tea leaves settle at the bottom of a cup.

To understand the magician's tendency to link events that for us have no logical connection, we need to recall that for most pre-moderns, everything happened for a purpose. Today we would say that every event has a cause, but

MAGIC AND MIRACLES

not every event has a purpose or meaning. If I stumble on the threshold of my front door as I leave for work in the morning, I think nothing of it. But a Roman may well have decided to alter his plans for the day, interpreting the stumble as a message from above. What we call chance events—events that seem to occur for no rhyme or reason—most certainly do have a rhyme or reason for the magically minded person. She instinctively assigns meanings to events, while moderns feel that they have fully explained an event once they have determined its cause, and, more often than not, that cause is empty of meaning. If I am climbing a mountain and a rock falls on my head, I do not interpret the blow as an expression of the mountain's opposition to my ascent. Indeed, in my thought-world, the mountain has no power of expression, and so I invoke a mechanical, non-meaningful explanation. The rock was slightly too heavy for the ledge it was resting on, and the ledge just "happened" to give way as I was climbing toward it. Gravity then brought the rock crashing down on my head. Beyond my injury, there is no larger significance to the matter. It was simply an "accident."

Compare this attitude with that expressed by William of Canterbury, a medieval thinker: "The Creator has so ordered the laws of matter that nothing can happen in his creation except in accordance with his just ordinance, whether good or bad."[22] The key to the difference between our modern outlook and William's is that, whereas he insists that God ultimately determines events, we are often content to let the laws of nature claim final responsibility for what happens to us. Granted, our insurance agent may call a hurricane "an act of God," but this phrase now simply means a catastrophe beyond our control, not something that God intended. Note, however, how differently things shape up once the older attitude is adopted. If the universe is governed by a divine and purposive intelligence, then it follows that events ought to bespeak that intelligence. But if natural law reigns, then talk of meanings and purposes becomes less plausible, for the laws of nature do not impress us as having some innate purpose or meaning. Can we, for example, ascribe meaning or purpose to the law of gravity? It feels strange to try to do so, because gravity seems like a blind or dumb force.

This perhaps explains why the formula "As above, so below," and its converse "As below, so above," are no longer persuasive. The "above" is no longer obviously divine or purposeful, and so the "below" can hardly be so. But if the above were purposeful, it would tend to fill or leaven the entire cosmos with purpose. And conceivably that purpose (or set of purposes) would be reiterated in many different ways and at many different levels. Hence, in the older worldview, the lines on the palm of my hand must "say something"; they must have some larger significance. Indeed, every part of my body is, at least in principle, laden with significance beyond its own obvious function. A palm reader, then, can

MAGIC, MYSTERY, AND SCIENCE

"divine" my future by studying the divine impress of lines upon my hand. An iridologist can do the same by looking at the variations in the irises of my eyes. A reflexologist studies the soles of my feet. Even the distribution of moles on my face signifies my character and future. Wherever one looks, the story of my life is written into my body.

It is as if my body encodes "me," and, curiously, this quest for a code is not so different from the modern belief that one's entire biological history is inscribed within the DNA sequence of a single cell. Will I get Alzheimer's disease? Will I lose my hair or go gray? Am I likely to develop a biochemical-related neurosis as I get older? The answers to all these questions and many more are to be found in one's genetic code, and that code is fully replicated in every cell of the body. Wherever one looks, the biological story of my life is written into my body.

This analogy between the attitudes of a modern biologist and a magician can only be taken so far, however. Both the biologist and the magician focus on the human body, but the magician takes a more expansive or "cosmic" view of it. Tending to see the universe in living terms, believing that it is tied together by a common purpose, and invoking the "As above, so below/As below, so above" formula, he posits a microcosmic-macrocosmic connection: the mini-universe that is one's body recapitulates the universe at large. Hence, it is not surprising that the stars may be said to influence one's behavior; as they move within the macrocosm of the larger world they also, in some sense, move within the microcosm of the human body.

Of all the principles of the magic worldview, this one is perhaps the most difficult for a modern thinker to comprehend. We sometimes say that "no man is an island," meaning that people cannot or should not try to isolate themselves from their social milieu. But the magician would say that we cannot isolate ourselves from our cosmic milieu; indeed, each human being is an entire universe, albeit miniaturized. Conversely, the universe is a human being writ large. Or, to take the thesis in a theological direction, the individual is a miniature of God, and God is an enlarged image of the individual. Everything within the universe is contained within the individual and vice versa. Manilius, an ancient poet, wove these ideas together in the following way: "Why wonder that men can comprehend heaven, when heaven exists in their very beings and each is in a smaller likeness the image of God himself?"[23]

A grandiose outlook, to be sure, and one is tempted to dismiss it as sheer megalomania. But there are reasons to pause before doing so. When Walt Whitman wrote, "I am large, I contain multitudes" and "With the twirl of my tongue I encompass worlds and volumes of worlds,"[24] he was echoing the timeworn cry of the mystic whose sense of consciousness suddenly and limitlessly expands. Mysticism is not magic, but it certainly can play into magic and

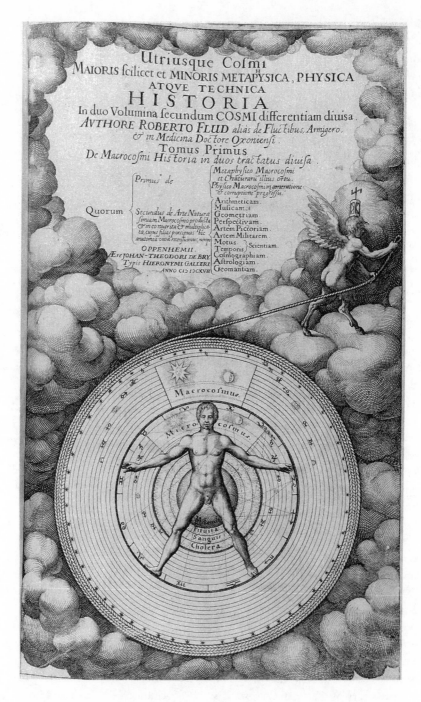

Figure 5. Macrocosm/Microcosm. The individual person spans the spheres of the universe (the earth, sun, moon, stars, and so on, are all contained within the individual). Surrounding the human figure in this illustration is the macrocosm of the actual universe of sun, moon, and stars.

perhaps it does so here. The expression "to become one with the universe," although trite, suggests euphoria, and, almost by definition, euphoria would mark the successful practice of magic. After all, the magician's goals were as lofty as any we can imagine.

Aside from this, however, the macrocosmic-microcosmic connection elicits a very practical recommendation, one that is bound up in the question of how we are able to know and understand the world. If the world were utterly alien to us, it seems probable that we would not be able to get any sort of epistemic purchase on it; we just would not "see" it in the first place.

That we can talk knowingly about it, however, suggests that we are like it, that we have an affinity with it, that our mutual likeness opens out onto a congeniality or "likeability" of being that makes understanding possible. Taken to the limit, this suggestion becomes the microcosmic-macrocosmic thesis: we are so much like the world that we know it from the inside out.

Again we can draw an analogy between the concerns of modern science and those inherent in the magic worldview. Today one hears a lot about the anthropic principle, which posits a pre-existing affinity between the cosmos and the life forms that have evolved therein. Life as we know it is the product of a very subtle interplay of circumstances, any one of which, if not operative, would scuttle biological development. In the face of what seems to be such a delicately contrived situation, some scientists have suggested that the universe was somehow "tuned" to produce life much like a piano is tuned to produce music. Whether this is so is beyond the scope of our inquiry. The important point is the concern for affinity or congeniality. In the mind of some scientists, an uncongenial or life-unfriendly (or, "life-unlikeable") universe could never have produced life. In the mind of a magician (and many ancient thinkers like Aristotle) an uncongenial universe—one with whom we share no kinship—cannot produce knowledge within the minds of its inhabitants. The mind must resonate with the world, and resonance implies similarity, perhaps even unity.

We can now appreciate the magician's hope to achieve omniscience. If the world is so much like us as to be us, then maybe everything is already within us, waiting to be realized. Paracelsus, the Renaissance doctor and alchemist, had something like this in mind when he stated that the heavens stamp into us an impression of themselves. So if you want to learn something, go within yourself. If you want to learn the properties of some herb, don't look at the herb; look within.[25] Omniscience is possible because we are not chipping away at a cosmic structure that dwarfs us; rather, that structure indwells and defines us.

Omniscience, however, is not the ultimate goal of the magician. Knowledge is useful because it facilitates the exercise of power, and the magician aspires to subordinate the universe to his or her will. If omniscience expands or exalts one

MAGIC AND MIRACLES

to cosmic dimensions, then one ought to be able to manipulate forces and objects within the cosmos. The possibility of such manipulation traded not only on a belief in macrocosm/microcosm, but also on a view of nature known as the Great Chain of Being. This outlook, which was prevalent in the West for centuries and hardly the exclusive preserve of magicians, described nature as a continuum reaching from lowest being (dirt and rocks) to highest being (God), and embracing everything in between. The poet Alexander Pope, in his *Essay on Man*, wrote:

> Vast chain of Being, which from God began,
> Nature ethereal, human, angel, man,
> Beast, bird, fish, insect! what no eye can see,
> No glass can reach! from Infinite to thee,
> From thee to Nothing![26]

Or, in schematic fashion:

God

Spirit Beings

World

Humans

Beasts

Zoophytes (half plant, half animal)

Plants

Metals

Stones

Suffice it to say, the Great Chain of Being links humans to nature, and nature to the hand of God. Humankind is placed in the center of the universe, and nature to the hand of God. When this idea is represented pictorially, humankind is often placed in the center of the universe, and nature is portrayed as a young woman wearing sun, moon, and stars. People are thus connected to God and the heavens just as they are to the earth and its creatures.

At least in principle, this linkage could be exploited for magical purposes. Cornelius Agrippa, a sixteenth-century magician, said that the Great Chain of Being is like a tightly stretched string—if you pluck it, the whole string vibrates. If God plucks the string, even the stones feel it. But so also "As below, so above." That is, if you influence something here below, that influence will reverberate heavenward to affect everything above. The nineteenth-century poet Francis Thompson wrote, "All things . . . linked are / Thou canst not stir a flower / Without troubling a star."[27] The seamless continuity of the Great Chain allows us to affect and even control beings and intelligences higher than us.

MAGIC, MYSTERY, AND SCIENCE

Indeed, the concept of the Great Chain of Being fits nicely into the larger magical theme that All is One. For the magician, the universe is a fundamental unity. This idea is sometimes called monism, but here we will simply refer to it as the doctrine of unity. You may wonder how magicians can assert that "all is one" when obviously opposites abound—male and female, light and darkness, and so on. These opposites, the magician believes, ultimately do not exist. At some point they meld into each other: light and darkness, male and female, heaven and earth, human and God. In the end, even good and evil do not exist, but are collapsed or blurred into unity. The aim of the magician is to reach that unity and thereby see things from the higher vantage point it offers, and here experience is the key. Within the context of magic, one must experience all things in the universe to be a completed person, to be a unity. The magician must come to terms with good and evil, light and darkness, love and hatred, kindness and cruelty, for these opposites are all aspects of a great unified whole.

Do all opposites ultimately collapse into unity? The question is an old one and one argument on behalf of such a collapse runs like this: although different, opposites depend on each other for their meaning and therefore participate in each other. Without evil, for example, we would not know or be able to name goodness. Therefore, evil contributes as much to the reality of goodness as goodness itself. The two lean on each other, perhaps lean *into* each other; maybe the two are even in cahoots. If one takes this view, then one will not attach absolute value to either good or evil, will not be daunted by either God or Satan, the Christian archetypes of good and evil. Thus undaunted, the magician will seek to assimilate these one-sided opposites into the larger unity that he believes is reality's true expression.

THE PRACTICE OF MAGIC

There are two major ways that one might practice magic, and they are not mutually exclusive. One is high or ritual magic; the other is everyday magic or what some thinkers call low magic.[28] Ritual magic could be called bookish or intellectual magic. A person who wants to perform ritual magic must be knowledgeable, dedicated, and persevering, spending perhaps a lifetime on her practice. A high magician would know and apply all the principles of the magical worldview that we have discussed in this chapter and would be willing to perform intricate ceremonies to obtain her goals.

Remember that the ultimate goal of a magician is power—to be as a god. In ritual magic, often the first step toward realizing this goal consisted in calling forth a spirit (or demon) so as to force one's will upon it. As in the Faust legend, once the demon was under his power, the magician could control and command it. But how would a budding magician learn how to do this? While

MAGIC AND MIRACLES

Figure 6. A high magician in his study. He summons a demon while drawing a magic circle to protect himself. The demon, complete with hooves and horns, enters through the door in the background.

MAGIC, MYSTERY, AND SCIENCE

tutoring or apprenticeship was a common way of passing on the practice of magic for centuries, by the Renaissance or early modern period, one could learn much from grimoires as well.

Grimoires are sort of do-it-yourself magic textbooks. They are manuals for performing ritual magic, although low magic is sometimes included, as well. Most of these works originate from the sixteenth through the eighteenth centuries, but a few date from even earlier. They may seem very odd at first glance, because they often mix piety with evil actions. They may instruct the magician to fast and offer prayer to God or to angels even while the purpose of the rituals is to call up evil demons, to murder someone, or to force a woman to submit to lovemaking. But the doctrine of unity blurs distinctions of good and evil, and, because power is the ultimate goal, the magician draws upon power wherever he finds it. If God or some angel is deemed more powerful than some demon in a certain instance, then a magician will call upon the power of God or that angel.

Given their strange objectives and the unusual images and expressions that mark their pages, grimoires are very difficult to read, and the instructions are not easy to carry out. But, according to Richard Cavendish, there are essentially three major stages to ritual magic: preparation of oneself, preparation of environment, and the ceremony.[29] To prepare oneself, the magician needs to concentrate all his energies on performing the magic ritual. Preparation often includes abstaining from sex for a certain period, fasting, and praying a great deal. In addition to having a "clean," perfectly focused mind, the magician also must have a clean body. Why? Although she may intend to torture or kill someone, she also may be calling on God or invoking divine names during the ritual, and "cleanliness is next to godliness," as it were. It was also believed that if the magician were physically unclean at all, the evil spirits he was summoning might find a way to seize him. A stain or smear of any sort might work against him as a kind of chink in his spiritual armor.

Along with preparing himself, the magician needed to prepare the environment or trappings of the ceremony. First, a proper place had to be decided upon, preferably a place associated with mystery or evil, such as a graveyard, a church, or a dark road. Second, the correct instruments had to be prepared, such as swords, staffs, and wands. These were to be instruments never used before; otherwise, things could boomerang from a previous owner's use. Third, the ceremony had to be performed at the right time, usually at night. Often, the time would be astrologically determined. Fourth, the magician had to dress properly. Usually, the grimoires recommend white robes, for ritual purity, but black might be used if the demons being called up were completely evil. Fifth, a magic circle had to be drawn. This was extremely important because the circle, drawn around the magician, kept him safe from the powers he called forth. According to the late-nineteenth-century magician MacGregor Mathers, if the circle is drawn incorrectly when a demon is being summoned, the magician will die on the spot in a horrible fit of strangulation or seizure.[30] A correctly drawn circle almost always had a border with the names of God inscribed within it, including the Tetragrammaton ("YHWH" = Yahweh or Jehovah) and other names of power that served to protect the magician. Like an electrician who handles and directs voltages that could easily kill him, the magician had to be extremely careful in his handling of power. He would not, for example, ever step outside the magic circle when channeling demonic powers toward his ends. That would be like risking electrocution.

The incantation was an extremely important aspect of the magic ceremony. By correctly calling upon a god or a demon—invoking its name—the magician believed she could somehow capture its essence. This belief issued from the assumption that names are not arbitrary labels but have been stamped upon us by God or other cosmic forces. Hence, a name encodes or captures one's fate and essence, and to control it is to control the person so named. Recall the story of Rumpelstiltskin, who lost himself, so to speak, when he lost his name. Once his name was guessed, he self-destructed by madly spinning himself into the earth. We generally understand the story as the mere guessing of a riddle, but the extreme note on which the story ends alerts us to the ancient belief that real power resides in names and so names themselves are powerful. We need also to observe that anciently riddles were often more than entertaining puzzles. The riddle of the Sphinx tested one's knowledge of self and those who failed the test died soon thereafter. Again, power was thought to reside within, in a name or in one's self-understanding, and names were portals to self-understanding.

While invoking the requisite names of power, the magician has to ensure that the incantation in general is properly carried out. Errors like a mispronounced name can lead to disaster, because they can be seized upon by malignant forces. Even the rhythm of the incantation is important, because it helps carry the power of the incantation. The life energy of a sacrificed animal also might help in this regard. Demons may resist a weak summons, but an incantation strengthened by the sudden release of animal energy will likely compel them. Going further, human sacrifice will liberate even more energy for incantational purposes—that at least was the determination found in some grimoires.

Low magic is a more common, simple, and everyday type of magic. It has none of the elaborate preparations and ceremonies of ritual magic. If low magic could be bought in a pawnshop, it would be found in the "Saturday-night specials" section. This magic is most often passed on by word of mouth, but some was written down and even found its way into the grimoires. Low magic

MAGIC, MYSTERY, AND SCIENCE

is more what we would normally think of as magic spells (e.g., on the TV show *Bewitched:* "By the point of Arthur's spear, make these pancakes disappear!"). Most low magic attempts to deal with the perennial problems of humanity—how to gain love, blast enemies, stay healthy, and get rich. Here, for example, is a curse directed against two Roman chariot teams. Perhaps the author of the curse has bet money against them:

> I conjure you, daemon, whoever you may be, to torture and kill, from this hour, this day, this moment, the horses of the Green and the White teams; kill and smash the charioteers Clarus, Felix, Primulus, Romanus; do not leave a breath in them. I conjure you by him who has delivered you, at the time, the god of the sea and the air.[31]

Or, for a ritual charged with animal energy, one could drown a cat whose death was thought to attract a demon. When the demon arrived at the scene, the magician would blame the cat's drowning on the enemies he wished to smite and the demon would leave to attack them. A more elaborate version of the ritual involved further handling and burying of the cat's body. In the case that follows, the hope again is to increase one's odds at the chariot races:

> Take the cat and stuff three scraps of paper into him—one into his behind, one into his mouth, and one into his throat. Write the appropriate formula with vermilion on clean paper and then [draw] the chariots and the charioteers and the seats and the race horses and wrap them around the cat's body and bury it. Light seven lights over seven unbaked bricks and give him a smoke offering of gum resin. And be of good cheer.[32]

Here is one way to keep from getting shot or taken captive, taken from a grimoire entitled *Egyptian Secrets: or White and Black Art for Man and Beast,* purportedly by Albertus Magnus: in June, on Saints Peter and Paul's Day, dig up some blue waywort roots fifteen minutes before twelve o' clock, and also procure the herb of this plant. If you carry this herb with you, and someone tries to bind or fetter you, then all ropes, fetters, and locks will spring open, and balls fired at you will not strike you. Another way to keep from harm is to eat some wild radishes before breakfast. If you do, no one will be able to flog you, and if you can manage to keep the radishes in your mouth, you will be able to vanquish all enemies. (And, depending on the potency of the radishes, perhaps friends as well.) One final example of low magic: to make yourself invisible, simply pierce the right eye of a bat and carry it with you. (It is not clear whether the eye or the bat should be carried.)[33]

This sounds like mumbo jumbo, which it is in more than one sense. Mumbo jumbo means both magic ritual and (for the uninitiated) the unintelligible

MAGIC AND MIRACLES

language and activity associated with that ritual. To understand how these strange prescriptions might be thought to have efficacy, we turn to two cardinal principles of magic.

TWO PRINCIPLES OF MAGIC

Magicians have long relied upon two interrelated ideas to explain how most magic works: imitative magic and the magical link. These two are not mutually exclusive and they both assume action-at-a-distance interaction. As one might guess, imitative magic involves making something that imitates the person to be affected and then doing to the thing what you want done to the person. The most well-known example of imitative magic is the use of the voodoo doll, which looks like or imitates the person to be harmed. Imitative magic using dolls is certainly not confined to West Indian voodoo. In England at one time, if citizens merely made a doll of a member of the royal family, they could be charged with high treason.

Imitative magic, however, is not limited to making dolls of a person over whom one wishes to exercise power. At times, it might be advantageous to establish a link between the targeted individual and the magic. For example, a voodoo doll would work much better if it not only looked like the victim (imitative magic) but also had actual hair or clothing from the victim. The hair or cloth would transmit magical power, allowing it to run from the doll to the intended recipient. It would function as a magical link in somewhat the same fashion that an autograph of Babe Ruth links one to Babe Ruth: it sets up a sympathetic connection between a particular individual and the magician. For this reason, the act of establishing a magical link is sometimes called sympathetic magic.

This explains why the twentieth-century magician Aleister Crowley was so fearful of anyone gaining access to his fingernail clippings or hair or anything else from his body. In the hands of an enemy, even an eyelash could become a conduit for the transmission of evil energy. Sympathetic magic, however, could help as well as harm. During the Middle Ages and the Renaissance, a magician might try to heal an injured soldier by preparing an ointment to "heal" the weapon that wounded him. The thread of sympathy that ran from the weapon to the wound could be relied upon to transfer to the wound the healing properties of the ointment, once it had been applied to the weapon.

THE REVIVAL OF MAGIC IN THE RENAISSANCE

Most modern people take a dim view of magic, and this attitude can be traced in part back to the Renaissance. Copernicus, Leonardo da Vinci, Michelangelo, and Andreas Vesalius were Renaissance figures, and they helped pioneer new perceptions and understandings of nature. If Western intellectual experience throughout the Middle Ages tended to be theocentric (with theology as "the queen of the sciences"), during the Renaissance it became more humanistic and secular. To be sure, God still figured prominently in the cosmic drama, but within that drama humans were learning to play more active and independent roles. And if humans were developing a stronger sense of autonomy, perhaps it is not surprising that before long they began to think of nature in mechanical terms. In both spheres—human society and the natural environment—self-regulation became a desirable attribute.

Early practitioners of science made impressive advances by learning to regard the universe as a machine. Earlier we noted that a clock, say, may initially impress one with its seemingly magical capacity for autonomy, precision, and regularity, but once the clock is reduced to its smallest workings, it no longer compels our wonder. We see it as a well-planned ordering of parts energized by outside force; it differs from a lever or pulley only in degree of mechanical sophistication. This realization—that things which seem living and mysterious may actually be complicated mechanisms—prompted the thesis that the world is generally lifeless. It is a huge machine, full of smaller machines.

But what to do with the thinker of such thoughts? Is he or she also a small but highly complicated machine? More often than not, those who subscribed to the mechanical outlook exempted themselves from its characterization. Perhaps their bodies were machines but their minds or spirits were repositories of intelligence, and this exception to the rule explained their enlightenment. According to his own report, René Descartes (circa 1630) was visited by the "Spirit of Truth," who informed him that mathematics was the key to unlocking the secrets of nature.[34] This epiphany inspired Descartes to rid nature of its poetic qualities and redefine it in quantitative, mechanical terms. The irony, of course, was that, at least in part, Descartes's naturalistic view of nature was rooted in a supernatural experience. In order to give us the lifeless world he felt was so vital to science, he had to become, in effect, an alien from another world.

This irony introduces us to the flip side of the Renaissance. To be sure, science did flourish during the Renaissance but so did magic, astrology, and alchemy. In fact, these occult branches of knowledge enjoyed more social approbation during the Renaissance than they did during the Middle Ages. Why? Because magic was an important part of Greek and Roman culture, and Renaissance thinkers wanted to emulate the classical world in every way. They disparaged the Middle Ages, the age between their own era and the glory of Greece and Rome, feeling that it was too unimaginative and too theocentric in its apprehension of nature. (Note that the propaganda of the Renaissance lives on: to call someone "medieval" is insulting, while to call someone a "Renaissance" person is a high compliment.) Furthermore, Renaissance scholars endeavored to place humankind at the center of the universe—not just cosmographically but also authoritatively—and magic accommodated this very well. Such striving became almost frenzied during the Renaissance, particularly after the works of the fabled Hermes Trismegistus reached Italy in the middle of the fifteenth century.

Classical texts of all sorts were highly prized during the Renaissance. Many of these had been brought back from Spain and the Middle East by Christian crusaders, and scholars were eager to have them translated from Greek or Arabic into Latin. One of the great patrons of this effort was the Italian ruler Cosimo de Medici. In 1453, Byzantium, the capital of the Byzantine Empire, fell to the Turks. When Greek-speaking Byzantine scholars fled the city, many of them brought ancient Greek works with them to the West. Cosimo, an old man by 1453, was impatient to read the great treatises of Plato before he died, for very few of Plato's works had been translated from Greek into Latin or Italian. Cosimo had one of these Byzantine scholars, Marsilio Ficino, begin translating Plato's works. But when a Greek manuscript of Hermes Trismegistus was brought to his attention, Cosimo immediately redirected Ficino's translation energies to this new find. Plato's wisdom was extraordinary, but that of Hermes was sublime.

Hermes Trismegistus ("Hermes Three Times Great") was believed to be a powerful Egyptian sage-magician who was slightly younger than Moses but much more ancient than Plato. His Egyptian origins and extreme antiquity helped explain the profundity of his teachings. Tradition had it that he had crossed paths with Moses and had incorporated that great prophet's wisdom into his own elevated understanding of the cosmos. Then his corpus of thought tumbled down from one generation to the next, sometimes being garbled in the transmission process. When his works were finally translated in the West, Hermes' enlightenment seemed more wondrous than ever, for the text clearly showed that he had prophesied of the coming of Jesus Christ. And almost all of the ideas we normally associate with Plato, well, they are found in Hermes' writings—Plato had obviously received them from Hermes. No wonder Cosimo wanted Hermes translated first. Why drink downstream from Plato when you can go directly to the source of Plato's wisdom—Hermes Trismegistus.

Hermes' prophetic powers, however, were eventually discovered to be the result of hindsight rather than foresight. After the Renaissance, scholars came to realize that the works attributed to Hermes were in fact written two or three hundred years after the time of Christ, and hence about five hundred years after Plato. Cosimo and nearly everyone during the Renaissance had creatively misunderstood the texts. To this day, we do not know the true authors of the

Figure 7. Hermes Trismegistus

Figure 8. The magus as master of the cosmos

works of Hermes because they all wrote under the pen name "Hermes Trismegistus" and thus produced a hodgepodge of texts known as the Hermetic
corpus. The final result is a wild brew of Greek philosophy, alchemy, and magic,
spiced with various flavors of cabalistic, Gnostic, and Neoplatonic thought.

Now that the exalted personage of "Hermes Trismegistus" has splintered
into several obscure individuals, the texts attributed to him are no longer very
compelling. During the Renaissance, however, the Hermetic corpus held forth
tremendous magical promise. It taught that a magus (one deeply versed in
magical arts) could take control of his own fate and ultimately of the universe.
Nothing was beyond his will, for magic can be understood as an attempt to collapse the tension between heaven and earth. Most of us feel "grounded" to the
earth and the limited opportunities it offers—recognition, wealth, and personal
comfort. We do not aspire to the grander possibilities of omniscience and om-
nipotence that are said to belong only to God. As the builders of the Tower of
Babel learned (an operation purportedly masterminded by Nimrod, a great magus), humans cannot successfully storm heaven and take control of the cosmos.

A magician, however, might argue that we have let the frailty of the human body trump the soaring imagination of the spirit. The earthly experience has a way of sizing down our dreams. Henry David Thoreau once stated that the "youth gets together his materials to build a bridge to the moon . . . and at length the middle-aged man concludes to build a wood-shed with them."[35] The hard knocks of adulthood teach him a lesson in dream management, and so he spends the remainder of his years leading a life of "quiet desperation,"[36] not daring to overstep his mortal limitations. If he is religious in a traditional sense, he waits for God to rescue him from those limitations. The magician, however, is not inclined to wait but tries to encroach on the Deity. In this respect, perhaps, he is not so different from the scientist who "plays God" by cloning animals or engineering better gene sequences. In either case, the practitioner is not content to let nature or supernature take its course, but deliberately steps in believing that she can cure a disease, turn lead into gold, unlock the energy of the atom, or project spaceships into the starry heavens.

"Magic and alchemy," writes Iring Fetscher, "were later dismissed . . . by the age of science, yet the wishes, hopes, and attitudes they expressed are thoroughly comparable with those of Bacon, Descartes, Newton, and so on. They, too, strove constantly to make man the 'master and owner of the world' (Descartes)."[37] In sum, the propensity to think and dream big is common to both magic and science and may help explain their juxtaposition during the Renaissance. As we have already suggested and will observe at greater length, some of the architects of early modern science were involved in magic. This is not to say they were full-fledged magicians, only that they were more alive to the possibilities of magic than most Westerners are today.

MAGIC AND MIRACLES

3

NUMEROLOGY, THE CABALA, AND ALCHEMY

My idea is that magic and experimental science have been connected in their development; that magicians were perhaps the first to experiment; and that the history of both magic and experimental science can be better understood by studying them together.

—Lynn Thorndike[1]

Concerning alchemy it is more difficult to discover the actual state of things, in that the historians who specialize in this field seem sometimes to be under the wrath of God themselves; for, like those who write on the Bacon-Shakespeare controversy or on Spanish politics, they seem to become tinctured with the kind of lunacy they set out to describe.

—Herbert Butterfield[2]

WHAT'S IN A NAME?

The power of names is the impetus behind both numerology and the Cabala; in both, a name may contain the very essence of an object or a person. By "names" we mean words in general: the ability to recast the world in audible tones and written characters. Now taken for granted, that ability once provoked wonderment, for language was felt to yield unexpected dividends: mere sounds and strokes of a stylus dissolved into luminous thoughts and richly detailed stories. Language consequently registered itself as part of the miracle of Creation, and some people sought to harness its marvelous powers in ways that go beyond rhetoric and modern storytelling. Because words were elemental (not invented after the fact of Creation), they could be manipulated in the same manner modern scientists seek to manipulate atoms and genes.

Moderns may think this bizarre, but closer examination reveals that our everyday discourse still carries vestiges of this view. Instead of saying that a loved one "died," we say he "departed" or "passed away." The word *died* seems too blunt, perhaps too much a part of death itself. It is almost as if the word participates in the reality of the thing it represents; the two interpenetrate. This, then, is the old magical view of words: they call forth or re-present (rather than merely represent) the entities they name. The word "death" embodies the death experience.

This equivalence between word and world—George Steiner calls it a covenant that has now been broken[3]—finds further illustration in the way we feel about our personal names. People who use them too quickly provoke our resentment. It feels as if they are taking liberties with something more than just a label; they are flaunting part of our core identity. Going much further, Nazi death-camp workers stripped their victims of names altogether, replacing them with impersonal and dehumanizing numbers. Much easier, after all, to gas "83612" than a girl named Jennifer Prague. Even today, we may unconsciously trade on the assumption that an unnamed child is not fully human. One author recalls a highly publicized case of a baby born with a physical impairment. The doctor, with the consent of the parents, ordered that the baby's food be withheld until it died. During all the media coverage while the baby still lived, she was never given a name: she was merely referred to as "Baby Jane Doe." Without a personal name, the child could not be legally registered as a unique individual. More important, she could not readily pass into public consciousness as such.

NUMEROLOGY

The basic concept of numerology is that personal names embody soul and destiny, and that such is revealed as names are translated into meaning-resonant numbers. This implies that our given names are never arbitrarily chosen. Rather, every name, even one given in a moment of whimsy, fits the individual upon which it is conferred by fitting into a vast set of cosmic pur-

NUMEROLOGY, THE CABALA, AND ALCHEMY

poses. A name, therefore, is an aperture through which one may look to discern an individual's life-role on the larger stage of things.

What makes this outlook persuasive is the supposition that everything (even the seemingly small and random details of our lives) is shot through with meaning. Given the war-related horrors of the twentieth century and contemporary strains of thought emphasizing alienation and cosmic loneliness, this view is no longer in vogue. Some optimists may disagree, but few of them (we suspect) would go so far as to argue that numbers are deeply meaningful entities. The modern predisposition is to make quantitative, but not poetic, spiritual, or mythic, sense of numbers. They are flat and impersonal, and this makes balancing the checkbook a chore rather than an opportunity to search out esoteric interconnections. The $61.29 phone bill resonates no spiritual or metaphysical truth; its value lies in its quantitative exactness, its failure to mean anything but its numerical content.

The numerological view of numbers is very different. Alfred Crosby explains how:

> Today we utilize numbers when we want narrow focus on a given subject and maximum precision in our deliberations. The old Europeans preferred broad focus and settled for imprecision in the hope of including as much as possible of what might be important. Often they were reaching not for a handle on material reality, but for a clue as to what lay beyond the scrim of reality. They were as poetic about numbers as about words.[4]

With this attitude prevailing, words or names could be numerically sounded for their poetic or spiritual content. The standard practice was to assign a number to each letter of a name and then to add and collapse the digits so as to produce a number between 1 and 9. Either first or last or both names in combination could be treated in this fashion. Take, for example, "Madonna," the name of the well-known rock diva.

1	2	3	4	5	6	7	8	9
A	B	C	D	E	F	G	H	I
J	K	L	M	N	O	P	Q	R
S	T	U	V	W	X	Y	Z	

Lining up letters with numbers, we get 4, 1, 4, 6, 5, 5, 1, which, when summed, equal 26. Since 26 is more than 9, we collapse its digits to produce 8. This number is Madonna's digital root, the integer most prized by numerologists because it is said to capture a name's totality. As an 8, Madonna supposedly shares the characteristics of other 8s, such as power, money, worldly involvement, material success (or failure), all of which seem to fit. (To be fair, however, we should note that 8s are also said to be uninspiring and lacking in charisma, qualities or "defects" not normally associated with Madonna.) But the digital root, while primary, does not exhaust one's identity and life-purpose, although it unveils the inner, secret self by stripping away one's public mask or persona. The consonants of a name are also important, for when added up in the same way, they give the "personality number"; that is, the essence of one's outer self. Similarly, the vowels sum up to the "heart number," which identifies the inner personality. Having a personality number of 9 and a heart number of 8, Madonna is set apart from most others whose digital root is 8.

But is she really? Skeptics object that this is nothing more than coincidence borne of a hit-and-miss approach: assign enough adjectives to a particular personality category and several are sure to match up with anyone put in that category. What's more, since people often remember the hits while overlooking the misses, the description seems to fit. In this vein, Richard Cavendish states that if one is amazed at how well numerology works, "[t]he reason is the looseness and woolliness of numerologists' language, which is so broad and vague that almost any set of characteristics can be fitted into any number combination. (The same thing is true of astrology and other forms of fortune-telling.)"[5]

Cavendish's point is well taken, but before we dismiss numerology on this basis alone, let us recall that its view of words and numbers may be quite different from our own. Valuing precision, we eschew "loose and woolly" language. Such signifies muddle-headedness or, even worse, an inclination to mislead. Perhaps only in the realm of poetry is imprecise language readily accepted, and then because it is evocative of rarely divined possibilities. Of course, there it is not labeled "loose and woolly" but, rather, figurative, because its function is to overcome sharp distinctions rather than create or reinforce them. When numerology is seen in this light—as more poetic than scientific— then its broad descriptions begin to make sense. Not aiming for sharp distinctions alone, numerology may avoid fault when it fails to achieve them. As long as it takes words and numbers as reservoirs of hidden meaning, it cannot be precise and predictive in the way physics, say, is.

Yet one may wonder how poetry can be extracted from numbers. The fact is we still use numbers in poetic or idiomatic ways, but generally do not attach much significance to them in such contexts. Who but a "1" would have a *one*-track mind, look out for number *one*, and be number *one*. A "2," naturally, would be indecisive (*double*-minded), a good subordinate (play *second* fiddle), and prone to lying and *du*plicity (*double*-tongued). This sort of reasoning applies to other numbers as well, though often the connections do not become obvious until we visualize numbers as dots on a die or pebbles in the sand.

NUMEROLOGY, THE CABALA, AND ALCHEMY

Such numbers are called figurate numbers, because they are felt to reveal the true figure or form of a number. Consider 3. What is the most aesthetically pleasing or beautiful way to arrange three pebbles? One response is to put them in a row (. . .). This arrangement affords insight into the traditional link between 3 and completeness or fulfillment. In Christianity, for instance, the Trinity represents the fullness of the Godhead, a completeness incorporating the three-in-one idea of beginning, middle, and ending. Further analysis indicates that numbers (with the possible exception of 1, which expresses unity) are sexed according to their odd and even natures. Comparing 4 and 5, how might we determine which is male and which female?

Notice that 5 has, as Plutarch politely phrased it, "a generative middle" dot, and thus is male. By contrast, even numbers like 4 (think also of 2 and 6 on a die) have "open, receptive middles," and hence are female.

This way of extracting meaning from numbers has a long history, going back at least to the Greek Pythagoreans. For them, numbers were first and foremost physical patterns that allowed each number to announce its elemental nature. People today tend to dismiss those patterns as arbitrary or biased, but this objection rests on the relativistic assumption that beauty is in the eye of the beholder. Were we to believe, as most pre-modern cultures did, that one's sense of beauty is a guide to truth, figurate numbers would be more interesting to us. What's more, we would probably wonder why numbers are now almost exclusively identified with markings like 7 or 19. They, after all, are indisputably arbitrary and as such keep us from seeing numbers in their pure and simple (figurate) form.

PYTHAGORAS AND THE PYTHAGOREANS

Pythagoras (circa 560–500 B.C.) is best known for his supposed derivation of the Pythagorean theorem: the square of the hypotenuse of any right triangle equals the sum of the squares of the other two sides. Whereas this alerts us to his mathematical interests, it fails to communicate Pythagoras's remarkable philosophical outlook. He founded a religious community in southern Italy, a brotherhood so secretive that its members were sworn to reveal nothing, perhaps on pain of death. Because of this and the antiquity of the group, our knowledge of the Pythagoreans is fragmentary. We do know, however, that they revered mathematics as a vision of nature. "All is number" is the Pythag-

MAGIC, MYSTERY, AND SCIENCE

orean refrain, a mantra expressing the mystic wonder of the way numbers seemed to inform and structure physical reality.

Caught up in a quest for eternal bliss, the Pythagoreans were an ethical order, concerned with purity and usually dressing in white. They believed in the immortality of the soul and its transmigration—the soul survived physical death and passed on to another body, but not necessarily a human body. This belief might explain why they refrained from eating animals, which could have been departed loved ones. Unlike the Egyptians, the Pythagoreans took a dim view of the physical body, believing it to be a kind of tomb in which the soul suffered redemptively for previous misdeeds. Salvation occurred via a spiritual leave-taking of the material world, and the study of numbers facilitated this leave-taking by introducing one to a mathematical constancy beyond (or beneath) the physical flux. Tracing this view of salvation back to Pythagoras, Bertrand Russell wrote that mathematics is "the chief source of the belief in eternal and exact truth, as well as in a super-sensible intelligible world."[6] Uncanny in its capacity to re-express the regularities of nature, mathematics seemed otherworldly in its origin.

There are at least three ways in which scholars have interpreted the Pythagorean claim that "all is number." Each view has some support, and the Pythagoreans could have held none, any, or all three simultaneously as far as we know. Perhaps they *literally* held that all is number; that is, that music, tables, dogs, horses, people—everything is composed of numbers. This is not so farfetched as it first sounds, because figurate numbers consisted of distinctive visual patterns like many other things in the world. Moreover, those patterns fit in with the Greek penchant for geometry: mathematical propositions, while perhaps leading the mind upward to a more sublime immaterial realm, were initially grasped as lines and points in the sand or on a piece of parchment. (Algebra, a more symbolic branch of mathematics, lay in the future.) Possibly this geometric rendering of nature was felt to capture the essence of an entity in a stark, minimalistic way, so that each object's particular number agreed with the fewest number of points needed to represent it. (Compare the constellations, which minimally represent a lion or horse, for example.)

If this view is correct, the Pythagoreans believed that numbers were integral to all physical entities. They are prior to those entities and lend to them their distinctive natures. Another possibility is that the Pythagoreans took the weaker view that numbers merely *represent* things. This is not to say that numbers are a human invention, for whether they indwell and compose things or simply represent them, they are marvelously effective in helping us understand the world and hence cannot be explained away by other means.[7] Even when applied to abstract ideas, they afford insight. Marriage, for instance, is represented by 5, the sum of the first female and male numbers (2 + 3). Being a

NUMEROLOGY, THE CABALA, AND ALCHEMY

male number itself, 5 marks marriage as a male-governed relationship. (No argument from the brethren here.) To cite another example, 4—a square—stands for justice, perhaps because an equal times an equal ($2 \times 2 = 4$) represents a balance of justice.

This tendency to see balance and symmetry in numbers opens out onto the third possible interpretation of "all is number." (Remember that no interpretation necessarily excludes another.) It may be that all things are ratios, or proportion—that all is *harmonic balance*. This is seen in the pleasing symmetry of figurate numbers. The paramount number was 10, and its cosmic significance showed up in the triangular arrangement of the tetraktys. The Pythagoreans even swore by the beautiful pattern of ten dots or pebbles.

The tetraktys forms a perfect (equilateral) triangle. Note also the numerical sequence of dots: $1 + 2 + 3 + 4 = 10$. These numbers, arrayed to produce a visual balance, defined the ratios of musical harmony.

A momentous discovery for the Pythagoreans was that music is governed by mathematical principles. When a musical string is plucked, a note sounds. Until Pythagoras, however, no one related string length with tone; perhaps it seemed that musical tones were too elusive to be captured by rule. Then Pythagoras (or his disciples) found that a halved string (one held down at its center) produces a note one octave higher than at its full length. The ratio here, of course, is 1:2, which corresponds to the first two levels of the tetraktys. Pythagoras furthered determined that a string, when divided into thirds and held at the two-thirds point, produces a very pleasing sound that harmonizes with the entire string—what musicians call the fifth. This proportion—2:3—is the second ratio of the tetraktys. The third ratio (the fourth in musical terminology) was found in like fashion: hold the string at the three-quarters point to produce a note that resonates nicely with the note produced by the string at full length. This gives us 3:4, the last (bottommost) ratio of the tetraktys.

If something as spontaneous and subjective as music has a numerical essence, why not everything? Why not suppose that the order or harmony of the world arises from the very ratios that lend to music its harmonious qualities? And by embodying those ratios, the tetraktys shone forth as a re-expression of the

MAGIC, MYSTERY, AND SCIENCE

cosmos. In fact, when further contemplated, it afforded the initiate a complementary vision of the world's creation. Starting at the top, one could retrace God's steps in ordering the universe—from single point, to line (requiring two points), to plane figure (three points), and finally to solid body (four points). This was God's geometrical path to a three-dimensional world filled with three-dimensional objects.

Given this outlook, it is not surprising that the Pythagoreans imagined the Creator God as a mathematician. This view was not only central to later numerology; it also shaped the thinking of Galileo, Johannes Kepler, and other founders of modern science. After declaring the universe to be written in the language of mathematics, Galileo wrote that unless one first "grasps the [mathematical] symbols . . . it is impossible to comprehend a single word of it; without which one wanders in vain through a dark labyrinth."[8] In the twentieth century, Werner Heisenberg (one of the architects of quantum mechanics) expressed his Pythagorean sympathies by writing that "[i]n modern quantum theory there can be no doubt that the elementary particles will finally also be mathematical forms, but of a much more complicated nature [than those supposed by Pythagoras]."[9] This may be nothing more than a metaphysical or aesthetic intuition on Heisenberg's part, but that is just the point: balance, harmony, elegance, beauty—or one's sense thereof—still play a role in our investigation of the world. It is a commonplace among physicists that Einstein's General Theory of Relativity is beautiful, and Einstein himself remarked that aesthetic considerations prominently figured into its development.[10] In this respect, Einstein and Pythagoras are kindred spirits.

Like numbers, names also suggest themselves as constitutive of Creation, and now the focus shifts from early Greek philosophy to a different but equally fecund tradition—that of Judaism.

THE CABALA

The corpus of esoteric documents known as the Cabala embodies a system of Jewish mystical thought originating in the late Roman period. During the Renaissance, many non-Jewish mystics began to use this system as well, and it has continued to attract interest ever since. (More recent proponents include Eliphas Levi and Aleister Crowley.) Cabalistic thinking tends to be obscure, perhaps because of its holistic, suffusive character. Relationships are emphasized as much as individual entities.

Central to the Cabala are the secret names of God, which, not surprisingly, are the most powerful names in the universe. According to some cabalists, the mere utterance of one of these names set in motion the creation of the universe. Projected into emptiness like a stone dropping into a still pond, the name initiated a wave-series of events that still reverberates. Or, to speak in Cabalistic idiom, when the unknowable God created the universe, he sent out an emanation of himself into the void, then further emanations, down and down, like the successive reflections of a beam of light on a series of mirrors. These emanations were both the universe and God, for cabalists (like Renaissance magicians) believed that God is one with his creation; he thus embodies all contradictions—good and evil, mercy and cruelty, light and darkness, and so on. The keys to grasping all this are the emanations themselves, ten in number and collectively known as the sephiroth. Because God shares himself as he emanates, the sephiroth are his ten attributes. Arranged pictorially, the sephiroth become the Tree of Life, which we will explain in a moment.

How do human beings fit into this state of affairs? We originate from God, our souls having descended at birth through ten spheres—corresponding to the sephiroth—into mortality. During this descent, we picked up characteristics from each sphere, so that, upon reaching the earth, our souls have a tenfold layering. (This involved an older view of the universe in which the earth was at the center, surrounded by concentric spheres like successive layers of an onion.) Although this layering ultimately belongs to God (because he is identical with Creation), it is yet infected with the various imperfections of the present world. Our goal, then, is to return to God by peeling off the layers; that is, reverse the process that predisposes us to error and imperfection. This, however, is not an easy task, for angels or spirits, residing on the spheres and having a vested interest in the status quo, seek to prevent the soul's ascent.

Hoping to outmaneuver the malevolent spirits, cabalists studied the Tree of Life, which not only brings the sephiroth into meaningful coherence but also reveals the twenty-two paths back to God. The paths interconnect the sephiroth, and their number coincides significantly with the twenty-two letters of the Hebrew alphabet. Thus, alphabet and sephiroth—both expressions of God's creative sharing—interlock to form a powerful image of the cosmos. Overall equilibrium and flow of life energy was achieved not only by balancing the visual pattern but also by arranging the sephiroth so that each sephira functions as a receptor and transmitter: it receives the preceding sephira (via one of the twenty-two paths) and then transmits its own energy, bundled with that of previous sephiroth, to the next sephira. This description, however, is a bit misleading, for it evokes the analogy of power line transmissions. Thinking more organically, cabalists felt that the sephiroth were sexed and even "bisexual" in their ability to both receive and project life-giving virtue.

Reminding devotees of the primacy of the twenty-two letters of the Hebrew alphabet, the Tree of Life encouraged contemplation of sounds and words as well as visual images. What sounds did God utter to bring the universe into existence? No doubt he spoke one of his names—probably the Tetragramma-

MAGIC, MYSTERY, AND SCIENCE

ton, which many felt to be the most important and powerful of all God's names. Not a name as such but the name of a name (it is Greek for "four letters"), the Tetragrammaton is generally spelled "YHWH" (Yahweh) or sometimes "JHVH" (Jehovah). In Hebrew it means "I am" and dates back to Moses's experience on Mount Sinai: when he asked to know God's name, God replied, "I am that I am."[11]

Implying that God is self-existing and that the existence of all else is derivative, YHWH was reverenced by Jews as God's sacred name for himself. As such, it could not be spoken glibly lest it be profaned. By the first century A.D., only the high priest pronounced it once a year in the holy of holies (the innermost and most sacred chamber of the tabernacle and synagogue). Care was taken to pronounce it correctly, although today scholars are unsure of the original pronunciation. Less daunted by the long, tortuous history of the Hebrew language, one modern magician, Aleister Crowley, professed to know its true pronunciation and on occasion kept potentially wayward disciples in line by threatening to pronounce YHWH in such a way as to destroy the universe. Evidently he felt that by saying God's name backward, he would undo or reverse the Creation.

Another candidate for God's creative utterance is the Shemhamphorash, which is the longest of God's many names. Again, this is a name of a name, one whose seventy-two syllables of three letters each (216 letters, total) are actually the words of three biblical verses all packed together. Exodus 14:19–21 describes the Israelite crossing of the Red Sea, and some cabalists insist that Moses invoked this passage as God's name in order to part the Red Sea. As a vessel of God's power, the Shemhamphorash is said to be useful in subduing demons, quenching fires, healing invalids, and slaying enemies. The rub, however, is that only the spiritually pure (like Moses) may command its tremendous energies; others will be blasted to nothingness.

Along with their constructive properties, the elements of creation have destructive potential. This dictum, now descriptive of atomic particles, once applied to Hebrew letters. Cabalists consequently immersed themselves in the Hebrew language. One could, of course, simply read important Hebrew texts such as the Old Testament to ascertain God's purposes, but textual analysis often yielded greater rewards. Believing that God had both written the Old Testament and encoded it with deep meaning, cabalists invented three codebreaking techniques that have subsequently found application in other domains of magic. These are gematria, notarikon, and temurah.

For the Pythagoreans, all was number. For the cabalists, everything reduced to Hebrew letters. In both cases, fundamental reality consisted of already existing entities that, when apprehended or discovered, sparked understanding. That is, numbers and names were not human inventions imposed on nature

NUMEROLOGY, THE CABALA, AND ALCHEMY

after the fact of creation, but elemental constituents fulfilling the role that subatomic particles now play in modern science. As such, they could be probed for insight and manipulated for power. In Hebrew, some letters functioned also as numbers (something like A = 1, B = 2), and this number-letter link formed the basis of gematria: convert a word or phrase into numbers and then match the sum of the word(s) with the sum of another significant word or phrase. By this means, cabalists found deep connections that otherwise would have gone unnoticed. For example, in the eighteenth chapter of Genesis, we read that while Abraham was sitting in his tent on the plains of Mamre, "he lift up his eyes and looked, and lo, three men stood by him." Who were the three men? The text does not identify them, but using gematria, cabalists determined that the phrase "and lo three men" adds up to 701—a number also derived from the phrase "these are Michael, Gabriel, and Raphael."

Another code-breaking technique is notarikon, which involves taking the first (or last) letter of each word in a phrase to make a new word that imbues the phrase with fresh meaning. This is much like forming an acronym, but acronyms are not always felt to illuminate the organization or activity they represent. (Sometimes they do, however, as in MADD—Mothers Against Drunk Driving.) Perhaps the best-known or most widely displayed notarikon today shows up (albeit in an unwritten way) in the fish symbol that adorns Christian churches and the automobiles of believers. That symbol is very old, going back to the early Christian era when most followers spoke Greek. The word for fish in Greek is *ichthys,* which could be expanded to *I*esous *Ch*ristos *Th*eou *Y*ios *S*oter, or "Jesus Christ, God's Son, Savior." The fish symbol captured this notarikon and functioned as a succinct and sometimes secretive expression of one's belief. Moreover, its link to Christianity was perfectly apt: Christ was a fisher of men, some of his disciples were fishermen before conversion, several New Testament miracles involved fish, and the Age of Pisces (Fishes) had supposedly begun at about the time of Christ's birth. (There will be more on this in chapter 4.)

Temurah is the last cabalistic technique for decoding Hebrew texts. Using temurah is much like making anagrams—switching letters around in a word to spell a different word. The obvious difference is that for modern people words composed of the same letters (though differently arranged) need not be linked in meaning. "Disk" and "kids," for instance, do not share some hidden significance merely because they share letters. This is because for us each alphabetic letter is a perfect blank; it has no meaning to breathe into the words it helps form. In some non-alphabetic languages (such as Chinese), however, ideas or meanings are built into the characters (ideograms), and so it is natural to expect that words that share characters will be semantically related. Hebrew is an alphabetic language, but cabalists believed that each letter had a root meaning

MAGIC, MYSTERY, AND SCIENCE

or value that fed into a word's overall meaning. Thus, the meaning of words was to be found in the twenty-two letters of the Hebrew alphabet, and when sets of letters were rearranged to form different words, semantic linkages were anticipated. After all, the root values stayed the same even when differently ordered.

Reasoning from these premises, one of our students supplied a temurah that might as well be enshrined at Graceland, Tennessee: *lives* unscrambles quite wonderfully into *Elvis*. Of course, cabalists would be wary of temurahs worked out in languages other than Hebrew; there is, after all, only one alphabet of Creation. A more responsible (but no less incredible) example of temurah comes from Richard Cavendish.[12] After the German army occupied Greece during World War II, Jewish communities in Syria feared that Hitler would soon invade their land. To forestall an invasion, Syrian Jews consulted several learned cabalists who worked feverishly through the night and finally hit upon a solution: rearrange the Hebrew letters in the word *Syria* to form *Russia*. (Something like "Syria" = "Rysia.") Soon thereafter, German divisions raced into Russia, and Syria escaped the brunt of the Nazi war effort. This extraordinary account illustrates the cabalistic belief that the Hebrew alphabet could be manipulated to alter events and tip the balance of power in one's favor. Because knowledge is power (an equivalence still taken for granted), knowledge of God's own alphabet afforded one tremendous power.

THE TAROT

To say that something is "in the cards" is to draw upon the cabalistic tradition of the Tarot and the popular practice of using tarot cards to tell fortunes. According to occultists, Tarot cards may help one read the future, but this is their lowest, least advanced application. Fully understood, the cards usher one into the dance of life—the very rhyme and reason of the world.

Based upon the sephiroth, the cards are said to bring God, humans, and the universe into mutual contact. Or, more correctly, they make us aware of the intimacy we already enjoy with God and his creation. Daily events often seem random and digressive—"out of the blue" happenings that do not advance our goals and sometimes hinder their realization. Why, for example, did my airplane seatmate spill his drink on me just as I was getting comfortable? Why did the weather turn cold and blustery the afternoon of the family picnic? Why did I call my date by the wrong name when I wanted to make a good impression? These are idle questions in the egocentric life-narratives we spin for ourselves, but when put in the larger context offered by tarot cards, answers emerge. The stray threads are gathered into the wider tapestry of God's purposes.

NUMEROLOGY, THE CABALA, AND ALCHEMY

There is, however, no standard way to interpret the Tarot (the vast multiplicity of tarot card arrangements). That, perhaps, would be like coming up with a rulebook for life. A similar uncertainty marks the origin of tarot cards; they have been traced back to nearly every ancient culture from China to North Africa. One legend attributes them to the ancient sages of Egypt, who, foreseeing the destruction of the magnificent Library of Alexandria by barbarians, decided to preserve their wisdom in a deck of cards that offered harmless amusement to the uninitiated. To others with occult sensibilities, however, the cards, when shuffled and arranged in patterns, brought the world's operation into microcosmic focus. By giving the cards to gypsies, who used them for their own crass purposes and spread them far and wide, the Egyptian sages found a way to perpetuate sacred wisdom under the guise of commonplace activity.

The standard tarot pack contains seventy-eight cards. Of these, fifty-six make up the Minor Arcana (*arcana* meaning hidden or secret), consisting of four suits of fourteen cards each. Modern playing cards, being derivative, roughly follow the Minor Arcana's format. The four suits are (usually) Cups, Wands, Coins (or Pentagrams), and Swords, corresponding to the more familiar hearts, clubs, diamonds, and spades, respectively. Each suit has cards numbered from one to ten and then four face cards: King, Queen, Knight, and Page (equivalent to the Jack). The Knight, of course, has no equivalent in modern face cards.

The remaining twenty-two cards are the Major Arcana, so called because they are believed to contain the deep, occult secrets of the Tarot. These feature fascinating, often bizarre, illustrations and titles such as "Devil," "Female Pope," and "The Hanged Man." Each bears a unique meaning or "personality," just as individual numbers in numerology do, or zodiacal signs in astrology. And like those numbers and signs, each card offers understanding of one's true self and destiny. Taken collectively, the twenty-two trump cards correspond to the twenty-two paths on the Tree of Life and, by extension, to the twenty-two letters of the Hebrew alphabet. Thus integrated into the world's foundation, the cards comprise life's many permutations, and the patterns of their arrangement are as diverse as the images of a kaleidoscope. One can place the cards on the Tree of Life to coordinate their various meanings with those of the sephiroth. Or, one may arrange them in a wheel or circular fashion so as to "recreate" the ever-spinning universe. In this pattern, the "Fool" card is placed at the center or hub of the cosmic wheel. The Fool watches the dance of life around him, but does not join in.

Although often depicted as a happy-go-lucky youth ready to skip off a cliff while blithely chasing a butterfly, the Fool is more than meets the profane, untutored eye. Not unlike Shakespeare's Tom o' Bedlam (the village idiot), Thoreau's Bill Wheeler (the town drunk), and the Beatles' "Fool on the Hill,"

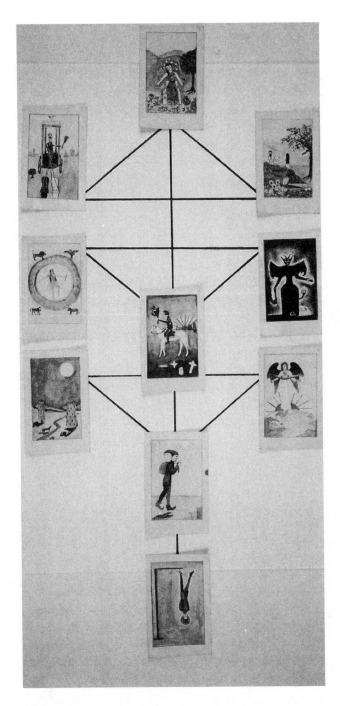

Figure 9. Tarot cards. A few of the Major Arcana arranged upon the
Tree of Life of the Cabala.

his foolishness is borne of a transcendent wisdom rarely attained by others; thus, he can lightheartedly "play" the fool while others, caught in the egocentric predicament, feel the weight of the world as they affect postures of respectability and understanding. This bemused detachment from conventional care makes the Fool supremely important in the current scheme of things, for even though he does not participate in the dance of life, his clear vision sustains it like a hub sustains the spokes and rim of a wheel. Should he ever leave his central position to join in the dance, the world would tumble in upon itself, and life as we know it would cease.

ALCHEMY

Alchemy also prizes that which is commonplace, lowly, foolish, and despicable, recognizing in such a hidden splendor. Today most people regard alchemy as a headlong, misguided, and perhaps even shameless pursuit of material wealth, but this distorts its true nature. Granted, alchemists sought to turn lead into gold, but they believed that such a transmutation would occur only as one's own soul was similarly transformed. The conversion of lead into gold, in other words, evinced spiritual purification. Often extraordinarily ambitious, alchemists—like Renaissance magicians, with whom they share ties—concerned themselves with immortality, knowledge, and power. Their Great Work was to become a god or as God or one with God. (Those more aligned with Judeo-Christian ideals aspired to conjoin with, or know the mind of, God.)

Can one really turn lead into gold? Thanks to advances in modern science, it is now possible, although the cost is so prohibitive as to make the process unfeasible. But alchemists did not envisage transmutation occurring via mechanical or engineering means. The process had to be natural, not coercive; it had to participate in the familiar expressions of change occurring all about us. A stick of wood, thrown into a fire, becomes smoke and ashes; a planted seed becomes a tree; a lump of dough, sprinkled with yeast, swells into a loaf and becomes bread under the action of heat; ingested food becomes part of one's body. None of these changes surprise us, but that is not because they are easy to explain: it is because they are commonplace. In brief, nature readily supplies examples of change no less striking than that attempted by alchemists. Moreover, the alchemist's attempt was carried out within the familiar bounds of nature, for therein lay the power to effect change.

But how might an alchemist tap and direct this power? He had, first of all, to understand nature's elemental operation, the way a few fundamental constituents interact to produce manifold diversity at a secondary, often more obvious level. The modern approach is to trace everything back to the periodic table of elements and then to probe or manipulate selected elements. Ancient alchemists proceeded in a similar fashion, though, as just mentioned, they were less prone (and less able) to subject nature to extraordinary circumstances; "high-energy" alchemy was neither a conceptual nor a practical possibility. Moreover, alchemists worked with far fewer fundamental elements. Instead of the hundred-plus that make up the period table, there were just four: earth, air, fire, and water. These roughly coincided with everyday experience. Things such as rocks, trees, and dirt clods seem generally to be opaque and to hold their shape so that they have a certain "hard" or solid presence about them—they hurt when we bump into them. By contrast, translucent water takes the shape of its container and more often than not yields to earthy bodies. Air or wind seems quite different. For one thing, air is harder to see than water. For another, it tends to expand beyond or escape from its container: it has the ability to go upward (toward the sky) while water and earth invariably go downward unless forced otherwise. Finally, there is fire, which also goes upward but which is manifestly different—even to the point of seeming otherworldly—from the first three elements.

That said, let us add that these four elements were felt to be ideal substances or states of being that can only be approximated. This means that water, say, never shows up in nature in a pure state. Even the clearest spring water contains traces of the other three elements, and such intermixing implies interaction or change. As Empedocles (the ancient Greek who first proposed this theory) said, the four elements continually run through each other, ever mixing and remixing to produce unceasing change in the world.[13] Alchemists believed that by skillfully directing the mixing of elements, they could incline the flow of change upward to substances like gold and thus help nature realize her highest possibilities.

During the Middle Ages and the Renaissance, alchemists drew upon another tradition of basic elements, often conjoining it with the older Greek outlook. All metals were thought to be composed of sulfur, mercury, and salt. Again, these are ideal substances in the sense that they epitomize principles or states of being. Sulfur embodies the active, burning principle—the hot, fiery, combustive state that seems to be nothing but active emission of energy or force. Mercury typifies the liquid, passive principle by virtue of its fluidity and vulnerability to outside force or pressure. Finally, salt, being relatively stable in a physical sense, exemplifies the inert, solid principle. Since everything consisted of the same three (or four) elements, it followed that gold could be produced once the requisite balance of elements or principles was achieved. Paracelsus, a Renaissance figure who practiced alchemy with an eye toward physical and spiritual healing (salvation), insisted that gold is a properly proportioned compound of mercury, sulfur, and salt—three fundamental elements that correspond with spirit, soul, and body, respectively.[14]

NUMEROLOGY, THE CABALA, AND ALCHEMY

Figure 10. The alchemist following in the footsteps of Mother Nature

Alchemists valued gold for reasons we still find compelling: it is eye-catching, ductile (malleable), and resistant to corrosion. But aside from these qualities there was another that no longer registers in popular culture. Sappho (circa 632 B.C.) wrote that "Gold is a god, immortal / that keeps its lustre ever."[15] The undying shininess of gold suggested fire—an unusually high proportion of the fiery element—which in turn conjured up all the metaphysical resonance of fire. For Plato, Aristotle, and many others, fire, while yet a terrestrial element, most nearly approximated celestial or divine reality. Removed from fire by artificial heating systems, we have far fewer occasions to let its seeming magic mingle into our thinking. Thoreau in his cabin complained of

MAGIC, MYSTERY, AND SCIENCE

the stove: it "not only took up room and scented the house, but it concealed the fire, and I felt as if I had lost a companion." He then quoted with favor Mrs. Hooper's poem, which reads in part:

Why art thou banished from our hearth and hall,
Thou who art welcomed and beloved by all?
Was thy existence then too fanciful
For our life's common light, who are so dull?[16]

The alchemist's imagination, more alive to fire than ours, instinctively associated metallic shininess with fire, and this association found empirical confirmation in the fact that the smelting of ores required fiery heat whose brightness apparently took up residence in the newly produced metal. Of all metals, gold possessed fire in largest measure, and so was the most spiritually precious.

That gold ore—gold in its natural state—was lustrous indicated that it had already absorbed a great deal of subterranean fire or heat. This heat, now deemed incidental to mechanical processes, was then regarded as the life-warmth of the earth. Metals therefore were thought to gestate in the earth's womb; they grew toward perfection and completeness just as infants grow in their mothers' wombs and planted seeds grow in the ground. This made sense because, for alchemists, nature had not yet been dichotomized into lifeless physical matter and living mind or spirit. Life was the rule; it suffused everything down to the very dregs of physical substance—rocks, dirt, and so on. Higher up the scale, metals were precious or semi-precious concentrations of life force gathered up from the bowels of an organic earth. We still carry vestiges of this view in our language: if we find a "vein" of gold, we dig back to find its source, the "mother lode."

In his discussion of the origins of alchemy, Mircea Eliade relates two ancient inventions that no longer seemed connected: both agriculture and metallurgy presuppose the earth's fecundity. Consequently, "[m]an feels himself able to collaborate in the work of Nature, able to assist the processes of growth taking place within the bowels of the earth. He jogs and accelerates the rhythm of these slow chthonian maturations."[17] The alchemist, no less than the farmer, tries to regulate organic processes toward favorable ends. For those who participate in this effort, Eliade adds, "[t]here is a feeling of venturing into a domain which by rights does not belong to man—the subterranean world with its mysteries of mineral gestation which has been slowly taking its course in the bowels of the Earth-Mother."[18] Alchemy thus becomes a sacred labor, an opportunity to nudge the world toward its bright, fully ripened destiny by the expert handling of primordial life energies.

This, however, was easier said than done; the growth of metals could be stymied or stunted for reasons not unlike those that plague plants and animals.

NUMEROLOGY, THE CABALA, AND ALCHEMY

Most likely, impurities and disturbances would vitiate or block the life force, thus rendering the metal incapable of further progression. Hence, the alchemist's task was to help lower metals grow naturally into gold. As already noted, this transformation could not occur without concurrent spiritual growth on the part of the practitioner: he, too, had to pass through a refiner's fire to realize his full god-like or gold-like potential. Otherwise, he would remain "leaden" and impure, like an organically stunted "base" metal.

Given alchemy's earthy emphasis on fundamental elements and metals, one might be surprised to learn that it also possesses a "cosmic" or astrological orientation. This arises from alchemy's wide-angle view of things; like many occult practices, the alchemical quest could be intoxicatingly grandiose, for the otherworldly resonance of metals pointed the mind skyward. Since antiquity, seven wandering stars—seven planets—had been observed in the heavens, and each of these was paired with one of the seven principal metals: gold, silver, mercury, copper, iron, tin, and lead. This linkage was a macrocosm-microcosm relation because the planets—their properties—informed the metals with which they were associated. One consequently handled a metal in a particular planetary context, perhaps with a sense of being transported heavenward. The astrological symbols for the planets were used for the corresponding metals, and the metals were often referred to by their planetary names (as mercury still is). Each metal grew under the influence of its patron planetary deity, thereby incarnating that planet's distinctive virtue.

Before listing which planets "gave birth" to which metals, we need to note that alchemy, with its geocentric cosmology, deemed the sun and moon to be planetary bodies orbiting about the stationary (non-planetary) earth. A planet was any heavenly body that "wandered" or moved in an irregular fashion, and most of the planets showed a clear affinity with a particular metal. The "golden" sun and the "silvery" moon were obviously connected with the two most precious metals, gold and silver. Mercury, the quickest, liveliest planet, and the one with the shortest orbital year, gave its name to the quickest, liveliest metal—mercury. Also known as "quicksilver" (i.e., "living silver"), mercury seems ready to race off at any moment, as the word *mercurial* denotes. Venus's connection to copper is not apparent, but that of Mars to iron is bound up in iron weapons of war (Mars' province), the bloodshed of war, and the planet's rust-red color. Jupiter, king of the planets, seems short-changed by having been linked to tin, but tin was considered precious before our age of tin cans. Finally, Saturn, the slowest of the planets, seemed naturally associated with the heavy metal lead. To transmute dull, slow lead into bright, beautiful gold was not easy. Indeed, it involved a long and excruciatingly difficult process that ended with the "Philosopher's Stone."

MAKING THE PHILOSOPHER'S STONE

What was the Philosopher's Stone? The expression is slightly misleading to modern ears because we associate philosophy with armchair abstraction. But in the earlier alchemical context, philosophy meant natural philosophy or something like today's natural science. Thus, the alchemist discharged his philosophical (scientific) duties by striving, through his investigation of nature, to produce a substance with the power to perfect or fully ripen physical matter. This substance was the Philosopher's Stone, although it was generally not portrayed as an actual rock or stone. Some practitioners described it as a red powder while others spoke of a permanent or "penetrating water"; still others portrayed it as the medicine or "food of immortality."[19] One text conferred more than six hundred names upon it. Whatever its nature, a more sublime or precious substance could not be imagined. The Philosopher's Stone was not gold *per se*, but something like God's own finger, healing, purifying, and perfecting everything it touches. When brought into contact with an inferior metal, it turns the metal to gold, and this change is emblematic of a comprehensive transfiguration of nature. Conceivably, the Philosopher's Stone—if ever developed—could usher in humanity's long-awaited paradisiacal era.

For the aspiring alchemist, however, the difficulty lay not only in knowing how to produce the Stone, but, more fundamentally, in knowing how to talk about and conceptualize it. Evidently too sublime for precise definition, the Philosopher's Stone is said to be everywhere around us, priceless, yet deemed worthless; to be a stone, yet not a stone; to be made of fire, yet composed of water. One sixteenth-century text states that it is

> familiar to all men, both young and old; it is found in the country, in the village, and in the town, in all things created by God; yet it is despised by all. Rich and poor handle it every day. It is cast into the street by servant maids. Children play with it. Yet no one prizes it, though, next to the human soul, it is the most beautiful and most precious thing upon earth and has power to pull down kings and princes. Nevertheless, it is esteemed the vilest and meanest of earthly things.[20]

This may seem the stuff of Zen riddles, and perhaps the intent of these descriptions was to stretch the mind in new ways. Emphasis was put on the everyday, readily overlooked character of the Stone. Apparently it was too elemental for ordinary comprehension, perhaps because it was deemed foolish and worthless; or perhaps because it was so deeply familiar that only inarticu-

NUMEROLOGY, THE CABALA, AND ALCHEMY

Figure 11. The goal of the alchemist. The king, painted red, probably represents the Philosopher's Stone.

late infants could descry it, like a "music heard so deeply that it is not heard at all."[21]

What's more, alchemists, unlike modern scientists, did not generally strive for clarity when talking about their research. The steep spiritual ascent to the Philosopher's Stone precluded the possibility of cooperative effort and shared understanding, at least at the higher, more esoteric levels. Truth itself winnowed out the weak, and that same truth could not be communicated secondhand. Recall that alchemists aspired to a sacred wisdom that stretched the soul to god-like parameters. Such wisdom could not be taken back to the masses, or even to less advanced adepts, for easy assimilation. Indeed, it might do harm if openly expressed, like light that dazzles and thereby blinds. Better to veil it

MAGIC, MYSTERY, AND SCIENCE

in pictures, symbols, and conundrums. Besides, if an alchemist were driven by the hope of monetary gain (and some were, notwithstanding their high-minded aspirations), then it made good business sense to keep his research successes secret.

These concerns made alchemy an essentially solitary endeavor. As they studied each other's treatises, alchemists guessed at hidden meanings, hoping to lift the veil of secrecy that charitably protected lesser minds from the truth. This led to mutual misunderstanding and the complaint that alchemy is impenetrable. In Chaucer, a disgruntled alchemist's assistant says, "Their scientific jargon is so woolly / No one can hope to understand it fully."[22]

Here is a sample of the jargon, drawn from the writings of Michael Maier, an alchemist living in the early seventeenth century: "From a man and woman, make a circle, then a square, then a triangle, finally a circle, and you will obtain the Philosopher's Stone."[23] From this we may infer that the Stone has male and female qualities and that it entails a progression through three geometric figures with the circle functioning as the alpha and omega of that progression. Perhaps the circle, long considered a metaphor of Deity, is to be discovered afresh at a higher turn of the divine spiral. But this is little more than creative guesswork. There are myriad other possibilities, and even if the "correct" one is realized, how exactly does the practitioner carry it out to produce the Philosopher's Stone?

Whatever the path taken to the Stone, one could count on years of mixing, separating, vaporizing, and collecting various materials, often over smoky, red-hot furnaces. And although alchemists failed to agree on specific details, by the late Middle Ages a general procedure had emerged that took the form of a three-stage process associated with three colors—black, white, and red. The black stage "killed" the initial matter, the white "resurrected" it, and the red "nourished and matured" it.

No doubt this outline proved helpful to many alchemists, but it did not ensure a successful start, for that involved the knotty question of what substance to begin with. One could, of course, begin with lead, but lead was generally regarded as an intermediate product. The preferred starting point was First Matter; that is, matter void of attributes. This idea, admittedly hard to conceive, goes back to Aristotle. He declared that everything about us is made of form and First Matter. Form supplies characteristics or adjectival qualities, and First Matter receives those qualities but has none of its own. It is like an empty slate taking on chalk, or molten wax into which a signet ring is pressed, a kind of pure, utterly featureless receptivity.

Where might an alchemist find such a strange substance? With this question, however, one heads off in the wrong direction: First Matter cannot be strange or exotic, cannot possess any qualities that would set it off from other things. It must therefore inhere in that which is bland and common. Of course, blandness and commonality are also qualities of objects, but in their flat sameness one finds an intimation of First Matter's adjectival emptiness. Alchemists consequently gathered up lowly, common, worthless substances—grass, mud, slime, spittle, feces, urine—from which to distill First Matter. These were not First Matter, but they closely approximated it. First Matter lurked just below the surface as a kind formless chaos ready to receive the impress of creation.

Having decided what to start with, the alchemist's first task was to kill it. In the black stage (nigredo), practitioners took the first step toward producing the Stone by stripping the muck they began with of all qualities and characteristics. By thus "killing" the initial substance, they freed its soul or divine spark; what remained—First Matter—could then be revived in whatever form they wished. Alchemists often applied Jesus' words regarding his own death and resurrection to this process: "Unless a kernel of wheat falls to the ground and dies, it remains only a single seed. But if it dies, it produces many seeds" (John 12:24). Without death, new life is impossible, and the miracle of plant growth entails the springing forth of a galaxy of life—many seeds—from the symbolic burial and death of a single seed. An analogous miracle follows from Christ's passion, death, and resurrection, the "good news" of which becomes the basis for multiple spiritual conversions and newness of life. Put in an alchemical context, the saying was felt to refer to the dying of initial substance and subsequent material conversions (changes) to gold, the metal generally associated with Christ. The "killing" of the material included reducing it to powder via calcination, then mixing it with mercury, and finally separating and mixing until nothing remained but a black blob of First Matter.

How could one be sure that it was dead? It stank like a rotting corpse, and alchemical symbols of the nigredo stage followed suit: a decaying body, a dead king being chewed on by a wolf, the crucifixion of a snake, and the dismembered body portrayed in figure 12. These dark images not only captured the death of the initial substance; they also expressed the deep melancholy that came over the alchemist as he passed through a corollary spiritual death.

After nigredo came albedo, the white stage involving rebirth and resurrection. In this phase, the alchemist immersed the dead First Matter in a liquid solution known as the "bath of rebirth." If performed correctly, the operation would turn the black blob into a white stone, sometimes identified as the white stone inscribed with a new name mentioned in the second chapter of the Book of Revelation. Michael Maier called it the "true crystalline rock without spot or darkness" and compared it to Apuleius's "midnight sun" and Ezekiel's "wheel of fire."[24] A common symbol for albedo was a person in a bath, with the moon representing the white stone. Again, the alchemist personally shared in the experience, this time by undergoing mystical resurrection and rebirth.

Figure 12. The black stage of alchemy—dismembering and killing the element

In the third and final phase of the process, the white stone metamorphosed into red gold—the Philosopher's Stone. This stage, known as rubedo (red—suggestive of sacrificial blood and ripening), required the alchemist to first nourish and care for the white stone, and then purge it by fermentation and heat. During its "feedings," the white stone might be mixed with such things as honey or human blood. Evidently it needed sustenance to steel it for its long journey through myriad complex operations, including repeated vaporizations, condensations, and exposure to extreme heat. Eventually, however, the white stone would turn into the red powder often associated with the Philosopher's Stone.

Just as a tiny bit of yeast can raise a whole loaf of bread, so a tiny bit of the

Stone (a few grains of red powder) could supposedly perfect and mature all that was inferior and underdeveloped. Turning base metals into gold was just the beginning. Having reached this level, the gloriously successful alchemist allegedly shed his human trappings and took on divine characteristics: he would freely travel about in an astral body, unrestrained by the physical limitations of flesh and blood.

With these possibilities in mind, some alchemists identified the Philosopher's Stone as the Elixir of Life, the "fountain of youth" potion that conferred youth, health, and immortality on all who partook of it. Paracelsus declared that he would live forever, evidently believing he had produced and drunk the Elixir. (Maybe not: he died at about the age of fifty.) Another self-proclaimed possessor of the Elixir was the Count of St.-Germain. The brilliant count seemed the model of an immortal, for he spoke many languages, was quite wealthy, and related stories of his ancient friendships with figures such as Jesus, Cleopatra, and King Richard the Lionheart. Unfortunately, he died in 1784, having lived (by his reckoning) more than two thousand years.

According to their contemporaries, some alchemists, such as Paracelsus, did indeed discover the Philosopher's Stone, but many others who claimed as much were charlatans. More than once the deception was carried off by secretly manufacturing bi-metal nails: the upper halves made of iron and the lower halves of gold painted with black dye. Later, before an eager (and wealthy) audience, the pretender would sprinkle a few precious grains of the Philosopher's Stone into a prepared solution—perhaps an acid. He would then dip an "iron" nail halfway into the solution and pull it out as partly gold. If the ruse worked, the striking sight of a half-gold nail might turn spectators into patrons. Kings sometimes supported alchemists, conferring upon them significant endowments after being convinced that the Great Work was nearly complete: soon *copious* quantities of the Philosopher's Stone would be available. (With this prospect always near at hand, however, the king might be strung along for years.)

As late as 1782, many European cognoscenti were still inclined to take the Philosopher's Stone seriously. In that year, James Price, a young chemist, doctor, Oxford graduate, and fellow of the Royal Society (the academy of scientists in England), created a tremendous sensation when, before prominent citizens, he conducted experiments showing (or seeming to show) that a small amount of red powder stirred into heated mercury produced almost thirty times its weight in pure gold. (He could do the same for silver.) Unfortunately for Price, the so-called Last of the Alchemists, alchemy was transmuting into chemistry by his time: his contemporaries included John Dalton, Joseph Priestly, and Antoine Lavoisier, all pioneers of the modern revolution in chemistry. The skeptical Royal Society challenged Price's results and insisted that the experiments be performed before selected observers. Price reluctantly agreed, and, after greeting the scientific delegation at his laboratory, he turned, drank a flask of prussic acid (a form of cyanide), and collapsed and died while his stunned visitors looked on helplessly.

No one knows Price's motivation for ending his life in this way. Possibly for him it was a dramatic high, the ultimate surprise ending that far eclipsed his striking alchemical demonstrations. Nor do we know exactly why Price sought to defraud others. Being a wealthy man, he had no monetary need to do so. If his incentives are unclear, so is the secret of his alchemical ruse. Perhaps he had read and enacted Chaucer's tale of a crafty alchemist, who, like Price, had produced an ingot of silver by adding a bit of the Philosopher's Stone to a pot of heated mercury. But Chaucer saw through the phony demonstration: the alchemist had previously filled a hollow iron rod with silver shavings and then stopped up its end with wax. When the rod was used to stir the hot mercury, the wax melted and "Out of the stick slid all the silver dust / And down into the crucible it fell."[25]

Opposite Price, however, were many alchemists whose motives were sincere. Among such was a famous threesome of the seventeenth century: the philosopher John Locke, the chemist Robert Boyle (of Boyle's Law fame and whose immense wealth precluded any financial need for alchemical gold), and Isaac Newton. These three men exchanged letters on alchemy and swore each other to secrecy. Newton, in particular, spent years, day and night, working at his furnaces in Cambridge. Indeed, the elusive pursuit of the Philosopher's Stone and the unriddling of biblical prophecy consumed more of Newton's time than his scientific work on motion, light, and gravity. For Newton and his contemporaries, however, science, as we now know it, was not clearly set off from alchemy (or biblical prophecy). All research resonated spiritual overtones in that it was directed toward apprehending the Creator's plan.

Accustomed to academic specialization and having thrown alchemy into the dustbin of history, we are now inclined to regard Newton's alchemical pursuits as an unfortunate waste of intellect and sterile of larger possibility. The truth may be different, however. Richard S. Westfall (author of *Never at Rest*, the definitive biography of Newton) saw Newton's varied interests intermingling to produce a comprehensive vision of nature that departed in significant ways from Descartes's mechanistic outlook.[26] Physical matter, by Descartes's lights, was lifeless, passive substance incapable of mediating change except by direct contact. But alchemy regarded physical matter as fully capable of acting at a distance to effect change. Why not? It was active and living, and therefore able to cast its influence beyond its strict material confines. As Newton studied various processes of nature (the tides, capillary action, certain chemical reactions, and so on), he found Descartes's thesis too stark—too poorly stocked

NUMEROLOGY, THE CABALA, AND ALCHEMY

with possibility—to yield satisfactory explanations of numerous phenomena. By contrast, the organic alchemical view of nature seemed consistent with many of his observations, particularly those that suggested forces acting at a distance. This (and other considerations) predisposed him to propose that two bodies, albeit not in physical contact, might act upon each other gravitationally. As we noted in chapter 2, this hypothesis was rejected as occult by some of Newton's contemporaries.

In his high old age, the much-celebrated Newton may have, in his private musings, credited some of his success in physics to alchemy. And having by then abandoned his search for the Philosopher's Stone, he probably shared, or at least could sympathize with, Chaucer's skepticism:

> Learned and simple, by my soul's salvation,
> Achieve the same results from transmutation
> Equally well, when all is said and done;
> They all fail absolutely, every one.[27]

Yet, as Westfall proposes, the excruciating spiritual and intellectual rigors of the alchemical quest *could be* transmutative, albeit in ways not anticipated. There might be a hidden alchemical principle at work in the Sisyphean ordeal of rolling a rock up a hill only to have it roll down again. What's more, while we do not have the Philosopher's Stone to multiply gold, we do have modern science to multiply plastic, computer chips, and nuclear energy.[28] Inasmuch as science is deeply rooted in alchemy, it would be naive to argue that one multiplication miracle has nothing to do with the other. Eliade sees continuity between the two pursuits: modern science "takes up and carries forward" the dream of alchemy, albeit in a secular rather than sacred fashion.[29] "Alchemy," he adds, "has bequeathed much more to the modern world than a rudimentary chemistry; it has left us its faith in the transmutation of Nature and its ambition to control Time" (to accelerate and even transcend temporal processes).[30] Modern science, no less than alchemy, lives from the Stone Age discovery that nature is responsive to *homo faber* (man the maker) and that mutual uplift can occur as human genius seeks to improve nature. The responsibility for that shared ascent has now been transferred to modern science.

4

ASTROLOGY: THE STARRY HEAVENS ABOVE

Who could discern and compass in his narrow mind the vastness of this vaulted infinite, the dances of the stars, the blazing vault of heaven, and the planets' everlasting war against the signs, had not nature endowed our minds with divine vision, had turned to herself a kindred intelligence, and had prescribed so great a science [as astrology]? Who, unless there came from heaven a power which calls us heavenward to the sacred fellowship of nature?

—Manilius[1]

To speak of astrology today generates mainly negative images of banal advice columns in newspapers, charlatans pretending to foresee the future, or New Age witches absorbed in an engaging world of make-believe. And yet there was a time when astrology was considered a science, even the highest of sciences, capable of assisting the noble study of theology.

—Laura Ackerman Smoller[2]

Divination is a term that embraces a host of occult practices—crystal gazing, palm reading, automatic writing, Tarot interpretation, channeling, and so on. Although different, all of these practices assume that the gods may visit individuals and thereby "enthuse" (*en-theos*) them with *divine* understanding. What once made such visitations plausible was the sense that the gods are operative in nature: How else to explain nature's awe-inspiring presence? How else to account for such imposing, human-dwarfing realities as mountains, rivers, oceans, forests, and stars collected together in celestial patterns, along with intrusive spectacles such as thunderstorms, earthquakes, volcanic eruptions, and plagues? The world, large both in its actual size and in its capacity to stretch the mind, could best be understood by consulting higher beings able to take its full measure. This was the aim of all divination practices.

Not that it was necessary to commune with the gods directly, although this might be the goal. Often it was enough to descry glimpses of their intelligence as it informed, reflected, and perhaps ordered the operation of nature. The universe was felt to be encrypted with divine patterns and deciphering these was the task of the diviner. Among the techniques applied to this purpose, none was more venerable and compelling than astrology. Anthony Grafton writes that "astrology probably represents the most consistent, unified and durable body of beliefs and practices in the western tradition."[3] Note the present tense—"represents." Grafton argues that astrology is still very much alive in the West, that it embodies a persuasive and intellectually challenging worldview which modern scholars are just beginning to plumb, and that it compares favorably with more recently developed sciences in scope and rigor. Thus its history should not be written off as an intellectual dead-end; it may tell us much as we try to fix our relationship with nature. This is not to say, however, that every schoolchild should be taught to cast horoscopes. What is important is understanding how the integrative nature of astrology, over the centuries, has proved compelling and edifying to people at all levels of society.

ASTROLOGY'S APPEAL

One can best begin to appreciate astrology by taking note of the wondrous nature of heavenly bodies. Suppose a person chanced upon a sphere of light hovering six feet off the ground. Upon investigation, she determined that the sphere remained aloft by its own power and moved in a regular, apparently preordained or knowing fashion. The sphere's brilliance and periodic, seemingly autonomous motion, along with its power to resist the pull of gravity, would bespeak either native intelligence or an intelligent designer. Even today such a sphere would excite wonderment and speculation. It might well be tagged as evidence of a higher, more sublime reality.

MAGIC, MYSTERY, AND SCIENCE

Figure 13. Divination. A diviner tells his king the future by reading portents in the sky (astrology), fumes from mountains (volcanoes?), and sounds and movements of fish.

The sun, moon, stars, and planets are that sphere multiplied many times over and put high above our heads. Most heavenly bodies are self-luminous and all move in ways that intimate divinity. Plato wrote that

> the [creator] god invented and gave us vision in order that we might observe the circuits of intelligence in the heaven and profit by them for the revolutions of our own thought, which are akin to them, though ours be troubled and they are unperturbed; and that, by learning to know them and acquiring the power to compute them rightly according to nature, we might reproduce the perfectly unerring revolutions of the god and reduce to settled order the wandering motions in ourselves.[4]

Aside from being objects of scientific interest, the stars are morally instructive. They elevate both the eyes and the soul. Moreover, according to Plato, the periodic motions of the stars and sun "caused the invention of number and bestowed on us the notion of time and the study of the nature of the world; whence we have derived all philosophy, than which no greater boon has ever come or shall come to mortal man as a gift from heaven."[5] Put differently, human reason drafts on the circuits of intelligence in the heavens: by the time we began to investigate the starry sky—to reduce it to rule and pattern—it had already patterned our thinking.

While Plato held the stars in high regard, he did not see them as the last stop in humankind's quest for understanding. The stars were important insofar as they unlocked the rational faculties and propelled the mind beyond the physical cosmos into an unseen, unchanging world of eternal truths. Here all was perfect, and the stars, when rightly apprehended by the aid of mathematics, opened the mind to that perfection. Hence Plato's statement that time is "the moving likeness of Eternity."[6] The regular, time-marking motions of astronomical bodies bespeak a better, eternal world that is beyond time and that is both the origin of the human soul and its destiny.

The cosmology of Aristotle, Plato's most famous pupil, is less caught up in spiritual possibilities, but it still assumes that heavenly bodies are divine. They are said to be composed of ether or quintessence, an uncreated, incorruptible element not found on earth. Hence, stars last and have lasted forever, and the circles they trace out allegorize their everlastingness—their lack of beginning and end. It followed that when humans contemplate the heavens, they drink in an intelligence that makes them intelligent; they imbibe eternal or everlasting truths. Since it embodied divine understanding, the starry sky for Aristotle was not so much an obstacle to understanding as it was the very occasion of understanding.[7] Set down at the center of the starry spectacle, we can look out, indulge our passion for knowledge, and be transformed in the process. "Man has a desire to understand," states Jonathan Lear in explaining Aristotle's outlook, "which, if satisfied, pulls him right up out of human life into divine existence."[8]

Aside from the preternatural beauty of the stars, what made Aristotle's view persuasive was the apparent eternality of the heavenly vault. "Everything born to a mortal existence is subject to change," wrote Manilius, and the earth is "despoiled by the passing years." The starry firmament, however, "is neither the least bit warped by its motion nor wearied by its speed. . . . No different heaven did our fathers see, no different heaven will our posterity behold. It is God, and changes not in time."[9] Granted, the stars moved in their courses, but the untiring regularity of that movement seemed to partake of God, whom Plato and Aristotle had characterized as a timeless Being.

After Aristotle, several hundred years would pass before Greek astronomy was brought to full bloom by Claudius Ptolemy, a Greek mathematician living in Egypt. In pursuing mathematics, Ptolemy was responding to Plato's view

Figure 14. An astrologer/astronomer at work

that mathematics is a ladder for climbing into eternity. The stars themselves—their visible glory—might lift an observer heavenward, but a mathematical understanding of their motions brings one to heaven's gate. So oriented, Ptolemy freely confessed that the lamp of his mathematical genius burned with a spiritual flame:

> I know that I am mortal and living but a day.
> But, when I search for the numerous turning spirals of the stars
> I no longer have my feet on the Earth, but am beside Zeus himself,
> filling myself with god-nurturing ambrosia.[10]

A nice sentiment, but does it hold scientifically? For Ptolemy, yes: science (natural philosophy) allowed mortals to peer, however briefly, into the mind of God. Facilitating this attitude toward ancient science was a model of the universe that now seems quaint: an ensouled, geocentric cosmos. Although mortal, humans occupied a central position in a universe mindful of their actions and desires; they were integrated into the cosmos in a meaningful (that is, intelligent and spiritual) way. It followed that a study of the stars might do more than yield facts about the world: it might also yield insight into one's place and destiny in life.

Expressed most simply and literally, the stars help humans realize their highest possibilities, just as the sun helps plants sprout and ripen. This outlook emerges in Scipio Africanus's dream-vision of his deceased father. Therein Scipio, a Roman military commander and politician living about 150 B.C., learned that intelligence or mind is one throughout the cosmos: what quickens our thinking also speeds the stars through their orbits. He was then told that a virtuous life "is your passport into the sky" and beheld at that moment the Milky Way, among which were stars never seen from earth.[11] Macrobius, in offering comment on Scipio's vision, explained that human souls descend to earth at birth by passing through certain astronomical portals; they may also ascend at death if they have conformed their lives to the heavenly harmonies they once knew firsthand in a pre-birth state.[12] This view is a variation on the widespread ancient belief that the starry multitude mirrors humankind and that every soul originated from a particular star to which it will return at death.[13]

The skeptic may protest that the astrological outlook, although charming, is decisively refuted by the fact that no evidence exists to support the idea of heavenly bodies affecting our lives. This is a common objection but it stares past our obvious dependence on the sun and the moon's influence on the tides and the biorhythms of many species. Ptolemy, echoing Aristotle, made this clear when he wrote:

> For the Sun, together with the surrounding environment, is always in some way affecting everything on earth, not only by the changes that

MAGIC, MYSTERY, AND SCIENCE

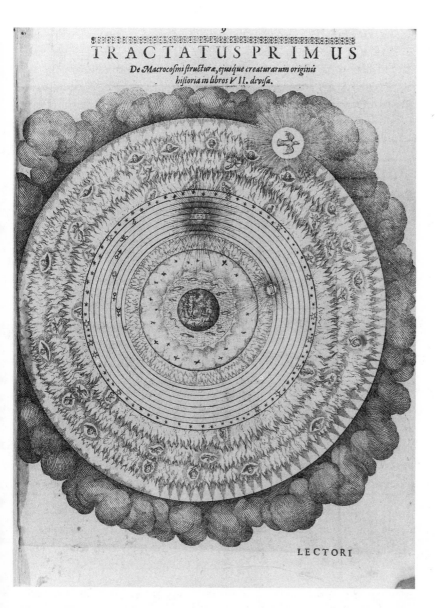

Figure 15. The Earth-centered universe, basic to Ptolemy and other astrologers. In this typical illustration, the sun, planets, and stars revolve around the Earth, with the fiery, empyrean heavens forming a frame of smoke around the stars.

accompany the seasons of the year to bring about the generation of animals, the productiveness of plants, the flowing of waters, and the change of bodies, but also by its dialing revolutions furnishing heat, moisture, dryness and cold in regular order and in correspondence with its positions relative to the zenith.[14]

If the sun so obviously plays into events on Earth, why not other heavenly bodies to a weaker degree befitting their fainter magnitude? Aristotle reasoned that the four earthly elements—earth, air, fire, and water—may in turn be characterized by four qualities—dry, wet, hot, and cold. In the statement just cited, Ptolemy has the sun parceling out these qualities "in regular order" as it orbits the Earth. Other planets similarly dispense them according to their character. Mars, for instance, radiates heat and dryness owing to its proximity to the sun and its reddish tinge, which bespeaks fire. The moon, by contrast, excites "damp vapours" on the earth (which often shows up as morning dew) and thereby induces "relaxation and putrefaction."[15]

Because heat and moisture promote growth, planets that exude these qualities were deemed beneficent; those radiating cold and dryness were thought maleficent, because these properties benumb life processes and bring on decay. Moreover, the moon and Venus, owing to their moist nature, were regarded as feminine planets, while Mars, Jupiter, and Saturn were masculine, even though Jupiter exuded moisture that produced "fertilizing breezes" upon reaching earth.[16] Since Mercury alternately radiated moisture and dryness in equal measure, it fluctuated between genders. The stars also changed gender according to whether they preceded the sun as it rose in the morning or followed it as it set in the evening.

One can imagine the celestial ether (the sublime, rarefied substance that, according to Aristotle, filled the heavens) carrying the planetary influences earthward where they would impinge upon the atmosphere to effect terrestrial change. The mechanism—if that is the right word—was not simple cause and effect as modern science portrays it, however. Note the touch of organic intimacy that figures into Ptolemy's description of the moon's effect on the Earth:

> The Moon, too, as the heavenly body nearest the earth, bestows her effluence most abundantly on mundane things, for most of them, animate, or inanimate, are sympathetic to her and change in company with her; the rivers increase and diminish their streams with her light, the seas turn their own tides with her rising and setting, and plants and animals in whole or in some part wax and wane with her.[17]

This brings the moon into sympathetic partnership—into kinship—with the Earth, and that violates modern sensibilities. All the same, our planet is subject to cosmic winds that blow through the solar system and to electromagnetic effects produced by the sun. In addition, the thinning ozone layer and global warming remind us that the earth is not a self-contained system immune from celestial influences. The difference, of course, is that those influences are now deemed inanimate and mechanical. They bathe the planet in ways obvious and subtle, but from a modern scientific viewpoint they arrive without purpose or meaning.

More than anything else, this shift in attitude toward stellar effects—not the disproof of such effects—has contributed to astrology's decline since the seventeenth century. It is hard to draw astrological meaning from a lifeless, mechanized universe. In recent decades, however, astrology has made a comeback, perhaps because the universe-as-machine metaphor is losing its appeal.

COSMIC HARMONY

In previous chapters, we skirmished with another idea that has contributed to astrology's longevity: cosmic harmony. This notion was once so pervasive as to be implicit in the thinking of the day; it was "presumed rather than overtly defended."[18] The Greek word *kosmos*—whence our *cosmos*—connoted order, beauty, attunement, and harmony. Everything fit together and thereby bespoke a designing intelligence, perhaps one (as with Plato) that had achieved cosmos by ordering or harmonizing primordial chaos so that oneness or unity emerged out of multiplicity. Manilius, a Latin poet living about the time of Christ, insisted that "by sacred dispensation the deity brings harmony and governs with hidden purpose, arranging mutual bonds between all parts, so that each may furnish and receive another's strength and that the whole may stand fast in kinship despite its variety of forms."[19] If this were not the case, "the Earth would not possess its stability, nor stars their orbits, and the heavens would wander aimlessly or stiffen with inertia."[20]

Much later, George Berkeley, trying to correct perceived deficiencies of eighteenth-century science, called upon the ancient Greeks—Pythagoreans, Platonists, and Stoics—to reintroduce the notion of cosmic harmony:

> There is, according to those philosophers, a life infused throughout all things . . . an inward principle, animal spirit, or natural life, producing and forming within as art doth without, regulating, moderating, and reconciling the various motions, qualities, and parts of this mundane system. By virtue of this life the great masses are held together in their orderly courses, as well as the minutest particles governed in their natural motion, according to the several laws of attrac-

tion, gravity, electricity, magnetism, and the rest. It is this [that] gives instincts, teaches the spider her web, and the bee her honey.[21]

In this kind of cosmos, humankind was perforce an integrated aspect of a larger whole. It was unthinkable, then, that humans had nothing in common with the stars, particularly as the patterned regularity of the stars came close to revealing the divine mind that had brought everything into common (cosmic) embrace. And with everything harmoniously interconnected, changes in the heavens were free to reverberate earthward. Indeed, the universal attunement was often thought to transfer change from one place to another by means of mutual resonance, one part causing others to vibrate sympathetically. "All things whatsoever observe a mutual order," Beatrice told Dante in the *Paradiso,* "and this is the form that makes the universe like unto God."[22] She further explained that his amazing ability (amazing to him) to fly up through the heavenly spheres toward God stemmed from his being caught up in the elemental inclination of the heavens—drawing near to God.

Suffice it to say, a web of interrelations (sympathies, tendencies, and inclinations) congenial to a belief in astrology informed and structured the universe. This outlook eventually gave birth to the microcosm-macrocosm principle, which held that humans are so deeply integrated into the universe as to be miniature reiterations thereof: the lines of cosmic harmony reconstituted themselves as human beings. It seemed reasonable, therefore, that "the human frame is apportioned among the signs";[23] that is, body parts correspond with planets or with constellations of the zodiac. Virgo, for example, was thought to govern the intestines. Such considerations, not surprisingly, were incorporated into medical theory so that astrology struck many as essential knowledge for treatment of both soul and body.

Incorporating astrology into the practice of medicine, Paracelsus explained that there "are a great many plants who are the earthly representations of astral influences corresponding to the stars, and which will attract the [healing] influences of the stars to which they are sympathetically related."[24] In the collecting of medicinal herbs, therefore, "[e]ach plant should be gathered at a time when the planet to which it is related rules the hour."[25] Along with an understanding of botany and human anatomy, this of course presupposed a knowledge of "the constitution of the starry heavens."[26]

Taken even further, the microcosm-macrocosm principle led to the view that the planets fulfill various organic functions within the cosmic body (macrocosm). Tamsyn Barton sums up one ancient thinker's outlook thusly:

> [W]hile the stars revolve like radiant eyes in the face of the universe, the Sun, playing the role of the heart, transmits and disperses out of himself heat and light as if it were blood and breath. The Earth and

MAGIC, MYSTERY, AND SCIENCE

sea act like bowels and bladder, and the Moon, situated between the Sun and the Earth, fulfills the function of an organ like the liver or perhaps the spleen, and directs the heat from the Sun to Earth, and the exhalations from the earth to the Sun, after refining and purifying them.[27]

Exhalations were often the medium for transmitting influences. The planets breathed their distinctive essences into the ether, which then bore them elsewhere to keep the cosmos in metabolic equilibrium. Given this steady give-and-take of organic activity, all of it holding the cosmos together, it is little wonder that astrology registered itself as a universal science. In the thirteenth century, Albertus Magnus wrote: "No humane Science or Learning doth perfectly attain the Ordination of the whole Universe; except the knowledge of the judgement of the Starres."[28]

Astrology is a throwback to an era when knowledge was packaged more holistically and comprehensively than it is today, no doubt because the universe was deemed a coherent, integrated whole with humankind smack dab at the center of things. Given this sense of interdependent oneness or mutual attunement, one could hardly presume that humans were interlopers on the stage of nature or accidental byproducts of random processes—that sort of chaotic dissonance might wreck the cosmic harmony and, along with it, the very notion of a divinely harmonized universe. This, incidentally, is another way of explaining astrology's demise. By turning the universe over to random (purposeless) processes, modern science snatches away astrology's axiomatic starting point.

ASTROLOGY IN THE WEST

Only in the last three hundred years have astronomy and astrology gone their separate ways, the former becoming science and the latter pseudo-science. Although the ideas informing the two disciplines have always been distinct, the bonds between them were strong enough that they were often referred to interchangeably. Astrology was seen as applied astronomy, or the practice of making judgments about the stars as they were charted by astronomers. Such judgments, of course, entailed drawing out the human (social, political, and religious) implications of changes in the heavens, but since virtually everyone assumed some sort of heaven-earth intimacy (while often differing on the exact strength and nature of that intimacy),[29] the two occupations freely interblended. In fact, some whom we esteem as great astronomers and mathematicians, such as Ptolemy, Copernicus, Tycho Brahe, Johannes Kepler, and Galileo, were not above casting horoscopes in a financial pinch. This is not to say that all these men embraced astrology wholeheartedly; Ptolemy certainly did but the others, living centuries later, harbored strong reservations about astrology without breaking with it completely. They were among those who enacted the Scientific Revolution, and with that momentous change astrology came to be regarded as occult superstition or, at best, pseudo-science.

As suggested above, astrology's demise in the West coincided with the passing of the Aristotelian worldview. That model of the cosmos, its perfect, heavenly spheres wheeling about us and each sphere bearing its own planet and guiding intellect, seemed particularly well suited to a belief in astrology. Not so, however, the Copernican system wherein the earth is just one of several imperfect planets circling the sun and heavenly perfection is wholly absent from the universe. It is hardly surprising, therefore, that in the West astrology has since commanded little assent until recently. In a 1934 poll, only 6 percent of the U.S. population expressed belief in astrology; in 1985, a similar survey found that 40 percent of the respondents concurred with the view that "astrology has scientific credibility."[30]

Why the resurgence of belief and interest in astrology? Some people simply like the big picture it offers. What's more, in that picture individuals really count for something, even if they are not part of the *glitterati*. There is also the consideration that modern science, which redefined the universe in mechanical terms, is now widely perceived in academe to be responsive to social and cultural influences that it cannot master or fully assimilate into any scientific model. We have gotten away, in other words, from "cardboard myths about science as pure observation and applied logic, divorced from realities of human creativity and social context."[31] This social constructivist view has created room to doubt science-inspired invective against astrology (and other occult practices). Against this background of doubt, recent studies have brought astrology forward as a subject with a rich and illuminating history.[32] A subtext of these new treatments is that the history of astrology should not be dismissed out of hand as irrational.

With this thought in mind, we note that the roots of astrology are very old, stretching back to ancient Mesopotamia. The Sumerians and Babylonians were observing the stars in a systematic fashion as early as 3500 B.C. for calendrical reasons—to determine when to plant crops and perform religious ceremonies. In the process, they came to realize that a few stars behave strangely. While most stars move in a "fixed" way by proceeding at a steady speed and in a constant direction across the night sky, planets (or "wandering stars") sometimes reverse their direction. This made it seem to the Babylonians that each planet has a mind of its own; it moves as it pleases. Accordingly, they deified the planets and believed that their movements both influenced and foretold events here on Earth. This is a particularly early instance of "As above, so below."

By relying on mathematical techniques and an ever-growing store of obser-

MAGIC, MYSTERY, AND SCIENCE

vations, Babylonian astrologers, who were members of the priestly caste, became expert at predicting stellar movements and happenings like new moons, planetary conjunctions, and eclipses. For all this, however, they never, it appears, thought of the stars and planets as we do: every change in the heavens was for them fraught with significance, was an omen or portent. The waxing and waning moon, for example, was a monthly ("moonthly") drama that embraced events on Earth (recall that the Egyptians saw it as the wounding and healing of Horus's eye), and part of the responsibility of the astrologers was to develop knowledge and rituals for coordinating human activity with this and other such dramas. Initially, their concern lay not with individuals but rather with nations or regions, probably because as servants of the king they sought to advise him of future events.

Astrology with a national or regional focus is known as mundane (or judicial) astrology. The astrologer might have warned the king of an impending drought or enemy invasion as foretold by the stars. (For a familiar example of such a warning, although arising from a different mode of divination, recall the biblical story of Joseph who, after listening to the Pharaoh's dreams, correctly predicted seven years of plenty and seven years of famine.) It was not until much later, probably not earlier than 410 B.C., that the first individual horoscope was cast by the Babylonians. Even so, only the king and perhaps a few nobles merited such consideration. In a culture that emphasized communal obligations, there was little reason to turn individuals into centers of astrological attention.

It was the Greeks who democratized astrology. The individualistic orientation they popularized is often called natal astrology because it is based on the planetary conjunctions at a person's time of birth. This departure put a sharp, personal point on a question the Babylonians had asked themselves: Is it possible to escape one's astrologically predicted fate? By answering no to this question, both Babylonian and early Greek astrologers adopted a stance known as fatalistic astrology. If imminent death were in the stars, one might very well begin to make the necessary funeral preparations.

Among the Greek philosophical schools, the Stoics accepted fatalistic astrology enthusiastically (to the extent Stoics were able to express enthusiasm). They believed that everything in the universe, including humanity, was subject to unchangeable laws of nature. It was hence best to accept one's fate *stoically* or calmly, keeping the emotions and ego in check at all times. Whether brilliant triumph was in the stars or disaster and death, so be it: accept the iron hand of destiny without self-exaltation and without self-pity. The realization that one's fate is sealed—that one is not free to change an already scripted future—sets one free from senseless worry.[33]

Not surprisingly, many Greeks (and others) rejected fatalistic astrology because it did not recognize free will. Their brand of astrology held that astrological fate, once known, could be avoided or outmaneuvered. If an upcoming trip held forth unwelcome surprises, simply postpone the trip until a more auspicious (astrologically favorable) time. This "free-will" astrology was very popular among the lower classes in the ancient world, whereas fatalistic astrology enjoyed considerable approbation among those who were wealthy and well educated. No doubt each stance served the social and emotional needs of its devotees: among the rich, personal wealth could be seen as the will of the gods; among the poor, self-advancement was possible because the stars locked no one into poverty.

MAKING A HOROSCOPE

Today most students of astrology prefer the free-will version of the art. And those who cast horoscopes sometimes point out that indeed astrology is an art, not an exact science, because a certain amount of subjective free play figures into the construction and interpretation of horoscopes. Although rules and criteria guide them, astrologers also rely on intuition and inspiration as they make their predictions. We now will explore the way in which horoscopes are "brought down to earth" from the starry sky.

Among the intellectual luminaries of Western thought, Claudius Ptolemy stands tall. As a Greek living in Egypt about A.D. 140, Ptolemy developed a geocentric astronomy that was sufficiently accurate (when adjusted periodically) to go unchallenged for the next fourteen hundred years. In the process of working out the ramifications of his system, Ptolemy wrote a book—*Tetrabiblos*—that codified astrological practice in the West. Almost all modern astrologers still derive their charts and horoscopes in the manner prescribed by Ptolemy, and if he were to return today, he could resume his practice of astrology without undue difficulty. (The story would be very different, however, were he to also take up astronomy.) Here, of course, we mean serious astrology, not the pabulum found in daily newspapers that presupposes a tiny fraction of the understanding implicit in the system worked up by Ptolemy.

One begins with the familiar, the zodiac. First elaborated by the Babylonians, the zodiac is the ancient name for a circular band of stars marked out by the sun, moon, and planets as they move along a common path known as the ecliptic. One will always see Mars, for example, moving through the same round of stars. The ancients divided this circular band into twelve equal segments of 30 degrees each. They further grouped the stars within each segment into constellations so as to produce the twelve signs of the zodiac: Aries, Taurus, Gemini, Cancer, Leo, Virgo, Libra, Scorpio, Sagittarius, Capricorn, Aquarius, and Pisces.

These designations, although prevalent in the West, are not universal but merely the Greek names that have been passed down to us. Other cultures invented different names and frequently different divisions and constellations. The one natural constant was the zodiac itself, thrown into relief by the sun, moon, and planets. Thereafter, human creativity took over to divide, group, and name the stars (constellations) of the zodiac in various ways. And as the word *zodiac* implies (*zodiac* is cognate with *zoo*), the Greeks "populated" the heavens with living beings so that the different zodiacal constellations emerge as animals or humans. These characterizations impart to the stars distinctive qualities that then spill over into astrological readings. A person born in Aries (the Ram), for instance, might be expected to develop ram-like traits, perhaps butting in where he does not belong or ramming his ideas through.

To be born in Aries, or any other zodiacal sign, means to be born on a day that that sign is directly behind the sun when it ascends in the east. The rising sun's brilliance, of course, obscures the stars, but pre-dawn observations (and solar eclipses) allow one to keep track of where the sun is in its yearly journey through the zodiac. Since the sun spends about a month in each constellation (sign), a person born in August, say, would most likely be born under the sign of Leo. (The months do not correspond exactly with the signs.) This would be that person's sun sign, which is said to be the most important astrological variable in shaping one's personality and destiny.

Another variable, also important, is the ascendant, which is the sign that is rising or ascending at the moment of birth. If you were born exactly at dawn with the sun in Aquarius, then both your sun sign and ascendant would be Aquarius. But if, say, you were born at noon, the sun and Aquarius would be directly overhead (because the sun continues to stay in Aquarius for about a month) and another sign would be ascending on the eastern horizon. In this circumstance, that very likely would be Taurus. It is not surprising that while nearly everyone knows his or her sun sign, few people know their ascendant. This is because the sun sign period is quite long—about thirty days—but the ascendant time frame is short: each sign spends only about two hours a day on the eastern horizon. It becomes imperative, therefore, to fix the moment of birth as precisely as possible; otherwise, one may select the wrong ascendant and throw off the entire reading. Furthermore, precise knowledge of the time of birth will allow the astrologer to determine the ascendant degree—how far the ascendant has advanced on the horizon. This will indicate the strength of the ascendant's influence on the newborn infant and, of course, afford a more accurate horoscope.

So far we have talked only about the sun and the zodiacal signs. It is time to factor in the planets. Recall that they also travel through the zodiac, and because they embody distinctive qualities, their zodiacal positions at the time of birth also must be marked. Suppose in the case we are developing, while the sun is in Aquarius and Taurus is rising in the east, the moon is in Libra (the moon and sun were considered planets in the ancient geocentric system), Venus is in Sagittarius, and so on. Things are getting complicated, and not just because more celestial entities have been thrown into the mix. Astrological qualities also must be interrelated. What metaphysical sparks fly when Venus moves into Sagittarius? The answer will depend not just on Venus and Sagittarius but also on the angular relationship of Venus with the other planets.

Such planetary relationships are called aspects, and while there are many possible aspects, the most important ones are conjunction (zero degrees separation), square (90 degrees), trine (120 degrees), and opposition (180 degrees). When two planets are in opposition, the net effect will generally be disagreeable or at least conflicted for the person involved—opposition bespeaks strife. When planets are in conjunction, their energies (good or evil) will generally be mingled or concentrated, particularly if both planets share similar qualities.

One can see that a horoscope is a map of the heavens as seen from Earth at the moment of birth. It encapsulates the relative positions of the planets against the backdrop of the zodiac, something any good astronomer could do with the aid of mathematics. There is thus a quantitative dimension to astrology that gives it a scientific feel. Numbers are important because they afford precise data. But to be astrologically significant, data must be interpreted, and we have already indicated some of the possibilities. This is where astrology moves into a realm of complexity that now appears distinctly non-scientific because the rules of interpretation seem as mercurial as the personalities they set out to explain. Astrology, in other words, seems to get bogged down in its all-too-human subject matter.

INFLUENCES AND SYMPATHIES

Modern astrologers disagree about whether planets and constellations actually influence us or merely mediate higher powers that first affect stars and planets. Either way, astrology subscribes to the "As above, so below" principle that sees the universe as a unity in which influences fly back and forth by virtue of common sympathies. In this context, *likeness* may replace *sympathy*, the idea being that a common bond of affection or likeability allows two distant entities to immediately affect each other. Sometimes influences also pass by means of antipathies or disaffections that charge the intervening space with tension. Magnets, which were long regarded as having occult powers, were seen to work this way, at least when it comes to attracting and repelling other magnets across space.

MAGIC, MYSTERY, AND SCIENCE

Influences and sympathies are always operative, according to astrologers, and always in flux because planetary positions and aspects are continually changing. Moreover, it is important to realize that every human personality is the product of stellar influences and so remains, to some extent, under their sway. It is a commonplace that no two snowflakes are alike: each began as a featureless drop of moisture and then crystallized as a snowflake under a unique set of atmospheric circumstances. Similarly, each personality crystallized under a different set of astrological influences. Since these influences are not "turned off" after birth but wax and wane as planetary configurations change, they continue to make a difference in our lives. Having impressed us at birth with their attributes, the planets and constellations remain sympathetically operative in our lives.

All in all, the sun sign exercises the strongest influence, but only as it blends with other influences. A person born under the watery sign Pisces (the Fishes) will tend to be indecisive and vacillating (like water) and perhaps a little slippery (like a fish). But these qualities might well be diminished or strengthened by the person's ascendant. Furthermore, each of the seven planets rules one or two of the zodiacal signs. Jupiter, for example, rules Pisces and Sagittarius, so Jupiter will leave an imprint upon anyone born under those signs. How strong and what sort of an imprint is hard to say precisely, although Jupiter bears connotations of material success, leadership, patriarchy, joviality, and magnanimity. Beyond this, Jupiter and the other planets are deemed hot or cold, moist or dry, male or female, day or night, and so on. And, finally, each planet rules a different part of the body. Jupiter, for instance, rules the brain; Mercury, the right ear.

Like the planets, the zodiacal signs have their own influences, and these of course merge with planetary influences in ways already specified. So far, perhaps, all seems intricate but manageable. For the novice, however, the complexity becomes truly dizzying with the introduction of quadruplicities (four-sign groups), which link the twelve signs of the zodiac with the beginning, middle, and end of each of the four seasons. Ideally, the sun moves into Aries on the vernal equinox (the first day of spring), into Cancer on the summer solstice (the first day of summer), into Libra on the autumnal equinox (the first day of fall), and into Capricorn on the winter solstice (the first day of winter). These four signs, then, constitute the *cardinal* quadruplicity, that set of four signs announcing the onset of each season. The *fixed* quadruplicity comprises the four middle signs of each season (Taurus, Leo, Scorpio, and Aquarius), while the *mutable* quadruplicity takes in the end signs (Gemini, Virgo, Sagittarius, and Pisces).

Why these groupings? For one thing, they reflect astrological belief in heaven-earth intimacy. The seasons, which moderns take merely as a sun-earth affair, were once felt to receive some of their distinctive character from the particular zodiacal signs through which the sun passed: the sun's entry into a sign strengthened its influence so that each sign (its qualities) prevailed on earth for about a month within a broader three-month (seasonal) span. Intuition further suggested that people born when planets were predominantly in the cardinal signs would be self-starters and innovators. They would, like the cardinal signs, announce and inaugurate new possibilities. Those born under fixed signs (planets in fixed signs) would tend toward fixity of purpose and conservatism. Mutable signs would naturally engender flexibility and perhaps instability.

Another grouping of the signs is the triplicities (three-sign groups), which are linked to the four elements—earth, air, fire, and water. For example, Aries, Leo, and Sagittarius are fire constellations, while Taurus, Virgo, and Capricorn belong to earth. Whether a person is fiery, watery, earthy, or airy depends on the extent that the respective triplicities are marked by planets at the time of birth.

Yet another astrological division, more familiar than quadruplicities and triplicities, is the houses. These have to do with mundane aspects or departments of life such as family, money, children, and health. The purpose of the twelve houses is to link the ascendant to planetary positions. Imagine a circle cut into twelve segments like slices of a pie. This circle could be the zodiac divided into the twelve signs, or it could be the houses. Generally the two circles will not coincide precisely because it is improbable that the ascendant just touches the horizon at the moment of birth. Ordinarily it will straddle the horizon, part of it above and part below. If the ascendant is 10 degrees advanced, say, then that— a point slightly above the horizon—is where the houses begin. And just as each planet falls into a particular sign, so will each fall into a particular house and thereby reveal the specific nature of its influence. Thus, if the moon is in the seventh house—the house that governs love and marriage—an astrologer might predict an oscillating love life, one that waxes and wanes like the moon.

Note that the houses do not fall out of the sky, as it were, as the zodiacal signs might be said to. The signs are humanly contrived in that there could be fewer or more of them and they could be differently constellated. But at least there are stars in the zodiac for the imagination to work with. The houses, by contrast, do not appear to have any such empirical touchstone; they seem to come completely from the imagination. (Some say that they have been inferred from centuries of inductive observation. If so, the observation was not controlled and systematic but, rather, steeped in anecdote and folklore.)

The last astrological category we wish to mention is the decans, which rival if not surpass the houses in their inscrutability. They originate in ancient Egypt, where they were used to help tell time at night, each one coming over the horizon about every forty minutes. All told there were thirty-six decans (40

MAGIC, MYSTERY, AND SCIENCE

minutes $\times$ 36 = 24 hours), and these coincided with the zodiacal constellations so that each constellation was occupied or ruled by three decans; or, to express the matter geometrically, the 30 degrees of each constellation was divided into three 10-degree decans.

Often astrologers use decans merely to indicate where a planet makes its appearance in a constellation—in the first, second, or third decan. On other occasions, however, adepts may consider their astrological import in conjunction with the constellation they rule. This, of course, complicates the analysis even further, and Manilius proposed that it is the decans that ensure that "no sign has exclusive control over itself: all share their powers with certain signs in equal portions, and in a spirit of hospitality, as it were, they form a heavenly fellowship and surrender the parts of which they are composed to the keeping of other signs."[34] In other words, Virgo, say, may be merely a mask or code for another sign or signs. "Heaven," Manilius adds, "is reached by no brief effort and does not favour short cuts: but the shape of one sign is placed in front of and conceals others, and dissimulates and hides its real influences and gifts." At this point, the complexity seems to verge to infinity, but, Manilius concludes, not without purpose: this obscurity will compel us to learn to see by the light of reason, relying on inner judgment rather than outward appearances.[35]

Summing up, a horoscope is a mingling together of sign sun, ascendant sign, planetary aspects and qualities, quadruplicities, triplicities, houses, and decans (and quite possibly other considerations that appeal to some astrologers but not others). Each variable indicates a new layer of complexity, and it is not as if any one layer is straightforward in its implications. A single zodiacal sign may encompass as many as two hundred adjectives or attributes, each of which may be correlated according to taste with hundreds of others arising from planetary aspects, and so on. Little wonder that astrology, like numerology, is often characterized as a scattershot theory of human personality: it can hit anything its practitioners wish, given a little ingenuity on their part.

PROS AND CONS

Its excessive flexibility makes astrology seem distinctly unscientific, but economists, psychologists, sociologists, and meteorologists routinely invoke conditional language while implicitly acknowledging the over-rich complexity of their subject matter. Moreover, these scientists, like astrologers, target phenomena that steadfastly resist perfect rule and prediction. It is therefore unfair, argued Ptolemy, to criticize astrology for its failed predictions. In some cases, the astrologers are simply incompetent—just as some medical doctors are. In other cases, even the most competent astrologer, like his peers in other fields, cannot assimilate all of the relevant data.

ASTROLOGY

In Ptolemy's mind, the fault therefore lies not with the discipline but with its practitioners who literally reach for the stars in trying to overcome their human limitations. Indeed, one might venture that astrology, owing to "the magnitude of its scope . . . and the faint resemblance that it bears to a divine attribute,"[36] is the most daring of all the predictive sciences and therefore the one most vulnerable to failure. Sounding much like an alchemist, Manilius struck this note when he wrote that astrology is not for the cautious or faint-hearted. To the novice who protests, "the task you bid me undertake is great and subtle, and you are plunging my mind back into deep darkness just when I thought a simple principle was enabling me to see the light," Manilius countered: "The object of your quest is God: you are seeking to scale the skies . . . you are seeking to pass beyond your understanding and make yourself master of the universe. The toil involved matches the reward to be won."[37]

In recent centuries, scientists have increasingly embraced statistical laws that describe large populations, the premise being (even—or especially—in quantum physics) that the world is "messy" or probabilistic—particularly at the level of individual components. Hence the need for percentages and provisional language when forecasting weather, stock market behavior, political elections, fluctuations in the unemployment rate, and so on. Astrologers similarly qualified their predictions, believing that general principles could be drawn from large numbers of reliable horoscopes. Anthony Grafton insists that during the Renaissance a single horoscope elicited little confidence, even from among those who championed astrology; nevertheless, "almost everyone . . . believed that a finite number of cases would suffice to settle all outstanding questions, rigorously and fully."[38] Given this, Grafton continues, astrologers performed many of the societal roles since taken over by economists, political theorists, psychologists, and ethicists.[39] These are among the "spin doctors" we see on the nightly news.

Related to the issue of astrology's predictive capacity is the question of whether the stars fully determine human behavior. If they do, then complete knowledge of the future is possible, at least in principle. Earlier we noted that many ancient Greeks departed from the Babylonian precept of astral determinism, believing that astrology could be a tool for avoiding unpleasant future events. In other words, the future was felt to be contingent on the present, and changing the present could change the future for the better. Medieval Christians concurred on this point, largely because any sort of determinism sabotaged their belief in free will and responsibility for sin. Many argued that evil stellar influences could be resisted because the stars merely incline or softly prompt human action rather than compel it. A similar position was that because the stars affect only our bodies (but not our souls), those who surmount the passions of the flesh also rise above astrological influences. If these consid-

MAGIC, MYSTERY, AND SCIENCE

erations were not persuasive, one could always rehearse Ptolemy's argument that our lives are not entirely scripted by the stars: all sorts of terrestrial influences also impinge on us.[40]

A very old objection against astrology is the problem of twins. Why do twins often differ in personality and destiny? They were, after all, born under the same astrological circumstances and their horoscopes are identical. One apologetic response is that since twins do not share *exactly* the same birth moment, they are not astrological clones. Tiny horoscopic variations may translate into significant life differences. Furthermore, the objection presupposes astral determinism, hardly a widely affirmed precept in the West. If the stars merely incline, then even astrological clones might well grow into different fates.

The battle problem, another ancient objection to astrology, concerns the end of life rather than the beginning. To some, it seemed implausible that a thousand men should die in battle on the same day and perhaps even at the same hour when each had a different horoscope. (Or, to take a modern example, think of an airliner crashing and several hundred people dying at virtually the same moment.) Did every horoscope predict or imply the tragedy from a different astrological basis? Ptolemy ventured the idea that sometimes larger factors can override a single person's horoscope—a larger fate can overtake smaller fates. But this *ad hoc* appeal to the inscrutability of the cosmos does not inspire much faith in astrological prognostication: individual horoscopic predictions are reliable granted they are not reversed by larger unforeseen developments. Again, we come back to the highly probabilistic character of astrology and the ability of individuals to freely chart their own fate within wide astrological limits.

A more modern problem concerns the houses. Because these do not coincide with any obvious feature in the world, they strike some people as arbitrary and unnecessary. Most astrologers just accept them without bothering to explain their origin or empirical basis (if indeed there is one). What astrologers themselves contest, however, is the size of the houses. Should they all be equal in size, each 30 degrees like the zodiacal constellations, or of varying sizes? As long as disagreement on the issue prevails, astrologers will produce different horoscopes from the same astronomical information: in one horoscope, Venus could end up in the sixth house; in another, in the fifth or seventh.

To an outsider, this might seem a decisive blow to astrology, but to adepts it is not particularly troubling. Over the millennia, astrological techniques have varied from culture to culture; what's more, the complexity of any one astrological system precludes a single right deduction from a given set of data. Instead of processing data in an uncaring, algorithmic way, astrologers (so this line of defense goes) develop an intuitive feel for it. What matters ultimately, then, is not the single detail of which house Venus is in, but the inklings and insights sparked into existence by a whole complex of details. In this sense, astrology is said to mirror life and the way we come to know other people by working past first impressions that are often false and narrowly construed. And no two people go about getting to know a common acquaintance in precisely the same fashion.

Given this emphasis on inspiration or intuition rather than formal method, it is hardly surprising that modern statistical studies of astrology generally return negative judgments. An apparent exception to this rule is the "Mars effect" study conducted by the French psychologists Michel and Françoise Gauquelin. After tabulating the birth times of 2,088 sports champions, the Gauquelins found that a higher than random number of champions were born when Mars was either near the eastern horizon or the celestial meridian (directly overhead). Astrologers anxious for scientific vindication often cite this study, but there is reason aplenty to exercise restraint. For one thing, the planetary position itself does not fall into any normal astrological category of influence (although it does correspond roughly with houses 12 and 9). For another, the finding has never been replicated. Indeed, other studies by the Gauquelins have produced opposite results. In one study they tested more than twenty-five thousand subjects to see if a relationship existed between one's profession and sun sign. In another they compared profession to position of the sun, the moon, and the ascendant sign at birth. Neither study produced a statistically meaningful correlation. Aries, it seems, is no more likely to produce soldiers than Libra, even though belligerence is said to typify Aries and pacifism Libra.[41]

Far from vindicating astrology, the Gauquelins's research renders it highly suspect from a scientific point of view. Michel Gauquelin offered this conclusion:

> Every attempt, whether of astrologers or scientists, to produce evidence of the validity of astrological laws has been in vain. It is now quite certain that the signs in the sky which presided over our birth have no power whatever to decide our fates, to affect our hereditary characteristic, or to play any part however humble in the totality of effects, random or otherwise, which form the fabric of our lives and mold our impulses to action. Confronted with science, modern and traditional astrology are seen to be imaginary doctrines.[42]

This reasoned judgment is unambiguous, but it is predicated on the view that science is a universal yardstick for measuring the validity of other endeavors. As suggested, this view has suffered erosion in recent decades. After rehearsing the recent history of particle physics, philosopher Andrew Pickering states that "there is no obligation upon anyone framing a view of the world to take account of what twentieth-century science has to say."[43] Pickering holds that worldviews spring from cultural preferences; that is, from the deep and ultimately unfathomable recesses of the human mind. This extreme relativism may be quite wrong, but the salient point is that many thinking people no longer regard science as the court of last appeal.

THE GREAT YEAR AND THE WORLD AGES

"This is the dawning of the Age of Aquarius." So runs a familiar refrain popularized in the late 1960s by the Fifth Dimension, a rock music group cognizant of New Age possibilities. In some quarters, the line became a mantra connoting a now-in-progress cosmic shift toward peace and love. This expectation may be nothing more than wishful thinking but it stems from age-old astronomical and astrological understandings that still rivet the imagination.

The astronomical effect underlying "the dawning of the Age of Aquarius" is the precession of the equinoxes. As the earth rotates on its axis, it wobbles slowly like an off-balance spinning top and thereby traces out a circle with its pole. This means the axis of the earth is slowly changing its orientation, drifting away from the North Star so that even this star, supposedly a fixed point around which all other stars revolve (from our perspective on Earth), eventually becomes a revolving star. (In the process, however, another star may take its place.) A second consequence of this wobble is that the sun, upon completing its yearly journey through the zodiac, fails to return to exactly the same point from which that journey began. This tiny discrepancy builds up over time so that after about two thousand years the sun will have shifted into a new zodiacal constellation on any given day of the year. Whereas once it was in Aries on the vernal equinox (March 21), it shifted into Pisces at about the birth of Christ and is now close to moving into Aquarius. Each of these periods, slightly longer than two thousand years, is called a World Age and all together they make up a Great Year of twenty-six thousand years.

The Great Year, then, is a cosmic periodicity having twelve parts or seasons corresponding to the twelve signs of the zodiac. In the astrological worldview, each of these seasons partakes of the qualities of its respective sign. Since the vernal equinox marks the beginning of spring and the birth of a new year, the sun's zodiacal position on that day defines the ruling sign—the sign whose distinctive influence will be felt on a cosmic scale throughout the World Age. From about 4000 to 2000 B.C., the ruling sign was Taurus and worship of the Bull was common in many cultures. When Aries (the Ram) replaced Taurus, militaristic civilizations arose, the most prominent of which was Rome. Then, as Pisces displaced Aries, Rome fell and a religion betraying its Piscean origin emerged: Jesus was a fisher of men, some of his apostles were fishermen by trade, fish figure into several New Testament miracles, and the Greek word for fish, *ichthys,* became an acronym for "Jesus Christ, God's Son, Savior" (*Iesous*

*Ch*ristos, *Th*eou *Y*ios, *S*oter). Now that Aquarius (the Water Bearer) will soon inaugurate a new World Age, astrologers tell us we may expect monumental change. Unlike the Bull, the Ram, and the Fishes, Aquarius is human and this bodes well for the human race and, by extension, for the entire planet.

Although this shifting of the zodiacal constellations with respect to the sun makes for great cosmic drama, it is, oddly enough, generally not incorporated into individual horoscopes, and so renders them grossly inaccurate from an astronomical point of view. The tendency among modern astrologers is to rely on a picture of the sky that is two thousand years out of date—that goes back to the time when the sun rose in Aries on March 21. Hence, the sun signs that modern people invoke so freely to explain their personalities today do not correspond with the *actual* constellations they were born under! A "Capricorn" born on December 31, for example, is really a "Sagittarius," if the sun's zodiacal position on that day truly means anything.

THE MULTI-STORIED UNIVERSE

Now that zodiacal *constellations* no longer coincide with zodiacal *signs,* is there warrant for taking astrology seriously? Of course, absolute precision in any endeavor, scientific or otherwise, is impossible, and the starry sky has driven home this truth over the centuries. When first studied long ago, the starry sky seemed the epitome of regularity and exactitude—this comes close to Plato's view. But then nothing fit quite as it should have. Ideally, there would be twelve lunar months in a solar year, but by the time the sun completes one revolution around the earth (thinking geocentrically) the moon makes about 12.36 revolutions. Even the sun's period could not be established with sufficient accuracy to keep the calendar in synchrony with the seasons. Then there are the planets, which were supposed to move in circular orbits (befitting their eternal, immutable nature) but sometimes did not. Add to this the precession of the equinoxes and one might well begin to wonder if the sky is a bottomless pit of perturbations, irregularities, and surprises—all meant, as Plato said, to train our minds and expand our spiritual horizons but also, perhaps, to vex and humble those who presume to squeeze the cosmos down to a fully rational system.

Ptolemy, probably the most accomplished astrologer in the West, implicitly acknowledged the imprecision of his craft when he argued that horoscopes would be more accurate in some respects were they drawn up from the astronomical circumstances that prevailed at the moment of one's *conception.* This, he continued, was generally not possible (who knows when he or she was conceived?), however, and so the time of birth would suffice.[44] A discrepancy of nine months might seem a fatal blow to any horoscope, but for Ptolemy it was not an all-or-nothing proposition. Since the sky was always revelatory of events on earth, it could always be profitably consulted as long as some information about one's beginnings was available. Better information, of course, yielded better results, but vague information need not squelch the search for astrological truth: that would be like refusing to peer into a tarnished mirror simply because of the imperfect reflection it casts back. This simile is particularly apropos of astrology because people once routinely characterized the sky as a mirror of the earth, and so it made sense to study it while trying to catch sight of one's reflection, however flawed, in the upper regions.

The important point is that belief in astrology flourished for centuries because it was congenial to the worldview that fostered it. When modern science discredited that worldview, astrology naturally lost its power to compel belief. Today any criticism of astrology employs the straightforward, confident language of science (à la Gauquelin's denunciation, above), the assumption being that reality is a single linear story made up of precise, single-valued meanings. Ideally, those meanings are mathematical values, which is to say they lack metaphysical or spiritual import. Such a worldview seems to offer little ground for astrological prognostication. Occultists, however, sometimes protest that the world is multi-storied and that science selectively captures just one story and then exalts it to the exclusion of all the others. The difficulty with this view from a scientific perspective is that it leaves too much to the imagination. What, for example, are we to make of the following statement by Leonardo da Vinci?

> You should look at certain walls stained with damp, or at the stones of uneven colour. If you have to invent some backgrounds you will be able to see in these the likeness of divine landscapes, adorned with mountains, ruins, rocks, woods, great plains, hills and valleys in great variety; and then again you will see there battles and strange figures in violent action, expressions of faces and clothes and an infinity of things which you will be able to reduce to their complete and proper forms. In such walls the same things happen as in the sound of bells, in whose stroke you may find every named word which you can imagine.[45]

Leonardo's ability to find "an infinity of things" in the irregularities of a stone wall is little different from the astrologer's ability to find a multiplicity of human fates in the motions of the stars. But is this ability solely a function of the imagination, or might the world (which, after all, includes the imagination) freely offer up a rich intermingling of many stories rather than just one story? *A priori* assumptions will guide the way in which this question is answered. One such assumption—that the world is riddled with evil—informs darker aspects of the occult. It is the subject of the next chapter.

5 ANCIENT EVIL

They are the evil Spirits in the creation
of Anu spawned. . . . They are the
Children of the Underworld.
Loudly roaring on high,
Gibbering below,
They are the bitter venom of the gods
. . .
No door can shut them out,
No bolt can turn them back,
Through the door like a snake they
glide . . .
Estranging the wife from the embrace
of the husband,
Snatching the child from the loins of a
man,
Sending the man forth from his home

—*Ancient Babylonian text*[1]

For it is ordained that none except the
gods shall live without misfortunes.

—*Sophocles*[2]

Recently in London's East End, two very similar cases arrived in hospital
emergency rooms—both were teens, both were from Bangladeshi families, and
both seemed possessed.[3] As the teens were in the modern West, both were
given phenothiazines, drugs that help control psychiatric disorders. But both
families had brought their children to the hospital only as a last resort, since
both believed their children were tormented by demonic jinn.[4]

When Zohra, a teenager, was first attacked, she thought someone was trying
to kill her at school and could neither eat nor talk for over a week. An Islamic
healer was brought in, and he concluded she was possessed by a jinni, an
invisible being, which he then attempted to expel by using a talisman of

Qur'anic verses. Zohra recovered the next day, and things seemed normal for a few weeks. Then she awoke one night screaming that a satanic being (*shaytan*) was in her room; when her father and brother entered, she cursed them, tried to hit her father, and broke down a door. She was even heard to say, "I'm getting married, put lipstick on me, I will kill you."[5] After being taken to the hospital, she was released a few days later and recovered.

The fifteen-year-old boy, Ali, was similarly treated by an Islamic healer after being hurled from his bed with such force that he lost his ability to speak. After seeming to recover, he later began acting erratically by throwing things and talking about knives. One night he screamed that his family members were pigs; fearing for their lives, the family called the police and later took Ali to the hospital. Like Zohra, he regained his sanity after medical treatment. But, while it was modern drugs that helped at the point of extreme crisis, both the parents and the patients continued to believe that the primary cause of the illnesses was demonic, not physical. Their view is deeply entrenched in history.

The belief in invisible, malevolent beings was all but universal in the ancient world, and it is still widely subscribed to. In antiquity, Egyptians, Babylonians, Hebrews, Greeks, and Romans all believed in various sorts of unseen spiritual beings who could cause injury, illness, and destruction. These views were enhanced in the Rabbinic, Christian, and Islamic traditions. Even during the Scientific Revolution, demons were considered both a subject of serious study and a possible source of scientific knowledge. Only in the eighteenth and nineteenth centuries did the belief in demons begin to decline sharply or, rather, the belief in their conspicuous and ubiquitous activity.

In this chapter, we look at several pre-modern cultures that readily traced the origin of evil (pain and misfortune) back to malevolent beings. Although the stories and remedies for warding off evil jar modern sensibilities, there is a kind of logic to them. The amulets and formulas were felt to work because evil agents were willful beings. They could therefore be checked by threats and reminders of their weakness in the face of superior powers. One may sometimes intimidate a snarling dog with a show of bravery because dogs generally respond to stern words and threatening actions. If all evil originated with snarling dogs—or creatures of similar mentality—then a show of force (amulets, threats, incantations, etc.) would do much to keep disease and misfortune out of our lives. And if the show of force failed, then perhaps force itself would succeed. A god might come to the rescue. Then again, one might not. Sometimes dogs do attack and achieve their purpose.

But what if, more often than not, evil comes about by purposeless, unknowing agents—say, a hurricane, or a disease-bearing flea with no capacity to appreciate the pain it causes? No show of force would be effective against it. The more appropriate response—the modern response—would be direct action. Not inclined to threaten or outwit evil beings that are said to create hurricanes, moderns simply deal with hurricanes themselves, which are felt to arise from chance perturbations within large, unknowing weather patterns. Similarly, the flea cannot be thwarted with mere words or ritualistic actions, since it is blind to human concerns. It must be pinched or poisoned.

As detestable as they are, fleas are not the real culprits, however. According to modern medicine, they are merely vectors of disease, along with mosquitoes, vermin, and the like—all of which convey microorganisms that invade the body. These microorganisms, completely driven by their own survival needs, have no inkling of the pain they are causing; their genetic programming, borne of eons of evolutionary adaptation, just carries them along. This is a very different picture from the pervasive pre-modern view that disease originates with evil spirits or demons that derive some sort of malicious satisfaction from watching their victims writhe in pain. Despite this, one should not conclude that ancient medicine was all a muddle. If aloe brings relief, what *immediate* difference does it make whether germs or demons—or little green men from Mars—are said to have caused the pain. The remedy is no less efficacious for having defeated an enemy that, by modern medical standards, does not exist.

DEMONS IN THE ANCIENT NEAR EAST

That there is much evil in the world was as much a truism for the ancients as for us. But what causes evil? For the Egyptians, the gods, while possibly dangerous at times, were not and could not be evil—evil verged away from the gods, toward disorder and non-existence. Even the god Seth, who killed his brother Osiris, was more of a "trickster" than a purveyor of absolute evil.[6] Thus, evil originated, for the most part, with evil humans (both alive and dead) and demonic spirits, not with the gods.

Ancient Egyptians believed that demons were wicked, dangerous, and invisible. Surprisingly, several texts imply that demons had physical bodies that could die. More specifically, according to some Egyptian physicians, headaches could be caused either by the dead or by demons. If caused by the dead, the sufferer was to implore the gods for relief by reciting a prescribed incantation or prayer. But if the headache was traced back to a demon, an exorcist threatened "to burn [the demon's] soul and consume its corpse."[7] Threatening to destroy its corpse seems an odd way to make a demon quake in fear, but, as we have already seen, for an Egyptian, the idea of the body's physical destruction was so ominous that elaborate mummification rituals were developed to protect against it. Demons were presumed to also want to preserve their bodies, even their dead bodies, at all costs.

Each door of an Egyptian household had a god to protect it from bad luck,

MAGIC, MYSTERY, AND SCIENCE

demons, and the dead.[8] But if an evil spirit did enter, one could say, "Mayest thou flow away, he who comes in the darkness and enters furtively, with his nose behind him, and his face reversed, failing in that for which he came!"[9] To protect her sleeping child, a loving mother might recite this touching charm at night: "Hast thou come to kiss this child? I will not let thee kiss him! Hast thou come to silence (him)? I will not let thee set silence over him! Hast thou come to injure him? I will not let thee injure him! Hast thou come to take him away? I will not let thee take him away from me!"[10]

Given that many people still pray for their children and other loved ones each night, the mother's recitation is hardly odd. When the idea is carried over into medical practice, however, it does mark a striking departure from modern attitudes. The Egyptians held that the primary cause of illness was attack by spirits (that is, demons or ghosts of the dead), though sometimes the gods themselves might send disease, as when Sekhmet sent plagues. Given this premise, it comes as no surprise that nearly all Egyptian medicine involved charms, amulets, incantations and prayers, and if need be, rites of exorcism.[11] Therefore, so far as healing was concerned, there was no airtight distinction between physician, priest, and exorcist.[12]

Like all other ancient healers, Egyptian physicians employed varying combinations of pharmacology, prayers to the gods, and excoriations of demons. The modern emphasis on *materia medica* (medical treatment that takes no notice of supernatural or spiritual forces) as the only source of "real" efficacy would have seemed quite bizarre, bordering on the ludicrous.[13] Since demons were real presences, they could enter through any of the body's openings to cause illness. Enemas were thus popular among Egyptians.[14] To prevent demonic entry through the mouth one might write a verbal amulet or spell on papyrus, immerse the papyrus in water, and then drink the inky incantation for protection.[15]

Of course, a good offense is often the best defense, and some amulets were quite offensive. The mother's charm cited above continues: "I have made his [the child's] magical protection against thee out of clover . . . onions . . . honey" and the eggs, jaws, and backbones of various fish.[16] This repulsive mixture was meant to frighten away harmful spirits. All sorts of stinking material could be used in these talismans, such as garlic[17] (reminiscent of Dracula's hatred of that pungent herb). And what could be more repellent than excrement, mentioned in the following Egyptian text: "O ghost, male or female . . . who dwelleth in this my flesh . . . get thee hence from this my flesh, from these my limbs. Lo, I brought thee excrements to devour! Beware, hidden one, be on your guard, concealed one, escape!"[18] Mesopotamians similarly found dog feces especially useful in driving off demons.[19]

Unlike excrement, honey is not repulsive, but according to Egyptians it was "sweet to men but horrible to ghosts."[20] They were right, at least if ghosts are equated with germs. Honey has been shown to be an excellent antibacterial unguent for topical wounds.[21] The logic was straightforward: since evil spirits caused disease and infection, and honey helped heal wounds, demons obviously hated honey. Egyptian doctors used it in 30 to 40 percent of all their medicines, both external and internal.[22]

In a form of sympathetic magic, demons could also be warded off by scrawling their activities on a pottery bowl, then shattering it. As the pot was broken, so also their power would be broken. This technique was also used against hated associates and overseers: many smashed bowls have been found with the names of foreign rulers, Egyptian rebels, chancellors connected with the pharaoh's harems, and even a tutor or two.[23]

In the event of symptoms suggesting demonic possession, Egyptian priest-physicians performed exorcisms. One of the most peculiar exorcisms recorded in late Egyptian literature shows up in the *Legend of the Possessed Princess*.[24] The story is probably a religiously motivated forgery, dating from Ptolemaic Egypt during the fourth to third centuries B.C., but it purports to have occurred at the time of Ramses II in the thirteenth century. Pharaoh Ramses II had taken a beautiful woman from faraway "Bekhten" (possibly Bactria) to be his wife. Sometime later, his wife's sister was reported to be very ill, and the Prince of Bekhten persuaded Pharaoh to send an Egyptian physician to come heal her. When, however, the physician diagnosed her as being "possessed of spirits" so powerful that he could do nothing, the Prince begged Pharaoh to send an Egyptian god to come. So, an Egyptian god made a long-distance medical house call.

Curiously, the god took seventeen months to reach Bekhten, since he rode in specially commissioned boats and chariots supplied by Ramses. Once the god arrived, he cast the disease-causing demon out of the princess in a very civilized manner—by responding to the demon's request for a going-away banquet. The Prince of Bekhten was so overjoyed at the outcome that he decided to not let the god go back to Egypt, but finally, after nearly four years, the god flew back to Thebes as a golden falcon.

For those living in ancient Mesopotamia, such as the Sumerians, Akkadians, and Babylonians, the gods were not so accommodating. Born of the blood of an evil, fallen god, humans had gotten off to a deplorable start.[25] Often portrayed as slaves of the gods, they were subject to the nearly inscrutable whims of their divine masters. Even the after-life, when mentioned at all, was no Egyptian paradise but a place of darkness and eating of clay.[26] And everywhere there was the danger of "sinning" against the gods.

The Mesopotamian concept of "sin" was far broader than the Judeo-Christian view.[27] Yes, the breaking of moral law was part of it—murder, for

MAGIC, MYSTERY, AND SCIENCE

example, could be a sin, particularly if the murder victim were a fellow member of the community. (Killing an outsider generally did not count as murder.) But any unwitting misstep in action or ceremony could be an affront to a god, and such a "sin" left one open to demonic attack.

By contrast, those who were conscientious in the performance of ceremony could win divine approbation. Nebuchadnezzar poked out the eyes of his enemies and impaled their living bodies on pikes, yet did not hesitate to declare to the great god Marduk that he had "continually sought the guidance . . . [and] followed the way of the gods," and that he was "the king whom you love . . . and who pleases you."[28] How did he distinguish himself so favorably in Marduk's eyes? Evidently by scrupulously following the gods' rituals and rebuilding their temples.[29] Ashurbanipal, an Assyrian king, depicted himself on a couch in his garden, which he adorned with his enemy's head hanging from a tree like a Christmas ornament.[30] Apparently the gods took no notice of this grotesque display; they were, however, pleased with the king's ceremonial observances.

Besides the gods, there were multitudes of demons ready to attack any Mesopotamian who sinned or otherwise lowered their spiritual guard. Demons could take on almost any shape: they might appear as an ass or a snake or a snarling dog pack, or as a fox slinking through the city at night.[31] Or, they might take no shape at all. Although they could be found nearly anywhere, they were most prevalent in dark, dangerous, and deserted areas: deserts, graveyards, caves, and ruins.[32] No home was safe from them, for they could slip under doors or through tiny cracks. Moreover, sorcerers could direct or "sic" demons on unsuspecting persons, either through elaborate ritual or simply by projecting the "evil eye" or even the "evil finger."[33]

Mesopotamians saw demons and evil spirits in the darkest of terms, "no light in their bodies," and utterly merciless (akin, perhaps, to the realistically terrifying creatures that populate modern cinema). They were neither male nor female, had neither marriage nor children, and "from their claws drips bitter gall, their footprints are [full of] evil venom."[34] "They have nothing in common with us," one scholar concluded, "they are . . . wholly other."[35] And if they attacked, these demons could cause illness, insanity, and death.[36] Diseases such as epilepsy were seen as demonic possession, and pregnant women were especially prone to demonic predation; thus the high death rates of both mothers and infants during childbirth.[37]

Like the Egyptians, the Mesopotamians had many possible defenses against demons, including small wearable effigies of the gods and amulets of special stones on special threads. One could even make a tiny replica of the demon, place it on a little boat and send it out (with proper incantations) into the water where, if all went well, it would sink along with the misfortune it spread.[38]

Protection also came in the form of a wide variety of "protective spirits" (which we might call "guardian angels" today), if they were invoked correctly, using talismans, invocations, and prayers. But luck, or what the Romans called *fortuna,* played into this as well. If you were lucky, you were said to "have a spirit." If, however, things went badly, the guardians were absent.[39]

Against demonic possession there were many exorcism texts, but some seem (like the Mesopotamian outlook in general) fatalistic and comfortless. One from Nimrod states, "When the exorcist proceeds to the house of a patient . . . [i]f he sees a white pig, this patient will live." If, however, "he sees a black pig," the patient will die by a certain time and in a certain way. To deliver a patient from a demon, the exorcist (according to other texts) could invoke gods well known for their demon-chasing power or could create and destroy magical wax effigies of demons.[40]

Here is a delightful exorcism used by a priest to help a poor fellow whose symptoms included "diseased flesh," vertigo, fever, and arthritis.[41] The text states that if a ghost, demon, or Evil Thing "has seized a man and persecutes him . . . and will not be separated from him, you shall take dust from a ruined town, a ruined house, a ruined temple, a grave, a neglected garden, a neglected canal, and a disused road, and you shall mix it with bull's blood and make an image of the Evil Thing." Since the image consisted of dust from the haunts of demons, perhaps the demon would feel more at home there than in the patient. The image was then treated rather nicely—but all as a trick. It was clothed in a lion's skin, adorned with a red jewel around its neck, given a leather bag full of provisions, and placed on the roof of the sick man's house. Once the demon had moved into the image (often after much coaxing and cajoling), the exorcist trapped the unwanted predator by drawing a circle of flour around the image and putting a new cooking pot over it. He then sealed the mouth of the pot and buried it "in a deserted wasteland."

By modern standards, such methods are decidedly unenlightened. But, as we noted above, prayer is not an uncommon practice, even in highly technological societies. So we may not be as far removed from "superstition" as we think. Perhaps the difference is that prayer and related appeals to Deity have become rather a last resort when problems are to be solved. When all else fails, supplicate a higher power. Also, the ancient polytheistic religions no longer flourish in the West. The strange gods of the Egyptians and Mesopotamians strike most believing (and non-believing) people as ineffectual. In biblical language, they are "vanities" having little or no power to answer prayers. It is fitting, therefore, that we turn now to Zoroastrianism, some of whose tenets parallel those found in the Western faith traditions that displaced polytheism.

Not far from Mesopotamia, priests in Persia were customarily the medical practitioners as well, since the evil Ahriman had created 99,999 diseases.[42] Ahriman was the malevolent enemy of the good god Ahura Mazda in the dualistic religion of Zoroastrianism. Zarathustra, the founder of Zoroastrianism (he was known as Zoroaster among the Greeks, hence the name) was said to be shocked at the polytheism and pagan practices of his time, much as Muhammad would be more than a millennium later. After receiving divine revelation, Zarathustra proclaimed that there was but one overarching god, Ahura Mazda, who had created all that was good and pure. Opposed to him in perpetual warfare was Ahriman, creator of everything evil and impure.[43] Each had lesser divinities under him: those under Ahura Mazda were roughly equivalent to angels, and those under Ahriman were "daevas," that is, demons.[44]

During the first six thousand years of the universe, Ahura Mazda was dominant and had thrown down Ahriman, who then arose for three thousand years and polluted the created world. Thereupon Zarathustra came forth and preached his redemptive message. As the end nears, each human must choose to follow the Truth or the Lie, for with the help of his pure devotees, Ahura Mazda will conquer Ahriman and evil, and this victory will usher in a resurrection of the dead, a final judgment, and a paradise for the righteous.[45]

The similarities of this salvation story to the doctrines of the great monotheistic religions of Judaism, Christianity, and Islam are obvious: angels, demons, resurrection, judgment, and a titanic eschatological struggle between good and evil in which humans play a vital role. Of particular interest is Ahriman, an adversary worthy of comparison with Christianity's Satan. Ahriman, Lord of Lies, attacked the beautiful creation of Ahura Mazda, introducing every evil thing found in the world, including poison, pain, disease, ants, locusts, winter, menstruation, and death. He turned creature against creature, insects against plants, wolves against cattle, and finally sent The Whore (a mysterious, feminine evil) who corrupted the first male "Adam," named Gayomard.[46] Curiously, this Whore had once revived Ahriman from lethargy by recounting the evil she had done. In return for this, Ahriman kissed her and thereby created menstruation, a serious ritual pollution for Zoroastrians.[47]

Like Mesopotamians, Zoroastrians had to contend with multitudes of demons. "A thousand death-dealing demons" were sent to attack the first man, Gayomard, alone.[48] Later Zoroastrians placed the number of demons in the millions. Unlike the Egyptians and Mesopotamians, however, for Zoroastrians the warfare between humans and demons was central. As one scholar put it, "Man in the actual world is thus presented as the main battleground for the spirits. The outcome of the battle is in fact entirely dependent on man, the ultimate victory is effected by man's ability to vanquish the demons within himself."[49] This is a tall order, but fortunately all pure followers are assigned guardian angels, the Fravashis, to help protect them.[50]

Given this emphasis on human worth and other parallel doctrines, it is tempting to assume that one religion—Zoroastrianism or Judaism—shaped the other. In fact, clear lines of influence are hard to establish and there are important differences between the two faiths. One difference is found in the paucity of references to demons in the Hebrew Bible ("Old Testament" to Christians). Further, Satan does not emerge as God's great opponent, a figure equivalent to Ahriman, for he is seldom mentioned in the Hebrew Bible and then only briefly.

Originally, the term Satan meant "adversary," and there is a spiritual adversary of Job (and of God) in the prefatory chapters of the Book of Job.[51] Many interpret this adversary of Job to be The Adversary, Satan himself; certainly the misfortune he inflicts befits the designation: murder of the innocent, pillage, and horrific disease. But, it may be argued, he simply plays the role of a "devil's advocate" by asking God's permission to test Job's faith. He does not loom up as one trying to dethrone God.

Elsewhere, Satan is mentioned only twice with certainty. In the Chronicles, he acted the tempter as he "rose up against Israel and incited David to take a census."[52] In the second instance, Satan stood beside the High Priest Joshua and accused him before God of being unworthy of the office.[53] Of course, there is also the temptation of Eve by the serpent in the Garden of Eden, but Satan's name is not mentioned there, and the snake and Satan are only linked in later developments of the doctrine.[54]

The Hebrew term for demons appears only twice in the Hebrew Bible, each time referring to wayward Israelites who made animal and child sacrifices to "false gods" that were actually demons.[55] (This term, "shedim," was a loanword from the Assyrian for good, protective spirits, which the Hebrews viewed as false and evil.[56]) While Phoenician and Canaanite worshippers of Baal practiced infant sacrifice,[57] Hebrew prophets sought to keep the contagion out of Israel. Even so, King Ahab and Jezebel, his notorious Queen from Phoenician Tyre, are said to have sacrificed a son to Baal.[58] And Solomon, who created worship areas for all his foreign wives, built a high place in Jerusalem for "Molech," the Hebrew term associated with these rituals.[59] According to the prophet Jeremiah, such hideous sacrifices took place at Jerusalem's Valley of Hinnom, a name which still means Hell in archaic English, Gehenna.[60]

In keeping with its lukewarm concern for demons, the Hebrew Bible tells of only one attempted "exorcism" of an evil spirit. After King Saul's disobedience to God, an evil spirit tormented him.[61] Attempting to allay this problem, Saul's attendants advised him to select a good harpist whose music could drive the spirit away. The chosen harpist was none other than David, the "Lord's anointed" and future king of Israel.

For a while, music soothed the savage spirit in Saul, but he soon grew jealous of the young harpist's military feats, which, ironically, were being set to music by others. And one day as Saul began "prophesying," he fell into an ecstatic state that prompted David to play his harp.[62] Overcome by envy and the evil spirit, Saul hurled a spear at David while he was playing, which David skillfully avoided.[63] After slipping away, the young musician was exiled from court on military maneuvers, evidently in hopes that he would be killed in battle. Despite this early failure in music exorcism, later Jews composed songs to chase or ward off demons; the *Dead Sea Scrolls* have several, attributed to David, Solomon, and "the Sage."[64] And Pseudo-Philo's *Biblical Antiquities* (first century A.D.) purports to give the actual song with which David soothed Saul.[65]

If demons get scant mention in the Hebrew Bible, the *Pseudepigrapha* fully remedies the lack.[66] A central concern throughout that collection of texts is the origin of evil and how demons may have sprung from the first evil act or contributed to it. Many of the pseudepigraphical works attest that evil demons were either fallen angels or the offspring of angels and humans.

"Pride goeth before a fall" is a familiar proverb,[67] and pride seems to be a special problem for angels, either fallen or unfallen. For example, in the *Apocalypse of Abraham,* the four-faced and fiery living creatures who sang before the very throne of God were sometimes envious and feisty. "When [these creatures] finished singing, they would look at one another and threaten one another."[68] Fortunately, the powerful angel who accompanied Abraham saw this and "turned the face of each living creature from the face which was opposite it so that they could not see each other's faces threatening each other. And he taught them the song of peace."[69] (How one turns the "face" of two four-faced creatures so that they cannot see each other is not explained.)

According to J. Z. Smith, even the archangels Michael and Gabriel bickered and threatened each other.[70] On occasion, God himself had to cut short their quarrelling, "for even the heavenly ones need peace . . . [since] each one in his turn says, 'I am the first.'" What is more, angels sometimes also resented humans. Shedding light (perhaps) on an enigmatic episode in the book of Genesis, the *Prayer of Joseph* explained that it was the angel Uriel's envy of Jacob that prompted his nighttime attack on the patriarch.[71]

Since, in these traditions, even the holy angels themselves were proud, envious, and contentious, it comes as no surprise that the demons were jealous of place and battled among themselves as well, "plundering and doing violence to one another."[72] As fallen angels, they would simply be following a pattern marked out by unfallen or not-yet-fallen angels. It is important to note, however, that in the *Pseudepigrapha* angelic jealousy is not directed toward God: this will come with early Christian thought and, of course, Milton's *Paradise Lost*.[73] Reminiscent of Uriel, the pseudepigraphic Satan is jealous of *humans*. In fact, according to Satan, his fall was all *man's* fault.

The clearest example is found in the *Life of Adam and Eve*.[74] The account, given by Satan, relates that when Adam was "made in the image of God,"[75] Michael brought Adam out before all the angels and said: "Worship the image of the Lord God, as the Lord God has instructed." Michael bowed first, and then asked Satan to do the same. Much to Michael's chagrin, Satan balked. When the exchange escalated, Satan indignantly asked, "Why do you compel me? I will not worship one inferior . . . to me. I am prior to him in creation; before he was made, I was already made. He ought to worship me." This retort appealed to many other angels, who joined Satan's ranks by also refusing to worship Adam. Trying to stem the mutiny, Michael warned that God would become angry if his command were not followed; to which Satan replied, if God gets angry with me, then "I will set my throne above the stars of Heaven and will be like the Most High." For this presumption, Satan and his followers were cast down to earth.

There are also other stories of fallen angels in the *Pseudepigrapha* and some of these identify lust rather than envy or pride as the fatal flaw. Two of the most puzzling verses in the book of Genesis are found in chapter 6: "the sons of God saw that the daughters of men were beautiful, and they married any of them they chose" (6:2), and "There were giants [i.e., Nephilim] in the earth in those days; and also after that, when the sons of God came in unto the daughters of men, and they bare children to them, the same became mighty men which were of old, men of renown" (6:4).[76] Who were these "sons of God"? Who were these "giants," and how, if at all, are the two verses connected? Numerous commentators have addressed these questions. Here is one fairly representative response by the author of the *Ethiopic Apocalypse of Enoch*.

Shortly after Adam and Eve's expulsion from the Garden, two hundred angels (the aforementioned sons of God) looked toward earth and were sexually aroused upon seeing the beautiful women.[77] Leaving their heavenly station, the angels came to earth, chose wives, and sired offspring. But their children grew to be giants, some reaching a height of 450 feet. At first humans supplied the giants with food, but, given their enormous appetites, this could not last for long. Unfortunately, when the humans tired of feeding them, the hungry behemoths helped themselves to anything at hand—humans, birds, beasts, reptiles, fish, and, ultimately, each other. Blood flowed freely and unbridled voracity multiplied.

With carnage and other evils polluting the earth, God sent the judgment of the great Flood on humans and giants, and captured the evil angels in nets for

MAGIC, MYSTERY, AND SCIENCE

later punishment.[78] That was not the end of the giants, however, for they were to become evil spirits on the earth and cause great trouble for humanity.[79] Enoch, by the way, went to heaven to plead the case of the fallen angels, and lost.

There are many variations of this story, some of them quite bizarre. But there is no need to multiply instances that no longer seem persuasive, particularly when the larger point is that belief in fallen angels and Satan became increasingly prevalent during late antiquity. The world's evil may be characterized in many ways, and long ago many people instinctively personified it by talking of demons, evil spirits, fallen angels, and Satan. This way of talking is central to Christianity, particularly as it was practiced by ancient and medieval believers.

SATAN, DEMONS, AND THE NEW TESTAMENT

Although the Hebrew Bible makes little mention of Satan and demons, the gospels of the New Testament incorporate many doctrinal developments of late ancient Judaism (which show up as well in the *Pseudepigrapha*). As in other cultures, demons have power to afflict their victims in ways both physical and mental. That said, not all diseases were ascribed to demons. The high fever of Peter's mother-in-law, for instance, was simply a fever.[80] And according to the Gospel of Matthew, Jesus healed "people brought to him . . . who were ill with various diseases, those suffering severe pain, the demon-possessed, those having seizures, and the paralyzed."[81] The implication seems to be that disease can occur naturally or non-demonically.

There are, of course, dramatic accounts of demonic possession. The most memorable concerns the Gadarene living near the Sea of Galilee.[82] This man exhibited superhuman strength, having broken all the chains used to bind him, and he dwelt among the tombs and desolate mountains—a favorite haunt of demons in earlier cultures. When Jesus approached, the demon within cried out to him, begging that he not be tortured before his time, a reference to the Final Judgment. Jesus asked his name, and he replied, "Legion, for we are many." Realizing they were about to be cast out of their victim, the pack of demons pleaded to go into a huge herd of pigs (an unclean animal to the Jews), whereupon Jesus simply commanded, "Go!" and into the herd they went. The nearly two thousand swine turned mad and ran pell-mell into the sea and drowned. The herders, no doubt, were not only shocked to see their profits sinking before their eyes, but also to see the squealing hogs drowning at all, for pigs are normally excellent swimmers.

This, in effect, was an exorcism, although New Testament authors do not apply that word to Jesus' ministry; perhaps because exorcism implies complex,

Figure 16. Jesus casting out demons. Demons fly out of the possessed man (in chains) and enter swine, which fall off a cliff in the background.

formulaic rituals, and Jesus used none.[83] He simply commanded demons out, and out they came—like ballistic projectiles. (The New Testament Greek for "cast out" is ἐκβάλλω, to throw or tear out violently; it is related to the English "ballistics."[84])

This straightforward approach comports with Jesus' aversion to elaborate public ritual and his message that power (or, the "kingdom of God") is within.[85] When some of his disciples tried and failed to cast out demons, he did not correct their ceremonial modus operandi (apparently they had none); he simply instructed them to fast and pray before trying again.[86] But, despite the implicit acceptance of demons in the world and recognition of their capacity to blight human experience, demonic possession and exorcism was not a cardinal theme

MAGIC, MYSTERY, AND SCIENCE

Figure 17. Lucifer. "The mighty angel" becomes known as Satan after his fall.

in the New Testament church.[87] In fact, there are few references to exorcisms in post-resurrection documents.[88] It is as if the hot war had become a cold war, or that Satan's tactics had changed from open attack and control to deceit and sabotage in occupied territory. His New Testament epithet, "The Father of Lies," suggests that he is adept at spinning out murky half-truths.

Even at the beginning of Jesus' ministry, Satan's attacks were subtle and cunning. The story of Jesus' temptation in the wilderness reveals a clever, questioning Adversary who hoped to win by intrigue and sleight of hand rather than open combat, coyly quoting scriptures and planting doubts: "If you *are* the Son of God . . ."[89] Less an accuser than an insinuator, Satan deceives by preying on our insecurities and luring us into self-deception. (For a classic modern illustration, see C. S. Lewis's *The Screwtape Letters*.)

Notwithstanding his low-key, shadowy approach, the New Testament Satan was said to have once been a bright angel. He fell, however, "like lightning from heaven"[90] after mounting a rebellion against God. Commentators linked his fall to a passage from the Book of Isaiah: "How you have fallen from heaven, O morning star [literally, 'shining one'], son of the dawn! You have been cast down to the earth, you who once laid low the nations! You said in your heart, 'I will ascend to heaven; I will raise my throne above the stars of God. . . . I will make myself like the Most High.' "[91] The initial interpretation of this Old Testament passage marked the King of Babylon as the haughty figure whom God had humbled, but, after the early Satan took on a more insidious, arrogant aspect, the scripture acquired new meaning.

The Isaiah passage is the major inspiration for calling the Devil "Lucifer" and attributing his fall to pride. The *Septuagint*, the Greek translation of the Hebrew scriptures, rendered the Hebrew word for "shining one" as "light-bearer," and, in his Vulgate version, St. Jerome turned this into "Lucifer," which captures the Greek meaning quite precisely and which was already in usage as an alternative Latin name for the planet Venus.[92] (It was an apt choice, for Venus, the brightest of heavenly bodies after the sun and the moon, almost seems to rival and challenge the sun just before dawn—then is obscured or humbled by the rising sun.) Over time, the bright cognomen became so closely linked with Satan that the King James Version simply retained it. Among Christians, *Satan* and *Lucifer* are interchangeable names for God's great opponent.

No description of the New Testament Satan would be complete without saying a bit more about his fall and ultimate fate. Evidently linking Satan with the serpent that tempted Eve, the author of *Revelation* characterized him as "an enormous red dragon" whose "tail swept a third of the stars out of the sky and flung them down to earth."[93] These stars are usually identified as angels who followed Satan. With two great forces massed, full-scale conflict ensued: "And there was war in heaven. Michael and his angels fought against the dragon, and the dragon and his angels fought back. But he was not strong enough, and they lost their place in heaven. The great dragon was hurled down. . . . He was hurled to the earth, and his angels with him."[94]

Although decided in heaven, the war continues here on earth. Eventually, however, Satan and his angels will be thrown into an abyss for a thousand years and then permanently consigned to a "lake of burning sulfur."[95] Only then will the world be free of the proud, once-bright angel who strove to depose God.

More than any other version of evil, the Satan of the New Testament, along with his hellish hordes, continues to animate Western imagination. Belief in his conspicuous activity in the world peaked during the Renaissance—at a time, ironically, when modern science was taking shape. We have already commented on this irony (in chapter 2), but will explore it further in the chapters on demons and witchcraft.

6 SATAN, DEMONS, AND JINN

And the Lord said unto Satan, Whence comest thou? Then Satan answered the Lord, and said, From going to and fro in the earth, and from walking up and down in it.

—*Job 1:7*

Today the word "demon" summons up frightening images of evil, primarily because Christian authors borrowed the Classical Greek term "daemons" to signify fallen angels. For the Greeks, however, demons were not necessarily evil. They straddled the line between good and evil, some falling on one side, some on the other. Thus, "daemon" could be interchangeable with the word "god," as when Homer used both terms to refer to the same goddess.[1] Moreover, humans could achieve daemonic status. Aeschylus spoke of the dead Darius as a divine daemon, and for Euripides, an esteemed wife who passed on into the next world was to be honored as a goddess or a "blessed daemon."[2] Even Hector's wife lovingly addressed him as "daemon."[3]

Among other things, demons were a way of making sense of reality. Things happen every day that moderns ascribe to various laws of nature, none of which can be directly observed or handled but must rather be inferred. Such was the case with demons: their reality was inferred from observed events. A wine barrel, just set down, explodes for no apparent reason, but each witness of the event reaches for a reason that makes sense within his or her culture. Perhaps a weak barrel stave, an overactive fermentation process, *or* a demon that was disturbed by the placement of the barrel. The first two reasons make sense to people in the modern West, while the last made sense to ancient Jews.

But what really happened? That question, one might venture, can be decided by scientific investigation. But this is a distinctly modern response. The ancient Jew might reply that rabbinical investigation should decide the issue. The question then becomes one of adjudicating between evidence gathered by each authority figure, whether scientist or rabbi. But this is more difficult than it seems, for what counts as evidence in one culture often comes off as nonsense in the other. In this particular case, a rabbi, called upon to investigate an exploding wine barrel some two thousand years ago, seems to have found clear evidence of demonic activity. Using trumpets, he exorcized the offending demon and asked why the creature had burst the cask. The demon replied, "What was I supposed to do, they set it on my ear!" The demon was charged for the damages, but as one might expect, he slipped away without paying.[4]

The smile that this story elicits would be reciprocated by an ancient Jew on hearing an unfamiliar story involving certain "laws of nature" that caused the explosion. But despite the wide difference marked out by demons and the laws of nature, there are surprising similarities between the two entities. One similarity has already been noted: both demons and the laws of nature are matters of inference, not direct observation. Also, demons are pervasive—they are virtually everywhere—just as are the laws of nature. Finally, demons, although fairly predictable in their activities, sometimes surprise us. Similarly, the laws of nature, although perhaps idealized as simple propositions, have yet to be fully mastered by human ingenuity.

Einstein once remarked that "physical [that is, scientific] concepts are free creations of the human mind, and are not, however it may seem, uniquely determined by the external world."[5] This is a good thought to keep in mind as we venture into the ancient world of demons and genies (jinn). There are many ways of playing dot-to-dot with the phenomena of nature and perhaps no one way is "uniquely determined" or mandated by the world. While natural phenomena are the same for all cultures, human creativity connects the dots in different ways.

DAEMONS IN ANCIENT GREECE

To appreciate what demons meant to the Greeks, one must reflect that most people occasionally sense that there is more to the world than what they directly apprehend. William Wordsworth, for instance, wrote that he had felt

A presence that disturbs me with the joy
Of elevated thoughts; a sense sublime
Of something far more deeply interfused,
Whose dwelling is the light of setting suns,
And the round ocean and the living air,

And the blue sky, and in the mind of man;
A motion and a spirit, that impels
All thinking things, all objects of all thought,
And rolls through all things.[6]

Admittedly, Wordsworth is an extreme case—few people seem so intimately attuned to the larger unseen presence he posits, but many nod in agreement while reading his poetry and so assent to the possibility that there is an elusive spiritual dimension to the world. For the Greeks, this dimension sometimes took the form of daemons, and many experiences that moderns now trace back to *inner* psychology—say, a bright idea, a sudden inspiration, or an unexpected mood change—were attributed to daemons or gods or similar *external* supernatural beings. This is why the philosopher Thales proclaimed that the living world is full of daemons.[7]

Plato formulated the framework of a daemonology in his *Symposium*, in which daemons were the intermediaries, in all senses, between the gods and humans.[8] Daemons were both the messengers of the gods to humans and the emissaries of humans to the gods. Thus, all forms of divination occurred through daemons, and all prayers, spells, and magical petitions were carried by daemons back to the gods. It is difficult to know, however, if all this was a common Greek view or one of Plato's many innovations. For Xenocrates, Plato's pupil and later head of the Academy, the World-Soul itself was a daemon and so also were all the souls of the planets.[9] But this is not surprising, as Plato himself disclosed that every person possesses a daemon in some sense. As he declared in the *Timaeus,* "God has given to each of us, as his daemon, that kind of soul which is housed in the top of our body."[10]

The most famous daemon was that of Plato's mentor, Socrates. Socrates' "divine sign," as he often called it, had been a voice within him since childhood.[11] Never prompting him to action, but deterring him from actions that were dangerous or harmful for himself or his friends, this daemon guided him in matters large and small.[12] At times, Socrates would stop speaking in mid-sentence, or remain seated, or refuse to accept a would-be disciple—all at this spirit's prompting.[13] Twice it warned him to tell a friend to stay seated at a banquet. Later the friend slipped away while Socrates was looking after other matters. Misfortune ensued, for unbeknown to Socrates, the friend had conspired with others to commit murder, a crime for which he was later executed.[14]

This was not a minor aspect of Socrates' personality. He claimed that this divine force impelled him to teach and advise others by "interfering" in their affairs, and it was on account of this divine sign or impulse that he was charged with impiety for introducing new gods.[15] What's more, it was because the daemon did not allow him to plan a defense, or prompt him to flee the danger

SATAN, DEMONS, AND JINN

of the trial, that Socrates claimed his impending death sentence was not an evil for him, but a positive good.[16] In brief, this daemon was central to Socrates' philosophical life and actions, and thus of great import to all later Western thought. It is worth asking: Would there have been (in terms of cultural impact) a Plato or an Aristotle without a Socrates, and would there have been a Socrates without his daemon? Could he have been so fearless, so stalwart, and, yes, so humorous in the face of death, without that distinctive inspiration that he felt linked him to the immortal gods?

Using Socrates as a mouthpiece, Plato implied that daemons were of the gods, and thus could not be evil.[17] But by the Hellenistic era, and increasingly during the Roman Empire, pagan Greeks began to believe that some daemons could be very nasty indeed. Plato's student Xenocrates had already proposed that daemons could be good or evil, and the later Platonists, Stoics, and Neoplatonists agreed.[18] This outlook proved quite useful to any who wished to protect the gods from criticism. Daemons, being spiritual, powerful, and knowledgeable, could become divine tricksters by impersonating the gods.[19] Thus, those repulsive myths concerning the capricious "gods" who raped or murdered for pleasure, could now be ascribed to evil daemons who were pretending to be Zeus or Bacchus for selfish reasons. Likewise, bloodthirsty "gods" who demanded human sacrifice or self-mutilation were really daemons, too.[20] The revisionists did not deny that spiritual powers were present at these rites, only that they were wicked spirits and not the gods themselves. Christian apologists also adopted this stance and mixed it with Jewish views.[21] So, to the considerable displeasure of the Neoplatonists and others, the Christians lumped *all* pagan spirits under the demonic rubric, daemons and gods alike.

As messengers of the gods, daemons were sources of divine foresight and were consequently tapped for information regarding future events. By the Hellenistic period, however, more coercive approaches began to flourish wherein sorcerers tried to use daemons to manipulate existing circumstances and, in some cases, to determine future events. Inasmuch as we discussed some of these methods in chapter 2, here we merely note that magicians sought to extend their power by creating tablets that called upon daemons to bind or weaken an enemy.[22] These inscribed lead tablets could also take the form of little figurines, and much like later voodoo dolls, they often had nails shoved in all sorts of painful locations (from the eyes on down) to inhibit the intended target.[23] Another practice, euphemistically termed "love magic," involved commanding a daemon to abduct the person of one's lusts—a spiritually aided rape.[24] Finally, sports figures could be targeted: daemons were frequently called upon to weaken wrestlers or enfeeble opposing charioteers.[25]

Once popularized, these practices could turn a profit. By the time of Plato, professional magicians charged fees for individualized tablets.[26] But it was the matter-of-fact Romans who began mass-producing tablets and dolls.[27] Naturally, counter-measures against these daemons, such as amulets, could be purchased as well.[28] With belief in magic flourishing, the link between the conjurations of some magicians and the world of the spirits was felt to be so potent, that in one instance an evil daemon materialized out of nothing but a curse.[29] And, finally, one of the greatest purported achievements of ancient Greek magic was the late classical *Spell of Pnouthis*, which contained what must have been the dream of many: a recipe for acquiring an "assistant daemon" of one's very own.[30]

DEMONS AND THE RABBIS

Unlike early Christians, the ancient Rabbis had little interest in Satan, but they were bedeviled by demons, millions of them. The *Babylonian Talmud*, a rich vein of demonological lore, warned that each person has one thousand on his left and one thousand on his right—just as the ancient Babylonians believed.[31] Like their Babylonian brethren, rabbinic demons, or *shedim*, lived in dark and filthy areas of the world, especially in ruins, waste water, and the shadows of multi-branched trees.[32]

Latrines and toilets were a special danger, and to protect oneself, it was always wise to pray, be silent, and behave modestly. But sometimes that was not enough. When Rabbi Abaye was a child, his mother trained a lamb to go with him to the latrine to help protect him, apparently so he would not have to go by himself. There was always safety in numbers against demons. Three people walking together at night were much less likely to be attacked than two, and the solitary person risked almost certain attack.[33] One rabbi's daughter made sure he was never alone at the toilet by cutting a hole in the wall so she could place her hand on his head to protect him.[34]

Any place with standing water was also a likely site for demons, and if water or food were left uncovered overnight it could easily become infested with them.[35] Thus, it was best to never drink from any standing water at night, and even water in a pitcher should have the top portion poured off.[36] If the water was covered, it was still best to knock on the lid before drinking (perhaps to scare off the demons).[37] Furthermore, an entire company of demons awaited those who let someone with unclean hands pour water over their own hands, or were handed a shirt by an unclean attendant.[38] So also those who touched their nostrils or touched blood without washing their hands risked demonic attack.[39]

All this might not be as foolish as it first seems, for it is probable that these practices arose from trial-and-error observation. After all, moderns, relying on the germ theory of disease, agree that having "unwashed hands," or leaving

SATAN, DEMONS, AND JINN

food and drink out and uncovered overnight, can bring harm. There are, in fact, several parallels between what we call "germs" and what were once called "demons." Both are invisible to the naked eye, both multiply rapidly, both are found in food, crumbs, and water left out for long periods of time, both can be transferred by touch, and both are a primary cause of illness. Moreover, the practical effect—a stomachache—is the same regardless of whether one eats food which is believed to have been contaminated by germs or by demons.

By contrast, there is vast difference between demons and germs when it comes to cosmological orientation. Christians, it will be remembered, believed that demons were fallen angels, but the rabbis insisted that they were both like and unlike angels. Like angels, demons had wings and could fly all about the world. But, unlike angels, demons shared three things with humanity: they could eat, they could have offspring, and they could die.[40] Later tradition said that demons could also marry, and one such marriage purportedly occurred in Jerusalem around 1916. After mischievous demons pelted strollers with stones in a courtyard, the courtyard was bedecked for a wedding and then locked for a month to allow plenty of time for the newlywed spirits to enjoy themselves.[41]

What exactly went on within the courtyard no one could say for sure, for demons were normally invisible unless they chose to reveal themselves in some form, say, as a human or a dragon. One imaginative demon took on the appearance of a winged goat horn, another that of a ladle spinning in liquid.[42] Then, too, if curious humans wished to see invisible demons, that could be arranged. One risky procedure entailed securing the placental after-birth of a black cat, burning it to powder and sprinkling it in the eyes. A less dangerous way to gain evidence of their presence involved scattering ashes around one's bed at night. The next morning, chicken scratches could be seen in the dust, for demons had feet like roosters.[43] Some demons, it was conjectured, may have even "evolved" or been generated from animals. A male hyena, after seven years, could turn into a bat, which in another seven years could become a thorn, and after several more intervals could finally turn into a demon.[44]

The most wildly popular demon of the Jewish tradition today is Lilith, the seducing vampiress and proto-feminist.[45] Known in modern circles as Adam's first wife (before Eve), she is barely mentioned in the rabbinic literature and her presence in the Hebrew Bible is dubious. The best-known stories come very late—in the cabalistic *Alphabet of Ben Sira* (eighth–tenth century) and the thirteenth-century *Zohar.* Nonetheless, she is of very ancient lineage, going back at least to the first millennium B.C., and perhaps to the ancient Babylonians.[46]

In the earliest records, Lilith is clearly evil. As one who stole and murdered children, she was the bane of every woman who nursed a child. Much later she was also depicted as Adam's first wife, the one that would not submit to

MAGIC, MYSTERY, AND SCIENCE

his authority and, upon leaving him, was replaced by Eve. Still later, she was portrayed as the evil spirit that seduced Adam during his sleep and thereafter produced demonic offspring.[47] The one constant in all these and other traditions is that Lilith hates children. In the *Zohar* she is depicted as a particularly chilling "vampire," longing to attach herself to the little faces of the sons of man.[48] To protect against her, parents often hung amulets on all four corners of their children's cribs, or on the walls.[49]

The Lilith stories are shocking, and no doubt that was part of their purpose. To be sure, her hatred of children was horrifying, but just as unsettling for a medieval reader would have been her defiance of established hierarchy: her rebellion against Adam was decidedly unnatural. Modern Jewish feminists, however, have drawn the opposite conclusion. They see her as a valiant, much maligned spirit bravely throwing off the yoke of patriarchy.[50] Accordingly, musical fairs have been organized in her honor and a Jewish feminist journal bears her name.[51] Although not yet in motion pictures, her troubled life has been fictionalized in novels, fantasy, and science fiction, and has even been the source of an innovative modern opera.[52] But even with this revisionist view, the old stigma lingers so that Lilith sparks opposing reactions. On one side of town, New Yorkers welcome her in the theater, while on the lower east side, they still buy amulets to hang about their children's cribs.[53]

DEMONS IN MEDIEVAL CHRISTIANITY

A mountain of material about demons poured forth from the pens of medieval theologians, far too much to summarize here. But, for the most part, the scholars stayed within the bounds of the early Christian perspective. We consequently will do the same by addressing views sanctioned by the Catholic Church, arguably the most influential institution of the European Middle Ages.

Medieval Christians portrayed demons both as terrifying, ubiquitous, nearly invincible forces of evil and as ridiculous, comical, gullible buffoons. Sometimes these characterizations coexisted in the mind of the same thinker. But even an inane demon posed a threat to the faith and had to be guarded against. Certainly, protection against demons was a central concern in popular Christianity. In the fourth century, Emperor Julian the Apostate mocked Christians by declaring that their theology "boils down to these two things: whistling to keep away the demons and making the sign of the cross upon their foreheads."[54] Writing only a few decades later, St. Augustine insisted that the gods and daemons of the Greeks were in fact demons or evil spirits.[55] He even implied that Socrates had been misled by an evil demon of the Christian variety, not a good daemon or divine sign as he supposed.[56]

Figure 18. Demons at work. In the medieval view, demons could be useful to have around. In this illustration, one performs barnyard chores while another holds a cloud of wind to help move a ship quickly. In the manuscript caption for this illustration, the sixteenth-century author writes that people who hold this view are deluded.

Furthermore, Augustine attested that demons were actively engaged in open battle with human beings, even in the area of his hometown of Hippo. Among the stories he related of demonic attacks and deceptions, the following memorably illustrates the power of demons to torment humans. At midday, a young man was watering his horse near a Christian monument when suddenly he was possessed by a demon and fell down as dead. Later that day, some Christians came singing hymns and praying. At the sound, the young man suddenly awoke, and the demon within him began shrieking that he would inflict evil on every body part of his host. Finally, through prayer, the demon was forced out, but not before the poor fellow's eye was left dangling from its socket by a slender white vein. Some urged him to see a doctor, but his brother-in-law said that God, who expelled the devil, could also heal his eye. They consequently bandaged it up and seven days later it was healed.[57]

This is a somber tale in most respects, but demons could also be comically impotent or tricksters easily tricked. According to the thirteenth-century *Golden Legend*, St. Lupus, while praying one evening, was suddenly overcome by a ravenous thirst brought on by the Devil. The saint called for some water,

MAGIC, MYSTERY, AND SCIENCE

but suddenly realizing the Devil's wiles, pressed a pillow down over the container of water. Trapped, the poor Devil howled and moaned all night, and in the morning, he was released—dazed and confused.[58]

Lest the reader take this as a child's tale, let us observe that the author of the story was Jacobus de Voragine, a well-respected Dominican theologian and Archbishop. He, like Pope Gregory the Great, wielded wide influence, and both men were inclined to portray the Devil as a buffoon. In one of Gregory's stories, a poor nun, wandering in a garden, pulled off a piece of lettuce and ate it without making the sign of the cross. Suddenly, a demon seized her. During the exorcism, the demon was cross-examined as to why he possessed her, to which he replied, "What have I done? What have I done? I was sitting upon a lettuce, and she came and ate me."[59]

One last story combines comical and chilling elements, although it was probably less comical and more chilling to its medieval audience than it is today. The twelfth-century Abbot Guibert of Nogent, who was often skeptical of relics and exaggerated tales, related that in the nearby district of Vexin a hunting party of nobles bagged an unusually heavy badger. But this was no badger, for on their way home, the nobles heard voices from the woods, saying "They are carrying off Caduceus!" Suddenly, hordes of demons attacked the group from all sides, freeing their comrade from the sack. Although the hunters managed to survive the frenzied onslaught, the story ends on an ominous note: "A short time after reaching their homes, [the nobles] were all dead."[60]

Along with ascertaining the behavior of demons, medieval theologians took up the question of what they look like. Today, when we hear the words "Satan" or "Devil," it takes a conscious effort *not* to imagine a ridiculous figure with horns, pitchfork, Vandyke beard, cloven hooves, pointy tail, and crimson tights. Early Christians did not think of Satan in these terms, any more than they thought of angels as chubby babies with dove wings attached. Satan was a powerful spiritual being with the ability to control his appearance should he wish to make one. Normally he would remain unseen, but if he did give an audience, he would most likely present himself as dazzlingly handsome, not as hideous or ridiculous.

In the Middle Ages, however, artists chose to personify Satan as a serpent (the tempter in Eden), a dragon (his image in *Revelation*), or sometimes as a hideous human with leathery wings. (Personification, after all, is the only choice one gets when drawing an invisible spiritual being.) Medieval mystery plays also drew upon stories like those cited above to portray the Devil as a buffoon. Because visual impact was key, the more frightening or ridiculous the costume, the better. Monstrous costumes, adorned with fangs, horns, and tails delighted the audience—and a face on the belly or buttocks was a sure crowd-pleaser.[61]

SATAN, DEMONS, AND JINN

But long before demons appeared on stage, they appeared to medieval monks in many forms, from apes and angels to pigs and priors.[62] For example, a Cistercian novice was tempted by the devil in the form of a monkey, according to Vincent of Beauvais.[63] And, in one bizarre case, while St. Norbert was exorcizing a young boy, an insolent demon appeared on the child's tongue in the form of a talking pea! This loquacious legume asserted he would never be cast out, but the saint called him a liar and the demon-pea was forced to depart.[64]

EXORCISM AND NIGHTTIME INCUBI

Getting demons to depart was no mean concern for believers. By the High Middle Ages, theologians believed that possession was only one of three major kinds of attack that demons could launch against humans (besides deceit and temptation, of course).[65] Demonic possession entails the spiritual being entering and taking control of a human—a spiritual hijacking, as it were.[66] Arguing that it was unlikely that believing Christians could be completely possessed or taken over by demons, some scholars went on to conclude that demons assault the faithful in two other ways: infestation and obsession.[67] Demonic infestation was deemed to be strongly akin to poltergeist activity, which consists primarily of strange noises and the breaking or disconcerting manipulation of household objects.[68] These were attacks on one's environment, but not on the person.

Obsession is a bit more difficult to define, partly because its visible signs often mirror those of possession. Medieval theologians, such as Aquinas, had long believed that, while Satan could control the body, he could not forcibly take control of the human will. This created a problem: What about all the stories of Christians who were "possessed," such as the aforementioned nun who ate the demon on the lettuce? The solution was "obsession," in which case the demon controlled the *body* of the unfortunate victim but *not* his soul or will. Sometimes this distinction revealed itself in bizarre ways.

One priest, for instance, noted that the beautiful singing voice of another priest sounded too perfect to be human. Suspecting the demonic, the first priest exorcized the singer, whose body promptly fell dead: a demon had been animating the corpse for some time.[69] Of course, it was far more common for the poor person's soul to be trapped against its will within a demonically obsessed body. And when this happened, the obsessed body might exhibit all the signs of a possession, such as a contorted face, projectile vomiting, inhuman voice, superhuman strength, and so on.

During some of the early modern witch trials, the difference between possession and obsession became a matter of life and death, for if demonic obsession was the bodily takeover of an unwilling victim, then demonic possession

Figure 19. An evil spirit cast out by prayer. An angel (on the left) forcibly carries the demon away.

implied the possessed was a *willing* participant. As David Harley explains, a possessed person was a sinner who actively allowed his or her own possession, which might even imply a pact with the Devil.[70] But, Harley notes, "direct obsession by the Devil was rarely invoked" in the trials; rather an obsessed person was almost always said to be *bewitched*.[71] Bewitchment was demonic obsession brought about by a witch who cast an evil spell on the afflicted individual. In this case, authorities laid no blame on the obsessed—the witch was at fault. This helps explain one troubling aspect of the trials for moderns: why people who were not witches, but only possessed, were nonetheless executed at times. By colluding with demons to bring about their own possession, they were as guilty as witches.

But if, in principle, even "directly obsessed" persons bore no responsibility

SATAN, DEMONS, AND JINN

for their bodily takeover, why the need for implicating witches? Apparently because victims still had to explain why they were targeted for demonic obsession in the first place. Better to have someone else instigate the attack than live under the suspicion of having attracted demonic interest simply on the basis of one's everyday activities—which then might be construed as morally dubious. (Pointing a finger of blame, however, did not always shift guilt elsewhere, for trial judges had to accept the accusation, which, after all, could be a Satanic ploy.) Moreover, there was a need to resolve the issue legally and religiously, to affix guilt to a definite party and assign punishment, and demons were much harder to round up and punish than human beings.

The concept of bewitchment is still invoked in some quarters. In 2001, Father Gabriele Amorth, the chief exorcist for the diocese of Rome, complained that new changes by the Vatican in exorcism rituals absolutely forbid exorcisms in cases in which a supposed evil spell has been cast. Father Amorth declared that "you might as well tell exorcists they can no longer perform exorcisms," for over 90 percent of all exorcism cases are at the instigation of others, through the use of evil spells.[72] Clearly, this agrees with what seventeenth-century people called "bewitchment."

Obviously, any assault, whether direct or witch-instigated, was fraught with peril. To protect its members from demonic attack, particularly possession, the Church developed rites of exorcism, which by the Late Middle Ages had become complex and stylized. To take one example, the Order of Exorcism from the 1614 *Rituale Romanum* (in a form that is little changed today) advises the exorcising priest to dress in a surplice and violet stole, and to sprinkle those present at the ceremony with holy water. Then the priest is to read certain scriptural passages and recite written prayers, which are reinforced at specified junctures by the sign of the cross, ✚. Next, the priest gives various adjurations for the demon to leave, using many forms of the names of God. What follows is just a small portion of the exorcism itself, meant to give its general flavor.[73]

> I adjure thee, thou old serpent, by the judge of the quick and the dead . . . by him who has power to send thee to hell, that thou depart quickly from this servant of God, [Name], . . . Resist not, neither delay to flee from this man. . . . And, although thou knowest me to be none the less a sinner, do not think me contemptible. For it is God who commands thee ✚. The majesty of Christ commands thee ✚. God the Father commands thee ✚. God the Son commands thee ✚. God the Holy Ghost commands thee ✚. The sacred cross commands thee ✚. . . . The blood of the martyrs commands thee ✚. . . . The de-

vout intercession of all saints commands thee ✝. . . . Go out, therefore, thou transgressor.

This much is well known; at least, it fits into a general pattern of popular understanding. What is less well known is that exorcisms were performed at all sorts of functions and in behalf of all sorts of entities. Homes, monasteries, and churches could all be exorcized of demons. Not only that, but exorcisms were also performed over all holy water, holy oil, purified salt, and altars.[74] Even pests such as mice, rats, and locusts could be exorcized.[75] In 1358, when a dangerous storm threatened the siege of Ansouis by the Gascons, Delphine of Languedoc performed a rite of exorcism on the storm itself! Apparently, storms could be "possessed" no less than humans.[76]

Moreover, nearly every Roman Catholic has had an exorcism performed on them, right up until the late twentieth century, although most probably never knew it. Until 1964, every child baptized was first exorcized, usually accompanied by the priest blowing three times into the child's face (a ritual called "exsufflation"—symbolically blowing away the Devil).[77] So, too, every adult convert went through a triple exorcism of demons.[78] And, finally, entire communities and regions could be exorcized.[79] As of September 2000, however, exorcisms can only be performed under a bishop's strict supervision, and may not be used in healing services, during mass, or any of the sacraments.[80]

This shift in attitude toward demons, or at least toward combating them, is reflected in the Church's recent adoption of "sensible" guidelines for identifying victims of demonic possession.[81] Although in use much earlier, these guidelines received official Church sanction in 1999, and they strike most people as reasonable. That is, they comport with the modern view that socially dysfunctional behavior has many causes, most of which have nothing to do with demons. First, the priest must ascertain that the victim is not actually suffering from some form of mental illness; if they are, a doctor, not an exorcist, is needed. Second, the possessed person will likely exhibit certain spectacular behaviors, such as suffering physical violence which seems demon-related, speaking or understanding unknown languages, revealing knowledge of distant events or hidden things, or demonstrating superhuman strength. Finally, the victim is likely to show extreme aversion to the name of God or Mary, and to crosses and sacred images. Even with these behaviors in evidence, however, the Papal Curia stresses that this form of direct possession is extremely uncommon, since Satan's preferred mode of attack is to deceive and mislead.

One may reasonably conclude from these changes that exorcism is no longer a major weapon in the Church's spiritual arsenal. This no doubt stems from an evolving characterization of Satan that renders him less likely to physically

SATAN, DEMONS, AND JINN

announce his presence in the world. Although the medieval Satan was crafty and subtle, he also did not shy away from physical confrontation when it served his purposes. He and his demons could throw objects, strike humans, and invade physical bodies of all description. They also had one other nasty trick up their sleeve.[82] According to medieval authorities, demons could have sexual relations with humans, and these amounted to spiritual seduction or, some would say, spiritual rape.

This judgment, however, raised serious questions, for demons (like angels) were surmised to be neither male nor female. Nonetheless, the nightmarish possibility was deemed real because demons could either assume the form of a human body, or, what is particularly repulsive, they could animate a human corpse. To a woman, a demon might appear in the dead of night as a handsome incubus (a "male" demon) and share her bed. To a man, the same thing might happen with the demon taking the form of a ravishing succubus (a "female" demon). It is particularly telling that *incubus* comes from the Latin for nightmare, "incubo," which is derived from the verb "incubare," to lie upon, because nightmares seem to lie heavily on the chest. As nightmare incubi and succubi went abroad at night, their victims felt themselves oppressed by great smothering weights.

Could these demons produce offspring with humans? Yes and no, said Thomas Aquinas, a late medieval Catholic theologian of immense significance.[83] Because they were spiritual beings, demons could not sire or bear children. However, they could do something else. A demon could first become a succubus, taking the semen from a man, then transform itself into an incubus and use that semen to impregnate a real woman. The offspring from this act was thought to be particularly evil by many—a child of the Devil. Even so, some esteemed individuals were reported to be the children of incubi. The mythical Merlin was said to be the son of a royal nun and a demon. Similarly, the very real Eleanor of Aquitaine was rumored (no doubt by her enemies) to be the daughter of an incubus.[84]

Perhaps it is not so odd that although no one talks anymore about incubi and succubi, similar nighttime assaults are still reported. In contemporary accounts, humans awake in the middle of the night to find themselves unable to move and under the control of extraterrestrial beings. In addition to collecting skin samples and the like, the aliens frequently rape or sexually use the humans in order to impregnate them or gather semen. Some abducted humans have also reported seeing and touching hybrid children. Let us note as well that fairy abduction stories flourished into the nineteenth century in Europe. Not of the Tinkerbell variety but more on the order of J. R. R. Tolkien's fairies,[85] these bold, high-spirited beings captured humans and whisked them off to fairyland. And often they did so for amorous reasons, as some commentators surmised

MAGIC, MYSTERY, AND SCIENCE

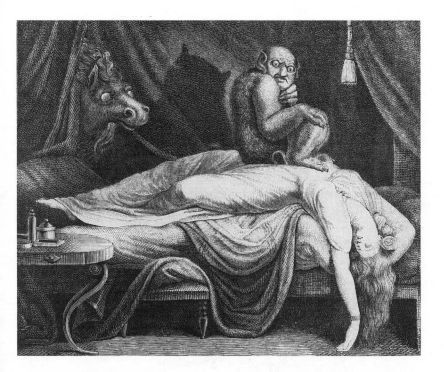

Figure 20. An incubus sitting on a sleeping woman. This is a nineteenth-century engraving based upon Fuseli's painting The Nightmare.

regarding Anne Jeffries (1649), who reportedly was snatched away on more than one occasion.[86] This belief in strong, dangerous fairies survived until quite recently: witness the case of Bridget Cleary, a young Irish woman, who in 1894 was beaten and burned to death by her husband, friends, and family, because they feared that the *real* Bridget had been taken by fairies and replaced by a witch.[87]

The subject of witches—inseparable from that of demons—is taken up in the next chapter. Before moving directly on, however, we pause to consider another fairly recent view of good and evil—Islam's world of the jinn.

SATAN, DEMONS, AND JINN

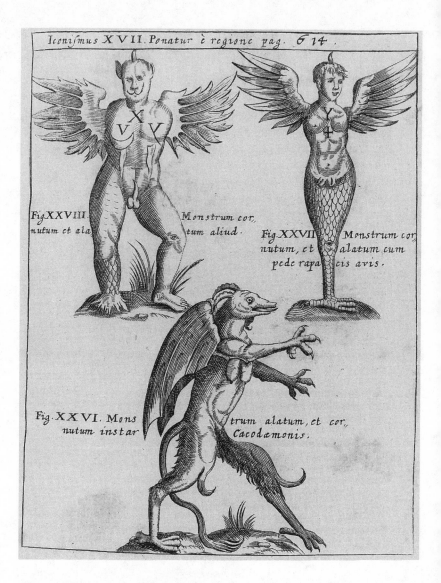

Figure 21. Demon spawn? These illustrations purport to show actual strange (monstrous) births and are included among illustrations of other strange births, conjoined twins among them. (Here, the artist is drawing from descriptions.) These images match the historical popular imagination in their inclusion of bird claws, horns, wings, and eyes on the knees.

MAGIC, MYSTERY, AND SCIENCE

All have heard of the magical genies of the *Arabian Nights,* such as the marvelous genie of the lamp. Now regarded by many as the stuff of imagination, genies or jinn[88] once commanded tremendous interest throughout the Near East and their existence was accepted matter-of-factly. They were not quite like any of the creatures we have described so far, but are an amalgam of bits and pieces of all of them.

According to the Qur'an, the holy book of Islam, jinn are invisible spirit beings neither human nor angel, but a separate creation made from "smokeless fire."[89] Like humans (and Greek *daemons*), jinn possess intelligence and free will; they therefore may choose between good and evil. By the time of Muhammad (circa A.D. 622), most jinn verged toward evil by choosing not to worship Allah. Also, like humans and *daemons,* jinn could die.[90] Obviously, then, they were not "fallen angels,"[91] for in Islam, angels are immortal and (apparently—we will see a possible exception to this) have no free will to sin against Allah.

Like the demons of Mesopotamia, jinn dwelt in forsaken places: ruins, deserts, and tombs. The Hadith (the authoritative words and deeds of Muhammad as reported by his companions) are replete with Muhammad's advice on how to protect oneself from evil spirits or jinn while going to the latrine (a concern for the rabbis as well, it will be recalled).[92] This unsavory aspect of jinn also showed up in their eating habits. Evidently they frequently scavenged through trash and refuse, for once a deputation of jinn begged Muhammad to tell his people not to use bones, dung, and charcoal while cleansing themselves after defecation; the jinn needed these materials for sustenance. Muhammad agreed to this request and directed his followers not to foul the jinn's fecal food.[93] One particular species of jinn, the ghouls, allegedly lived among tombs and feasted off the dead, sometimes even murdering for fresh meat.[94] Or so many Muslims believed, although, according to the Hadith, Muhammad denied the reality of ghouls.[95]

Like the demons of ancient Egypt and Mesopotamia, evil jinn were seen as a primary cause of disease and their presence could be detected by pain or fever.[96] Because they could also occupy the body and even control the mind, jinn-possession was considered a likely cause of mental illness, as it still is for many Muslims. Talismans afforded protection against possession, and these incorporated verses from the Qur'an along with standardized prayers to be recited before activities that made one vulnerable, such as showering or sexual intercourse.[97] If, however, a jinni had already taken up residence in the body, he might be dislodged in the following way. An appetizing meal was to be prepared for the possessed, who would then take a few bites of it to whet the appetite of the jinni. The food should then be taken far away and given to dogs or other animals. If all goes well, the jinni, overcome with a desire to finish the meal, will follow the food out of the human body and into the animal.[98] This method, although credible to many, was suspect in the eyes of Islamic exorcists: it would succeed only if Allah's power were invoked.[99]

Though invisible, jinn could take on many forms to become perceptible to human eyes. Often they were seen riding across the desert in whirlwinds of sand.[100] They also could take on animal shapes, such as that of a cat, dog, scorpion, or donkey. The form of a snake was a particular favorite. Because some snakes were actually jinn, Muhammad supposedly set forth a procedure for distinguishing between good and bad snakes—useful knowledge if a snake invades one's home.[101] More furtively, jinn could also shape-shift into humans.

Like the fallen angels of the Hebrew Bible, jinn were quite willing to transgress the line separating species to have amorous affairs with humans.[102] Many commentators insisted that the Qur'an itself taught that Jinn and humans could and did have sexual relations. This judgment rested on several considerations, one of which was the Qur'anic promise that those who reach paradise will enjoy "Dark-eyed virgins . . . whom neither man nor jinnee will have touched before."[103] Evidently there were human women touched or deflowered by jinn. This view was so common by the tenth century that Ibn al-Nadim's gigantic catalog of "all" the books in Arabic, the *Fihrist*, has a section called "Names of Those of Mankind who Loved the Jinn and Vice-Versa," and another on "Lovers of the Jinn."[104]

Although explanations are not supplied, sexual relationships between jinn and humans could apparently produce hybrid children. According to the Hadith, the Prophet Muhammad once asked his young bride Aisha whether the *mugharribun* had been seen recently. When she asked the meaning of *mugharribun*, he answered, "those in whom is a strain of the Jinn."[105] Also, according to an eleventh-century source, the Queen of Sheba was half-jinn.[106]

Besides children, poetry also issued from the interaction of humans and jinn. A female of the jinn reportedly stalked the young Hassan ibn Thabit. While he was walking through the streets of Medina one day, this jinnia leapt on him, held him down, and forced him to recite three lines of poetry.[107] From that day forward, he was a poet—the accosting spirit was literally his inspiration.[108] And he was not just any minstrel: he became the court poet for Muhammad and the early Islamic movement.

Muhammad himself suffered through similar experiences. While meditating in a cave one day, he was suddenly seized by a spirit being who pressed him down three times, demanding he recite several beautiful lines. For some time thereafter, Muhammad fretted that this forceful angel Gabriel might really be a jinni.[109] In one version of the story he became so distraught he contemplated throwing himself off a cliff in suicide.[110] Fortunately, his faithful wife Khadija helped convince him that this being was not a jinni, but from God.[111] More-over, the Qur'an itself proclaimed that Muhammad was not jinn-possessed.[112]

Besides evil jinn, there was another, much more formidable spirit being—Iblis—who had plagued the human race from the beginning.[113] The Qur'an reports that Iblis was present when Adam was created, and (here the story should sound familiar) when Allah commanded all the angels to bow down to Adam, Iblis refused to prostrate himself. He then defended his disobedience with the claim that "I am nobler than he. You [Allah] created me of fire, but You created him of clay."[114] So Iblis fell and became Shaytan (Satan), "the stoned one."[115]

This story was deemed so important that the Qur'an repeats it, in full, seven times.[116] At first blush, it seems Iblis was an angel who willingly chose to disobey God, but one of the narratives clearly identifies him as one of the jinn.[117] This ambiguity has inspired much comment. Modern Muslim scholars frequently insist that Iblis is definitely *not* an angel.[118] But some early authors split the difference, saying that the jinn were a type of angel made of fire, rather than light, and that Iblis became their leader. Al-Tabari reported that God sent the angelic Iblis with a mighty army down to earth to quell a group of rebellious jinn.[119] Upon accomplishing this tremendous task, however, Iblis swelled with pride, refused to pay obeisance to Adam, and fell to become Shaytan, the leader of the shaytans, the evil jinn.[120]

Immediately after his fall, Iblis/Shaytan is said to have tempted Adam and Eve in the Garden, thereby bringing about their expulsion.[121] He then ex-tracted a stay of execution, so to speak, from Allah. Free to tempt humankind until the Final Judgment, Shaytan and his minions wreak havoc throughout the land.[122] Their task, as set forth in the Qur'an, is to whisper, seduce, and lead humans astray.[123] What is more, the Hadith indicates that Shaytan wants to get *inside* us and (like the demons of Mesopotamia and Egypt) he can enter through the bodily orifices. Because the mouth is so accessible, yawning is from Shaytan and hated by Allah.[124] Shaytan can also slip into the upper nose and sinuses while we sleep, and possibly make his entry elsewhere during a call of nature or during sex.[125] One hadith recounts that when Muhammad was asked why a certain man had slept through morning prayers, the Prophet replied that Satan had urinated in the poor fellow's ears.[126]

In spite of their aptitude for evil and mischief, jinn (even the wicked shay-tans) could be useful when properly controlled. The Qur'an reports that King Solomon was given power over huge numbers of jinn to do his bidding.[127] They assisted in the construction of waterways, fountains, and even the king's mag-nificent temple.[128] In fact, they were working so hard for Solomon when he died that they did not notice his death until they saw a worm eating away at his staff and his corpse fall over. This led to some consternation, for apparently

SATAN, DEMONS, AND JINN

they begrudged the free or voluntary labor performed after their taskmaster's death.[129]

Although perhaps amusing to modern readers, these stories (and many more could be cited) bespeak a worldview that should not be taken lightly. Jinn were part of the natural order and a means of explaining a wide range of happenings, some everyday and some anomalous. That they could not be easily apprehended should not be cause for dismissing them outright. There is a story about a nineteenth-century steamboat captain who tried to enlighten his African boat workers on the mechanics of steam energy: the fire imparts energy to the water whose agitated molecules then fly up to move the engine's pistons. This explanation did not impress the workers, who had already arrived at a similar, albeit animistic, account: when the hot fire made the tiny demons in the water "hopping" mad, they jumped up against the pistons. When the captain protested that he could not see the demons, the workers countered that they could not see the molecules. This story reminds us that every world-picture invokes conceptual entities that elude our direct apprehension; further, much depends on initial assumptions. If the world strikes us as fully alive, then its constituents will be living entities like jinn. If not, they will be more like lifeless atoms and molecules.

That jinn were once regarded with utmost seriousness becomes clear upon examination of documents that debate their place in human society.[130] Since jinn had free will and were intelligent, they could be inspired by the verbal majesty of the Qur'an and convert to Islam. When this happened, questions arose. Some Muslims reasoned that since forty believers were needed to hold a Friday service, any converted jinn attending could be counted among the forty. Arguments ensued, however, between those who could see the jinn present and those who could not.[131] Jinn also showed up, as it were, at the mosque schools. One great Muslim teacher in sixteenth-century Morocco was said to have had seventy thousand believing jinn students over his lifetime (as reported by another *shaykh* [sheik] who had befriended four of this great number).[132]

Because Islam aspires to bring all human endeavor within the embrace of its principles, and since the Qur'an matter-of-factly acknowledges the existence of jinn, it was inevitable that questions should arise regarding their dealings with humans. After all, the two species ate some of the same foods, competed for similar resources, exchanged labor and gifts, and even, on occasion, intermingled sexually to produce hybrid children. In a community of humans and jinn, what passed muster as religiously appropriate (and therefore legally sanctioned) interactive behavior?

Was it right, say, that humans marry jinn? There were opinions on both sides of the issue. Some, such as the eighth-century mystic Hasan al-Basri, insisted that such marriages were acceptable provided the human were a faithful Muslim.[133] Waving off abstract considerations, the fourteenth-century zoologist Damiri argued that the question was already largely decided by actual circumstances: he was personally acquainted "with a *shaykh* who was the wedded husband of four female demons."[134] The issue was something of a can of worms, for it led to other questions regarding the legal status of hybrid children. Moreover, even without taking up these knotty, trans-species problems, scholars still had to ponder the legal rights of jinn and their "full-blooded" jinn children.[135]

Judicial review of these issues did not stop at the end of the Middle Ages. As late as the turn of the twentieth century, legal textbooks were grappling with the issue of jinn-human marriage in Egypt and the Ottoman Empire.[136] The Ottoman Turks decided against these relationships by reasoning that, because jinn were able to materialize as male *or* female (were free to alter their sexual appearance), homosexual unions might result.[137]

Legal or no, reports of jinn marriages in the Near East still circulate. A Turkish student of our acquaintance stated that his mother remembers a man who married a jinnia.[138] Another fairly recent source relates that a Moroccan married to a jinnia had two children by her. Not particularly sociable (at least with humans), she turned herself into a frog whenever visitors came over.[139]

If these stories strike a ludicrous note, the reader may wish to consider that similar stories regarding extraterrestrials circulate in the modern West. Steven Spielberg's *E.T.* has attracted millions of viewers, many of whom, by their own admission, do not believe in space aliens. Why bother seeing the movie then? Because in every culture certain stories, no matter how improbable, ring true while others do not. Westerners can readily imagine visitors from outer space because that possibility concurs with the scientific hope of exploring the galaxy and establishing contact with extraterrestrial civilizations. Imagining visitors emerging from a snake, frog, or whirlwind is more difficult, however. According to science, these events are more than improbable: they are impossible.

For many Muslims, however, wondrous visitors *might* emerge from spaces other than outer space; their culture is not adverse to such happenings. A case in point is Fethullah Gülen, a respected Turkish religious scholar and controversial political figure who believes in jinn.[140] Gülen promotes a liberal Islam that can coexist with other religions and flourish in a democracy; he recently met with the pope to help further interfaith dialogue between Muslims and Christians.[141] Taking jinn very seriously, he has proposed that humans learn to cooperate with them. The reward of such collaboration, he continues, would be improvements in the fields of mining, telecommunications, space exploration, and (given the jinn's immense age) historical studies.[142] This view, although dissonant to modern Western ears, was almost exactly what many scientists proposed concerning Spiritualism in the nineteenth and early twentieth centuries. And, as we note in the next chapter, some scholars of the Scientific Revolution proposed that we begin "thinking with demons"[143] in order to fill out our understanding of the world.

7

WITCHES AND
WITCH-HUNTS
IN THE WEST

> Thou shalt not suffer a witch to live.
>
> —*Exodus 22:18*

Hell is—other people!

—*Jean-Paul Sartre*[1]

In the United States, Halloween has domesticated, commercialized, and trivialized "witches" as broom-riding old ladies who cackle when they laugh. But several hundred years ago, witches were not taken lightly. Regarded as agents of Satan, they were felt to menace the existing spiritual and political order. And, sprinkled among the general populace, they threatened to overcome communities from the inside out, just as cancer cells overcome once healthy bodies. Now witches inspire more amusement than fear, and the fear they once inspired is generally deemed groundless. But experiencing fear and understanding it are often separate occurrences. The Red Scare—fear of communism—informed much Western thinking during the twentieth century and prompted U.S. leaders to wage war in Vietnam at a cost of fifty-eight thousand American lives. Looking back, it is easy to second-guess the Vietnam War and to chalk it up to groundless paranoia. This response, however, stares past the fact that, until the late 1960s, most Americans fully supported the war, having absorbed an ideology that portrayed the Soviet Union as "the evil empire."[2]

In retrospect, the Soviet Union looks more like a paper tiger than a military leviathan hell-bent on world conquest. And we may chuckle at the Cold War "hysteria" (as it is now called) of the 1950s and 1960s, some of which took the form of backyard bomb shelters and "duck and cover" emergency procedures in public schools. But for people of that era, the Soviet Union was just as menacing and sinister as terrorist underground networks are today—or as witches were in the sixteenth and seventeenth centuries.

The literature on the history of witchcraft is immense and has become a thriving cottage industry for academics; for example, two recent collections of articles, edited by Brian P. Levack, run to six and twelve volumes respectively.[3] And this does not include the mountains of monographs produced over the last few decades.[4] So what follows is necessarily a cursory overview of the concept of the European witch and the rise and decline of the great witch-hunts. Perhaps the most vexing aspect for any brief introduction to the topic can best be summed up by resuscitating the old adage (with apologies to the rabbis) "Two historians, three opinions." This, however, is a sign of health in the field—the multitude of monocausal explanations proffered over the decades has given way to more nuanced approaches.

But first, where did the European concept of the witch come from, and, second, why did the great witch-hunts take place in the Renaissance and early modern periods and not in the Middle Ages (as is often believed)? For answers, we must look to the long history of witchcraft in the West.

GREEK AND ROMAN WITCHES

The belief in witches and sorcerers is common to almost all early cultures, and the witch-hunters of Europe inherited some of their views from ancient Greece and Rome. For the Greeks, the lines between a witch, a sorcerer, and a magician were not easily drawn, nor were any of these persons pre-determined as necessarily good or evil. Witches could aid in love magic, cast spells to heal or harm, and call upon daemons for knowledge or power. They could also summon up the dead to foretell the future in a form of divination called necromancy.

According to the Greeks, the strictures of time did not inhibit the dead; thus, they could be called upon to reveal both past and future. Odysseus, for instance, performed a necromantic ritual by summoning souls from Hades to tell him his future.[5] But, while necromancy carried no stigma in *The Odyssey*, later Greeks and Romans saw it as a hideous and unlawful evil to which only witches would stoop. Lucan's tale of Erictho the Witch performing necromancy is particularly blood-chilling.[6] It is also instructive as a pre-Christian description of an evil witch. The ghastly Erictho buries people alive, murders to get fresh blood, slits open pregnant women to sacrifice their babies, and feasts on human corpses by scooping out eyeballs and gnawing on fingers. And all this is couched in an epic about civil war and rebellion.

MAGIC, MYSTERY, AND SCIENCE

Evil witches and magicians did not just show up in fictional epics. In one of his judicial orations, Cicero charged Vatinius, a friend of Julius Caesar, with sacrificing young boys in necromantic rituals. Cicero's concern was both moralistic and political, for, in his mind, such atrocities fueled civil strife by inviting darkness and chaos into the world.[7] By the first century A.D., Pliny the Elder lauded fellow Romans for their ongoing attempt to do away with magi (magicians).[8] One instance concerned the Roman Senate's resolution, shortly after a plot against the Emperor Tiberius was foiled, to exile astrologers and magicians from Italy owing to the political intrigue they inspired. Indeed two of that scurrilous number were executed.[9]

The second-century author Apulius wrote a marvelous tale, *Metamorphoses, or The Golden Ass,* in which beautiful Thessalian witches could smear themselves with ointment and turn into birds. The main character of this comedy, Lucius, tries to do the same, but when smeared with unguent, he turns into a braying ass and spends the rest of the book trying to become human again. Unfortunately, in real life, Apulius was brought to court on the charge of using magic to both obtain a wealthy wife and kill her son for the inheritance. In his *Apologia,* he maintained his innocence and his hatred of all magic, arguing that it was dark and evil by its very nature and was known to be so in the *Law of the Twelve Tables.*[10] This very ancient codification of Roman law did indeed prohibit, on penalty of death, singing incantations against others.[11] Obviously Roman concern with magic stretched back many centuries.

This concern persisted in the legal codes of the Late Roman Empire. A woman during the time of Constantine could only initiate a divorce if her husband was a murderer, a tomb destroyer, or an evil magician.[12] (All three crimes were capital offenses, so a divorce would seem superfluous, except for dowry reasons.) Christian Emperors of the fourth century, such as Constantinian and Valentinian, continued to make the pagan Roman distinction between white magic and black magic (*haruspicina* and *maleficia*), tolerating the former and condemning the latter. But under the tolerated category of white magic, which included relatively harmless forms of divination, they now gathered all pagan "superstitions" as well. In A.D. 438 the *Theodosian Code* removed this distinction, however, by stipulating that the death penalty awaited all those who practiced *any* form of divination or magic, including haruspices, augurs, chaldeans, and magi who all (according to the code) bring about *maleficia* and invoke demons.[13]

ROMAN PERSECUTIONS OF CONSPIRACIES: A PATTERN OF CHARGES

Earlier, we noted Cicero's political concern with necromancy. The Romans in general dreaded political conspiracies, and by the first century B.C., stories

WITCHES AND WITCH-HUNTS IN THE WEST

circulated of secret societies that practiced human sacrifice and even cannibalism for political ends. The historian Diodorus Siculus (circa 90–21 B.C.) tells of Apollodorus, who formed a conspiracy to become the tyrant of Cassandreia around 278 B.C.[14] Apollodorus had his band of political conspirators swear an oath of loyalty to one another over the murdered body of a child. Then they collectively ate the child's entrails and drank his blood mixed with wine to seal an unbreakable bond—the deed was so foul that none could betray the others and hope to escape punishment. This same tale was applied again and again to various political conspirators by such ancient authors as Plutarch, Sallust, and Cicero, all of whom wished to viciously stigmatize non-conformist elements.[15]

Similar slander was brought against the Jews as early as the Hellenistic period.[16] In his *Against Apion,* Josephus refuted as ridiculous the following story told by Apion, a fervent enemy of the Jews. Apion had appeared before Caligula representing the Alexandrian Greeks in a case brought against the Jews of their city.[17] His wild tale, no doubt a fabrication, relates that each year the Jews would kidnap a Greek, hide him in their Temple, fatten him up for a year, and then sacrifice him and eat his entrails. Not only that, but they would swear an oath to God to hate all other races, especially the Greeks. This "unspeakable law of the Jews," as Apion called it, bears all the marks of the old cannibalistic, political conspiracy stories noted above.

Like their Jewish predecessors, early Christians were also slandered with similar stories and more. The Romans not only accused them of killing and eating infants but also of having drunken feasts followed by incestuous orgies. Norman Cohn's *Europe's Inner Demons* details these accusations and attributes them to a tendency to treat "the other" as anti-human. "In most societies . . . ," Cohn avers, "to say that a group practices incest, worships genitals, kills and eats children, amounts to saying that it is an incarnation of the anti-human. Such a group is absolutely outside humanity; and its relationship to mankind as a whole can only be one of implacable enmity."[18]

Certainly, the early Roman historian Tacitus viewed Christians as bestial, because they were reputed to be so deeply misanthropic. When much of Rome burned in A.D. 64, many Romans blamed the Emperor Nero, who consequently fastened the guilt on the Christians. In taking up the issue, Tacitus stated that the Christians were "a class hated for their abominations" and that "an immense multitude was convicted," not so much for burning the city, but for their "hatred against mankind."[19] Several decades after the fire, Pliny the Younger, as Proconsul of Bithynia, had some Christian slave women tortured to find out what occurred during their gatherings. In his letter to the Emperor Trajan, he reported that after their ceremonies, Christians would depart and then "meet again to take food; but it was ordinary and harmless food."[20] Evidently one of the points of interest was whether Christians feasted upon human flesh.

How could the followers of Jesus be accused of such evils as orgies and cannibalism? Well, they did celebrate something they called a "Love Feast,"[21] which in the first century accompanied what is now termed the eucharist, communion, or Lord's supper. Since it was against Roman law to be a Christian, they usually met in private at these "feasts." Thus shrouded in secrecy, the affairs took on a sinister aspect to those already suspicious of this strange, new religion. Bread and wine taken in remembrance of Christ were accompanied by strange words about "eating a body and drinking blood." With wine misconstrued to sweep away moral inhibitions, the ensuing "love feast," in which whole families participated, suggested to outsiders a deep and inhuman descent into evil.[22] Enemies felt no compunction at filling in sordid details, such as dismembering and eating babies, for good measure.

Throughout the second century, Christian apologists, such as Justin and Tertullian were forced to reply to such accusations.[23] This was no small matter, for Senator Fronto, the tutor and advisor of Emperor Marcus Aurelius, made a speech accusing Christians of cannibalism and incestuous orgies, which may have fueled Aurelius's persecutions of the Christians.[24] Even in the heat of martyrdom, Christians sought to refute the insidious charges. Eusebius writes of Attalus, who "when he was put in the iron chair and was being burnt and the reek was rising from his body, called out to the spectators in Latin: 'Look! eating men is what *you* are doing; *we* neither eat men nor indulge in any malpractices.' "[25] By the beginning of the third century, Christians were able to exonerate themselves of these accusations, but Cohn insists that the idea of a secret, anti-human society persisted well into the Middle Ages. Eventually Christians would level similar charges against members of their own community.

WITCHES IN THE MIDDLE AGES

Like Romans, Germans also had a great fear of evil sorcerers and witches. In the sixth-century *Laws of the Salian Franks,* for example, anyone who was proven to have killed another through magic spells was fined the full *wergeld* of a free Frank, the exorbitant sum of 200 solidi.[26] Ominously, the law also warned that "[i]f a witch eats a man and it is proved against him," the fine is also 200 solidi.[27] Even a person who used spells to *attempt* murder, or had used incantations to make a woman barren, was fined roughly a third this amount.[28]

But the charge of witchcraft was not to be made lightly, for if one called "another man a sorcerer (*herbugium*)—that is . . . one who is said to carry a brass cauldron in which witches brew" and could not prove it, the fine was more than 62 solidi.[29] And if a free woman was called a witch (a *stria*) without

WITCHES AND WITCH-HUNTS IN THE WEST

proof, the accuser incurred a fine three times as great—nearly the cost of a murder![30]

By A.D. 643, the concept of man-eating witches had come to include the belief that witches could literally consume a man from within—like a cancerous sickness. But in the *Laws of the Lombards*, promulgated in that year, this was flatly said to be impossible. "Let nobody presume to kill a foreign serving-maid or female slave as a *striga*, for it is not possible, nor ought it to be at all believed by Christian minds that a woman can eat a living man up from within."[31] Similarly, many Christian clerics in the Early Middle Ages saw belief in witchcraft as a delusional pagan fantasy; this is clear from a variety of sources, such as handbooks of penance and early Irish Canon law.

One law of an early medieval Irish Synod (ascribed to the time of St. Patrick) declared that anyone who believed that witches and vampires were real was to be excommunicated, and the same fate lay in store for anyone who even accused another of being a witch.[32] Likewise, a Spanish penitential from the turn of the ninth century excommunicated all who believed magic could be used to produce lightning, storms, or drought.[33]

Of course, not all in the early church disbelieved in witches and wizards. But even when their reality was not in doubt, penitentials (books prescribing rules of penance) required penance, not death. *The Burgundian Penitential* (circa 700–725) states, "If, indeed, anyone is a wizard, that is, a conjurer-up of storms, he shall do penance for seven years."[34] (Magnanimously, just the first three were on bread and water.) Only five years of penance were required of a "mathematicus" (wizard/diviner) who caused someone to go mad by invoking demons.[35] And at the Fourth Council of Toledo, in 633, the most severe punishment for priests and bishops who consulted a magician, or even practiced magic and divination *themselves*, was to be placed in a monastic house under perpetual penance,[36] a relatively light sentence compared to those passed down during the early modern witch-hunts.

Charlemagne's life-long struggle to Christianize pagan Saxony impelled him to enact draconian laws against all forms of paganism. For instance, the pagan practice of burning the dead was made punishable by death, as was eating meat during Lent.[37] But, like authors of the penitentials, Charlemagne's clerical advisors viewed belief in witchcraft as a pagan fantasy. This leads to a curious irony: under Charlemagne (circa 800), burning a witch was a capital offense. One of his capitularies declared that "[i]f anyone is deceived by the devil, and believes after the manner of pagans that some man or some woman is a witch and eats people, and if because of this he burns her or gives her flesh to someone to eat or eats it himself, let him pay the penalty of death."[38]

The ninth-century Bishop Agobard of Lyons also disbelieved in witchcraft and sorcery and wrote a book against some of the pagan superstitions of the time.[39] He mentioned that many in his diocese believed that certain people called *tempestarii* were able to call up destructive storms, wind, and hail. This was a standard form of *maleficia*, but what is truly bizarre is that the *tempestarii* were said to give the destroyed crops to men in *flying ships* from Magonia.[40]

For its striking similarity to modern space alien accounts, this story still fires the imagination of UFO believers. The bishop even tells of alien abductions, albeit in reverse. He reported that "several madmen who believe that such absurd things are real" brought him three men and a woman in chains. Their captors claimed these unfortunates had fallen out of the flying ships and that the bishop should have them stoned to death.[41] Fortunately, Agobard confounded these mad abductors through brilliant argument and the "Magonians" were released.

While Carolingian clerics disbelieved in witches and tried to dissuade the laity from belief as well, the Carolingian royal court was sometimes another matter. During the reign of Louis the Pious (ninth century), Paschasius related that the royal court was so overwhelmed with divination that even the queen was accused of being a witch: "There was witchcraft everywhere. Policy was based not on sound judgment, but on auspices, and forward planning on auguries. . . ." Even so, Louis's punishment of these witches was quite mild: "Lot casters, seers, interpreters of omens, mimers, dream mediums, consulters of entrails, and a whole crowd of other initiates in the malefic arts were driven out of the palace."[42]

The point to be stressed is that medieval people were generally less perturbed by witches than is commonly assumed. Even when they took witchcraft and sorcery seriously, they did not resort to the extreme measures that marked the early modern period. The highly influential *Canon Episcopi* (from its initial words), probably part of a late-ninth-century Carolingian capitulary, drives this point home.[43] In treating the question of whether witches fly about in the dark, the document states that Satan seduces certain silly women to believe that they ride on beasts during the night to meet the goddess Diana and do her bidding.[44] In other words, the experience is not real but delusional. Furthermore, the *Canon Episcopi* continues, anyone who insists that witches really do fly at night has erred from the faith and should be ejected "foully disgraced from their parishes."[45]

As late as the thirteenth century, some saw night-flying as implausible, even rejecting the view that the soul flew off while the body stayed behind. For example, in Jean de Meun's portion of the wildly popular medieval *Romance of the Rose* (circa 1277), he was adamant that sorceresses did not fly off bodily three times a week to follow "Dame Abundance." Nor was it their souls, rather than their bodies, that did the night-flying, as they claimed. Jean said the sorceresses "would have us believe that while their souls / Are on these trips their bodies must not be / Turned over" or their souls will not be able to re-enter their bodies and they will die. This was "monstrous foolishness," Jean argued, for when the soul leaves the body, the body dies. Thus, these women die and revive three times a week, he mocked, and "may well claim / Great frequency of resurrection days!"[46]

Other medieval accounts show a strong skepticism toward bewitchment as well. Philip Schaff relates one such story from Vincent of Beauvais (circa 1250).[47] A woman approached her priest with concern, telling him that she and some other women had been bewitched, and they had even gotten into his bedroom one night through the keyhole. The priest, unable to convince her that this was merely a fantasy, locked the door behind her and began beating her with a stick, shouting, "Get out through the keyhole now, if you can!" Typical medieval humor—droll and slightly misogynistic. Yet, there is little like it during later centuries of witchcraft trials, not until the Enlightenment when both witch and priest were mocked. It is important to keep this story in mind, for people could be both deeply religious and openly skeptical of witch-craft. Vincent, after all, was a Dominican monk.

We should not leave the Middle Ages without noting that, while witches did not command great interest during that era, heretics did. The Fourth Lateran Council of 1215 may be described as the dog that didn't bark—at least not at witches. Under Pope Innocent III, papal power and influence was at its climax, and yet at the Council there was no mention of witchcraft or sorcery.[48] What did perplex Innocent and the Council, however, was heresy, especially that of the Waldensians and the Cathars.

The Waldensians hoped to rediscover the pristine Christian gospel and ini-tially did not intend to antagonize the Church. At first, they even sought papal recognition. But eventually they were identified as an apostate sect to be exter-minated. Their sins? Peter Waldo, after whom the Waldensians took their name, had sections of the Bible translated into the vernacular and encouraged followers to study the Bible for themselves, believing that the Holy Spirit would give divine guidance. He also believed in the priesthood of all believers, that the sacraments could be administered by lay members, that the preaching of crusades was wrong, and that prayers for the dead, the taking of oaths, and the adoration of the saints were unbiblical.[49]

The other apostate sect, the Cathars, figure into modern Gnosticism and are discussed, along with the Knights Templar (another group to be deemed heretical), in chapter 13. For present purposes, we stress that the persecution of the Waldensians, Cathars, and Knights Templar bears similarities to the later persecution of witches. Chief among these is the characterization of the targeted factions. A papal bull portrayed Waldensian worship as fully Satanic.[50] Adherents were accused of worshipping the Devil with an obscene kiss on the behind, as the latter morphed into a giant toad, a duck, or a man said to be ice-cold.[51] Also, the alleged heretics were said to desecrate the host, which they secretly carried in their mouths from Catholic mass. Finally, the worshippers putatively fell to eating infants and enjoying wild orgies, all with all. Similar charges were brought against the Cathars and Knights Templar, who, unlike the Waldensians, did not survive the crusades launched against them.[52]

This late medieval persecution of heretics gave inquisitors and judges a template for handling later demon-worshipping secret societies—such as night-flying witches. A paradigm had crystallized.

THE BEGINNING OF THE WITCH-HUNTS

The persecutions of the High and Late Middle Ages were not completely "unreasonable." There was a chain of logic that stretched from simple error and superstition to the demon-worshipping Sabbat (or Sabbath) of Satan. Persons holding wrong beliefs erred from the faith, and if they refused to repent, they were heretics who opposed God. Moreover, those who opposed God allied themselves, whether knowingly or unknowingly, with God's great adversary: Satan. The "Father of Lies" would tend to lead these deviants into ever-greater blasphemies and inversions of truth, such as the unholy kiss, cannibalism, orgies, devil worship, and pacts with Satan, which in turn make way for both spiritual and political rebellion.

For inquisitors, discovering heresy or witchcraft was like discovering cancer: the malignant growth was either nascent or fully present. Thus, if under torture, a heretic confessed to one of these anti-human actions, there was no reason to doubt it—the prognosis was already known. And, just as cancer cells cannot be gently coaxed away but often must be painfully and invasively eradicated, so Satan's hold on the soul had to be wrested loose by forceful means. Thus, in many places, torture was a standard aspect of the interrogation, or healing, procedure.

Seen from the vantage of the twenty-first century, torture makes little sense, if only because it seems to decide the issue in advance: even an innocent person will confess to a crime when tortured. Perhaps, however, if we—and this is a huge stretch—invested as much faith in the "spiritual doctors" of earlier centuries as we do in modern physicians (who can detect cancer in people who feel themselves perfectly healthy), then torture might shape up as some sort of chemotherapy meant to cleanse the body politic as a whole.

Here the importance of the community must be underscored. Until the eighteenth century, there was little if any inkling that all men and women, regardless of social class, enjoyed inalienable rights that made them equal as individuals before the law. It was the community that seemed real and worthy of defense, and individuals were significant insofar as they contributed thereto. This was particularly true when the community was perceived to be under assault, and Satan was the great assailant. Hence, says one authority, "the emphasis" in the early modern witch trials was "not upon helping the victim [the individual witch], but in ridding the world of those who work for the devil."[53] (There *was* an emphasis on helping the victim in, of all places, the Spanish Inquisition. Contrary to common opinion, Spanish and Italian inquisitors executed very few witches—they were far more likely to give penance than to burn. Thus, it was far better to fall under the Spanish Inquisition than to be accused of witchcraft by the more "secular" and politically minded judges to the north.) Evil in the world was proof of the Devil's existence, and just as cancerous cells coexist with healthy cells in a diseased body, so evildoers were felt to coexist surreptitiously with God-fearing folk in an obviously imperfect world.

Accordingly, if under torture an alleged witch confessed to some foul deed, that reaffirmed a fact made obvious by the very real presence of evil—Satan had infiltrated the community. The reasoning was not illogical (however weak the links) given the initial premises. Madness perhaps, but there was method to it.

The genesis of witchcraft madness may be dated to 1258 when some inquisitors requested permission to search out witches along with heretics. The pope said no—*unless* some link could be found between witchcraft and heresy.[54] Thenceforth, a small but powerful segment of the ecclesiastical elite began to see witchcraft, not as a self-delusional fantasy, but as a reality and the ultimate heresy. Among those taking this stand were certain Franciscans and Dominicans. They fused old folklore views of witches into the paradigm that had emerged with the persecution of heretics—that is, evil magicians were now accused of being Devil-worshippers as well. This in itself, however, did not immediately spark large-scale witch-hunts, which began only in the early modern period.

In 1426, Bernardino of Siena, a popular Franciscan preacher, instigated a search for witches in Rome.[55] The reluctant populace began to point fingers only after being threatened as potential accomplices. Perhaps a hundred people were questioned, mostly women. Two were executed, one of whom not only confessed to a pact with Satan but also to sucking the blood of children and grinding their bodies into magic powder.[56] Still, there was no mention of a Devil-worshipping Witches' Sabbat, nor did this lead to further trials, although the preaching continued.[57]

During the same period, Joan of Arc was burned as a witch, and rightly so, according to Johannes Nider, a contemporary of Joan's and a Dominican professor at the University of Vienna.[58] What was particularly disconcerting to

MAGIC, MYSTERY, AND SCIENCE

Nider was that Joan seemed to have a familiar spirit (what she called her "saints") and that she dressed in men's clothing. The latter connoted the damning sin of rebellion, Nider said, "considering that she openly professed herself a woman and a maid" and yet refused to dress like one.[59] Left unsaid were the words of 1 Samuel 15:23: rebellion is as the sin of witchcraft.[60]

In his book called *The Ant Hill* (circa 1437), Nider not only mentioned Joan of Arc's burning but also the trial of several Swiss witches who worshipped Satan and desecrated the sacraments. Among them was a married pair of witches in Bern, Switzerland.[61] The husband confessed he was led by "the masters" early one Sunday morning to a church to renounce his baptism and faith in Christ, to "do homage to the magisterulus" (i.e., the little master, the Devil), and to drink from a flask containing the liquid of murdered infants. Although repentant, he was nonetheless burned as a witch. Brother Nider goes on to say that the penitent's "wife, however, though convicted by the testimony of witnesses, would not confess the truth even under the torture or in death; but, when the fire was prepared for her by the executioner, uttered in most evil words a curse upon him, and so was burned."[62]

THE *MALLEUS MALEFICARUM* OF HEINRICH KRAMER

Despite changing attitudes toward witches, many secular clerics clung to the old view that witchcraft was a silly delusion requiring penance, not burning. Such was the opinion of George Golser, Bishop of Brixen, in the Austrian Tyrol, who came into conflict with Heinrich Kramer. Kramer, known in Latin as Henricus Institoris, was a Dominican Inquisitor of Heretical Depravity, and later the coauthor of the infamous *Malleus Maleficarum*, "The Hammer of Witches."[63]

Like Italians fifty years earlier, German rulers and clerics at first resisted witch-hunts. In 1484, however, Pope Innocent VIII promulgated a papal bull supporting Dominican inquisitors who apparently had been blocked in their duties while searching out witches in northern Germany.[64] The intent was to "remove all impediments" and grant full authority to two handpicked inquisitors to search for, imprison, and punish witches. These were Henricus Institoris (i.e., Kramer) and Jacobus Sprenger, whom the pope called his "beloved sons."[65]

The papal bull issued a long list of *maleficia* that witches "of both sexes" were capable of, such as destroying crops and animals, inflicting torturous pain, and causing impotence and barrenness. Still, it made only a few oblique references to witches being in league with the Devil, and there is no mention of Devil-worship, night-flying, infant-eating, or huge Sabbat gatherings—that is, of an organized, secret society of cannibalistic anti-Christian heretics who wor-

WITCHES AND WITCH-HUNTS IN THE WEST

shipped Satan himself.[66] This apparent oversight was later remedied by Pope Innocent's "beloved sons," Kramer and Sprenger, in their *Malleus Maleficarum*.

Upon arriving at Innsbruck in Bishop Golser's diocese, papal bull in hand, Kramer rounded up more than fifty suspected witches within a month.[67] Of this number, only two were men. The skeptical bishop Golser, who was in Brixen, sent handpicked commissioners for the trial. When the official commission convened, Kramer began asking the first woman highly detailed questions about her sex life. The commission halted the proceedings, using Kramer's own papal bull against him by insisting he look for heresy, not sexual improprieties.[68] When the commission reconvened, Bishop Golser employed an excellent defense lawyer who used legal technicalities to thwart Kramer. The commission let the women go, but Kramer refused to leave the city.[69] After informing Kramer that he could not guarantee his safety if riots ensued, the bishop ordered him out.[70] In a separate letter to a priest, Golser called Kramer a "senile old fool."[71]

But there was an unexpected consequence of the Innsbruck trial, as Eric Wilson notes.[72] Sadly, while the good bishop had won the round, he may have inadvertently spurred more trials and burnings. Kramer, stung by this humiliation, spewed forth the *Malleus* with an eye toward guarding future inquisitors both from meddling bishops and lawyers, and from charges of incompetency and evil.

The *Malleus Maleficarum*, first published in 1487, has long been portrayed as the church's official witch-hunter's manual that both instigated and guided the witch-hunts of the early modern period. It was not and did not. Furthermore, its outrageous misogyny is often depicted as typical, but in fact it is extreme even for a period known for its anti-female bias. Earlier historians may have given it undue credit, because it is highly quotable and easily accessible.[73] Nonetheless, as a codification of earlier beliefs, it did have considerable impact on later demonologists and witch-hunters who found it a handy and self-serving reference.

Kramer, the failure and fool of inquisitors, overcame this blow to his reputation with a steady stream of falsified data. He puffed up the number and importance of his persecutions, and he affixed Pope Innocent's bull to the front of the book to make it appear sanctioned by the Church.[74] Some surmise that his coauthor, Jacobus Sprenger, had relatively little to do with the work and may have been added for respectability; furthermore, the attached endorsement letter from the College of Cologne was, in part, a forgery.[75] Kramer even praised the secular and ecclesiastical rulers of the Brixen diocese on how zealously they worked to exterminate witches.[76] To admit they had booted him out of town and let the alleged witches go free obviously would not have been helpful to his project.

MAGIC, MYSTERY, AND SCIENCE

Kramer's life is an object lesson in how personal vengeance may be allied with religious zeal to overpower good judgment and compassion. Those suffering most, the accused witches, were no longer viewed as deluded souls but as patently wicked beings. In direct opposition to the *Canon Episcopi* and medieval tradition, Kramer's *Malleus* said witches really might fly around at night, and they do have intercourse with the Devil.[77] Furthermore, the *Malleus* implied the greatest of all heresies was to *disbelieve* in witchcraft.[78] If one admitted doubt on this point, there were grounds to suspect apostasy, for such "errors savour of heresy."[79]

Going even further, the *Malleus* redefined judicial procedures to bolster the position of inquisitors vis-à-vis alleged witches and any who might try to help them. Inquisitors (such as Kramer himself) were to be judges of these cases, although bishops could share the responsibility and secular authorities could carry out the sentence.[80] As to defense lawyers, they were not to bring forth any "legal quirks and quibbles" (as had occurred at Innsbruck), nor were they even to be given the names of the accusers.[81] Such lawyers were only to defend "just" cases—they must not defend alleged heretics, under the threat of excommunication.[82] These deterrents ensured that few witches had a defender; they were in the hands of the judge, who was often the prosecutor as well. Kramer rationalized these seeming injustices by arguing that witchcraft was a *crimen exceptum*, an offense so extraordinarily dangerous that normal judicial cautions had to be ignored.[83]

Immense danger, for instance, was said to reside in the apocalyptic fact that Satan was using women as a delaying tactic to ward off the Day of Judgment and his own eventual punishment. How? By reducing the population so that God could not reach the specific number of souls he intended to save! Under Satan's guidance, witches cast spells of impotence to stop procreation; they also masqueraded as midwives to steal and kill unbaptized babies, thereby thwarting their entry into heaven. And since by these stratagems "the number of the elect . . . [is] more slowly completed," the end of the world and Satan's own judgment are also delayed.[84]

As one may readily infer, Kramer's malice toward women knew no bounds. Women, he asserted, were far more likely to become witches because they are unusually prone to superstition and excess. Moreover, he continued, they are easily overcome by sex and pleasure, owing in part to their childish intellectual faculties.[85] "When a woman thinks alone, she thinks evil," Kramer claimed.[86] In support of this outlook, Kramer went to remarkable lengths. He tells, for example, the story of a man whose wife had drowned in a river, but in searching for her body, the husband went upstream, not downstream. When asked why, the man replied that his wife had been so contrary in life that he assumed she would continue being contrary in death. Originally told as a joke, the story

WITCHES AND WITCH-HUNTS IN THE WEST

struck the humorless Kramer as clear evidence of female obstinance and rebellion.

Another example will suffice to underscore the pernicious effect of Kramer's warped judgments. According to the *Malleus*, witches would cut off male organs and keep them in boxes or in nests in trees, where the organs were fed grain and moved about like worms![87] One witch allowed a poor fellow who was lacking his member to choose a replacement, but "when he tried to take a big one, the witch said: 'You must not take that one . . . it belonged to a parish priest.' "[88] This coarse medieval joke, told at the expense of priests, was catalogued by Kramer as further proof of the evils of witchcraft. He added, however, that witches could not really emasculate men—it was all a demonic deception. Nevertheless, by tricking the eyes of victims, Satan misled men into believing they lacked the sexual means of fulfilling their religious duty to procreate.

THE EVIL DEEDS OF WITCHCRAFT: *MALEFICIA* AND DEVIL WORSHIP

In the early modern period, witches became agents of satanic evil rather than (as they were earlier) mere perpetrators of localized harm and mischief. That is to say, their crimes progressed from *maleficia*—casting spells on fellow villagers, say—to worshipping Satan and thereby fully allying themselves with aboriginal evil. The first sort of misbehavior fit in with a general belief in magic and was consequently tolerated as an inevitable aspect of human imperfection. Since the second sort, however, implied a large-scale, organized attempt to destroy God's (political and religious) Kingdom on Earth, it could not be allowed by political powers to flourish in any degree.

What were the specific crimes of Devil-worshipping witches? On a grand scale, witches were said to cause all manner of plagues and diseases, fatal to both humans and animals.[89] Or, they might destroy crops with hailstorms, insects, and rodents. On a smaller scale, individual diseases, deformities, deaths, and accidents were often traced back to witches. If a child developed an ugly growth, or fell into a stream and drowned, it might be witchery.[90] Even two teats drying up on a cow was cause for suspicion.[91]

Needless to say, such disasters could destroy agricultural societies. But family life was at risk, too. As Kramer argued in his *Malleus*, witches could cause impotence, failure to conceive, miscarriages, stillborn babies, and even the death of newborns.[92] These offenses were awful, but inquisitors and demonologists, believing that witches *did not act alone*, were persuaded of even more horrendous transgressions.

The notion that witches worshipped the Devil and entered into pacts with him hardly disturbs anyone's sleep today. But, at the time, demonologists, theologians, and increasingly large numbers of the laity, saw Devil worship as catastrophic to Christendom and the prevailing political order. That is, it was not just blasphemy: it was treason against both God and humanity. With some demonologists estimating 1.8 million witches across Europe, it is no wonder that the most royal of demonologists, King James I of England, exclaimed that there was a "fearefull aboundinge at this time in this countrie, of these detestable slaves of the Devill, the Witches or enchaunters," and that they merited "most severly to be punished."[93] Two witches from Lorraine confessed that, at their Sabbats "they were sometimes present among so great a number of witches that they felt no small pity for the human race when they saw it assailed by so many enemies and betrayers."[94]

Echoing earlier accusations hurled at heretics, demonologists asserted that witches secretly congregated at regular intervals, called Witches' Sabbats, and did all sorts of ghastly things. To get to these meetings, witches often flew upon the backs of demons shaped like rams, pigs, oxen, or black horses. Others had simpler conveyance such as shovels or brooms.[95] To still others, the Devil gave ointment to smear on a short stick and when a witch put the stick between her legs, off she flew.[96] Whether witches could *really* fly was a matter of debate among demonologists. Some believed they physically traveled to the Sabbats, others that only their spirits flew, leaving their bodies at home. Nicholas Rémy resolved the issue for himself by saying either could be true, but the evil Sabbats themselves were *real* either way, and the witches should burn for it.[97]

Once at the Sabbat, new witches committed themselves to a pact with the Devil. Demonologists came to see this as a conversion to Satan that inverted Christian Church practices.[98] After cursing both God and the Virgin Mary, the new Satanic converts would be rebaptized and renamed, and after denying their old godparents, they were given new godparents[!] by Satan. Then standing in a circle, they swore allegiance to the Devil, promising to sacrifice to him and to bring back a gift of something black to him each year. Also, they requested that their names be struck from the Lamb's Book of Life and written in the black Book of Death. Finally, as a seal of this new covenant with Satan, they would receive the Devil's mark on some part of their body, just "as fugitive slaves are branded."[99]

Veteran witches were required to report their evil deeds since the last Sabbat and were beaten by Satan if the evil was below standard. Then they allegedly did what Jews, ancient Christians, and medieval heretics had supposedly done: feast on infants, engage in orgies, and plant the "kiss of shame" on Satan's backside. During this latter rite, the Devil was said to appear as a stinking goat or dog, and witches approached him in unnatural fashion, perhaps skittering forward like crabs, but upside down and on their backs.[100]

Furthermore, the ceremonies offered little intrinsic pleasure. At the feast, all

WITCHES AND WITCH-HUNTS IN THE WEST

Figure 22. Witches and demons feasting on babies

Figure 23. A witch causing maleficia. *She sinks a ship and destroys crops and livestock.*

Figure 24. Witches at their cauldron, causing a storm (hail?). Note that they add a rooster and a snake to the fiery concoction.

Figure 25. A Witches' Sabbat. Note the flying, the feasting on babies, the "kiss of shame" (at right), and the backward dancing.

was filth and stench. The wine was black "like stale blood." The food was hard to keep down, and any who managed it felt hungrier than ever. Then came the dirty dancing, often back-to-back as a perversion of the natural order or circling to the left in jerky, frenzied movements.[101] Finally, each witch paired off with a demon lover for a tiring, painful, and ice-cold sexual experience.[102] And then they were back off to their homes before the cock crowed.

All this makes for a revolting and highly picturesque display of evil but, unlike *maleficia*, which were part of popular culture, it was mere fabrication. The only evidence for the existence of large-scale Devil-worshipping societies comes from coerced and delusional testimonies.[103] It is important to note also that the concept of a Witches' Sabbat did not catch on everywhere. In England it arrived late, which is probably why night-flying barely figures into indigenous folklore: English witches had no place to go.[104] On the other hand, animal "familiars" play prominently into English trials but receive scant mention on the Continent.[105] These were said to be demons dwelling with witches in the

MAGIC, MYSTERY, AND SCIENCE

Figure 26. Demon embracing a witch

WITCHES AND WITCH-HUNTS IN THE WEST

Figure 27. Naming names. Matthew Hopkins, witch finder general, with a witch on trial revealing the names of her demonic familiars.

MAGIC, MYSTERY, AND SCIENCE

shape of animals (a cat, dog, toad, or mouse, say) and doing their bidding. Stories developed that they would drink blood from a demonic teat on the witch's body. One witch, who had five such teats but seven familiars, complained that "when they come to suck they fight like pigs with a sow."[106]

This is a light note now, but several centuries ago it and similar details compelled grave thought that often resulted in unspeakable pain. Consider the case of Father Urbain Grandier, best known from Aldous Huxley's *The Devils of Loudon*.[107] At his trial, a Devil's pact was produced. The document was written backward (of course), in Latin, and signed in blood. In it, Lucifer promises Grandier "the love of women, the flower of virgins, the chastity of nuns, worldly honors, pleasures, and riches. He will have sex every three days." It is dutifully signed by Satan, Beelzebub, and other princes of Hell, and notarized by Baalberith, Recorder.[108] This is all very humorous until one realizes that for the authorities of Grandier's day, the pact was exactly what it purported to be. And so Grandier was tortured until marrow ran from his crushed bones and then was burned alive.

FINDING A WITCH: PRICKINGS, MARKS, DUNKING, CRYING, AND TORTURE

Because Satan and his demons were elusive, devious, and supernatural, only God could destroy them. But humans could catch up with fellow-humans who allied themselves with Satan. The first step was to identify a suspect, who, in all likelihood, was someone already disliked by neighbors and thus a kind of lightning rod for community resentment and frustration. (As suggested below, only when witch-hunts escalated wildly did other dynamics come to dictate witch selection.) This would begin an evidence-seeking process that could take several forms.

One way to identify a witch was to find the aforementioned Devil's mark on the body.[109] This mark, said the Jesuit Martin Del Rio, might look like a spider or a cat, the footprint of a hare or a toad, or just a mole or a flea bite. (Who doesn't have a blemish that could be construed as such?) To hide the mark, Del Rio further insisted, the Devil would put it in secret parts of the body: "On men's bodies it is often seen under the eyelids, the lips, the armpits and the rectum. In women it is seen on the breasts or the genitals."[110] To find the elusive mark on women suspects, courts often called in respected midwives.[111] And sometimes victims' bodies were completely shaved, a procedure that no doubt produced a few marks of its own.

A related method of discovering witches was pricking. According to demonologists, Devil's marks were insensitive to pain; some authorities also said they could not bleed. But since blemishes might or might not be Devil's marks, each had to be pricked. The investigators pressed sharp instruments into marks,

WITCHES AND WITCH-HUNTS IN THE WEST

blemish after blemish, until one failed to bleed or produce a painful reaction in the alleged witch.[112] If every prick produced pain, this could be explained away as a counterfeit reaction: witches could feign pain. Thus, Devil's marks were not always reliable indicators of witchcraft and tended to be sought only to confirm other damning evidence. If they showed up, that might well clinch the matter; if not, one could not assume automatic acquittal. Del Rio argued that Satan did not *always* brand his followers with a mark and, wily fiend that he was, would sometimes remove a mark prior to a witch's arrest. Others disagreed, but there was enough interpretive leeway on the matter to ensure that if a judge wanted to burn a witch, he probably could.[113]

Like many aspects of the witch-hunts, the idea of a Devil's mark could be abused in more than one way. Some witch-prickers were reputed to be highly skilled in identifying Devil's marks, and some were even paid by the number of identified witches—an incentive begging to be exploited.[114] Two fraudulent witch-prickers, John Kincaid and John Dick, helped instigate the Great Scottish Witch-Hunt of 1661–1662, in which 660 were accused, and perhaps one hundred died.[115] The persecution ceased only after the duplicitous pair came under suspicion and were thrown in prison.[116]

Two other procedures—one major and the other minor—were sometimes used to discover, or confirm, a witch. The frustrations of proving witchcraft led to the revival of an old form of trial by ordeal known as "swimming" or "dunking." Like all trials by ordeal, dunking called upon God, rather than humans, to act as judge.[117] To bring off the trial, officials sprinkled holy water into a pond or stream, thus making all the water holy. The accused witch was then bound and either thrown into the water tied to a rope or put on the end of a balanced beam and dunked into the water. If she floated to the surface, it was presumed that the holy water had rejected her, whereupon she was dragged out and condemned (and thereafter executed). If she sank (and sometimes drowned), however, it was said the holy water had accepted her as an innocent soul.

King James approved this method, saying that God had appointed a supernatural sign to reveal the monstrous crime of witches: "the water shal refuse to receive them in her bosom, [those] that have shaken off them the Water of Baptisme. . . . No not so much as their eyes are able to shed teares (thretten and torture them as ye please)."[118] And that is the second, more minor, sign of a witch—she is not able to cry, even when tortured. The *Malleus* concurred, but cautioned that a witch could "assume a tearful aspect and smear her cheeks and eyes with spittle to make it appear that she is weeping; wherefore she must be closely watched by the attendants."[119] In other words, judges should not be moved to sympathy by (apparently) weeping suspects.

But more than ambiguous tokens such as counterfeit tears and Devil's marks,

MAGIC, MYSTERY, AND SCIENCE

judges wanted strong *legal* proof of witchcraft. Roman law required either two reliable witnesses or a confession for a conviction. As it was often difficult to find two reliable witnesses of witches' crimes (crimes generally witnessed by Satan and other witches—all unreliable), a confession was the only sure legal alternative. This, more often than not, meant torture, but Roman law allowed for torture in certain extenuating circumstances.

In some (but not all) countries, witchcraft came to be seen as one of those circumstances—an exception to the general rule that torture not be used for judicial purposes. The reasons have already been noted: witchcraft was considered a special case because it was so heinous and so difficult to gather hard evidence about.[120] The legal bounds of torture were sometimes stretched, however, with an eye toward extracting a more reliable "voluntary" confession. Prisoners subjected to the rack for a while might be given a respite to weigh the merits of confession. Or, if the mere sight of instruments of torture prompted a confession, such was considered free and voluntary.

In England and its colonies, as well as in Scotland, torture was illegal; thus the major tortures, such as the rack and strappado (tying a victim's hands behind her back with a rope threaded through a tackle-and-pulley in the ceiling, then jerking her up and down in the air—sometimes with weights hanging from the feet), were not used. (Or at least they were not used legally: many Scottish trials used torture nonetheless.) But what we might call non-physical tortures, such as being kept awake and questioned for days, were sometimes used to great effect.

Even though a few individuals refused to confess even under extreme torture, we may be sure that many capitulated to the pain and offered false testimony against their will. Three points, however, should be noted here. First, some victims confessed without torture apparently because they were already tormented by self-doubt and religious guilt; accusation or denunciation by others was enough to decide the issue. Second, torture could sometimes be shockingly ineffective. For example, between 1565 and 1640, when the Parisian Parlement put a total of ninety-nine accused witches to torture, *none* confessed![121] And third, confessions could be doubly insidious: they not only consigned confessors to a painful death but often whipped up the frenzy by producing names of other suspects to be tracked down and tortured.

What is more (and this is where things might backfire on accusers), when judges asked for names of accomplices, they gave the condemned power to make a vengeance list.[122] Such lists were seldom used as stand-alone evidence for that very reason (except in some run-away hunts in Germany). In small communities, disliked persons could stave off charges of witchcraft by threatening to name their accusers as fellow witches. One Lorraine woman reportedly said "that if she were arrested 'she would accuse others whether they were

Figure 28. The strappado. Note the weights on the floor that could be added to increase the pain. Lifting people with their arms in this position is a "come along" method still used by police to drag away protestors.

good women or not.' "[123] Thus, it was not uncommon for villagers to wait years before denouncing a suspected neighbor, all the while hoping that enough community consensus would develop to counteract the shocks of a vengeful confession.[124]

WITCHES AND VICTIMS

Looking back at the great witch-hunts, we wonder at how things could have gotten so unhinged. What impelled seemingly well-intentioned people to turn so viciously on those about them? And who were the victims? That is, what did a witch look like? What was it about a person's appearance, behavior, gender, and social position that predisposed others to suspect witchcraft?

Since notions of witchcraft varied from place to place, no single profile fits universally. But let us begin with the modern stereotype of a witch and see how well it holds up. It has long been a truism that during the early modern period the vast majority of accused witches were women. These women have usually been portrayed as poor old widows, ugly and friendless, who were often employed as wise-women or midwives. Recent, area-specific research has overturned many of these views. While impoverished old spinsters may be typical of English witches, for example, it was less so elsewhere, and midwives were sometimes more likely to be accusers than accused. Even the automatic equation of witches *as* women has begun to weaken.

Like Kramer's *Malleus*, some modern authors have linked women and witchcraft so closely that they have portrayed the witch-hunts as thinly veiled "women hunts" whose true intent was gendercide.[125] Considering that, on average, four out of five executed witches were women, "women hunts" does not seem inappropriate at first blush.[126] In some regions, such as Denmark, Sweden, and Essex (England), over 90 percent of those executed were women.[127] The trials *were* misogynistic, of that there is no doubt. But were they driven by extreme misogyny, or do the numbers merely reflect the general misogyny of the age? If hatred of women alone caused the trials, why didn't they begin much earlier, end much later, and kill a far higher proportion of women? And why did the hunts include large numbers of men and children? Clearly, as Christina Larner points out, "the crime of witchcraft, while sex related, was not sex specific."[128]

Larner's view achieves plausibility once it is considered that in some localities men were more likely to be identified as witches than women. In Estonia, males made up 60 to 65 percent of witches executed; in Russia, 70 percent; and, in Iceland, 95 percent![129] In Finland, more men than women were accused of witchcraft until quite late in the period; only with the adoption of the

WITCHES AND WITCH-HUNTS IN THE WEST

Continental concept of the Witches' Sabbat in the 1670s did women begin to outnumber men.[130]

Even in Western Europe there were significant regional departures from the witch-as-woman rule. The most severe persecutions took place in Switzerland, where one's chance of burning was a staggering one in a hundred in any given year![131] Yet, in Switzerland, nearly 40 percent of those executed were *male*.[132] In France, the figure climbs to 50 percent and shoots up to 75 percent in Normandy (in northwest France).[133] But witches were not always imagined as we have come to imagine them. From an English point of view, the stereotypical Norman witch was quite curious: a male shepherd whose menacing magic derived from stolen eucharists and toad venom.[134] (One wonders how differently discussions about witches would be today in the English-speaking world if witch folklore had developed as it did in Normandy or Switzerland.)

These departures, however, are just that. The fact remains that female victims outnumber male four to one. Stuart Clark has proposed that this gender imbalance stems in part from the Renaissance penchant for classifying everything into polar opposites.[135] Renaissance demonologists, like their magician counterparts, bifurcated the world into opposites that reflected gender differences. "Courageous" and "intelligent," for example, were paired with "male," while "talkative," "vain," and "shrewish" were linked with "female." Because these (male) demonologists certainly were not going to pair "witchcraft" with "male," they codified their unspoken, and perhaps unconscious, misogyny.[136]

Of course, we also classify today. Hearing that someone was beaten to death in an alley behind a bar, most of us instinctively assume the perpetrator was male unless told otherwise. If asked why, we might shrug and say that men are more inclined to violent crime than women—look at the statistics. Men, particularly young ones, are over 80 percent more likely to be arrested for violent crimes.[137] So, also, demonologists of the day would have said women were more predisposed to witchcraft; it is in their nature, look at the arrest statistics.

If women suffered most during the witch trials, old women suffered more (in proportion to their number) than their younger counterparts.[138] Some of those executed were over eighty years of age, and this in a time when far fewer people lived to old age.[139] Generally speaking, however, these women were not despised vagabonds moving through the countryside. They may have been unloved, but they were nearly always well-known members of the community, and though not well off, they were not the very poorest either.[140] Moreover, nearly half of all accused witches were married.[141] This fact is important because it challenges Keith Thomas's "charity refused" model of witchcraft that posits that begging old spinsters were accused as witches after having cursed their neighbors for refusing to give alms.[142]

Also, there is no evidence that midwives and so-called wise-women and cunning folk were specifically targeted during the witch trials. Kramer had argued that midwives were ideally situated to cause abortions, kill unbaptized babies, and provide infant victuals for Sabbat feasts.[143] It is true that midwives aroused widespread concern owing to their ability to nudge newborns either toward life or death (by the early modern period, they were often required to swear before a cleric not to perform abortions, or "suffer any woman's child to be murdered, maimed, or otherwise hurt"[144]), but apparently this concern did not fester into witch hatred. If anything, midwives were underrepresented at the trials.[145]

Something similar may be said of cunning folk. These were people who practiced magic, seemed to have unusual powers, and sometimes were consulted by neighbors to counteract evil bewitchments (spells). Of course, anyone aspiring to practice "helpful magic" might wind up being accused of practicing dark magic. From the trial records, however, there is no evidence that cunning folk in Europe came under unusual scrutiny during the witch-hunts.[146] Alan Macfarlane, for instance, noted that of the forty-one known cunning folk in Essex, only four were accused of witchcraft, and this out of a total of four hundred trials.[147]

Even more surprising, perhaps, is that cunning folk and midwives were often called upon as subject matter experts during the trials. Who better to detect witchery than one who knew the ways of magic but worked to thwart its evil effects? And midwives, as noted earlier, were frequently asked to distinguish ordinary bodily blemishes from the fateful Devil's mark that signified satanic allegiance. These responsibilities gave cunning folk and midwives unusual clout that could easily be abused, and some scholars have depicted them as willing, or even fearful, pawns in the judicial proceedings. No doubt they sometimes were. But the Lancaster witch trials of 1634 show they also could be fiercely independent.

Twenty people were accused of witchcraft by a boy of ten.[148] Of the sixteen women, thirteen were found to have Devil's marks in their genital area by local midwives. After some concern about the verdicts, the court ordered four of the accused women to be taken to London for a second opinion. There they fell under the gaze of a panel of ten no-nonsense London midwives. These women, knowing that they were disagreeing with their Lancaster counterparts, said that they found no Devil's marks on the four examinees.[149] (Evidently William Harvey, prominent physician and anatomist, and King Charles I were also present and could see no marks either.) All of the accused were later acquitted.

Unfortunately, this display of courage is made exceptional by the general fact that over time women became increasingly likely to accuse others of witchcraft and testify against them.[150] Why? Perhaps because housewives were well situated to witness (seeming) *maleficia* against a household, such as cows dying

WITCHES AND WITCH-HUNTS IN THE WEST

prematurely.[151] Or perhaps, as Larner suggests, women, "dependent for their livelihood on the goodwill of men," simply caved in to male misogyny.[152] This sounds, to modern ears, like a forced, external conformity, and certainly it was for some. But many women, as well as men, actually believed the misogynist stereotypes taught them. (No matter what *we* think about these pernicious stereotypes.) Accordingly, they accused other women as witches, not because they were compelled by male-dominated courts, but because of their unquestioning acceptance of prevailing values. Indeed, some women willingly confessed to witchcraft in the trials, believing themselves to be witches in part because they had failed to live up to wifely and motherly ideals.[153]

Children might also be accusers and were frequently arraigned as witnesses when it was believed that they, innocently or not, had been led into witchcraft by their parents. In some instances, they were called upon to identify adults present at the Sabbats. Giving the power of life and death testimony, with impunity, to minors could be extremely hazardous. In Sweden, mass trials were fueled by the testimony of groups of children, some of whom were paid as witch-hunters. And a number of the older children apparently coordinated the testimony of the rest, so that they would all agree in court.[154]

But children, although generally exempted from persecution, sometimes were victims themselves. Nicholas Rémy, the author of *Demonolatry* and witch-hating judge *par excellence* (by his own account he condemned more than eight hundred witches to death in ten years[155]), believed that offspring of witches were almost certainly witches as well, and irredeemably so. Under a law he thought too lenient, children of witches were stripped and beaten while they watched their parents burn at the stake.[156]

Rémy contended that children of witches naturally follow their parents into the craft. He told the story of a man planting cabbages with his eight-year-old daughter. She did so well that he praised her, whereupon she boasted that she could do far greater things, such as call down rain anywhere in the garden. She then "dug a trench and pissed in it, and beat the water with a stick," and sure enough, rain suddenly fell in that part of the garden. When the father asked who had taught her, she replied, her mother, who knew far more than this. A few days later, the father dressed them all in their best on the pretense of going to a wedding. Once in town, he handed both his wife and daughter over to the judge to be tried as witches.[157]

When on the relatively rare occasion children were targeted as witches, the persecution could be fierce. In the Zuberer-Jackl (Jack the Little Sorcerer) trials, held in Salzburg from 1677 to 1681, some 140 people were burned at the stake, mostly beggars and roving bands of children.[158] The numbers fit neither the "British" nor the *Malleus* witch stereotypes. Seventy percent of those executed were under the age of twenty-two, and, likewise, 70 percent were male.[159] And, although the Elector of Bavaria offered a handsome reward for his capture, Little Jack was never apprehended.[160]

Fifty years earlier, in the German city of Würzburg, not only were scores of teenage boys and girls rounded up and executed for witchcraft, but about three hundred children between the ages of three and four were "said to have had intercourse with the Devil."[161] This turn of events reflected an increasing tendency for children to be involved in large-scale hunts in southern Germany after the turn of the seventeenth century.[162] Bishop Binsfeld of Trier contributed to this development by approving the torture of children under the age of fourteen to obtain confessions and testimonies against adults.

Let one horrifying episode illustrate what such torture might entail. In 1600, the Munich Commissioners had Hänsel Pappenheimer, a ten-year-old boy of poor parents, brought before them and beaten with a rod until he finally "confessed" against his brothers.[163] Yes, Hänsel admitted, his brothers had been chopping the hands off young children and even killing pregnant women to gain the hands of their unborn babies—all for the nefarious magical purpose of making "thieves candles" out of them.[164] All the Pappenheimer family were soon put to the rack and found to have made pacts with the Devil, committed horrific murders, and, of course, taken up witchery. At their executions, while young Hänsel was forced to look on, his family (and others caught in the web of lies) had their flesh torn with red-hot pincers—even his mother's breasts were not spared. His father, as the alleged leader, had his limbs broken on the wheel and then was impaled from underneath with a thin, pointed pole. He was then dragged, still alive, to the stake, joining his wife and others there. As the flames engulfed them, little Hänsel sobbed, "My mother is squirming!" Afterward, Hänsel was taken back to a cell and "questioned" for more information. A few months later, he, too, was burned at the stake.

PUTTING THINGS IN PERSPECTIVE

As awful as the witch trials and executions were, they should not be taken as license to assume that most people of the era were bereft of sanity and compassion. After all, every century has witnessed its share of mass horrors, some sanctioned by political or religious authority and justified by such apparently high-minded ideals as Manifest Destiny, ethnic cleansing, and *Lebensraum*. Despite these, many people lead admirable lives while resisting the inhumanity that inevitably flares up about them.

If the Pappenheimer family execution had been the norm throughout all of Europe, then we might expect that hundreds of thousands, even millions, of people were similarly executed. In fact, one oft-cited estimate for the total number of witches burned is nine million. This figure was apparently pulled

WITCHES AND WITCH-HUNTS IN THE WEST

from thin air by the nineteenth-century feminist and iconoclast Matilda Joslyn Gage in her diatribe against Christianity.[165] It was then picked up by Gerald B. Gardner, the modern founder of the Wiccan movement, and subsequently popularized by Starhawk and other counter-culturists.[166] It even made an appearance in *Ms.* magazine and continues to live in cyberspace—many Wiccan and Neopagan websites use this huge number as an apologetic when speaking of "The Burning Times."[167]

Judging from trial records, the best estimates by historians today are that perhaps as many as sixty thousand people were executed over the space of three hundred years, and the number was certainly under one hundred thousand.[168] (As more local records are examined, these figures continue to edge down slightly.) Of course, even a single execution is intolerable, but sixty thousand or one hundred thousand such executions is a far cry from nine million. And with these more accurate numbers in mind, we may reasonably respond to the question of how likely it was that a particular woman would be executed for witchcraft? Judging strictly from statistics, the likelihood of a woman dying in childbirth or drowning was far greater than that of being burned as a witch.[169] Even in areas where intense persecution raged, the odds of being burned were not as great as we might expect: perhaps one in fifty thousand women suffered that fate.[170]

This is not to excuse the witch trials, only to put the numbers in perspective. It is eye-opening to realize that a modern American woman is nearly five times *more* likely to be murdered than a seventeenth-century European woman was to be burned as a witch.[171] Any attempt, then, to portray the witch trials as "an organized mass murder of women" seems rather overblown.[172] The real question may be (as Robin Briggs has stated), why were there so *few* witch trials, given the limitless number of possible suspects. In England, for example, far more women may have been executed for infanticide than for witchcraft.[173] During Queen Elizabeth's reign, about eight hundred criminals per year were executed in England.[174] Of these, fewer than two per year were witches, and yet Elizabeth's reign was the high water mark for witch prosecutions until the English Civil War.[175]

But if the witch trials were not "women hunts," why did they occur? Historians have long searched for a touchstone. There have been many single-cause theories (the Spanish Inquisition, Calvinism, the formation of the centralized state, among others) that seemed quite reasonable at one time or other. All, however, have collapsed under the scrutiny of recent scholarship.[176] As is often the case, it is tempting—and simplistic—to point a finger of blame at a single large-scale institution when the complicated truth of the matter lies closer to home. Current research indicates that while large, spectacular witch-hunts have long attracted attention, the vast majority of accused witches were tried

MAGIC, MYSTERY, AND SCIENCE

and burned alone, and, more often than not, in rural settings rather than cities. Apparently, these single defendant trials were driven not so much by the ecclesiastical or political elite as by exasperated neighbors who had feared and distrusted a suspected witch for many years.[177] The title of Robin Briggs's survey, *Witches and Neighbors*, emphasizes just this point.

This finding correlates with the emerging fact that Europeans in the early modern period were learning to be litigious. Even the middle and lower classes were less likely (than they had been earlier) to settle their local disputes out of court.[178] They consequently used the legal system to exact vengeance on troublesome neighbors whom they had come to perceive as witch-like malefactors and threats to the community.[179]

There were, of course, large-scale hunts as well (although, in sum, they took far fewer lives), and these generally radiated out from a large city. Nearly always in these persecutions, victims were accused of attending Witches' Sabbats and tortured for confessions and names of other attendees. And once a critical mass was reached, most of the customary stereotypes of the witch broke down: almost *anyone* could be a witch. The Mass Hunt at Würzburg, for example, executed people of every rank and status, from the children of nobility to wizened old clerics—males, females, young, old, students, teachers, laborers, married, and widows—none were spared.[180]

Mass hunts suggest mass hysteria, and no doubt there was some of that. But oft overlooked is the importance of the individual judge, particularly when he had no one to answer to. Richard Golden points out that most large-scale hunts were directed by single persons.[181] Unchecked and highly zealous, these could ignite a firestorm of persecution when, under slightly different circumstances, saner minds might have prevailed. As mentioned above, Rémy sent more than eight hundred witches to their deaths in ten years, and he may have sent as many as two thousand to the stake in the course of his career.[182] If so, his tally is *more* than all the witches killed in England, France, and Spain *combined*.[183] Only the Archbishop of Cologne, Ferdinand of Bavaria, killed witches on a comparable scale—about two thousand executions in thirty-eight years.[184] Seven other German Prince-Bishops (of Bamberg, Würzburg, and Mainz) oversaw the worst of the large-scale witch hunts, totaling nearly four thousand victims among them.[185] Thus, only nine men were responsible for some 10 to 20 percent of all witch trial deaths. And while sowing misery, none of the nine had an effective check to his power from secular or ecclesiastical authorities. So, even in mass hunts, individual persons often loomed large, especially when power was concentrated under their authority.

Ferdinand did his work of death in central Europe, a fact consistent with the finding that the farther from central Europe, the smaller the hunts.[186] There is, of course, one set of witch trials very far from Europe but nonetheless central for most Americans: Salem, Massachusetts. By serving as an exemplar for nearly every evil from Puritanism to McCarthyism, Salem has gained mythic status in the United States. It too needs a bit of perspective. During the trials of 1692, nineteen were hanged, two died in prison, and one was pressed to death. Previously, a total of twenty-two people had been executed for witchcraft in the Colonies (if one includes three America-bound victims executed by fearful sailors aboard ships before they ever got to the Colonies).[187] Given that the New England population in the 1690s was just under one hundred thousand (the entire colonial population was about a quarter million), the American colonial witch-hunts, including Salem, rank well behind those of Iceland—hardly a hotbed of witch hatred.[188]

DECLINE OF THE WITCH-HUNTS

Witch trials were irreducibly complex. If almost any factor were missing, the process would collapse, or perhaps never begin. If a judge linked *maleficia* and demonic worship but the common people did not, or if the judge did not believe God would allow witches demonic power though the commoners did, then the trials were not likely to continue. Nor would large-scale trials take off if judges rejected confessions extracted by torture or accusations of condemned prisoners. And where belief in the Sabbat and its links to blasphemy and treason were absent, large-scale hunts were improbable. For example, Finland had nearly two thousand witch trials, but there was no naming of names and there were no mass witch-hunts—evidently because there was almost no mention of a Witches' Sabbat.[189] Taken in sum, this suggests that any search for *the* single reason why the trials began or ended is doomed to failure.

Why the witch-trials went away is as difficult to grasp as why they began. The facile response of the nineteenth century, that the rise of science and reason in the seventeenth century banished belief in witchcraft, is held by fewer historians today.[190] This view *seems* right, but that is because people tend to assimilate the past to their own contemporary fantasies. After assuming that science and witchcraft are mutually exclusive categories, moderns instinctively project that assumption back on earlier centuries. The result in this case is an outlook that depicts the decline of witchcraft as the flip side of the rise of seventeenth-century science. Since the two are natural antagonists, so this line of thought goes, one or the other had to emerge triumphant.

But the era in question—the seventeenth century—does not offer up a preponderance of modernistic thinking on the issue. Not only was seventeenth-century science compatible with belief in witchcraft, but some notables of the Scientific Revolution, such as Robert Boyle and Joseph Glanvill, may have encouraged and reinvigorated a belief in witches as a bulwark against incipient deist and atheist ideologies.[191] Along with Henry More, these fellows of the Royal Society (England's premier scientific institution) collected, studied, and theorized about witchcraft in the same way they did about the possibility of the vacuum, magnetic action at a distance, and the nature of light.[192] Glanvill even pictured investigating demons and witches as a "kinde of America," a new frontier of knowledge.[193] He and Boyle believed that science was the one tool that could verify their existence and shed light on their activities, whether natural or supernatural.

Moreover, there is the irony that materialistic conceptions of nature—those that distanced the world from notions of spirit and divinity—actually encouraged belief in occult and supernatural possibilities for some. These conceptions were part of the intellectual fare of the seventeenth century, but they were often deemed too stark to account for a world that seemed to vibrate with color, harmony, and life's ecstasies and agonies. Witches were one way of filling the emotional void left by scientific materialism, and, for many, a way made altogether plausible by the apparent failure of materialism to (literally) live up to the world it aspired to explain.[194]

Not all, of course, were vitally interested in science and the philosophical judgments it pronounced upon the world. And neither were people always scrupulous, vigilant, or consistent in the way they defined and designated witches. Like "communist" or "child molester" in our own day, the term "witch" was so inflammatory as to stigmatize whomever it fell upon, innocent or not. It is not surprising, then, that the word was rancorously hurled back and forth in contexts other than witch trials. A handy weapon in worldview warfare, it was used by both sides in the English Civil War and by believers of every stripe during the great religious wars of the early modern period.[195]

Eventually, it seems, witchcraft became so politicized and so deeply associated with public smear campaigns that skeptics—those "in the know"—were able to laugh it off as more tactic than reality. This transition from public excess to private disbelief, from the cynical, calculated use of witchcraft to cynicism about it and anything savoring of it (religion included), may be noted in the French Catholic exorcism dramas played out before the masses in France. These were ostensibly staged to heal demonically afflicted souls, but their true political and religious intent was to bring French Huguenots (Protestants) back into the Catholic fold by demonstrating the spiritual superiority of the Roman Church.[196] After claims, counter-claims, and cantankerous rounds of fanatical bickering, conversions to skepticism increased. Michel Montaigne was one of many to follow. After being allowed to question an old woman accused of witchcraft, and even seeing a mark insensible to pain, he concluded: "One overvalues one's conjectures if one makes use of them to burn a man alive."[197]

Thus, religious "enthusiasm" came to be seen as something to be moderated by reason, or even dismissed by it. During the eighteenth century, Deists and anti-clerical rationalists could dismiss great swaths of orthodox belief by the mere mention of "witchcraft" and a knowing roll of the eyes. For many of the elite, however, conversion to disbelief in witchcraft was prompted as much by intellectual fashion as by reason—derisive laughter at any kind of miraculous religion was a net wide enough to capture belief in witches, too. In a very real sense, Deists and "rationalists" mocked witchcraft to death, and, along with it, a great deal of religious belief.

The curious lesson that emerges from this development is that reason, like witchcraft, may be deployed effectively as an ideological weapon. And often those who use it in this manner fail to fully understand its strengths and limitations. But it is this ignorance that empowers the haughty sniff or withering stare that often reduces opponents to meek silence.[198] "Oh, don't tell me you still believe in witches" (or in Aristotle, the soul, morals, Western rationality, etc.).

Among those who voiced concern over this misuse of reason, this *non-rational* rejection of the miraculous and the supernatural under the banner of reason, was the evangelist John Wesley. In 1770, he came upon a young woman who was possibly obsessed or possessed. Contemplating her condition, Wesley recorded the following in his journal:

> When old Dr. A———R———[i.e., Dr. William Alexander] was asked what her disorder was, he answered "It is what formerly they would have called being bewitched." And why should they not call it so now? Because the *infidels have hooted witchcraft out of the world;* and the complaisant Christians, in large numbers, have joined them in the cry.[199]

Fearing that he was swimming against a rising tide, Wesley warned that "the giving up [of] witchcraft is in effect giving up the Bible."[200]

Not all in the reformed tradition would have agreed. Nearly two hundred years earlier, some of the Anglican clergy had been skeptical of witchcraft and possession cases on doctrinal grounds, believing that the "age of miracles" had ceased long before.[201] Even John Calvin had hinted at the "cessation of miracles" with the apostolic age, arguing that extraordinary miracles attested to the authority of the apostles before the written gospel.[202] In any event, witchcraft, once a rich and explosive mix of magical, religious, and scientific possibility, now presents itself as a wrong turn in the history of Western civilization. No doubt in many ways it was, but one of the ensuing course corrections—the nay-saying, anti-religious rationalism of the eighteenth century—has since come to be seen by some as an over-correction.

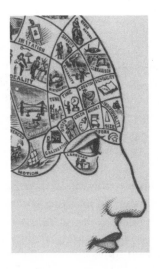

8

SPIRITS, SCIENCE, AND PSEUDO-SCIENCE IN THE NINETEENTH CENTURY

Any one with a healthy sense for
evidence, a sense not blunted by the
sectarianism of "Science," ought now,
it seems to me, to feel that exalted
sensibilities and memories, veridical
phantasms, haunted houses, trances
with supernormal faculty, and even
experimental thought-transference, are
natural kinds of phenomena which
ought, just like other natural events, to
be followed up with scientific curiosity.

—William James[1]

By the nineteenth century, science was becoming impossible to ignore, even
for an otherworldly occultist. The occult, meanwhile, had plummeted from its
zenith during the Renaissance to its nadir during the eighteenth century—the
"Age of Reason" as it called itself (although some at the time saw reason, or at
least the inordinate veneration of reason, as a new form of irrationality and

even self-idolatry). The educated now derided many of the older occult views, and with some justification: the Scientific Revolution of the seventeenth century had ushered in a new worldview whose natural laws and predictive capabilities far surpassed any previous mode of apprehension. Many marveled when a comet appeared in the night sky in 1758, but this time the source of wonder resided primarily in Edmund Halley's correct prediction that a comet would appear, not in the comet itself. No religious prophet or occultist had ever been able to foresee events with such accuracy, at least not in such a public and unequivocal manner.

For more than a century after the Scientific Revolution, Newtonian physics was seen as the key to understanding the universe, including humanity. The resulting "Newtonmania," combined with the burgeoning Industrial Revolution, compelled many in the Age of Reason to believe that the "scientific method," if used properly, could heal humanity of its ills and fulfill its fondest dreams. This method, albeit nebulously defined, came to include the formulation of mathematical laws of nature, empirical observation and experimentation, and the collection and classification of almost everything on the planet.

Because of its past success and immense future promise, science cast a hegemonic shadow over other intellectual endeavors during the late eighteenth century and throughout the nineteenth century. As a result, the occult, along with philosophy, theology, and art, suffered tremendous internal tensions. To what degree should science be accommodated? Embracing it meant tapping into its widespread prestige and thereby winning almost instantaneous social approbation, but outright acceptance of its principles might irreparably compromise the integrity of whatever non-scientific belief system one wished to promote.

Generally speaking, occultists, while otherwise willing to accommodate science, resisted two science-spawned ideologies. Neither was science proper, but, given the triumphs of science, both struck many people as right and true. One was scientism, the belief that science alone arbitrates truth and therefore what is not science is not worth knowing.[2] The other doctrine, also unpalatable to occultists, was the mechanical worldview—that all is lifeless matter in motion. (Many in the Age of Reason equated this philosophy with science itself.) For some, this outlook was too severe, for it warranted the implication that God, the soul, and free will were false notions. Taken a bit further, it suggested that human beings were mere robots.

Writing in 1902, William James stated that "[n]ature has no one distinguishable ultimate tendency with which it is possible to feel a sympathy. In the vast rhythm of her processes, as the scientific mind now follows them, she appears to cancel herself."[3] Mechanical at bottom, nature went nowhere. Thus, to some extent, nineteenth-century occultism was "a flight from reason," at

MAGIC, MYSTERY, AND SCIENCE

least insofar as reason sought to evacuate nature of life and inner purpose. But it was also an accommodation to scientific reason, for many occultists felt that science would eventually come to embrace the spiritual and immaterial in its quest for universal understanding. In the hands of impartial truth-seekers, the scientific method would open a path into the occult and reduce its seemingly erratic and haphazard character to rule. Accordingly, many people practiced and investigated the occult in a "scientific" manner. Mesmerists conducted experiments, phrenologists subjected the human head to rigorous measurement, Spiritualists kept careful record of what unfolded during séances, and all three groups invoked scientific terminology to describe their findings.

Of course, it is only in retrospect that we are able to identify these nineteenth-century "failed sciences" as occult endeavors. In their heyday, they struck many people as the most recent areas of human interest to come under science's ever-widening aegis. That said, they do have occult tendencies or parallels (which we will highlight) that put them at odds with science's stark, mechanistic vision. In our own time, similar new interests—think of ESP phenomena and near-death experiences—have sprung up and flourished with the hope of receiving scientific sanction while at the same time reacting back on science to make it more open to spiritual or immaterial possibilities. Will these subjects eventually be accepted into the fold of scientific understanding or be exiled to the wilderness of the occult? The jury is still out.

Now in exile, mesmerists and phrenologists would have vigorously rejected the occult label. Indeed, both disciplines wavered on the edge of scientific respectability throughout the nineteenth century—some parts falling into science, others falling out. Mesmer's apparent aptitude for healing by unseen, unknown powers seems occultic, as does phrenology's supposed ability to determine a person's personality from the topography of her skull. Yet modern science has surely accepted both the hypnotic trance of mesmerism and phrenology's belief that different regions of the brain preside over different organic functions. Spiritualism, by contrast, has contributed little or nothing to science, and we now often think of it as an unorthodox religious movement infiltrated by con artists. But many of its devotees were scientifically inclined thinkers and even scientists who felt that Spiritualism represented modern science's greatest opportunity since its inception three centuries earlier. What could be more momentous and far-reaching in its life-enhancing ramifications than a demonstration of the existence of another world—a spirit world—with which the human race could now interact? Christopher Columbus had discovered a new continent, and Spiritualists felt themselves on the brink of an even larger discovery.

The rub was that so much of Spiritualism could not easily withstand the public light of science. The Spiritualist medium, sitting in a darkened room, slipping into a trance, soliciting an unseen spirit guide, and requesting information about the dead and the living: the parallels with necromancy (the age-old practice of communicating with spirits of the dead) are deep. All the same, followers hoped that Spiritualism, once properly disciplined by science, would yield up its store of treasures. The disjunction, however, between Spiritualism's advocacy of immaterial, otherworldly beings and science's commitment to a mechanical interpretation of this world proved too great: within decades of its birth, Spiritualism came to be seen as the very antithesis of science.

This tension between those who unconditionally champion science and those who try to limit its authority or leaven it with spiritual promise continued throughout the nineteenth century and has not abated to this day. Plato called it the ancient quarrel between (natural) philosophy and poetry,[4] and we can see an early modern version of it in 1784, when the king of France appointed a scientific commission, including Antoine Lavoisier and Benjamin Franklin, to investigate the strange healing powers of Franz Anton Mesmer.

MESMER AND MESMERISM

Mesmer earned his doctorate in medicine at the University of Vienna in 1788. His thesis concerning the magnetic influence of the planets on humans conjoined Newton's universal gravitation with Paracelsus's cosmology; it was a mix of the old and the new, and so was Mesmer. Putting his ideas into practice, Dr. Mesmer soon discovered that he could heal his patients by passing magnets over their bodies, thereby freeing them of anything that blocked the flow of the subtle magnetic fluids coursing through the universe. Although this may sound bizarre to us—what, after all, are "subtle magnetic fluids?"—Mesmer was well within the science of his time. Heat, gravity, electricity, ether, and magnetism were all thought to consist of subtle or superfine fluids; or, perhaps, they consisted of tiny particles whose mass action was fluid-like.

The fluid hypothesis rang true because, even though we cannot actually see these phenomena, they do seem to behave as fluids. Put a hot bar of iron next to a cold one and after a while the two bars will reach a common temperature. Evidently, heat *flowed* from the hot to the cold bar. Or, move a magnet from underneath a table and watch as it affects steel objects on the table. Some force or substance must be passing through the solid wooden table—something rarefied or subtle. (No doubt you have covered the end of a flashlight with your palm and noticed some light actually passing through your hand; light thus also seems very fine or subtle.) For Mesmer, the magnetic fluid was a universal life force, which, if harnessed properly, could promote healing and health.

Notwithstanding its link with science, Mesmer's approach did not endear him to the Viennese medical profession. An expansive thinker, Mesmer was intent on revolutionizing the healing arts and so, to those more committed to tradition, he often came off as a charlatan. Seeking a more progressive milieu, he left his friends in Vienna, including Mozart, and moved to Paris, where he quickly made his mark as a daring and innovative physician. It did not hurt that he had a personality to match: he was socially adept, always ready to publicly demonstrate his remarkable skills, and ever alert to new opportunities for self-promotion.

In many ways, Paris was ready for Mesmer. The French were enchanted with all the unseen powers and substances that science surrounded them with, particularly Newton's gravity, Benjamin Franklin's electricity, and the invisible gases that allowed people, incredibly, to fly. The flight of balloons so enthralled the French that many of them believed science could accomplish anything. Mesmerism thus became one more scientific miracle, surprising but fully congruent with other recent, initially incredible, breakthroughs. Robert Darnton tells of a man who said he had invented "elastic shoes" that allowed him to walk across the River Seine: many who heard the claim embraced it uncritically.[5] This was the beginning of the age of invention, and the French were learning to anticipate a scientifically transformed future.

By the time he arrived in Paris, Mesmer had discovered that he could dispense with magnets in healing his patients. He could concentrate the magnetic fluids within his own body—use his own "animal magnetism"—to act upon those within other bodies. Armed with this new power and its attendant mystique, he became the rave of Paris. Patients at Mesmer's salon of healing were ushered into rooms with mysterious lighting, thick rugs, and rows of mirrors. They would gather around large wooden tubs filled with iron filings wherein vessels filled with "magnetized water" were arranged like spokes on a wheel. Iron rods protruded through the lids of these tubs, allowing patients to touch the magnetized rods to the ailing parts of their bodies. Mesmer or an associate would then apply his animal magnetism by moving his hands in the air around each patient or by touching the patient's "magnetic nodes" to realign them.

All this set the stage for the healing climax, which was called the "moment of crisis." When this occurred, some patients fell into mesmeric trances, others convulsed on the floor like epileptics, and still others went into hysterical fits. Attendants then carried the patient into a mattress-walled "crisis room" to recover. (Gossipy tongues wagged about what went on in these rooms.) Many who went through the experience claimed to be healed—so many, in fact, that some French doctors grew suspicious of Mesmer and labeled him a quack. Responding to their charges, the king of France assigned a commission or committee of doctors and scientists to investigate mesmerism.

Snubbing Mesmer and against his protests, the committee chose to investigate one of Mesmer's former disciples (a Dr. Deslon) who had since set up his

SPIRITS, SCIENCE, AND PSEUDO-SCIENCE

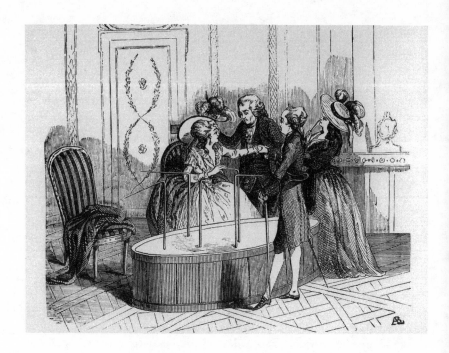

Figure 29. A mesmeric tub with iron rods protruding from vessels of "magnetized water"

own rival practice. After the committee decided against mesmerism by insisting that it had no scientific basis, Mesmer's fame began to diminish and he withdrew from public life. Still, the outlook he spawned—mesmerism itself—continued to flourish on the Continent and in England and America. It had yet to run its course and would soon lead to a genuine scientific discovery.

One of Mesmer's students, the Marquis de Puységur, observed that some mesmerized patients appeared to be asleep but were highly responsive to the suggestions of the "magnetizer" (the person inducing the mesmeric state), answering his questions, "seeing" things that were not there (having sensory hallucinations), and being very willing to obey his wishes. Puységur noted the many similarities between this "magnetic sleep" and the natural state of sleepwalking, the major difference being the suggestibility of the subject. We now, of course, call this "magnetic sleep" hypnosis, but at the time the subject was

MAGIC, MYSTERY, AND SCIENCE

called a "somnambulist" (literally, "sleepwalker"). Later, mesmerists discovered that the somnambulist could be given suggestions that would take effect post-hypnotically. Furthermore, the mesmerized subject could, by suggestion, be rendered impervious to pain.

This latter fact seemed particularly significant, as anesthesia had not yet been developed. In 1842, an English doctor mesmerized a patient before a leg amputation; the patient exhibited no pain, only a low moan.[6] Incredibly, the doctors of the London Medical Society declared the pre-operative mesmerization a hoax, saying that the man only pretended to feel no pain! Further denunciations followed as Dr. Esdaile, an English doctor in charge of a hospital for the poor in India, performed hundreds of painless operations.[7] Generally speaking, the medical profession was contemptuous of mesmerism, whether it was presented as a healing therapy or as an anesthetic. To be fair, however, many mesmerists exaggerated and misrepresented their accomplishments, and it was hard, even for impartial observers, to separate fact from fantasy.

For some mesmerists, immunity to pain was only the beginning. They claimed that mesmerized patients could look within their own bodies, diagnose their own illnesses, prescribe cures, and offer comprehensive prognoses that amounted to seeing their individual futures. Highly sensitive somnambulists reportedly could exercise their powers on behalf of others by discerning disease, recommending and even effecting cures, foretelling the future, and communing with spirits of the dead. (Some were even said to be able to read books with the backs of their heads or with their toes!)

These exceptional somnambulists were soon called *sensitives*. In the United States, many mesmerists traveled from town to town with their professional sensitives, earning a living by diagnosing and healing the illnesses of the locals and performing other mesmeric wonders. Often, the traveling mesmerist practiced other voguish medical arts, as well, such as phrenology.

PHRENOLOGY

Phrenology was a scientific theory linking mind (soul, personality) and brain. The development of this revolutionary concept—connecting thoughts, feelings, and behaviors with the physical anatomy of the brain and then to the shape of the head—owed much to the mechanists of the Scientific Revolution and their goal to explain everything as physical matter in motion. Although phrenology is now passé and, by modern standards, uncharitable (how unfair to judge the character of others by their outward physical features), the mechanistic, materialistic agenda it promoted still flourishes. Today, scientific materialists look *within* the human body for the mind's physical blueprint, and the

SPIRITS, SCIENCE, AND PSEUDO-SCIENCE

fundamental constituents thereof may be neurons, genes, organic molecules, or other tiny bits of matter whose behavior is determined by mechanical principles.

Phrenology's founder was Franz-Josef Gall (1758–1828). Like Mesmer, Gall was also a doctor from Vienna whose views were rejected by fellow Austrians but enthusiastically received by the people of Paris. Trained as a neuroanatomist (one who studied the various regions of the brain), Gall was well respected by his scientific colleagues; what many did not like, however, was his claim that the bumps on one's head revealed the real person. These were sufficient to afford a full understanding of mind or personality.

Why did Gall believe this? Proceeding from the premise that the brain is the physical organ of the mind, he reasoned that the brain pushed outward so as to impress its essential character on the skull. Furthermore, he thought that different personality traits were localized in particular sections or areas of the brain. One's head, then, expressed the strengths and weaknesses of one's mind and was therefore a map of one's behavioral destiny.

To discover which sections controlled what behaviors, Gall visited prisons and hospitals, feeling people's heads to match their crimes or illnesses with their bumps and lumps. He soon found that robbers and kleptomaniacs had a certain "organ" of the brain (expressed as a bump) that was much larger than average; this, he concluded, explained and signified their tendency to steal. Before long, Gall found other distinctive organs of the brain—twenty-seven in all—and the resulting explanatory system was nothing less than an atlas of the brain. There was an organ of "combativeness," an organ of "amativeness" (sexual desire), and so on. Since the size of each organ could vary from small to large, the resulting bumps afforded insight into one's character or mind. Thus, for example, if the "self-esteem" bump was large, expect a very prideful person. ("Self-esteem" did not have the unambiguously positive ring it now possesses.) Not surprisingly, the lower, base instincts that humans shared with animals were at the base of the brain, while the intellectual and spiritual organs were nearer the top of the cranium.

Among other things, phrenology sought to explain why ethnic groups and races were marked by peculiar temperaments—why some were noble, others lazy, still others aggressive, and so on. Narrowing the focus, some police departments hired phrenologists and physiognomists (physiognomy was a related "science" more concerned with facial features) to match up suspects with recent crimes. Phrenology also offered predictive guidance on individual relationships. Hiring a maid? Check the heads of prospects so as to ward off potential thieves. Choosing a mate? Make sure your skulls are compatible.

Now a question of great import: If your combative and thieving lumps were large, were you forever destined to fight and steal? Gall would have given a

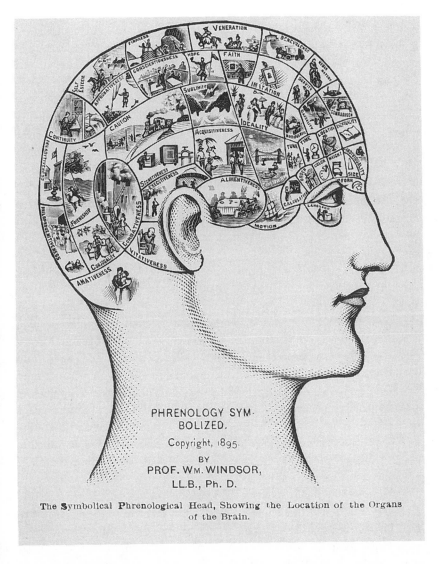

Figure 30. A phrenological "map" of the brain (and thus the skull) indicating the locations of the "organs" of behavior

SPIRITS, SCIENCE, AND PSEUDO-SCIENCE

qualified "Yes," saying you cannot modify the brain; but you might also have a lump of human kindness that keeps you from harming others—a balance of bumps, so to speak. With these considerations, we confront again the issue of whether human behavior is grounded in free choice or determined by unalterable factors. It served no purpose for a phrenologist to decide the issue solely in terms of human freedom, for then he lost the explanatory and predictive powers that made his science useful; and, as Thomas Huxley explained, "[t]he power of prediction . . . is commonly regarded as the great prerogative of physical science."[8] By contrast, if future character and behavior were already "locked in" by unalterable factors, the phrenologist could do nothing but make predictions—if indeed he fully understood those factors. By stressing that each bump may act on all the others, that the whole is more than the sum of its parts, Gall complicated the phrenological picture and thereby erected a hedge against sure-fire, fatalistic predictions.

The question of free will, of course, still challenges science, but the turf on which the question is contested has changed. Today, we wonder increasingly about genes and their capacity to determine both our biological *and* our psychological make-up. The tension, in other words, between scientific prediction (based on knowledge of deterministic processes) and human freedom has not gone away. Even so, there often comes a point at which science turns from passive understanding to active intervention and knowledge opens out onto new freedom. Now geneticists talk about the elimination of hereditary diseases and the genetic "correction" of disabling characteristics. There is, of course, a host of issues to be dealt with here and much concern about science trespassing its "lawful" bounds, but the scientific prospect of expanded freedom mitigates the deterministic thesis that mechanical cause-and-effect constitutes the whole of nature.

Striking a blow for freedom, J. K. Spurzheim (1766–1832), one of Gall's disciples, disagreed with his mentor by claiming that human beings have free will. He believed that, to a certain extent, people could change the shape of their skulls and thus their behavioral destinies; the brain's configuration was not permanently fixed but could be modified by thought and deed. A small organ of benevolence, for instance, might be enlarged by the conscientious practice of kind acts. One could only go so far, however. Slight modifications were the rule, perhaps because these could be "inferred" by experts such as Spurzheim, while large changes required dramatic alterations that were rarely if ever observed. Small though they were, the presumed modifications nevertheless offered a glad message to those interested in self-improvement.

Breaking away from Gall, Spurzheim traveled to Great Britain and later to the United States, convincing many of his view of phrenology. During the first half of the nineteenth century, many scientists and non-scientists hailed phrenology as a landmark science. Even Queen Victoria and Prince Albert wanted young Prince Edward's head evaluated, and George Combe, a follower of Spurzheim, gladly obliged. Combe, however, took a more deterministic view of phrenology, as is evidenced by his diagnosis of the young prince. He said Edward had sizable "organs of ostentativeness, destructiveness, self-esteem, combativeness and love of approbation," and thus "he will be liable to vehement fits of passion, opposition, self-will and obstinacy, not as voluntary acts, but as mere results of the physiological state of his brain, which he can no more avoid that he can prevent a ringing in his ears."[9] Suitably impressed, the royal family engaged a phrenologist as royal tutor for their children.[10]

In the United States, Spurzheim's phrenology excited much positive interest because of its emphasis on free will and self-help. Americans have always been partial to both science and self-improvement programs. They, therefore, anxiously awaited Spurzheim's first lecture tour of the country in 1832. To their disappointment, he died just two months after arriving in Boston. He was given a magnificent public funeral attended by both the president of Harvard University and the entire Boston Medical Association.[11] (Moreover, the Harvard Medical School paid him the high [posthumous] honor of pickling his brain.)

Despite Spurzheim's death, phrenology's popularity continued to grow in the United States. Soon phrenological centers were established in many major cities, while traveling doctors of the discipline visited the countryside. Like many "cutting-edge" scientific offshoots before and since, phrenology simultaneously inspired controversy, commanded respect, and held forth great promise. Lest we—no longer privy to the age that spawned it and beyond the reach of its erstwhile appeal—associate phrenology exclusively with the gullible, uninformed masses, we need to recall that it was championed by the likes of Edgar Allen Poe, Horace Greeley, and Walt Whitman. And, as any avid reader of the English classics knows, phrenology frequently turns up in Victorian fiction; even Sherlock Holmes must fend off a doctor who longs to read his head. Yet, by mid-century, phrenology had begun its long decline, first among scientists and then among the public. Before its demise, however, the traveling phrenologists/mesmerists were to exercise a key influence on the rapid spread of Spiritualism.

SPIRITUALISM

Of Spiritualism, Arthur Conan Doyle, the creator of Sherlock Holmes, wrote:

I consider [it] to be infinitely the most important thing in the world, and the particular thing which the human race in its present state of development needs more than anything else. Nothing is secure until the religious basis is secure, and that spiritualistic movement with which I am proud to be associated is the first attempt ever made in modern times to support faith by actual provable fact.[12]

Short of achieving eternal bliss, what could be more marvelous than securing religious faith with scientific fact? For Doyle and others, the moment was at hand. Spiritualism offered science empirical phenomena that were not, it seemed, amenable to naturalistic explanation.

The Fox Sisters

The beginnings of this momentous movement were surprisingly humble; it began in a small cabin in the little town of Hydesville, New York. Situated upstate, Hydesville was part of the "burnt-over" district—so called because of the numerous religious revivals that had swept through it. Here the Church of Jesus Christ of Latter-day Saints (Mormons) originated in 1830; the religious fervor also gave birth to the Millerites, who predicted the Second Coming would occur in 1843 or 1844. Had that prediction been fulfilled, presumably the need to make contact with the unseen world of spirits would have been obviated. In any event, on the night of March 31, 1848, the Fox family of Hydesville was disturbed by strange rapping noises. The two young daughters in one bed, and their parents in another in the same room, had gotten little sleep for several nights because of the bumping and rapping, but this night was different.

Margaret and Catherine (Kate) Fox, the daughters of John and Margaret Fox, responded to the noises by calling out, "Do as I do." Rapping once, they heard one rap in reply; two raps elicited two raps. After working out a simple yes-no code with their unseen visitor or presence, the girls, along with their mother, proceeded with an interrogation. They thus became acquainted with the spirit or ghost of a peddler who had been murdered years before the Foxes had moved into the house and whose body, he said, was buried in the cellar. Although his story was gruesome, the spirit meant the family no harm; indeed, he seemed quite friendly.

Soon thereafter, Mrs. Fox called in many of her neighbors to confirm the spirit's presence and his truthfulness. Responding with the correct number of taps, he answered such questions as "How old am I?" or "How many children do I have?" Most witnesses were astonished. Not long thereafter, the Fox daughters and their mother traveled to Rochester, New York, to visit the girls' married sister Leah, who was nearly thirty years older than Catherine. Surprisingly, the ghost made his presence felt there as well. Before long, people from neighboring communities were coming to see this communication between the living and the dead. Apparently, the two girls were *mediums;* that is, intermediaries between living persons and spirits of the dead. As their fame grew, the sisters, now accompanied by Leah, traveled from city to city, charging admission for their demonstrations. They made as much as $150 a night, a handsome sum for the time.

Soon other people discovered that they, too, were able to hear and respond to rappings from beyond, and within three or four years, the rappings and tappings of the dead were heard throughout the East Coast, in the Midwest, and even in England. The Spiritualist movement was underway. The oldest Fox sister, Leah, founded the first Spiritualist society and did much to stimulate Spiritualism's early growth.

Predictably, skeptics suggested that the sisters were staging an elaborate hoax, and so the girls were tested by professors, physicians, and other interested and supposedly qualified individuals. Instead of deciding the issue, these tests provoked fresh interest and controversy. Some examiners concluded the noises were genuine intrusions from an unseen realm. Others, conjecturing that the noises came from the popping of joints underneath long dresses, made the girls fully extend their legs and place their feet upon pillows (thus making it difficult to pop joints). Sometimes the doctors also held the girls' knees. In both cases, no raps were heard. But no wonder, some Spiritualists replied, the spirits were obviously offended by such rude treatment of their friends.

It was not until forty years later, in 1888, that Margaret Fox confessed that the rapping had been a deception. This was soon corroborated by her sister Kate, who said, "Spiritualism is a humbug from beginning to end. It is the greatest humbug of the century."[13] What had begun as the girls' prank on their mother quickly drew in neighbors and then paying strangers. Afraid of being found out and basking in their newfound fame, the sisters had discovered various ways of making noises, including using the joints of their toes, ankles, knees, and fingers. So engaged, they would (like a ventriloquist) divert their audience by looking off in a particular direction: it seemed as if the noises were coming from an unoccupied location.

Margaret and Kate alleged that their older sister Leah had quickly discovered their deception but had urged them on as their fame grew and opportunities for tours and demonstrations mounted. They made this claim or confession, however, after they found themselves marginalized by the very movement they had fostered. Unprepared for the rapid growth of Spiritualism and unable to direct its course, they were pushed aside by other figures. (Leah, by contrast, was still comfortably ensconced in the leadership of the movement, and she denied her sisters' allegations.) Financially strapped, the middle-aged Margaret

SPIRITS, SCIENCE, AND PSEUDO-SCIENCE

and Kate went on tour divulging their erstwhile "spiritual" tricks, but these exhibitions were poorly attended; Spiritualism exposed was less interesting than Spiritualism. Finally, Margaret became a medium again, and many Spiritualists, overlooking her defection, welcomed her back. She and Kate died as alcoholics in the 1890s.

This wrangling and admission of past deceit did little to dissuade believers. Most simply ignored it, for the spirits had long since moved beyond simple rappings to far more spectacular actions. They now turned and tilted tables, tooted horns, and rang bells. And that was just the beginning.

Séances: The "Laboratories" of Spiritualism

By claiming access to unseen powers, Spiritualism held forth many of the same opportunities as mesmerism and phrenology. It is not surprising, then, that, in the decade after its birth, scores of mesmerist "sensitives" became "mediums" almost overnight. It was simply a matter of catching the larger wave of Spiritualism, for many somnambulists were already communing with the dead in their hypnotic trances. Thus emerged the paradigmatic image of a medium: self-entranced, speaking for departed souls or higher intelligences, mediating or "channeling" information from beyond. One such sensitive-turned-medium was Andrew Jackson Davis, best remembered for his description of "Summerland," the beautiful abode of the spiritual realm. Davis also communicated the spirits' demand that mortals do more to help the poor. (The spirits, both then and now, always seem to be in the avant-garde of social, political, and environmental causes.)

Why did Davis's revelations and Spiritualism in general find an enthusiastic following? One reason is that a spiritual void had opened up in the eighteenth and nineteenth centuries as orthodox Christianity's truth claims were eroded by historical criticism, philosophy, and science. Many consequently left organized Christianity, believing it to be either untenable or overly conservative. Furthermore, Spiritualism required no statement of faith or catechism, so one could retain core Christian beliefs while pursuing the novel and uniquely Spiritualist opportunity of communicating with the dead. Another reason for Spiritualism's success lay in its ability to mesh with science; purportedly, it offered physical proof of a spiritual world. To find this proof, one need only attend a séance.

Fully developed, séances were the "laboratories" of Spiritualism—places for scientific fact-finding about the realm of spirits. Initially, they were faddish, fun-but-spooky occasions during which friends gathered in dark rooms to solicit spirits, who then would manifest their presence by rapping and table-tilting. (Today the Ouija board affords this outlet.) Soon, however, séances became more formal and elaborate, particularly among professional mediums.

MAGIC, MYSTERY, AND SCIENCE

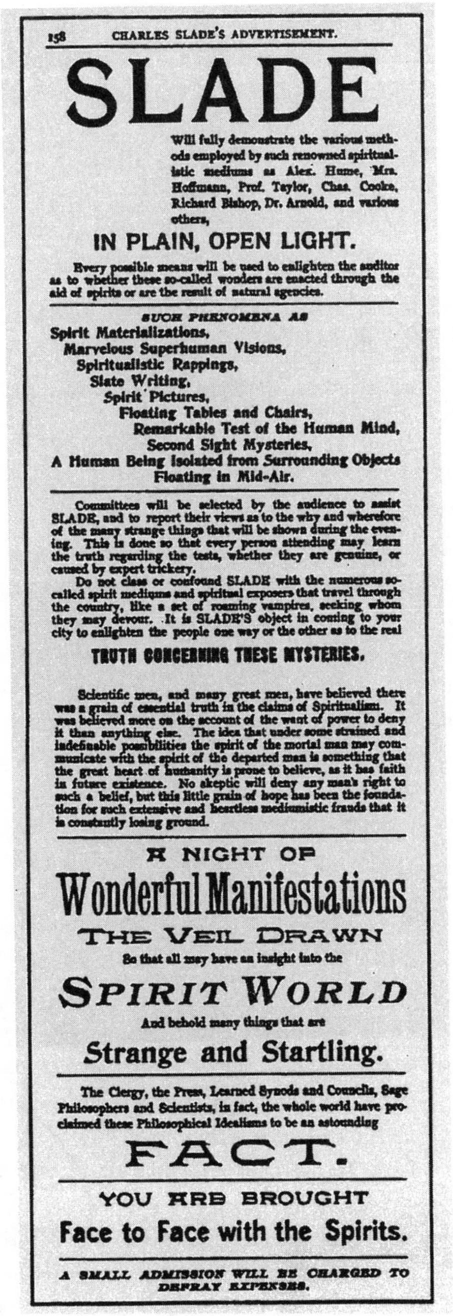

SLADE

Will fully demonstrate the various methods employed by such renowned spiritualistic mediums as Alex. Hume, Mrs. Hoffmann, Prof. Taylor, Chas. Cooke, Richard Bishop, Dr. Arnold, and various others,

IN PLAIN, OPEN LIGHT.

Every possible means will be used to enlighten the auditor as to whether these so-called wonders are enacted through the aid of spirits or are the result of natural agencies.

SUCH PHENOMENA AS

Spirit Materializations,
Marvelous Superhuman Visions,
Spiritualistic Rappings,
Slate Writing,
Spirit Pictures,
Floating Tables and Chairs,
Remarkable Test of the Human Mind,
Second Sight Mysteries,
A Human Being Isolated from Surrounding Objects
Floating in Mid-Air.

Committees will be selected by the audience to assist SLADE, and to report their views as to the why and wherefore of the many strange things that will be shown during the evening. This is done so that every person attending may learn the truth regarding the tests, whether they are genuine, or caused by expert trickery.

Do not class or confound SLADE with the numerous so-called spirit mediums and spiritual exposers that travel through the country, like a set of roaming vampires, seeking whom they may devour. It is SLADE'S object in coming to your city to enlighten the people one way or the other as to the real

TRUTH CONCERNING THESE MYSTERIES.

Scientific men, and many great men, have believed there was a grain of essential truth in the claims of Spiritualism. It was believed more on the account of the want of power to deny it than anything else. The idea that under some strained and indefinable possibilities the spirit of the mortal man may communicate with the spirit of the departed men is something that the great heart of humanity is prone to believe, as it has faith in future existence. No skeptic will deny any man's right to such a belief, but this little grain of hope has been the foundation for such extensive and heartless mediumistic frauds that it is constantly losing ground.

A NIGHT OF

Wonderful Manifestations

THE VEIL DRAWN

So that all may have an insight into the

SPIRIT WORLD

And behold many things that are

Strange and Startling.

The Clergy, the Press, Learned Synods and Councils, Sage Philosophers and Scientists, in fact, the whole world have proclaimed these Philosophical Idealisms to be an astounding

FACT.

YOU ARE BROUGHT

Face to Face with the Spirits.

A SMALL ADMISSION WILL BE CHARGED TO DEFRAY EXPENSES.

Figure 31. A nineteenth-century advertisement for a séance

SPIRITS, SCIENCE, AND PSEUDO-SCIENCE

These individuals, apparently gifted with unusual powers, commanded respect by reason of their singular rapport with the dead. Hence, they were the "stars" of the séance, and generally the session was held at their homes.

At a séance, the medium sat at the head of the table while others joined in by linking hands. The room was kept almost completely dark, as the spirits were said to shy away from lights and the direct gaze of mortal beings. Once, however, they felt comfortable enough to make an entry, they were free to express their presence in several ways. They might speak out, make noises, materialize as a ghostly form, or levitate the medium. Or they might communicate verbally by giving oral or written messages through the medium, who would be in trance. Mediums who relayed messages in this fashion were called trance (or mental) mediums, while those whose séances were characterized by the physical effects of a spirit's presence were called physical mediums.

To safeguard against trickery, those seated on either side of a physical medium would not only hold her hands but also often use their feet to control her feet. Sometimes the medium even allowed others to tie her to her chair. The suspicion was that she might, under the cover of darkness, surreptitiously move about and produce ghostly effects. Since things often got quite animated during the séance, with the medium receiving sharp bursts of spiritual energy from time to time, it was important that her movements be controlled, particularly if a séance cabinet was nearby. The cabinet, generally standing behind the medium's chair but obscured by a curtain, was filled with banjos, trumpets, bells, writing slates, and various other items, all meant to facilitate spirit communication. Such paraphernalia are suggestive of what might unfold during a séance: participants reported trumpets sounding, bodies floating through the air (the heels thereof brushing past observers' foreheads), tables jumping about erratically, and deceased relatives materializing before one's eyes!

After participating in a séance involving three mediums, Sir William Crookes reported that:

> We were arranged round the table in such a way that each medium was held by a trustworthy person and the rule was *very rigidly* enforced that all hands had to be held during the darkness. . . . At first we had very rough manifestations, chairs knocked about, the table floated about 6 inches from the ground and then dashed down, loud and unpleasant noises bawling in our ears and altogether phenomena of a low class. After a time it was suggested that we should sing, and as the only thing known to all the company, we struck up "For he's a jolly good fellow." The chairs, table, and thing on it kept up a sort of anvil accompaniment to this. After that D.D. Home [one of the mediums] gave us a solo—rather a sacred piece—and almost before a

dozen words were uttered Mr. Herne [another medium] was carried right up, floated across the table and dropped with a crash of pictures and ornaments at the other end of the room. . . . Home's singing appeared to drive away the low-class influences and institute his own good ones. After a minute or two I suggested that we should all sing again, and proposed the song first sung, "For he's a jolly good fellow." Immediately a very sweet voice, high over our heads quite out of reach of anyone present even had they been standing, and as clear as a bell, said, "You should rather give praise to God." After that we were in no mood for comic songs. We tried something sacred, and as we sung we heard other voices joining in over our heads.

Crookes goes on to report other phenomena: an accordion flying swiftly about the room and playing "one of the most exquisite sacred pieces I ever heard"; sweet voices whispering in the participants' ears; a little illuminated hand bell floating about; and lights darting about. Then, as "the power increased," spiritual hands began to stroke the participants' faces and move objects about. One participant managed to grab one of the hands as it was removing a book from his pocket, but, says Crookes, it "was *only a hand,* there being no arm or body attached to it, and it eluded his grasp [jerked free] and carried the book right across the table."[14]

Crookes, a man of science, concludes his report by stating that "it is impossible to describe to you all the striking things that took place, or to convey the intense feeling of genuineness and reality which it caused in our minds." Both small and great, illiterate and intellectual, were impressed by the séances. But it was not the spectacular spiritual effects that drew many to the sessions; it was spiritual hope. While other religions spoke vaguely of reunion with departed loved ones in the indefinite future, Spiritualism affirmed reunion as actual, present fact. This helps explain its immense appeal and the desperation with which many believers, even in the face of fraud, continued to cling to it. One glimpse, however tenuous, of a deceased friend or family member, often sufficed to negate the prospect of eternal oblivion.

Even for—perhaps, especially for—those attuned to the agnostic nuances of scientific materialism. Spiritualism's most ardent supporters frequently came from the upper classes and the intelligentsia, and many of these were scientists. The famed biologist, Alfred Russell Wallace, who played an important role in Charles Darwin's public announcement of his evolutionary theory, was so taken with Spiritualism that he once allowed himself to be duped by an amateur magician pretending to be a medium. Well-known physicists who similarly championed Spiritualism included Oliver Lodge, remembered for his work on radio waves, and William Crookes (author of the description just offered), who

SPIRITS, SCIENCE, AND PSEUDO-SCIENCE

discovered the element thalium and whose invention of the Crookes tube set the stage for the discovery of the electron and X-rays. All these were scientific advances, but for many they possessed a spiritual luster not at odds with the tenets of Spiritualism. X-rays, Becquerel rays (radioactivity), and other, newly hailed forms of radiation (some of which proved to be spurious) seemed to corroborate the existence of an unseen world of spirits.

Of course, many other famous individuals believed in Spiritualism, the English poet Elizabeth Barrett Browning and the French writer Victor Hugo among them. (Hugo insisted that he communicated not only with his deceased daughter but also with Dante, Shakespeare, Jesus, and doves from Noah's ark.) Also of interest are the conversions to Spiritualism of the American social reformers, Robert Owen and his son Robert Dale Owen. Both father and son had been free-thinkers and agnostics, and both were more interested in the here and now than the hereafter, as is evidenced by their roles in founding the utopian society of New Harmony, Indiana. Yet the father converted to Spiritualism at the age of eighty-two, and the son followed suit a few years later.

With so much interest in Spiritualism, perhaps it was inevitable that an organization should arise to critically assess its claims. In 1882, several English scholars founded the Society for Psychical Research (SPR) with the intent of conducting scientific studies of hallucinations, ghosts, ESP, hauntings, dowsing, communication with spirits, and other unusual phenomena. Three years later, the American Society for Psychical Research (ASPR) sprang up on the other side of the Atlantic with a similar purpose. Among the mediums investigated by these organizations were Eusapia Palladino and Margery Crandon, whom we will spotlight. Among those investigating and investing faith in Spiritualism were Arthur Conan Doyle and Harry Houdini, two famous figures at the turn of the century whose friendship was shattered by contentions within the movement. These two individuals also figure into our story.

Eusapia Palladino

The reader has probably noted by now our tendency to characterize Spiritualist mediums as women. This is because most were women. The Fox sisters, of course, were the first mediums, and that no doubt established an initial template. We also should observe that mediumship came with certain social rewards (at least within a select community) not normally available to nineteenth-century women.[15] In a time when women were allowed almost no say in politics or religion and their employment opportunities were severely limited, mediumship must have seemed extremely appealing to some. How better to earn one's own living, and without having to rely on men? Not only that, but as an important spiritual figure, the woman medium could promote various religious, political, and social changes with impunity. After all, she was

Figure 32. One of Eusapia Palladino's levitating tables

merely relaying wisdom from the Great Beyond. Given this freedom to speak out, it is not surprising that some women mediums were harbingers of such concepts as female suffrage, the rights of the poor, birth control, and free love.

Although not an outspoken advocate of social change, Eusapia Palladino (1854–1918) nevertheless broke the mold as a woman. She is remembered as one of the most gifted physical mediums of the nineteenth century. Born in southern Italy, she got off to a most unfortunate start in life: her mother died giving her birth, her father was murdered, and she grew up uneducated and illiterate. Notwithstanding these setbacks, Palladino developed into an athletic, vivacious, attractive, and (to some) erotic adolescent. At the age of thirteen, she took a job as a servant for a family involved in Spiritualism. When she was invited to sit in on one of the family's séances, remarkable phenomena occurred, and she was hailed as a medium among the local denizens.

SPIRITS, SCIENCE, AND PSEUDO-SCIENCE

Greater fame came years later when Cesare Lombroso, an Italian scientist and criminologist, took an interest in her. At the time, Palladino was working as a full-time medium in Naples. While participating in her séances, Lombroso became convinced of her powers and introduced her to a wider audience. Soon she was tested by many scientific societies throughout Europe. Although everyone was impressed, opinions differed over whether the observed effects were real or very cleverly contrived.

Palladino's séances were conducted in the aforementioned manner—in near darkness and with a curtained cabinet behind her chair. She usually allowed gentlemen on either side of her to control her hands and feet. This was no easy task, for when Eusapia's spirit guide, "John King," would come, she would go into wild gyrations, her hands, feet, and body flailing all about. The men tried desperately to control her movements while simultaneously attempting to observe corollary spirit phenomena. Inevitably, the experience was complicated by the question of what constituted proper behavior under such circumstances. What measures should a man, in the name of science, take while attempting to control an explosively active woman? No doubt both parties shared an approximate understanding of where good behavior left off and indecency began, but only Palladino was in a position to turn decorum to her advantage. In any case, once she got started, tables would fly up into the air, the curtain covering the cabinet would billow out, spirit hands would pinch participants' faces or arms, and spirit kisses would be given through nearby curtains.

The SPR finally decided to test Palladino and invited her to Cambridge, England. Sitting in on several of her séances, SPR members detected many tricks but could not explain every unusual occurrence. Afterward, Palladino freely admitted that she was not above occasional duplicity. She liked to toy with skeptical investigators and entertain séance sitters when spirits refused to come. Her supporters chimed in by saying that while she often resorted to trickery, she also sometimes produced effects that were truly supernatural.

In 1909, Palladino moved to the United States and, while plying her trade, submitted to tests at Columbia University. There in the scientific laboratories she came under the scrutiny of physicists, psychologists, and magicians. A psychologist at one séance reported assorted tugs, pinches, and touches to his body; then a table three feet behind Eusapia began to move. Suddenly there was a blood-curdling scream, said the psychologist, as if someone had been stabbed. As it turned out, the shriek was not planned. An observer concealed in the cabinet, and told to watch for strings and the like, had grabbed Palladino's foot when he saw it reaching back toward the table—and then she screamed. Magicians seated under the table later reported that Palladino, unbeknownst to others, had slipped her foot out of her shoe and used the free foot to pinch arms, strum instruments in the cabinet, cause the curtain to billow

MAGIC, MYSTERY, AND SCIENCE

out, and even throw tables in the air. Apparently she had unusually strong and limber legs. She also had a way of making sitters on her left and right believe they were holding separate hands when in fact they were holding the same hand; she had worked a hand free to make mischief. Despite these revelations of deceit, Palladino (and many of her supporters) continued to insist that not everything about her séances could be explained away as fraud.

Surpassing even Palladino as a master of strange effects was Daniel Dunglas Home (1831–1886), one of the mediums mentioned above in Crookes's narrative. His celebrated feats included bathing his face in hot coals, elongating his body, and making pianos, tables, and his own body float through the air. According to one report, he levitated out one third-story window and back in through another. What's more, no one ever detected trickery of any sort. Home is perhaps the only physical medium whose record is unblemished by scientific exposé, although we should note that he was not tested as rigorously as Palladino. Nor was he scrutinized by Harry Houdini, who sought to cleanse Spiritualism of all impostors.

Sir Arthur Conan Doyle and Harry Houdini

When Home died, Houdini was only twelve years old and had yet to make his mark. He would soon do so as a brilliant magician (although not of the Renaissance variety) and his fame brought him into contact with Arthur Conan Doyle. It is hard to think of two people more physically and socially mismatched. Doyle was a tall, imposing, well-bred Englishman, a highly educated physician, and a talented writer. Houdini, born of Hungarian parents, was short, stocky, and self-educated. These differences notwithstanding, the two men became fast friends for many years and professed the highest respect for one another. Both were deeply interested in Spiritualism, but they struggled to harmonize their dissimilar views of it.

On matters of Spiritualism, Doyle contrasted sharply with his fictional protagonist Sherlock Holmes, who employed cold logic to the exclusion of all else. Real life, evidently, is more complex than detective work. The bright, affable Doyle was easily duped by bogus mediums, a fact readily admitted by his Spiritualist friends. One of the most outspoken and visible missionaries of Spiritualism, Doyle donated much of his own fortune to further its cause. He also spent his last fourteen years lecturing and writing books (thirteen in all) on the subject. He often said he hoped posterity would remember him for his Spiritualist work, not for Sherlock Holmes. Holmes personifies, in an interesting and slightly amusing way, the archetypal scientific investigator, while Spiritualism comes off as a preserve for woolly-mindedness and charlatanism. Doyle would be disappointed.

Houdini was perhaps the greatest magician and escape artist of all time.

SPIRITS, SCIENCE, AND PSEUDO-SCIENCE

Early in his career, while still relatively unknown, he sometimes pretended to be a medium and used his magic to trick others. All that changed when his mother died. Unconsoled at her passing and desperate for renewed contact, Houdini turned to Spiritualism. He traveled extensively, seeking out mediums able to call forth his mother's spirit. Initially hopeful and believing, he discovered to his sorrow that séances were more pretense than substance. He himself, after all, had once played the game that he now grew to detest. It is often said that Houdini was anti-Spiritualist and anti-mediumist, but this is not quite true. He truly believed in the possibility of contacting the dead—he yearned for it—but woe to the medium who tried to trick him, especially concerning his mother. He became the bane of mediums across the country, for if they were impostors, he felt it his duty to expose them.

Doyle objected to Houdini's treatment of alleged fakes, feeling that the success of a séance hinged in part on the faith invested in it by participants. One consequently should come to the experience believing that "I am in the presence of a new revelation from the Great Beyond; I must approach it in a spirit of reverence and prayer."[16] Doyle advised Houdini that Spiritualism should "be approached not in the spirit of a detective approaching a suspect, but in that of a humble, religious soul, yearning for help and comfort."[17] Doyle even insisted that this principle helped explain Houdini's success as a magician—it was belief in a higher power that enabled Houdini to pull off as his brilliant escapes after being buried alive in locked cases underwater. Houdini's magic, in other words, had a spiritual basis. Houdini countered that he relied only on his own skill and cunning. He did not, nor did he pretend to, call upon spiritual forces to accomplish his feats.

Eventually the warm friendship between the two men cooled. During the summer of 1922, the Houdinis gladly accepted the Doyles' invitation to vacation with them in Atlantic City, New Jersey. One day, Sir Arthur invited Harry to participate in a séance with Doyle's wife, who believed she might be able to contact Houdini's mother. Houdini agreed to sit for the séance, doing his best to put aside his skepticism, both for friendship's sake and because he hoped to communicate with his mother. After Doyle opened the séance with prayer, his wife's arms began to shake uncontrollably and bang on the table. Taking a pencil in her violently trembling hand, she proceeded to receive automatic writing from the spirit world. Page after page was placed under the pencil, and soon it dawned on the participants that these scrawlings were meant to be a letter from Houdini's mother. The fifteen-page message, which began with a cross at the top and which was written in English, expressed all that he might hope for: a mother's love for her son and the promise that she would ever be with him.[18]

Houdini said little, not wanting to offend, but inwardly he was not con-

MAGIC, MYSTERY, AND SCIENCE

vinced. First of all, his mother could not read, write, or speak English. And, being Jewish, she would not have drawn a cross at the top of the letter. Houdini, trusting in the Doyles' sincerity, suggested that Lady Doyle had produced the letter from her subconscious mind.[19] Sir Arthur was incensed and censured Houdini for ingratitude and bad faith. The friendship deteriorated, and the two men staked out opposing positions on the question of Spiritualism, Houdini attacking and Doyle defending. Both would become involved in determining the merits of Margery Crandon, the last great physical medium.

Margery Crandon

Mina Stinson Crandon (1889–1941), who took the pseudonym Margery, was the best—and the most controversial—American physical medium. Married to a distinguished Boston surgeon, she was beautiful, educated, and refined. No doubt these assets figured into her success, for she was far better than Eusapia Palladino at winning the sympathies of her sophisticated investigators. In her trances, Margery's deceased brother Walter allegedly assumed the role as spirit guide. Walter was very different from the medium; his gruff voice and coarse language would make a decent girl blush. This incongruity alone convinced some investigators.

The Crandons controlled the conditions of Margery's séances, which were held in their home and in complete darkness. For the most part, the sessions entailed the same spiritualistic effects that Eusapia Palladino had produced, but Margery went one step further. She, with the help of Walter, produced ectoplasm, a material that issues from the medium's orifices—the ears, mouth, nose, navel, and between the legs. As its name suggests, ectoplasm is purportedly a living substance, and mediums who produced it claimed that it allows spirits (who, after all, are nonphysical) to be seen and to move objects. No doubt the sight of it flowing from a medium's body provoked wonder, but mediums begged sitters not to touch or examine it closely. Having originated from the medium, it was part of her life force, and any untoward action against it might cause the medium to sicken or even die. In the many photographs of ectoplasm, including those of Margery's, the substance looks much like chewed-up cheesecloth. (Some have hinted that that is exactly what it was.)

In the 1920s, the journal *Scientific American* offered $2,500 to any medium able to convince its committee of experts that communication with the dead was possible. Arthur Conan Doyle brought Crandon to the attention of the secretary of the committee, J. Malcolm Bird, who was so persuaded (some say "smitten") by her that he became her most loyal supporter. The committee, which included an MIT physicist and a Harvard psychologist, investigated Crandon and soon were impressed by her abilities. One committee member, Harry Houdini, had not been notified of the investigation, however. When

SPIRITS, SCIENCE, AND PSEUDO-SCIENCE

Houdini read Bird's report in the newspaper stating that even Houdini himself was at a loss to explain Crandon's feats, he furiously canceled his engagements and joined the investigation.

In the first few séances, Houdini suspected fraud but could not produce hard evidence. Later, he built a large box for Margery to sit in. Looking rather like a sauna box, it had only three holes to the outside, one for the medium's head and two for her hands. After a sharp exchange between Houdini and Dr. Crandon, Margery agreed to sit in the box while conducting séances. Walter's physical manifestations ceased, but his verbal presence was much in evidence. At one point, he accused Houdini of planting an expandable ruler in the box that Margery sat in. Why? To frame her; once found, the ruler could be explained as part of Margery's attempt to manipulate her environment. Walter became abusive, shouting "Houdini, you Goddamned son [of] a bitch, get the hell out of here and never come back. If you don't, I will."[20] When the box was opened, a ruler was found. Both parties denied putting it there, and this imbroglio soon brought the séances to an end. The committee's final decision was that Margery had not proven her case (four votes against, one for).

Nevertheless, Crandon continued to attract attention, thanks in part to Doyle. After hearing Doyle deliver a stirring address on mediums, J. B. Rhine, the famous parapsychologist, and his wife traveled to Boston to sit in on one of her séances.[21] Rhine was shocked at what he deemed fraudulent behavior on Margery's part and wrote an article saying that she was probably an impostor.[22] Doyle was so angered by the article that he ran a reply in a Boston newspaper. The black-bordered announcement simply said, "J. B. Rhine is a Monumental Ass!"[23]

In 1926, Margery outdid herself. Walter declared that if he were given hot wax during a séance, he would return it with his thumbprint impressed upon it. Sure enough, when the request was granted, a thumbprint was produced. Opponents of the Crandons conjectured that the print belonged to one of the couple's inner circle. Meeting this charge head on, Dr. Crandon employed E. E. Dudley to take fingerprints of all their associates. No matches were found. Dudley, an admirer of the Crandons, continued this work off and on until, six years later, he discovered Walter's thumbprint exactly matched that of the Crandons' dentist. Although Margery had been caught in an obvious falsehood, like Eusapia Palladino, she did not fall into immediate disrepute. Infallibility was not one of her claims, and perfection is an unfair expectation of anyone. Her merits as a medium are debated to this day.

Leonora Piper

Gradually, physical mediums gave way to trance or mental mediums (although with some notable exceptions, such as Margery Crandon, a relative latecomer among physical mediums). Possibly the shift was defensive in nature: the feats of physical mediums readily lent themselves to scientific scrutiny; trance mediums, by contrast, offered less physical evidence of their abilities— no flying tables, floating bodies, ectoplasm, or thumbprints. In trance mediumship, the spirit takes control of the medium and hence is called the "control." Information from the spirit world is then channeled through the medium to séance participants. (Often physical mediums had controls, too, such as John King and Walter, but these sought to prove their existence by physical feats.)

One of the most famous trance mediums was an American, Leonora Piper.[24] In 1886, she came to the attention of the Harvard psychologist and philosopher, William James, who, along with Richard Hodgson, the secretary of the ASPR, investigated Piper for many years. During her séances, Piper seemed to take on other personalities and to know things beyond her waking ken, things that only the control might be expected to know. One of her controls was "G.P.," thought to be George Pellew, a young English friend of Hodgson's who had suffered a sudden and untimely death. With G.P. as control, Piper provided information that seemingly would have been privy only to Pellew, such as the identification of thirty friends out of a crowd of 150 strangers and the whereabouts of a tin box containing some of Pellew's private papers. This so impressed Hodgson that he announced his conversion to Spiritualism.

Not all were persuaded, however. Pellew's living relatives said that Piper's information was mere drivel. In the family's sittings with her, she could answer the easily guessed queries, but when it came to deeply personal questions involving family matters, she often gave the wrong answer or no answer at all. She and her supporters, however, could chalk up misinformation to garbled communications; even in daily conversation, misunderstandings occur. Moreover, Piper had other controls, including Julius Caesar and a French physician, "Dr. Phinuit," who curiously knew very little French and even less medicine. In 1905, some of Piper's controls prophesied that Hodgson had a long life ahead of him and that he would marry and have two children. A few months later, he was dead. She lived on into her nineties, and, like other mediums, grounded her claim of authenticity not to an unbroken string of flawless performances but to having beaten the law of averages over the long haul. In a colorful world that often fails to reduce to black-and-white certitudes, Piper and her like will always be able to find a niche.

SPIRITS, SCIENCE, AND PSEUDO-SCIENCE

9 NEW AGE PRELUDES: UP THE GARDEN PATH?

These truths of ancient novelties, of new worlds, new stars, new systems etc. . . . are the beginning of a new age.

—*Thomas Campanella, 1632,*
responding to the publication
of Galileo's Dialogue on the Two
Great World Systems[1]

The relativity principle in connection with the Maxwell equations demands that the mass is a direct measure for the energy contained in the bodies: light transfers mass. A remarkable decrease of the mass must result in radium. This thought is amusing and infectious, but I cannot possibly know whether the good Lord does not laugh at it and has led me up the garden path.

—*Albert Einstein*[2]

What passes for New Age today is old in two senses. First, it is purportedly the sublime wisdom of ancient cultures and brotherhoods—wisdom much dimmed and distorted by intervening centuries and therefore in need of rebirth.

Second, its modern provenance is not as recent as many suppose, for the New Age synthesis occurred in the late nineteenth and early twentieth centuries. In addition to Western occult themes already mentioned in this book, that synthesis incorporates elements of modern science and Asian thought. To a significant degree, the spiritual center of gravity shifts eastward, particularly toward India and Tibet. For many Westerners, these countries are religiously exotic, and their technological backwardness and outward poverty suggest compensatory inner powers and sacred treasures.

If one person were to be singled out as the herald of New Age thinking, it would be Madame Blavatsky (1831–1891), who claimed to see the vast expanse of the past through the eyes of her spiritual masters. Blavatsky is so controversial that however she is described, some believer or disbeliever will disagree. Well, almost. All would agree she was a mysterious, charismatic person with a penchant for offbeat experiences and eclectic, universal explanations. Past that, everyone's footing is a little unsure. (She would have liked it that way, having revised her life story several times.) Madame Helena Petrovna Blavatsky, or HPB as she liked to be called, is best remembered as the cofounder and leading spirit of the Theosophical Society. This organization was formed to bring about the brotherhood of all peoples, to study the mysterious powers of humanity and nature, and to heed the teachings of the Ascended Masters or Mahatmas—quasi-spiritual beings living on a higher evolutionary plane than our own.

Because HPB's writings are voluminous and broadly eclectic, any summary of her thinking can just skim the surface. In brief, she concocted a heady brew of Western occult thought, Eastern religion, and the science of her day, being careful to stigmatize Christianity as an enemy of truth. From the occult, she affirmed aspects of Spiritualism, the Cabala, and Renaissance Magic, while attributing mystic views to the Egyptians, the Pythagoreans, Plato, and Paracelsus. From science, she borrowed *au courant* terminology and developed a goal-oriented evolutionary theory. And, from India and the East, she introduced (or re-introduced) to the West such concepts as reincarnation and karma. Her goal was to fuse aspects of Eastern and Western thought into a single worldview.

HPB'S INCREDIBLE LIFE

There was always something intriguing about this hefty, chain-smoking woman. Perhaps it was her mesmerizing eyes; even in her photographs, they still seem to hypnotize. HPB was born as Helena Petrovna Hahn in the Ukraine to aristocratic parents: her mother was a princess and novelist, her father a captain of horse artillery. At the age of sixteen, Helena married a Russian governor named Blavatsky. Within a few months, she had left him,

Figure 33. Madame Blavatsky

but kept his name. For the next twenty-five years, the record is unclear, so what follows is a sampling of what some of her biographers say. For a time, HPB worked as a circus bareback rider in Constantinople. Later, she taught piano lessons in London and Paris; at one point she was an entrepreneur of ostrich feathers. In Egypt, she became a medium, smoked marijuana and hashish, and, according to some, took lessons in snake handling. She also traveled about Europe as the lover of an opera singer. In the course of her travels, she became acquainted with Daniel Dunglas Home, and said that he converted her to Spiritualism.[3]

If her own conflicting accounts can be trusted, Madame Blavatsky journeyed around the globe—visiting Mexico, Canada, Egypt, and inner Asia, among other places—in order to learn from sages and gurus. Her ultimate objective was to reach Tibet to undergo initiations with her Masters, the Mahatmas, who had been guiding her every step of the way. She said she realized this goal and stayed in Tibet for several years. Or, since her chronologies do not leave room for this, she traveled in her astral body to Tibet almost every night for several years.[4] This, at least, was the thinking of some of her disciples.

When she traveled to the United States in 1874, she arrived as a medium, with her spirit guide, "John King" (who seems also to have worked with Eusapia Palladino). But with increasing frequency she spoke of the god-like beings—the Mahatmas—who had instructed her in Tibet and who wished her to be their messenger. While promoting their cause, she met Colonel Henry Steele Olcott, an American with a keen interest in the supernatural, at a home that had been recently favored with spiritual phenomena and was consequently attracting much public interest. Olcott, who was there as a journalist, reported that, among the visitors, there was "a stout and remarkable looking woman, wearing a perky hat with plumes, a *grande toilette* satin dress with much trimming, a long heavy golden chain attached to a blue enamelled watch with a monogram . . . in cheap diamonds, and on her lovely hands, a dozen or 15 rings."[5]

The two developed a somewhat conflicted friendship that led to the founding of the Theosophical Society in 1875. Not wanting to be confused with Spiritualists, Theosophists insisted that their goals were very different. While the former often communed with the dead on trivial matters, Theosophists sought to recover the exalted wisdom of the ancients.

Under the direct guidance of her Masters, HPB spent the next two years writing a massive book—*Isis Unveiled* (1877)—detailing that wisdom. Long ago, she claimed, a single universal religion informed and encompassed all human culture. This religion, known to both Plato and the Hindus, was far more comprehensive than any religion today, for it blended religion, science, wisdom, and power into a seamless whole.[6] Thus, all contemporary religions,

NEW AGE PRELUDES

along with modern science, are merely derivatives of this one, original truth—the "secret doctrine."

Her second major work, *The Secret Doctrine* (1888), continued the saga, but in a slightly different way. While the earlier work had relied more on Western thought as it pertained to religion and the occult (witness the Egyptian goddess *Isis* in the title), *The Secret Doctrine* was decidedly Eastern in its provenance and outlook. This is not surprising, for in the intervening years, Blavatsky had taken up residence in India. The relocation was in keeping with her interest in all things oriental, but it seems also to have been precipitated by her falling out with Daniel Dunglas Home, who then wrote a book characterizing HPB as a charlatan and the Colonel as her dupe. HPB felt that the book had "destroyed her in Europe—as it did in America."[7] The setback, however, was opportune, for the two Theosophists wanted to go to India to draw closer to their sources of ancient wisdom.

Once on the subcontinent, they set up the headquarters of the Theosophical Society at Adyar, near Madras, India. Owing to their reverence for Eastern religion, Blavatsky and Olcott played an important role in revitalizing and promoting India's indigenous culture. They made friends everywhere and stirred up nationalist pride in their newly adopted country, both because of their anti-British attitude and their fascination with native texts and customs. It was there as well that *The Secret Doctrine* came to completion, whereby, as HPB put it, all religious, scientific, and philosophical truths were "made to merge back into their original element."[8]

THE KUT HUMI LETTERS

The move to India brought Madame Blavatsky nearer to Tibet and, not surprisingly, upped the spiritual wattage of her communion with the Ascended Masters. Miracles became commonplace: a teacup might suddenly appear or even a Master himself, heralded by the tinkling of mysterious "astral bells." Most impressive of all were the letters sent by Kut Humi, one of the two special Masters in constant contact with HPB. These letters would sometimes materialize out of thin air and drop onto the table, or sometimes they would materialize within a sacred shrine in Blavatsky's sitting room. Among other things, they carried messages aimed at persuading prominent Englishmen in India to help the Theosophical Society.

In 1884, HPB and Olcott returned to Europe in triumph; many were fascinated by these two figures bearing wisdom from the East. When they arrived in England, the Society for Psychical Research (SPR) asked if they could test HPB's spiritual abilities. She agreed at once. The Colonel spoke to them about

MAGIC, MYSTERY, AND SCIENCE

astral travel and related matters, further ratcheting up interest in Blavatsky. Then defamatory, even devastating, news reached them from abroad.

Back in India, Emma Coulomb and her husband, Alexis, had been left in charge of Blavatsky's quarters. Mrs. Coulomb, an old friend and employee of HPB in the Society, had gotten into a dispute with other members there and was subsequently expelled from the headquarters at Adyar. In retaliation, she published several highly revealing letters that she claimed Blavatsky had written to her and her husband, which exposed HPB's "miracles" as frauds. In one letter, Blavatsky instructed Mr. Coulomb to make a dummy suit to wear outside the house in the moonlight; upon seeing the strange apparition, visitors from within the house could be told that Kut Humi had just hurried past the window. Also, the Kut Humi letters, thought to materialize in odd places out of thin air, were actually dropped through slits in the ceiling by the Coulombs. Even more damaging were details offered about the letters that suddenly appeared in Blavatsky's shrine.

The shrine in HPB's sitting room was purported to have a false door that opened into a hole of the wall adjoining her bedroom. Thus, she could write the letters at her leisure and surreptitiously deposit them in the shrine. Vehemently denying this, some of Blavatsky's devoted followers rushed to the shrine and were relieved to find it fully intact. To show that it was exactly as it appeared to be, one follower confidently pounded on the shrine. Suddenly a panel flew off, revealing a secret spring-loaded mechanism. Accusing the Coulombs of tampering with the shrine prior to their expulsion from Blavatsky's residence and feeling that it could not be salvaged, the faction burned it. Thus, only the origin of the false panel was in dispute, not the panel itself. Blavatsky's followers attributed it to the Coulombs, overlooking the fact that when the Coulombs had opportunity to rig the shrine, they had no motive, and when they had motive, they had no opportunity (because they had been expelled).

The SPR sent Richard Hodgson directly to India to investigate the incident. Later to be involved in the investigation of Lenora Piper, the young Cambridge-educated Hodgson impressed many and, prior to his return from India, was favorably perceived by HPB herself. Then, on the basis of his report, the SPR concluded: "For our own part, we regard [Blavatsky] neither as the mouthpiece of hidden seers, nor as a mere vulgar adventuress; we think that she has achieved a title to permanent remembrance as one of the most accomplished, ingenious, and interesting imposters in history."[9] Some have tried to discredit Hodgson's investigation by portraying him as an arch-skeptic, but this does not comport with the fact that he converted to Spiritualism while studying Piper. In any event, Blavatsky quickly returned to India to set matters straight. She accused the Coulombs of launching a smear campaign against her, complete with forged documents. Intent at first on suing them, she decided upon a softer approach after conferring with lawyers and fellow Theosophists. Then, when threats of legal action by the Coulombs surfaced, Blavatsky was hastily bundled off to Europe again. She would never return to her beloved India.

Far from deciding the question of HPB's bona fides, this episode complicated it. Like many occultists, Blavatsky blurred conventional boundaries and thus impressed devotees as a unique, futuristic soul beyond the reach of customary moral considerations. Ambiguity can bring freedom, and along with Blavatsky's self-declared mission of interblending traditional categories of knowledge, there was the issue of her masculine appearance and behavior. Some clucked that she had lesbian tendencies (she herself claimed to be a virgin), and fellow Theosophists wondered if her seeming androgyny were not central to her prophetic destiny: Olcott described her as "a very old man . . . a most learned and wonderful man . . . a Hindu man."[10] Not easily brought into focus, HPB enjoyed special dispensation among her followers to act in unconventional ways.

THEOSOPHY'S TIES TO SCIENCE AND THE EAST

"The Secret Doctrine," wrote HPB, ". . . teaches that every one of the higher, as of the lower worlds, is interblended with our own objective world; that millions of things and beings are, in point of localization, around and *in* us as we are around, with, and in them."[11] By saturating even the smallest detail of the universe with unsuspected significance, this holistic outlook opens the way for other occult doctrines. Rather than enumerate principles already covered, however, we wish to focus on the two other major aspects of theosophy: its appropriation of contemporary science and its borrowings from the East. Of course, Blavatsky did not feel that she was "borrowing" or "appropriating"; instead, she was bringing the broken shards back together, restoring and reintegrating truth's ancient fullness. Or, to use her own metaphor, she merely "supplied the string for the bouquet."[12]

Science provided Blavatsky with her progressive, goal-driven vision of history. This is not to say, however, that Blavatsky's outlook meshed perfectly with that of science. Darwin's theory of evolution was earth-centered, materialistic, and could be interpreted as random (mindless) and non-progressive. HPB felt that it obscured as much as it revealed and that most scientists—Darwin himself—failed to grasp or even dimly intuit the cosmic and spiritual import of the evolutionary process. They saw the outer, naturalistic shell of that process but ironically missed the rich inner vibrancy—life itself. In HPB's mind, the universe passes through successive cycles, all patterned similarly but each at a higher turn of the evolutionary spiral. Moreover, since cycles overlap, we have

MAGIC, MYSTERY, AND SCIENCE

dim memories of the far-flung past, although these often are written off as myth or childish fantasy. Hence the need for Ascended Masters, and someone like Blavatsky, to lift us out of our ignorance.

In these cycles, the universe passes through spiritual and physical stages, allowing its creatures to evolve through similar planes of existence. First, two spiritual planes, then three physical planes, then two higher spiritual planes. Corresponding to these planes or stages are seven root races on the Earth (other beings or races are found on other planets); four are past, we are the fifth root race, and two are yet to come.[13] That places us on the last of the physical planes.

What were the earlier root races like? The first and second are hard to describe. HPB stated that they "must remain beyond the comprehension of minds trained in Western thought."[14] She portrayed the first root race as a kind of spiritual ooze, individuated as ethereal bodies but lacking consciousness. These astral jellyfish lived in the "Imperishable Sacred Land," which still exists but on a different plane from our own.

In her story of the races, sex (particularly the misuse of it) plays a major role. The first race was sexless, and was eventually subsumed into the second root race, the Hyperboreans. These also were sexless, but evidently reproduced by budding. Their name refers to the beautiful green continent they lived on—Hyperborea—that was located where the North Pole now is. At one point in *The Secret Doctrine*, HPB described the Hyperboreans as boneless, at another, as "gigantic semi-human monsters."[15]

From the Hyperboreans evolved the third root race, the Lemurians. Taking their name from a supposed continent (or land-bridge) that once existed between Africa and India (the biologist Ernst Haeckel posited it to explain lemur distribution), the Lemurians were egg-laying creatures, at least at first. Blavatsky explained that they began as oviparous hermaphrodites but gradually separated into males and females. At the peak of their evolution, Lemurians were powerful, giant beings whom we now vaguely recollect in our stories of the gods. They, however, initiated their downfall by breeding with lower animals for sexual pleasure and engendering what we now call apes. (Apes are humans with bad karma.) As Lemuria passed out of existence, another continent, Atlantis, arose in its place at a higher turn of the evolutionary drama.

The inhabitants of Atlantis, the Atlanteans, were the fourth root race. We would recognize them as fully human, but they had greater physical and psychic powers than us. Indeed, some Atlanteans still had use of a spiritual third eye—which all Lemurians had—but as the two physical eyes came to dominate the sense of vision, the spiritual eye atrophied and retreated into the brain. Unfortunately for most of us, the third eye is dead, but its remnant lives on as the pineal gland.

Figure 34. The lost continent of Lemuria as depicted in a 1940 issue of the science fiction/fact magazine Amazing

Prospering on the continent of Atlantis and elsewhere, the powerful Atlanteans built many of the marvels of the ancient world, such as Stonehenge. But, like the Lemurians before them, some played out their sexual fantasies by copulating with animals. They also became idolatrously attached to physical matter and soon fell to worshipping themselves, thus further hastening the diminution of their spiritual abilities. Destruction came by water as their continent sank into the ocean. HPB declared, however, that this was not "because they had become 'black with sin,' but simply because such is the fate of every continent, which—like everything else under our Sun—is born, lives, becomes decrepit, and dies."[16] Atlantis's destruction is indelibly fixed in the Western imagination, thanks in large part to Plato, who claimed to have heard the story from Egyptian priests.

We are the fifth root race, having descended from the Atlanteans with a slight gain in spirituality. Occupying the last of the physical planes of existence, we are at an awkward stage, still very trapped by materiality and largely ignorant of the evolutionary distance yet to be traveled. But some sub-races of the fifth root race are more advanced than others. People in America, Blavatsky said, are leading the way, hastening the day when the sixth root race will appear. This race, fundamentally spiritual in nature, will not be awed and infatuated by physical matter but will master and direct it in life-enhancing ways. Eventually it even will grow "out of its bonds of matter, and even of flesh,"[17] and then at some point in the far distant future the seventh root race will appear to consummate the cosmic drama. This will all occur, and is occurring, according to the law of karma, and so cannot be refuted by the puny theories of materialistic science.

Curiously, Blavatsky seems not to have expected most educated people to believe this, even after giving it a scientific gloss. Occult understanding, she declared, is reserved for the few, for those willing to buck the tide of popular opinion and endure scorn. This stance enabled her to pre-dismiss criticism by insisting that anyone not privy to the "secret doctrine" would myopically disagree with her. And when criticism subsequently came her way, she and her devotees took that as proof of her messianic calling. Great figures, after all, are always misunderstood and maligned.

KARMA AND REINCARNATION

In the twentieth century, the doctrines of karma and reincarnation gained currency in the West, thanks in large part to Blavatsky. Karma is the cosmic law of adjustment, the immutable law of cause and effect in the moral sphere. Why do bad things happen to good people? The doctrine of karma purports that we are punished for past misdeeds, often those committed in previous lifetimes, and thus the suffering that attends calamity can be redemptive. Of course, we may also be rewarded for virtuous acts performed long ago. In either case, the universe is balancing the scales of justice and thereby ensuring that all creatures receive their proper due.

This is one response to the problem of evil. Misfortune is not random, the result of senseless turns of the "wheel of fortune." Nor will we be rescued from evil by a savior god who vicariously suffers penalty for our sinful acts performed during a single mortal probation. We ourselves pay the penalty over many mortal probations or incarnations, gradually working off our karmic debts (if all goes well).[18] Karma, then, is inextricably tied to reincarnation, although being fenced in by the here and now, we cannot read the long ledger of good and bad deeds—extending over many lifetimes—that leads to our present situation. Under this scheme, patience or resignation becomes a primary virtue: if lived well, this life will be a step up, but very likely not the last of many, many steps leading to Nirvana and the release from suffering it represents.

How many incarnations go into the realization of Nirvana? To answer this question, go down to the beach for a weekend and count the waves as they lap against the sand. The number probably will not do justice to the question, but it will drive home the repetitive, mind-numbing weariness that attends the idea of reincarnation in the East. Oddly, in the West, many believers romanticize reincarnation by recalling exciting, sometimes dangerous past lives spent in Egypt, Tibet, or Atlantis. But, from an Asian point of view, reincarnation is nothing to celebrate: the idea is to get off the wheel of rebirth. "This world is a bridge: pass over it, and do not build your house upon it," says an old Indian proverb.[19] If caught in a web of illusion—as they often are—romantic, adventurous lives build up the karmic debt to be paid off and thus lengthen the painful term of mortal experience.

For most, the idea of karma is appealing—initially, at least—because those who perpetrate evil get a full dose of their own medicine. Adolf Hitler, for example, might come back as the death-camp victim of some future Hitler, perhaps six or seven million times, or as a mouse to be ripped apart by an owl. Readers may customize this revenge fantasy to their hearts' content, but true believers in karma will find it an idle and perhaps even deleterious pursuit. Over the very long haul, the universe will extract from Hitler the "uttermost farthing," just as it will from all of us. No need, therefore, to dream up payback scenarios for other people.

This stance may dilute our desire to "get even" with others but it also tends to induce a sense of passivity or resignation—a trait not highly valued in the West. If the universe balances all accounts, why the human pursuit of justice? Furthermore, what about the numerous, almost uncountable inequities or injustices that surround us at every moment? Should we try to correct them? No, say many believers in karma. Clearly seen, those inequities harbor opportunities to pay off karmic debts incurred in previous lives. They are prison terms that must be served before progress becomes possible. To step in before the debt is fully paid, therefore, is to temporarily unbalance the scales of cosmic justice. Translated in everyday terms, this means we should pass by the starving beggar and let him pay full penance for previous misdeeds. Alleviating his misery only perpetuates it, for inevitably (probably in his next incarnation) unpaid debts will send him back to the gutter.

There is in all this an element that resists rationalization, a kind of logical slippage that is perhaps its saving grace. Conceivably, the beggar incurred his karmic debts by passing by beggars in a prior incarnation, and now it is *his* turn to feel the pain that he once ignored in others. Helping others, then, even those

MAGIC, MYSTERY, AND SCIENCE

who deserve their plight, keeps us from incurring a similar plight in some future life. One way out of this quandary—Should I seek to relieve the karmic suffering of others?—lies in the traditional Indian practice of self-immolation (*suttee*). In 1990, many upper-caste students resorted to the supreme act of protest in India: they publicly burned themselves to death to demonstrate their opposition to a proposed job-quota system that would allow "untouchables" (the lowest caste) to gain government positions.[20] At first, this might seem like pure caste hatred, and that is part of it, although bigots in the West never purposely inflict pain on *themselves* while attempting to achieve their prejudicial ends. By putting the issue in a wide, larger-than-this-life context, the doctrine of karma allowed the students to feel that they were performing an act of kindness toward the untouchables; they were helping them pay off karmic debts by keeping them locked up in poverty and social degradation. Not incidentally, this benevolence would redound to the students' own spiritual liberation so that all might take a step closer to Nirvana.

Viewed skeptically, karma, at least as it is practiced in India, is just a tool for dampening social unrest and keeping lower castes in their place. If this life is not the whole story but a small chapter in the story, then people are more inclined to bear their afflictions patiently. Furthermore, those with relatively few afflictions—the upper castes—may style themselves as rightful heirs to rewards earned in previous lives. The rub is that those rewards come at the expense of people—the lower castes—living now. But this is exactly as it should be, replies the true believer: for the time being, untouchables must take the low road to Nirvana.

THE THEOSOPHICAL SOCIETY AFTER HPB

After Blavatsky's death in 1891, Charles Leadbeater and Annie Besant emerged as new leaders in the Theosophical Society, alongside Colonel Olcott, who would pass away in 1909. Leadbeater had joined the Society in 1883, but failed to impress its members until turning to the task of elucidating Theosophist doctrine. He then, with the help of the Masters, laid down a system of thought that included the ceremonial introduction of advanced concepts. Some older members, such as Olcott, resisted this change, inasmuch as theosophy had once stood for the steady flow of new ideas, in deliberate opposition to fixed ritual and dogma. Interestingly, Leadbeater's inspiration subsequently led him to Australia, where he took holy vows as a bishop in the Liberal Catholic Church. This proved to be an embarrassment to the Society, but Annie Besant stood by Leadbeater, believing that he had not strayed from the Theosophist path.

By the time she met Blavatsky, Annie Besant was well known throughout

Figure 35. Annie Besant

MAGIC, MYSTERY, AND SCIENCE

England as an advocate of socialist and secular values. A gifted orator, she sought to improve the position of women and workers, believing that many Victorian Christians used their religion to perpetuate social injustices. Upon meeting Blavatsky, she began to nurture the hope that social change might be effected through supernatural intervention—she, like Blavatsky, functioning as an instrument of otherworldly agencies. She spent her last forty years in India, adulated by millions, moving among crowds as a kind of high priestess in her daily attire of white robes, and seeking to win Home Rule for India (political independence from Great Britain). In contrast to Mohandas K. Gandhi, whom she knew in the political arena, Besant couched her vision of the future in millennial terms: what happened in India would ripple out into the larger world to usher in a new world order. Theosophy, then, was the seed crystal of something much bigger.

In preparing for this new world order, Besant and Leadbeater were guided by their Masters to find the Great Teacher, the future messiah of the twentieth century. This turned out to be a fourteen-year-old boy whom Leadbeater met on the seashore near Adyar: Jiddu Krishnamurti. Besant and Leadbeater took their new protégé under wing, schooling him in Theosophist ideals (often under strenuous circumstances) and sending him to England for formal education. Although Krishnamurti possessed a humane, sensitive personality, he also questioned the messianic role he had been thrust into and sought to work out a life purpose that was fully his own. At times a lackadaisical, dreamy student, he did not advance as quickly as his mentors wished, and in 1929 he renounced their claims upon him, shook himself free of the Theosophical Society, and moved to California. In time he did become a teacher of international renown, and so—according to some—fulfilled the destiny first glimpsed by Besant and Leadbeater.

Given its relatively small membership (about forty-five thousand at its peak in the 1920s), the Theosophical Society exercised a disproportionate influence on popular culture in the West. Much of what we now regard as New Age originated with Madame Blavatsky and her disciples. The sense that Asia (particularly India and Tibet) is a cradle of sacred wisdom, that "what goes around comes around" (karma), that the soul migrates from one body and life experience to another (reincarnation)—these are now familiar outlooks in the West, even if they are not widely subscribed to. Throw in yoga, chakras, auras, the third eye, astral bodies, Ascended Masters, and the channeling of past lives, and a new conduit of religious experience opens up, one that to many still seems fresh and vibrant. But, as theosophy grew, it also mutated and combined with other streams of thought. We turn now to Rudolf Steiner and his attempt to create, in his own words, an "occult science."

ANTHROPOSOPHY

Rudolf Steiner was born in 1861 in the Austro-Hungarian Empire. Pensive and shy, he responded readily to the truth claims of science and appreciated the rigor and exactitude with which those claims were conveyed. He felt, moreover, that by its very success in explaining nature, science bespoke a supersensible world—an inner world awaiting our spiritual exploration. Steiner glimpsed as much as a young boy upon being introduced to Euclidean geometry: "That one can work out forms which are seen purely inwardly, independent of the outer senses, gave me a feeling of deep contentment. . . . To be able to grasp something purely spiritual brought me an inner joy. I know that through geometry I first experienced happiness."[21]

Interestingly, Albert Einstein and Bertrand Russell, in recalling their first encounter with geometry, described a similar happiness and wonder. And, while both took it as proof that a principle of intelligence or rationality informed nature, neither would have agreed with Steiner that geometry (and all of science) opens out onto spiritual agencies. This conclusion was almost innate with him. Awed by the beauty of nature and feeling himself in direct contact with these agencies, he was distressed by contemporary science's commitment to a purely material, mechanical cosmos. His life-long pursuit was to pull back the curtain on materialistic science so that all could see its larger spiritual context.

Along the way, he immersed himself in the writings of Johann Wolfgang Goethe, the great German poet who had sought to dethrone or at least limit Newton's theory of colors. For one thing, Newton (like Galileo, John Locke, and others) had contested the centuries-old commonsensical assumption that colors actually exist in nature, independent of our perception of them. Colors arise, said Newton, as incoming sense data trigger color sensations in the brain—that is all there is to it. The data themselves, before they reach the brain, are colorless, because the world itself is colorless. As proof for this view, one might argue that atoms have no color, and they alone constitute the whole of nature. Therefore, color must be smuggled in by the mind as a kind of secondary and ultimately false effect.

Goethe was put off by such reasoning, as were many Romantic thinkers of the day whose inclination was to see nature as "God's living garment." John Keats registered his disdain thusly: "In the dull catalogue of common things, Philosophy will clip an angel's wings."[22] In Keats's time, "philosophy" often meant natural philosophy or science and the attendant impulse to treat the world as a complex machine, void of poetic qualities. Later in the twentieth century, A. N. Whitehead would echo the Romantic sentiment (still a minority opinion) by writing that "we forget how strained and paradoxical is the view of nature which modern science imposes on our thinking." Thereby, nature becomes "a dull affair ... merely the hurrying of material, endlessly, meaninglessly."[23]

That was the substance of Goethe's complaint, and Steiner's, too. Materialistic science had turned nature into "a dull affair" by offering its adherents a strange doublethink. On the one hand, scientists readily concede that nature's appeal to the mind and senses is the very reason they venture forth scientifically. On the other, they are not prepared to credit that appeal with a life or voice of its own. So, in Goethe's phrase, scientists "destroy the inward life [of nature] to offer from without an insufficient substitute for it";[24] the map (scientific theory) becomes more real than the territory (nature), because the former obviously conveys intelligence while the latter is assumed to be mindless. In the case of vision, nothing calls out to us so strongly and primally as color. It, after all, is what we see without asking, what even infants see with the greatest of ease. And yet this calling-out is void of life or spiritual content, according to materialistic science.

Steiner attempted to rectify this incongruity by developing an occult science. Here "occult" refers to the normally unseen spiritual world that animates physical nature. Like the Theosophists, however, he sought to distance himself from Spiritualism. To be meaningful, communication with spirits had to be a full-time, laborious pursuit entailing much more than occasional séances. What good is a conversation with Plato if one has never bothered to study his writings? Moreover, communication need not be confined to deceased persons (although Steiner felt that such was likely to occur as one was falling asleep or awaking). The universe was filled with numerous spiritual beings at various hierarchical or evolutionary levels, all of which reveal themselves to receptive minds. Suffice it to say, the physical world, for Steiner, was not so much an obstacle to spiritual communion as the very occasion of it. "Fundamentally speaking," he said, "we are continually surrounded by spiritual happenings and beings. Physical phenomena are merely the expression of spiritual facts. Things that appear to us in material form are but the outward sheaths of spiritual beings."[25]

The apprehension of these spiritual beings required a kind of "cosmic clairvoyance," a wide supersensory perception that Steiner seemed to possess innately. Like others before and since, he claimed to be able to pick up an old object—a brick or coin, perhaps—and discern its history: where and when it had been manufactured, who had possessed it, and what wars or catastrophes it had passed through, and so on. (This alleged talent, known as psychometry, has led to "psychic archeology," a practice very much on the fringes of modern science.) The basis for this ability was the Akashic Chronicle, a superfine, spiritual tissue or parchment pervading the cosmos upon which events leave their imprint, albeit not in a secondhand, "reported" way. As a living record of all that has happened—all that, spiritually speaking, is still happening—the Akashic Chronicle affords its viewers direct witness of past events.

Given Steiner's proclivities, it is not surprising that he allied himself for a time with Annie Besant and headed up the German contingent of the Theosophical Society. Several important theosophical teachings coincided with his own: karma, reincarnation, the seven root races, exalted Beings ready to share their wisdom, an upwardly evolving cosmos, and the imminence of a worldwide spiritual awakening. Moreover, Steiner, like Blavatsky, eclectically developed his themes, obviously believing that traces of truth lay littered all about him. But there were differences as well. Although familiar with the Bhagavad Gita and other sacred texts of India, Steiner was less enamored of Asia and the resulting emphasis on Hinduism and Buddhism, whereby Christianity suffered by comparison if not by outright rejection. As he grew older, Steiner came to regard Christ as the pre-eminent figure of all cosmic history and assigned cardinal significance to what he called the "Mystery of Golgotha," wherein something happened to awaken human beings to their spiritual milieu.[26]

Besant had already expressed dissatisfaction with Steiner's more Eurocentric focus when he officially broke ties with the Theosophical Society, taking with him many German-speaking followers. The break, occurring in 1909, coincided with Besant's and Leadbeater's selection of Krishnamurti as the messiah of a new world order, a destiny that perhaps Steiner had reserved for himself. In any event, Steiner founded the Anthroposophical Society, headquartered in Dornach, Switzerland, and dedicated to bathing modern science with a spiritual luster. His cosmology, like Blavatsky's, is complex, even dizzying, and reiterates ancient motifs now considered occult or superstitious. Betraying a Pythagorean fondness for certain basic numbers, Steiner talks of the seven states of consciousness, the seven life kingdoms or conditions, the four elements, the three creative functions, the ten cabalistic sephiroth, the nine angelic orders, and so on.[27] These orders, kingdoms, functions, and elements, moreover, are linked to the planets or zodiacal constellations in a vast system of evolving consciousness.

Everything putatively began on Saturn, which was once composed of nothing but fire, the most creative and fundamental of the four Aristotelian elements. As warmth, an intrinsic property of fire, is something we feel both inwardly and outwardly ("I feel warm and this thing feels warm"; the three remaining elements do not permit this sort of bivalent discourse), fire is the "soul element," and Saturn brought the outward material world and the inner spiritual world into conjunction. Then fire "densified" into the material forms of air, water, and earth, albeit on other planets. The Earth is the fourth planet in the evolutionary cycle, following Saturn, the sun, and the moon. Higher

MAGIC, MYSTERY, AND SCIENCE

stages of consciousness await us on other planets as we pass from one incarnation to the next.

One may object that the sun and moon are not planets, but this response, according to Steiner, reflects an atrophying of the spiritual imagination. In the Copernican system, the sun and moon, strictly speaking, are not planets, but this system is simply a mathematical, mechanical description of the heavens, and one that takes leave of the Earth in order to see the world from an "objective" point of view. With Copernicus, we move into a spectator mode of consciousness, feeling that the world-drama is something we can observe impartially by the aid of science. Thus, subjective, inner, spiritual experience is eclipsed by objective, outer, material reality—by that which yields to scientific analysis. But truth, said Steiner, comes with the realization that we are always at the center of things as participants. This realization was built into the geocentric system that preceded Copernicus, but was lost as "human insight into the spiritual reality behind outer happenings . . . ebbed away."[28]

An essential aspect of Steiner's geocentric worldview was the microcosmic-macrocosmic connection. If the universe is holographic or holistic—if the cosmic whole informs all of its parts—then centrality is inescapable: each of us is at the very center of existence. And echoing Paracelsus, Steiner insisted that since "[e]verything that occurs in the human being is a copy of macrocosmic processes that have to do with his existence," the spiritually adept person may observe the planets from both within and without.[29] Needless to say, this emphasis on the mutual immanence of all things challenges the classical scientific assumption that the universe is an assemblage of distinct parts in mechanical interaction.

Steiner envisaged a time when people will look back and say: "In the past, there were human beings who thought it correct to place the material Sun in the center of an ellipse and to rotate the planets in ellipses around it. They constructed a cosmic universal system even as earlier people had done before them. But today, we know that it is all mere saga and legend."[30] That time has not arrived, nor may it ever. Still, thousands of Anthroposophists worldwide find Steiner's cosmic outlook richer and more real than that offered by modern science.

GURDJIEFF AND THE FOURTH WAY

Theosophy intersected with the development of other occult systems, including that of the highly enigmatic G. I. Gurdjieff, author of the strange, meandering (and somewhat autobiographical) *Beelzebub's Tales to His Grandson*. Born in the Caucasus about 1872, Gurdjieff spent his early adult years searching for esoteric wisdom throughout Central Asia and the Middle East.

NEW AGE PRELUDES

He recounts some of his travels in *Meetings with Remarkable Men,* a book that blurs fact with allegory. Claiming to be affiliated with a group that called itself the Seekers of Truth, Gurdjieff journeyed to Egypt, Tibet, Jerusalem, Persia, India, Mecca, and a host of other places looking for ancient brotherhoods, digging up old records, and studying with Christian monks and Sufi mystics. Traveling across the Gobi Desert in search of a buried city and blinded by sandstorms, the Seekers discover they can see above the storms by climbing to the top of a stepladder. They then devise stilts to accelerate their progress and, although they never find the city, they come away with a heightened appreciation of their problem-solving abilities.[31]

Gurdjieff claims to have been much taken with the prospect of finding an obscure school or brotherhood whose wisdom, passed down for generations, keeps the forces of cosmic darkness at bay and unlocks the riddle of existence. This, above all, motivated his quest and sent him into regions of political upheaval and civil war. Often escaping serious misfortune by his wits—he stated that in tight situations he could always detect and exploit others' psychic weaknesses—he nevertheless sustained gunshot injuries on three occasions and otherwise endured "unbelievable sufferings," including numerous infectious and dietary diseases.[32] Undeterred, he pressed on until, by his own account, he secured the understanding he sought. For the remainder of his life—from the age of about forty onward—he attracted disciples thirsty for truth. Migrating from Russia westward, he finally settled in France, where he purchased a permanent site near Fontainebleau for his Institute for the Harmonious Development of Man.

Like Blavatsky, Gurdjieff inspired controversy. Many saw him as a charlatan and opportunist of the first magnitude, and there is evidence that he worked his way through theosophical literature while developing his own occult views. He stated that he had found errors in Blavatsky's *Secret Doctrine* and, upon meeting her, had excited her romantic fantasies.[33] It is doubtful that the two ever met, but Gurdjieff was not above reinventing himself as the occasion required. In fact, a cloud of suspicion has always hung over his early, adventurous years: detractors contend that he traveled from country to country as an undercover agent for tsarist Russia, not as a "Truth Seeker." Even Gurdjieff's followers acknowledged that his behavior was often artificial and chameleon-like, but prolonged contact engendered the sense that here was a man of almost bottomless understanding. His eyes were mesmerizing (like Blavatsky's) and his imperial manner reminded disciples of their inability to comprehend his every action. As a result, they willingly suffered under the apparent whims of the master's mercurial temperament. His seemingly senseless demands, he told them, were meant to strip them of their pretenses and shock them into enlightenment.

MAGIC, MYSTERY, AND SCIENCE

Part of that enlightenment involved the realization that human beings are asleep—even when they think they are fully awake. Our lives are so conditioned by social patterning that we cannot remember who we are; individual reality—the "I"—is smothered by a cocoon of learned responses that turn us into zombies robotically (deterministically) passing through the motions of acceptable behavior. Only "super efforts" will free us from the cocoon, and these entail constant self-vigilance and the voluntary embrace of pain and confusion. Soporifically happy, we must violently attack the comforting bands of ignorance that swaddle us.

It was assumed that Gurdjieff had already woken up, and he left accounts of that momentous event. During his *Wanderjahre*, he reports, he developed tremendous psychic powers: "[B]y only a few hours of self-preparation I could from a distance of tens of miles kill a yak; or, in twenty-four hours, could accumulate life forces of such compactness that I could in five minutes put to sleep an elephant."[34] Still, he could not "remember himself," despite long bouts of concentrated effort. Seemingly blocked at every turn, he finally succeeded in thinking a "new thought" based on a "universal analogy" relating God and man: "He [God] is everywhere and with Him everything is connected. I am a man . . . created by Him in His image!!! For He is God and therefore I also have within myself all the possibilities and impossibilities that He has. . . . He is God and I am God!"[35] This revelation flashed into Gurdjieff's soul "like the sun,"[36] making it obvious (to him at least) that self-remembering could be achieved. Presumably, the revelation itself was a moment of self-remembering.

Disciples unable to grasp the full import of this account—and none could—were nurtured on elementary practices such as the Stop exercise. Whenever Gurdjieff called "Stop!" everyone froze in place for an indefinite period of time, the aim being to interrupt one's sleep-like, mechanical motion and thus make it obvious. Another tactic involved learning the "sacred dances" Gurdjieff had collected while searching for lost wisdom.[37] These were felt to embody aboriginal life rhythms at odds with the robotic motions of everyday society; they thus could facilitate self-remembering. Katherine Mansfield, best known for her short stories and tempestuous love affairs, wrote that one dance "contains the whole life of woman . . . it gave me more of woman's life than any book or poem."[38] Mansfield would die at the Institute in Fontainebleau, but not before plumbing the depths of her own artificiality and then ascending into the rarefied air of self-remembrance. This at least was her deathbed testimony and loved ones felt they saw it in her countenance.

Along with the group exercises, there was also need for private concentration and discipline. Gurdjieff set the pattern by developing sets of "will-tasks" to be carried out in three-month increments. To the uninitiated, these might seem a

NEW AGE PRELUDES

blend of the sane and the ridiculous. Here is one of Gurdjieff's sets, customized to his own purposes:

(1) To patiently and persistently study "the deep-rooted minutiae of the common psyche of man."
(2) To, upon interacting with other people of whatever familiarity or social station, discover their " 'most sensitive corn' and 'press' it rather hard."
(3) To eat freely and fully, accepting all kinds of food, but afterwards working up a feeling of pity for at least fifteen minutes toward others who have "no means of having such food."[39]

If these "will-tasks" do not seem to jibe with Gurdjieff's self-proclaimed aim of lifting humankind heavenward, that might be because he wished to throw others off balance into fresh understanding. Because linear thought, much prized in the West for its precision, leaves most of reality untouched, Gurdjieff sometimes slipped into the role of a trickster, the rascal—in his own words, "the Sly Man"—purveying what has since been called "coyote wisdom." Truth is not remote from lived experience, something subject to mere academic or rational transfer; rather it is extracted from confusion and strained personal relationships. The master must therefore become a positive deviant, at times insulting, befuddling, and discombobulating his disciples so that whatever wisdom they acquire is borne of their own refining experience.

Recalling his "reconstruction" of Asian wisdom, Gurdjieff stated that he wished to "add the mystical spirit of the East to the scientific spirit of the West."[40] It was therefore necessary to break the hegemony of Western reason in sudden, surprising, and ultimately mind-stretching ways. Despite that, Gurdjieff was a master at appropriating and conjuring up scientific jargon to promote his ends. In announcing the program of study at the Institute for the Harmonious Development of Man, he listed the following approaches: hydrotherapy, phototherapy, magnetotherapy, electrotherapy, dietotherapy, psychotherapy, duliotherapy (said to mean "slave-therapy"), as well as certain chemico-analytic, physico-metric, and psycho-experimental medical procedures.[41] He also wrote that lectures would be given on the

> [a]pplication of the psychological method to different sciences; cosmological philosophy; universal mechanics. Science of relativity. Science of number. Science of Symbols. Astrophysics, mathematics, chemistry ancient and modern (alchemy); ancient medicine, modern Oriental medicine. Comparative study of religions. Mythology. Idolatry. Ancient esoteric schools and modern Oriental schools. Psychology of art. Ancient and modern philosophy.[42]

MAGIC, MYSTERY, AND SCIENCE

The sweep is impressive, particularly when dance, painting, foreign languages, gardening, and other sundry topics were also included, but it seems to have been more of a wish list than a fully functioning curriculum. Besides, Gurdjieff often said he offered his students not a menu of intellectual delights but a method or system of self-enlightenment presupposing the circumvention of traditional learning experiences. This meant showing them how to wake up and then stay awake, what he sometimes called "esoteric Christianity" or the "The Fourth Way." The first three ways had all been tried but with limited success: (1) the way of the fakir—mortification of the physical body; (2) the way of the monk—the prayer of faith; (3) the way of the yogi—ascension to higher consciousness. Each of these ways overbalances its practitioners and thereby keeps them from realizing full enlightenment. In the Fourth Way, however, all aspects of the truth-seeker are simultaneously opened up and kept alive so that harmonious development blossoms into self-remembering.

For all its ineffable significance, self-remembering seems to have been that mystical moment when one's ego dissolves into the oceanic vastness of the cosmos. One of Gurdjieff's devotees explained that the "first characteristic of self-remembering" entailed the realization that "man is not center. He is not separate. Sitting in a room, he is aware of the whole room, of himself as only one of the objects in it. . . . This is not love, but it is the beginning of love."[43] Another student reported that, while walking outdoors,

> all anxieties and cares of ordinary life dropped away; at the same time I saw myself and my relations with people quite clearly; I saw the pattern of my life, my organism moving as it were along its appointed path. There was time no longer, and an understanding of the whole of life seemed possible for me. It was as if for a few moments I had entered into my real life; and the outer life, which had seemed so important and took up all my time, was not the real life but something ephemeral, a sort of cinema film with which I was identified. Only the inner something was eternal—I, the real self of me. I AM.[44]

While "I AM" echoes God's self-annunciation—"I Am that I Am"—in the Old Testament, it also jibes with a book by Gurdjieff entitled *Life Is Real Only Then, When "I Am."* The whiff of truth coming out of the I AM experience is not illusory, according to Gurdjieff, because all of reality is holistically intermingled. Therefore,

> [t]here is no need to study or investigate the sun in order to discover the matter of the solar world: this matter exists in ourselves and is the result of the division of our atoms. In the same way we have in us the matter of all other worlds. Man is, in the full sense of the term, a

NEW AGE PRELUDES

"miniature universe"; in him are all the matters of which the universe consists; the same forces, the same laws that govern the life of the universe, operate in him; therefore in studying man we can study the whole world, just as in studying the world we can study man.[45]

This, of course, is an old occult principle, one of several in Gurdjieff's system. His numerological inclinations steered him toward a "law of three" and a "law of seven," the interaction of which, he said, defined the operation of the cosmos. The law of three keeps things in evolutionary progress by overcoming the stalemate of action versus reaction—a third force neutralizing and resolving two opposing forces. The law of seven expresses the seven stages of the "Ray of Creation"[46] through which all things pass, whether it be the cosmos itself, the birth and development of an idea, or the movement toward full self-awakening. The musical scale with its seven tones reflects this universal process and reveals its non-linearity: the octave does not divide into evenly spaced intervals and so there is no such thing as the smooth and steady transition from one stage to the next. In fact, "shock points" occur at the half-steps (between E and F and B and C): these involve the sudden introduction of outside energy into the process. If received correctly, these will get us across the interval. If not, they will send us back to earlier stages. In any case, over the long haul "we must start and start again until we make an octave."[47]

Upon these two laws and the assumption of a consciously evolving universe Gurdjieff built a diverse cosmology incorporating a wide array of arithmetic, physical, astrological, and psychological considerations. As "the fundamental hieroglyph of the universal language"—the symbol that best sums up the structure of existence—he created an enneagram by collapsing the two laws together. The result is a circle marked by nine points. Three points, representing the law of three, derive from the insertion of an equilateral triangle, and the other six from an irregular figure whose points signify the six intervals between the seven notes of the octave. One may discover in the nine points the progression of the octave with its two shock periods. Looking further, James Webb felt that "Gurdjieff's enneagram is an adaptation of the [Cabalistic] Tree of Life."[48] Suffice it to say, the symbol, like all occult symbols, is amenable to many readings. It struck some devotees as a total revelation and affirmed the master's claim to ancient esoteric wisdom: he had found the elusive brotherhood and penetrated its inner circle. He was now trying to perpetuate the tradition by creating his own inner circle.

As intriguing as this may sound, full understanding of the Fourth Way is said to require wholehearted discipleship. Gurdjieff's explanations are often maddeningly obscure, but, of course, words cannot be expected to bring one

MAGIC, MYSTERY, AND SCIENCE

Figure 36. An enneagram

near to the beatific experience: action is needed. This entailed pledging oneself to Gurdjieff and then at some point, perhaps, being driven away from him as his teachings were internalized. Although no one ever knew for sure, Gurdjieff's penchant for shocking students into wakeful enlightenment may have taken the form of thrusting them out of the fold for their own self-growth. He alienated many disciples, often under traumatic and scandalous circumstances, but some of these later spoke as if their parting from the master was the painful next step toward self-remembering. The alternative reading is that Gurdjieff was simply out of control. His exalted position at the Institute—some followers

NEW AGE PRELUDES

felt he was infallible, saying that he even planned his car wrecks with an inscrutable higher purpose in mind—allowed him to act in excessive and abusive ways.

Was Gurdjieff an impostor, a self-appointed, self-deluded messiah, or was he the peerless sage whose full measure cannot be taken by ordinary mortals? Was he a borderline lunatic among reasonably sane people, or an eminently sane person in a collectively mad world—someone who managed to escape from the asylum and then returned to free others? These questions go back to Plato, whose cave allegory depicts an enlightened escapee returning at great personal risk to those content to live in darkness. Many intelligent people latched on to Gurdjieff, often put off by his unpleasant manner but awed by his presence and his talk of the Fourth Way. One skeptic observed, however, that these people were just those "whose adherence is *not* a recommendation."[49] Many were Theosophists or others similarly inclined to cast a wide net in the pursuit of truth. And, for some, Gurdjieff represented a step up from Blavatsky. Her many accomplishments notwithstanding, she was merely a mouthpiece of Ascended Masters; he by contrast spoke for himself and presented himself as the living embodiment of truth. One individual who passed through theosophy into the Fourth Way turned out to be a much-adulated figure in his own right and a stern critic of modern science's failure to expand with its own expansive discoveries.

OUSPENSKY AND THE FOURTH DIMENSION

In many ways, P. D. Ouspensky is easier to grasp than Gurdjieff. Although impassioned, his writings proceed along clear lines of thought. His personal manner, too, was forthright and open; he could be curt and even caustic with students but never devious or manipulative. A basic decency clung to Ouspensky: he was interested in truth but never adopted the calculating posture of "the Sly Man." Gurdjieff saw this as one of his weaknesses.

The two men met in St. Petersburg in 1915. Gurdjieff was giving lectures in the city and Ouspensky had just returned from a tour of Egypt, Ceylon, and India, spending six weeks with Annie Besant at the Theosophical Society headquarters in Adyar. Thirty-seven years old, Ouspensky had already published a major book and was regarded as a perceptive connoisseur of new ideas.[50] The book, announced as a "key to the enigmas of the world"[51] and generally well received, failed to quiet his restless mind and so he had visited the Sphinx, the Taj Mahal, and other shrines, trying to absorb their sacred message and fix his place in the universe. Contemplating the seeming insubstantiality of his life, he doubted that the Sphinx could see him—even if he were to stand in front of it until death.[52] While in Ceylon, however, a Buddha

MAGIC, MYSTERY, AND SCIENCE

with sapphire eyes briefly but penetratingly gazed into the deepest recesses of his being.[53] And the Taj Mahal taught him that the soul goes on forever, both temporally and *spatially*. The resplendent edifice dissolving into the natural creation contained the finite remains of the empress's body, an obvious sign that her soul was now blended back into the universal All.[54]

Ouspensky took his trip "in search of the miraculous"; that is, to find a brotherhood or school whose adepts could then instruct him in the ways of truth.

> I could not explain it clearly, but it seemed to me that even the begin-
> ning of contact with a school may have a *miraculous nature*. I imag-
> ined, for example, the possibility of making contact with schools of
> the distant past, with schools of Pythagoras, with schools of Egypt,
> with the schools of those who built Notre Dame, and so on. It seemed
> to me that the barriers of time and space should disappear on making
> such contact. The idea of schools in itself was fantastic and nothing
> seemed to me too fantastic in relation to this idea.[55]

Not until returning to his native Russia did the miraculous occur upon meeting Gurdjieff. Here in Ouspensky's own backyard was the link he had sought to the storied wisdom of the past, and he later recalled that Gurdjieff "produced in me an unexpected desire to laugh, to shout, to sing, as though I had escaped from school or from some strange detention."[56] He immediately threw himself into the task of learning the master's "system" and announcing it to the world.

It is often remarked that Ouspensky did for Gurdjieff what Plato had done for Socrates. Certainly Ouspensky was assiduous in explaining Gurdjieff, but the latter's blunt and vulgar behavior kept the two men apart in their latter years. Ouspensky established a school in London to teach the Fourth Way and attracted many disciples of his own. Ironically, his wife, also a follower of Gurdjieff, assumed the role of shocking students into enlightenment, a task fitted to her forceful, even intimidating personality. In time, two distinct groups evolved, one more comfortable with Ouspensky's cerebral approach and another with an appetite for emotional vicissitude.

A major aspect of Ouspensky's approach entailed grasping the significance of the fourth dimension. This was a theme that he had developed before meeting Gurdjieff, whose teachings reinforced Ouspensky's conviction that portentous truths lay just beyond sight and hearing—perhaps hidden up in the fourth dimension. The concept was momentous because it provided a means of intuiting how transcendental reality might invisibly encompass and inform mundane experience. Moreover, the fourth dimension was the product of recent scientific and mathematical thought; as such, it seemed a legitimate portal to cosmic truth. All the same, educated thinkers generally failed to step across the threshold, a fact Ouspensky attributed to modern science's myopic commitment to positivism and materialism. His elaboration of the fourth dimension, therefore, rested on the belief that philosophically blinkered scientists viewed science too narrowly. "I felt," he said, "that there was a dead wall everywhere . . . [and] that professors were killing science in the same way as priests were killing religion."[57]

The idea of the fourth dimension sprang from the development of non-Euclidean geometries during the nineteenth century. Until then, Euclidean geometry had endured for more than two thousand years as a seemingly faultless description of physical reality's mathematical structure. Space consisted of three dimensions, all extending rectilinearly as far as the mind could imagine. The rectilinear character of space is proven by the fact that light, the agency that takes us beyond the bounds of immediate consciousness, travels in straight lines: we do not have to make adjustments as we walk toward distant objects— we just follow the line of sight. The three-dimensional nature of space is equally obvious: any point in space can be fixed by the intersection of three axes running at right angles to each other. Call one axis length, another width, and the third depth. Since a fourth axis or dimension cannot be imagined (try to step off mentally in some wholly new direction that is not a composite of the first three dimensions), the possibilities of space seem to be exhausted.

But, although a fourth dimension is physically unimaginable, it is possible to mathematically invent universes of four, five, or even an infinite number of dimensions, and once such activity got underway, it excited the interest of people like Ouspensky who were looking for scientific validation of their metaphysical predilections. The most common means of tapping the fourth dimension's transcendental significance drew upon firsthand experience with two- and three-dimensional objects. Thus, our own world could be thought of as a three-dimensional slice of the hyperspace (four-dimensional) realm. Or, to shift the imagery slightly, the present world could be understood as a three-dimensional shadow cast by four-dimensional reality. One might also assert that four-dimensional objects (hypersolids) are bounded by (three-dimensional) solids, just as solids are bounded by two-dimensional planes. Similarly, it might be that hypersolids rotate about planes, just as solids rotate about lines. Such conceptualizations of the fourth dimension required one merely to think in terms of lower-dimensional objects and then move up a dimension and strike mind-expanding analogies (an application of "As below, so above").

For some thinkers, however, analogies were insufficient to drive home the full import of the fourth dimension. These individuals took the view that indeed the fourth dimension could be, at least in part, imagined if the aspirant

MAGIC, MYSTERY, AND SCIENCE

were willing to work hard. C. H. Hinton was the leading advocate of this outlook, and his publications shaped Ouspensky's thinking on the subject. According to Hinton, hyperspace was to be apprehended by the "mental or inner eye."[58] His system for training the novice entailed the study of different arrangements of multi-colored cubes, the purpose of which was to free the individual of certain "self-elements" that had distorted his apprehension of the world since infancy. As one progressed in the system, he gradually transcended normal ways of comprehending objects and, like the prisoner who escapes from Plato's cave, begins to see things as they really are. The ultimate vision, at least for the trainee, came with the apprehension of the hypercube or tesseract, which could be visualized through the manipulation of the aforementioned cubes. One was to build a tesseract from an intricate arrangement of those cubes and then—in order to "see" it—pass the tesseract through three-dimensional space. Just as a sphere passes through a plane in two-dimensional slices, so the tesseract would pass through three-dimensional space in three-dimensional slices. And, just as a two-dimensional being could infer the shape of a sphere from the size of its slices as they first increase and then decrease, so a human being could infer the shape of a tesseract from the progression of slices—differentiated on the basis of color patterns—passing before her inner eye.

Ouspensky drank in all this as if it were nectar, but then added a significant modification: the fourth dimension was not another spatial dimension but the apparently ever-flowing stream of time. This reformulation followed on Einstein's identification of time as the fourth dimension, made just a few years earlier. The impulse, however, was somewhat different. Einstein added time as another coordinate, realizing that the pinpointing of events necessitates a temporal value as well as the three traditional spatial values. For Ouspensky, the idea distilled out of several drug-induced mystical experiences, which convinced him that everything *remains* extended in time, despite the appearance of retreating into the oblivion of the past. Nothing drops off or fades away; therefore, we are elongated in time just as we are in space. We are, he realized, "atoms of a great being, 'the great man' " that ever exists.[59]

The problem, said Ouspensky, is that even though time is not in process but rather "*the Eternal Now* of Hindu philosophy,"[60] we are able to experience it only in tiny increments. Hence, it seems a moving series of distinct moments. But this cannot be correct, for no single moment may be grasped. The past is gone, the future has not yet arrived, and the present moment is so fleeting as to register itself only as it slips away. The time line that we imagine, then, participates in the illusion of a one-dimensional geometric line—so thin as to have no width, each point real because lines must consist of points, but ultimately unreal because lacking width points lack physical magnitude. For time

NEW AGE PRELUDES

to be real, Ouspensky reasoned, it must be planar rather than linear, just as any "real" geometric line must be planar or two-dimensional. Extending perpendicularly from the time line, therefore, is the planar expanse of eternity, broadening events and giving them the substance or magnitude to be more than just illusory happenings. Hence, those events are eternally present.

One of Ouspensky's enduring concerns was the transitory and ultimately destructive (entropic) character of time. He anticipated that contact with an ancient wisdom tradition would collapse the barriers of time and space and give him an eternal perspective. Science, he felt, could do the same, for true knowledge comprehends religion, philosophy, science, and art.[61] Unfortunately, modern science suffered at the hands of positivism, a thought-inhibiting state of mind. Ouspensky argued that positivism had begun as a way of exploring "new avenues of thought" but then had petrified into the dogma that only material objects are real and worthy of scientific consideration. And now there are "academies and universities dedicated to its service. It is recognized; it teaches; it tyrannizes over thought."[62] Some day, however, "positivism will be defined as a system by the aid of which it was possible not to think of real things and to limit oneself to the region of the unreal and illusory."[63] Science opens out onto eternity, but its practitioners studiously avert their gaze toward transitory material entities.

Even if Ouspensky's criticism is wide of the mark, his yearning for a transcendent, timeless reality—one that cancels out physical disintegration and death—figures into science at some fundamental level. Einstein found solace in his theory of relativity, which suggested to him that events are ever-present in the space-time continuum. When Einstein's friend Michele Besso passed on shortly before his own death, he wrote:

> The foundation of our friendship was laid in our student years in Zurich, where we met regularly at musical evenings. . . . Later the Patent Office brought us together. The conversations during our mutual way home were of unforgettable charm. . . . And now he has preceded me briefly in bidding farewell to this strange world. This signifies nothing. For us believing physicists the distinction between past, present, and future is only an illusion, even if a stubborn one.[64]

Ouspensky could not have said it better.

10

ESP AND PSI PHENOMENA

The physical man may hear and understand the voice of another man at a distance of a hundred steps, and the ethereal body of a man may hear what
another man thinks at a distance of a
hundred miles or more.

—Paracelsus[1]

One conclusion was forced upon my
mind at that time, and my impression of its truth has ever since remained unshaken. It is that our normal waking consciousness, rational
consciousness as we call it, is but one
special type of consciousness, whilst
all about it, parted from it by the
filmiest of screens, there lie potential
forms of consciousness entirely different.

—William James[2]

Is it possible to reduce the human mind to scientific rule? Psychologists say yes
and appear to have made much progress toward that end. Furthermore, the
general public readily acknowledges psychology as a bona fide science by turning to therapists and analysts when personal difficulties arise or trial experts are
needed to assess abnormal social behavior. These people, by dint of their training and their ability to talk knowledgeably about human personality, command
our respect, notwithstanding occasional slurs to the effect that they are the
modern equivalent of Stone Age shamans.

But if psychology has found an uncontested niche in the pantheon of scientific disciplines, not so parapsychology, which is the study of "psi" phenomena. According to *The Encyclopedia of Parapsychology and Psychical Research*,[3] the word "psi" is "broad enough to encompass all the events and abilities of human beings and animals [that may be] termed paranormal," but it does not imply that the events and abilities *are* paranormal. That is, even though psi phenomena are presently unexplained, they are not inherently outside the range of scientific explanation. These phenomena are telepathy, clairvoyance, precognition, and psychokinesis. The first three effects are grouped as forms of extrasensory perception (ESP); the last, psychokinesis or PK, apparently has nothing to do with "sensing" anything and so stands by itself as a separate effect. It involves the mind's alleged ability to move or affect physical objects, like the gambler who supposedly "wills" the roll of the dice.

Today, some universities offer courses in parapsychology, though precious few (mostly in Europe) have parapsychology departments. The discipline has its share of critics, many of whom wonder if it has brought any clarity to the issues that inspired its birth.[4] Do we talk more insightfully about so-called psi experiences than people did one hundred or even one thousand years ago? Or does a façade of sophisticated experimentation, statistical analysis, and scientific jargon mask our continuing ignorance and possible self-deception?

Critics have tagged parapsychology an occult and unscientific pursuit for at least two reasons. First, some say the presumed existence of psi effects has no evidential backing; parapsychologists, therefore, have hitched their wagon to a star no one has ever actually seen. Even though Aristotle misunderstood the motion of falling bodies, they were at least within his (and everyone else's) realm of experience and, consequently, appropriate objects of scientific inquiry. Psi effects, however, are so fleeting and elusive that one may reasonably doubt their existence: they may be nothing more than rare coincidences. Two events happen to "click" or intersect, not because they are causally related but rather because the laws of chance favor their intersection over the long haul. If one regularly "senses" that one's ailing grandmother has recently died, odds are that news of her death will follow the "premonition," and the coincidence of the two events may seem uncanny and scientifically inexplicable. Yet numerous unfulfilled premonitions or hunches are generally quickly forgotten and so do not count against the highly memorable exception to the statistical rule. This is one way of accounting for psi effects, and even if it is resisted, the fact remains that those effects, unlike falling bodies, are not public events. They cannot be readily observed or reproduced.

A second reason for questioning the scientific status of parapsychology concerns its attempt to discover capacities of the mind historically associated with the occult dream of omniscience and total universal power. Wouldn't it be

MAGIC, MYSTERY, AND SCIENCE

wonderful to read others' thoughts, to see into the future, to know the winning lottery sequence in advance, to detect the presence of things through a "sixth sense" that does not diminish with distance, and to move physical objects, even stars and planets, by mere mental exertion? Such powers would bring one wealth, fame, power, and a literally mind-expanding understanding of the cosmos. But, alas, say the critics, all this is wishful thinking that has no place in science—except, perhaps, as a stage to be grown out of along the way to adulthood.

Taking a cue from Shakespeare, believers in psi often respond that "there are more things in heaven and earth" than materialistic science can fathom. Furthermore, scientific theories undergo constant revision: the heliocentric worldview was almost unthinkable before Copernicus, as were plate tectonics, the Big Bang theory, quantum discontinuity, and relativistic time dilation at the turn of the twentieth century. There is no reason, then, to accord sacrosanct status to any scientific precept. Indeed, we should be suspicious of anyone who uses science to make absolutist pronouncements, to utter the "last word" on any issue, for science enjoins intellectual humility.

These are not easy matters to sort out, particularly now that the background understandings that engendered the birth of modern science have been called into question. Paramount among these is Descartes's mind-matter dichotomy. Is mind utterly remote from material substance, confined somewhere in the brain as the mere receptacle of incoming sense data and therefore not mingled into the physical world? This may seem right and even commonsensical, but that perhaps is because the idea has enjoyed a long intellectual vogue and is now part of our social conditioning. And what about the related assumption, also seminal to modern science, that physical matter is lifeless? If this view and the mind-matter dichotomy were reversed, would that open the way for a mindful, sentient world where psi effects are part of the natural order? Suffice it to say, believers and skeptics dispute more than just the existence of those effects but also the very character of science. William James, a well-known psychologist, philosopher, and investigator of paranormal phenomena, wrote this:

> Why do so few "scientists" ever look at the evidence for telepathy, so-called? Because they think as a leading biologist, now dead, once said to me, that even if such were true, scientists ought to band together to keep it suppressed and concealed. It would undo the uniformity of nature and all sorts of other things without which scientists cannot carry on their pursuits.[5]

James might have added that scientists would not be able to carry on as they have in the recent past; nature's uniformity would be recast in ways that might

ESP AND PSI PHENOMENA

very well invalidate traditional assumptions and modes of scientific conduct. Science would still continue, but very possibly with newly acquired occult sensibilities. For many, however, this would be a giant step backward because (to follow David Ray Griffin) the "modern worldview . . . not only excludes [psi], but was in part *created to exclude it*."[6] The construction of modern science in the sixteenth and seventeenth centuries proceeded from the assumption that thoughts could not escape from the brain in physically unmediated ways to act upon other thoughts or upon material bodies. If science were to concede this point now, much intellectual progress would be rolled back. As Sigmund Freud remarked to Carl Jung, scientific acknowledgment of psi would unloose "the black tide of mud . . . of occultism."[7] Freud's comment puts the issue in its proper historical context, particularly now that some investigators link psi to near-death experiences, out-of-body experiences, UFOs, channeling, and other occult themes.

J. B. RHINE AND THE BEGINNINGS OF PARAPSYCHOLOGY

It was J. B. Rhine—the man Sir Arthur Conan Doyle called a "monumental ass"—who transformed the scientific study of spiritualist mediums into the scientific study of psi. The difference between the two, really, is a matter of who controls what or whom. Even in highly controlled séances, such as Eusapia Palladino's at Columbia University or Margery Crandon's in the Houdini box, the medium decides the flow of events. One night, a message from the dead might be received; the next night, perhaps, an ectoplasmic hand appears. Investigators had to be ready for anything and respond accordingly. In modern testing for psi, however, parapsychologists control the variables, including what phenomena will be studied. They also, following Rhine's lead, seek to grasp undiscovered mental capacities of humans and animals, not spirits from an unseen world.

Rhine (1895–1980) grew up in rural Pennsylvania, New Jersey, and Ohio, and as a young child heard stories about spiritualist mediums. His father, who had once attended a séance, was dismissive, but his less-educated mother put stock in the supernatural. Although his early educational opportunities were limited, Rhine made the most of them and impressed his teachers, one of whom—Louisa Wessecker—he married after serving as a Marine in World War I. Together the couple attended the University of Chicago, where both earned doctoral degrees in the biological sciences. At the time, John Watson's behaviorism rocked the campus. The theory purported that there is no spirit or soul, that humans are sophisticated machines, and that their behavior can be fully explained by mechanical principles. Although Rhine had abandoned the Christian beliefs of his childhood, he nevertheless found Watson's thesis too

Figure 37. Professor J. B. Rhine apparently testing a dog's psi ability

severe and eventually responded by taking up the study of what was then called "psychical research." Among other things, he wanted to show that the mind's psychic abilities are non-physical—they do not diminish with distance or the passage of time.[8] Thus, one could claim that some aspect of human personality is indifferent to physical law and, more important, to physical decay.

The Rhines are best remembered for the work they did at Duke University, where, as part of the psychology department, they devoted themselves to the study of psi. Early on, Louisa absented herself from the research to raise four children, but J.B. threw himself into full-time testing and analysis. He sought to find individuals who were psychically gifted. The standard test involved Zener cards (named after Rhine's colleague, K. E. Zener) with five faces: circle, square, plus sign, wavy lines, and star. (It was felt that these cards, unlike normal playing cards, could be easily distinguished and imaged.) Rhine would shuffle the cards, place one face down on a table, and ask the subject to identify it. After twenty-five calls or guesses, the results were tallied. Mere chance

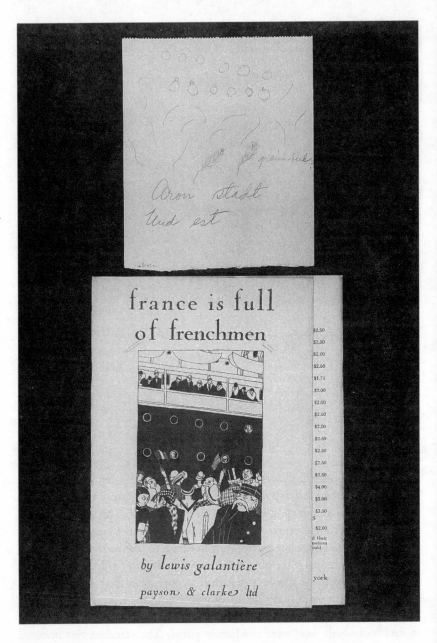

Figure 38. *A match in telepathy. The noted author Upton Sinclair believed that his wife had telepathic powers, or what he called "mental radio." Shown here is one of her best "hits." Bottom: a book's cover illustration, which Sinclair "sent." Top: Mrs. Sinclair's drawing of the message she "received." Most of Mrs. Sinclair's other images do not seem very accurate.*

Figure 39. Zener cards

dictated a 20 percent (one in five) success rate, or five correct guesses. Anything consistently above that would seem to indicate extrasensory perception.

One subject, Adam Linzmayer, once scored twenty-one correct, and Rhine knew that such was "virtually impossible by all the rules in the book of chance."[9] The rub was that Linzmayer could not perform consistently. The gift, if he actually possessed one, was fickle. Sometimes he scored high by looking out the window, other times he scored poorly (no better than chance) after being pressured into further testing. (The tests involved hundreds of calls.) Another subject, Hubert Pearce, registered similar scores and sometimes purposely scored low—perhaps one in twenty-five—just to show that he could defy the odds in either direction. Like Linzmayer, however, Pearce was unable to perform consistently, and as replication is all-important in science, his "good" performances were not widely accepted as evidence of ESP. Indeed, some thinkers interpreted them as instances of sloppy experimentation or even dishonesty.

Figure 40. Rhine looking on as Zener cards are used to test psi abilities. Rhine's experiments became increasingly rigorous and included screens between testers and subjects to reduce the possibility of cheating and "sensory leakage."

Critics have pointed out that Rhine's early experiments were, as a rule, poorly designed.[10] Simply laying cards on a table in the subject's presence allows for too much "sensory leakage." Even if the subject does not catch a glimpse of the card as it is placed on the table, he might (consciously or unconsciously) read cues from the tester's behavior or from the backside of the cards. In some cases, where attempts were made at greater experimental rigor by having the tester and subject in adjoining rooms, the tester's room was not secured to keep the subject from seeing into it and the subject was left unattended. That is, no one knew for sure what he was doing during the tests, an oversight that easily could have been avoided and one that left room for potential doubt. Also, the cards sometimes were not shuffled until the end of the day; the subject might therefore have discerned card sequences after just a few tests. This would explain the tendency of some subjects to improve their scores with further testing.

A final consideration, still highly relevant, involves similarities between psi testing and séances, notwithstanding Rhine's attempt to distance his work from the investigation of spiritualist mediums. Frequently, researchers seem to affect the experimental outcome by their very presence and attitude. Those who are believing and sympathetic tend to elicit better performances from subjects than those who are skeptical. Susan Blackmore, a modern student of psi who has turned from belief to skepticism, found no evidence of psi when she repeated positive experiments of others, and she wondered if her disbelief upset the subjects.[11] Many parapsychologists, insisting that psi cannot be treated, à la gravity, as a lifeless, mechanical force, agree: psi presupposes sympathetic interconnections conduced by shared belief, and skepticism short-circuits such. This stance, however, harks back to the spiritualist claim that mediums could be rendered ineffectual by disbelievers. What's more, some parapsychologists have argued that psi testing should not be too restrictive: the subject will perform better if allowed to relax and move around a little. This may be so, but a little freedom may also open the way for much trickery, as Eusapia Palladino demonstrated.

These similarities need not be taken as damning evidence of psi, however. Not all spiritualist phenomena could be traced to trickery, and there is no reason to suppose that a single research methodology can take the full measure of every anomalous effect. Like laughter, psi may flourish impromptu and be smothered by tight controls and preset agendas. Michael Crichton, author of *The Andromeda Strain* and *Jurassic Park,* makes this point while telling of a spoon-bending party he attended. There everyone threw straight spoons into a common pile, then picked up a spoon and tried to bend it, using only mind power (PK).[12] Although others, even children, easily bent their spoons, Crichton could not and, tiring of the effort, simply watched the party while still holding on to his spoon. Then someone congratulated him. He looked down and saw that the spoon had gone limp. He picked up another; it, too, wilted over. And so did another and another, until Crichton finally got bored and went looking for refreshments. He later concluded that PK works best when the mind is not intensely focused.

This, of course, is anecdotal, and the very idea of a spoon-bending party hardly inspires scientific confidence. Yet, Critchon's point that the mind occasionally "works" best when relaxed and softly focused seems true. William James pointed out that when a name escapes us, we instinctively try to retrieve it: "But sometimes this effort fails: you feel then as if the harder you tried the less hope there would be, as though the name were *jammed,* and pressure in its direction only kept it all the more from rising." The solution, of course, is to "[g]ive up the effort entirely; think of something altogether different, and in half an hour the lost name comes sauntering into your mind . . . as carelessly as if it had never been invited."[13] James found that religious conversion sometimes occurred this way: the breakthrough experience, often mystical in nature, came about after the petitioner gave up trying to reach God. He consequently proposed that if "there be higher powers able to impress us, they may get access to us only through the subliminal door."[14] Possibly psi effects reach us in the same way, below the radar of our scientifically attuned consciousness.

DEFINITIONS AND PERPLEXITIES

Needless to say, modern parapsychologists have learned from Rhine's early methods and evolved beyond them. Rhine himself led the way by constantly improving his experiments. As he did so, the positive psi results declined but never completely disappeared, and he died feeling that he had documented the existence of psi. Many modern parapsychologists feel the same way about their own research. Still, they have yet to silence their critics, most of whom appreciate the tremendous potential of psi phenomena—should such be verified—to upset standard assumptions about the world. Let us take a closer look at what psi entails.

As already noted, *psychokinesis* involves mind acting on physical matter. According to science (its underlying philosophical principles), this cannot happen: mind can apprehend and know matter but it has no capacity to physically affect it. Of course, things can happen in the brain, at the mind's instigation, whereby the body is set in motion to turn a doorknob or perform some other physical action. This, however, is vastly different from turning the knob by thought alone. Were this shown to be possible, scientific understandings such as physical causality and energy conservation would have to be reconsidered. What's more, longstanding practices that presuppose mental or spiritual influences effecting physical change—prayer, voodoo, the casting of magic spells, and so on—would seem to receive scientific confirmation.

Telepathy, if it occurs, entails reading another person's mind. In experimental circumstances, a sender attempts to transmit information by thought alone to a receiver behind a barrier or in another room. Many people can recall instances when they "sensed" a friend's thoughts, but this is not necessarily telepathy. Subtle visual or verbal cues may have played into experience. For these to be ruled out, the two individuals should be cut off from all sensory forms of communication with each other.

The term *clairvoyance* means "clear seeing" in French; that is, the ability to clearly "see" objects and events not apprehended by the five physical senses. Unlike telepathy, clairvoyance involves only one person, a receiver whose mind or consciousness presumably oversteps its sensory limitations. Sometimes, however, it is not easy to distinguish between the two. If one person "sends" an image of a duck and another "receives" it, what exactly has occurred? The receiver may have read the mind of the sender, or she may have discerned the duck clairvoyantly—she may have seen it directly through "remote viewing" (another term for clairvoyance).

The third type of ESP is *precognition*, or "knowing beforehand." This involves seeing events before they happen—seeing the future. Although this sounds unusual, it may be related to one of the most common of all psi experiences, *déjà vu*, which means "already seen" and refers to the feeling of having experienced or known a place or an event before. Most adults report having had déjà vu experiences, some of which involve entire conversations or several interrelated events. The difficulty comes with trying to link those experiences to unambiguous evidence of earlier thoughts, dreams, or experiences. Almost by definition, déjà vu entails indistinct or dreamy feelings that defy factual recapitulation, so the vaguely familiar experience may not be "pre-known" at all. Rather, it might be the result of a slight, short-lived hallucination. Or, turning back to the occult, it might be a residual memory of an earlier life, one that corresponds closely to the experience in question. This would make déjà vu more retro-cognition than pre-cognition; that is, remembrance or witness of happenings in the remote past. Should we interpret déjà vu as something we knew before it occurred, or as something we recall when it occurs? The evidence is as nebulous as the experience itself, and a few commentators, suggesting that to foreknow a future event is to render it probabilistic (knowledge of the future changes the present and thereby "resets" the future), wonder if precognition and déjà vu are not concepts of "doubtful intelligibility."[15]

In recent years, some researchers have proposed that categorizing psi into different forms is artificial and misleading. Everything might be collapsed into clairvoyance, if that term embraces both the ability to view things beyond one's spatial ken *and* a capacity to see backward and forward in time. Or, everything might arise from psychokinesis, mind acting not only on physical objects but also on other minds embedded in a field of universal consciousness.[16] Although these proposals model science's inclination to search for fundamental entities whose comprehension unifies our experience of the world, their content strikes many as scientifically outlandish and even scientifically irresponsible. Let the psi genie out of the bottle—free the mind from its four-centuries-long confinement in the brain—and there is no end to the scientific mischief that might ensue.

Whereas, in Rhine's day, skeptics could dismiss his psi claims by pointing to poor experimental design, today they often point out that positive results do not prove psi (or any other hypothetical entity) in any absolute sense. Small errors and unexpected variables are likely to crop up in even the most rigorous experiments, and so any talk of psi confirmation must be taken with a grain of salt. Furthermore, there are always the studies that go unreported—those that

ESP AND PSI PHENOMENA

fail to find evidence of psi and consequently fail to elicit interest among researchers who are looking for it. Such studies are consigned to file cabinets and forgotten; they thereby pile up as unseen evidence against psi.

Responding to these objections, psi advocates point out that no branch of science is immune to experimental error and uncontrolled variables; furthermore, novel findings always get more press than familiar understandings, particularly in journals dedicated to scientific advancement. Why then should parapsychology be singled out as a field that is fatally flawed when the flaws at issue are descriptive of science in general?

No doubt some of parapsychology's difficulties arise from a lack of consensus as to what might constitute proof of psi. Certainly an ESP superstar, the likes of which Rhine hoped to find in Linzmayer and Pearce, would constitute proof if he could dramatically display his talent to believers and skeptics alike in highly controlled settings. But, as Rhine realized to his dismay, the talent, if there really is one, is fugitive; it almost seems to "blow where it listeth."[17] And, even when Linzmayer and Pearce were performing well, they still missed more cards than they guessed correctly over a hundred or so trials. They were not the confident, all-knowing psychics of popular imagination but hopeful stewards of a precarious gift.

This assumes, of course, that they were not cheating or picking up on sensory cues. The salient point, however, is that when psi effects are confirmed in the laboratory, the margin of confirmation is almost always quite slim. The subject does not hit a home run every time at bat as the psychic stereotype might suggest. Nor does she know information in the crisp, factual way that a Jeopardy participant knows it. Instead, the knowledge is intuitive, half-formed, and often wide of the mark, but sometimes correct or close enough to be counted as correct. Unusual environmental factors—such as the tester's personality or perhaps even fluctuations in the earth's electromagnetic field[18]—are said to also play into experimental outcome, and all these considerations have led some thinkers to propose that the net of science is not well configured to catch psi effects. "Where attempts are made to establish the reality of paranormal phenomena," writes Eric Carlton, "it is disputable whether the usual scientific canons of evidentiality are even appropriate."[19] Objective knowing yields readily to objective testing, but what about intuitive guesses that exceed the statistical law of averages by only one or two percent? Is that evidence of psi or a consequence of experimental error, and how might we distinguish between the two?

To take a concrete example, consider one analysis of PK experiments that tested subjects' ability to mentally influence the roll of dice. As the participant focused on a tossed die, another control die was tossed and then results of the two dice were compared for significant statistical difference. Chance dictated a one in six success rate after many trials, and this is what subjects scored on the control dice (toward which no mental influences were directed). On the dice that were the focus of the subjects' attention, however, the success rate was 1 percent higher than chance expectation. This may not seem like much of a difference, but, given the number of trials, the odds against such were calculated at more than a billion to one.[20] Although these odds are certainly impressive, they are the consequence of many small fleeting instances, none of which seems very remarkable in its own right.

In other words, if psi exists, it manifests itself in the laboratory in tiny, almost apparitional ways.[21] To "see" it is to see something else that it could be, like experimental error. For this reason, the suggestion that psi be studied outside the laboratory strikes many as plausible. It "must be explained on its own terms, not in terms of the laws and principles that account for the objective phenomena of the physical world."[22] This is Fred Frohock's thinking, and his book, *Lives of the Psychics*, aims to describe psi in the rich and spontaneous milieu of everyday life as opposed to the tightly controlled setting of the research lab. This departure from scientific tradition is reminiscent of the shift that occurred in Catholic monasticism during the Late Middle Ages. Whereas initially monks sought spiritual truth in the cloistered, world-defying walls of the monastery, thereafter many ranged abroad to find it among peasants and townfolk. Perhaps psi also cannot be found within the modern scientific equivalent of the medieval cloister.

Given psi's spiritual resonance and that psi research stemmed from the investigation of spiritualistic phenomena, the comparison is apt. But it also leads one to wonder if psi is as elusive as spiritual truth, whose reality or non-reality is purely a matter of personal experience. Addressing the question before psi effects were partitioned off from spiritualistic happenings, William James once conjectured that

> the Creator has eternally intended this department of nature to remain *baffling*, to prompt our curiosities and hopes and suspicions all in equal measure, so that, although ghosts and clairvoyances, and raps and messages from spirits, are always seeming to exist and can never be fully explained away, they also can never be susceptible of full corroboration.[23]

This agnostic outlook finds an echo in modern science. Niels Bohr, a Nobel laureate in physics who read James's works, proposed that the universe enjoys just enough freedom "to hide its ultimate secrets from us."[24] We consequently will forever play catch-up with nature because the "minimal freedom" which allows nature to operate in ways that attract our interest also enables nature to escape our scrutiny once it becomes overbearing. Psi effects certainly attract

ESP AND PSI PHENOMENA

our interest, but in some ways they also seem to retreat at our approach, whether as real events or as mirages arising at certain intersections of mind and matter (like the illusion of water on the highway on a hot day). One response to their fleeting nature has been to broaden the domain of their operation. If they are truly extrasensory, then we must trace their origin to a realm beyond sense experience.

UNUS MUNDUS

Despite his misgivings about our ability to make sense of psi effects, William James sought to bring them within the orbit of human understanding—even if it were not the orbit marked out by the science of his day. He questioned the classical model of the brain and its assumption that consciousness is the product of neurophysiological processes. As every person's brain is physically distinct from all others, this assumption led to the view that each brain is a tiny consciousness theater cut off from other theaters. That is, consciousness is strictly a private, "inside" affair. Two people can interact through the senses but neither can step into the other's consciousness to know firsthand that person's inner experience.

But suppose, said James, that the brain does not produce consciousness but merely mediates or transmits it. The consciousness in this case would not be individually produced but universally available roughly in the way that light is universally available to a prism. As James puts it: "Consciousness in this process does not have to be generated *de novo* in a vast number of places. It exists already, behind the scenes, coeval with the world."[25] He proceeds to enumerate several advantages of this alternative outlook, one of which is that it renders psi phenomena less problematic. The psi connections would be implicit in the universal consciousness, ready to be made explicit under given circumstances. Not incidentally, the idea of universal consciousness naturally leads on to other religious or occult possibilities. When the brain becomes unusually transparent or receptive, then one might undergo the kind of consciousness-expanding experiences spoken of by saints and mystics. And when one's physical body dies, James points out, "individual" consciousness may be thought to return to its "mother-sea."[26] Such are the implications of a world sympathetically knit together by a universal consciousness.

Almost by definition, psi presupposes a world of sympathetic interconnections. Science recognizes interconnections as well but portrays these as brute forces of nature, like gravity and electromagnetism. In either case, the world coheres, but according to different principles. Gravitational and electromagnetic forces are "real" because they produce effects that are both readily observable and amenable to mathematical description. What's more, to some extent those forces may be mechanically modeled; even though we cannot see gravity in intermediate space (in between the physical bodies it acts upon), we can imagine a "field" through which it moves or traveling "gravitons." At no point in any of this does gravity emerge as a living entity, and so explanations remain cool and dispassionate. Emotion or personal meaning does not figure in, because the world is an emotional blank.

Refusing to accept the impersonal, uncaring cosmos of early-twentieth-century science, Carl Jung fashioned an outlook that, above all, emphasized and validated personal meaning. A central concept thereof is synchronicity, which he termed "an acausal connecting principle."[27] That is, something more fundamental than mechanical necessity or causal relation brings the cosmos into unity, and this is *meaningful* coincidence. Both *synchronicity* and *coincidence* connote events occurring at the same time, but coincidence, as generally understood, signifies the interesting but *accidental* (non-meaningful) intersection of two events. For example, when terrorists destroyed the World Trade Center towers and part of the Pentagon on September 11, 2001, commentators quickly observed that the numerical month and day—9/11—coincided with 911, the standard emergency call number in the United States. No one, however (to our knowledge), read any meaning into this coincidence; it seemed mere happenstance.

For all we know, it was indeed mere happenstance. Occasionally, however, coincidences are so compelling as to elicit a sense of destiny or providence. Jung, who practiced psychiatry in Switzerland, experienced many coincidences whose significance and improbability, he believed, defied scientific explanation; thereby the universe conspired to gently nudge him and others toward self-fulfillment. On one occasion, he was working with a young woman whose troubles stemmed from her tendency to block out poetic or mythic considerations in favor of reason or logic. As she related a dream in which she was given a piece of golden jewelry fashioned after a scarab beetle, Jung heard a scratching on a nearby window and saw a large insect. Opening the window, he let the insect fly in and caught it. It was, Jung reports, "the nearest analogy to a golden scarab that one finds in our latitudes, a scarabaeid beetle, the common rose-chafer (*Cetonia aurata*), which contrary to its usual habits had evidently felt an urge to get into a dark room at that particular moment."[28] The treatment could then proceed successfully, for the event had shattered the patient's intellectual armor, which in fact was straitjacketing her emotional life.

Skeptics respond that statistics favor the rare occurrence of experiences such as this; there is no need, therefore, to read more into them than the chance intersection of two causally unrelated streams of events. Because hundreds of psychiatrists advise patients every day, it would actually be surprising if something like this did not happen on occasion—just as it would be surprising if no

ESP AND PSI PHENOMENA

one ever won the lottery or beat the odds at Las Vegas. For Jung, however, this response missed the point entirely. Certainly any coincidence, no matter how unlikely, can be chalked up to chance by outside observers who have no personal stake in it. But when the universe seems to pay an individual a personal visit, when it shows itself mindful of someone's desperate need, to that person the statistical explanation rings hollow. "One can never fathom an emotion [or, experience] or divine its dictates by standing outside it," wrote William James. "Each emotion obeys a logic of its own, and makes deductions no other logic can draw."[29] We might add that standing outside an event is central to the scientific aim of dispassionate objectivity.

This is not to say the skeptical attitude is wrong, just that its logic is not all-embracing. Jung, feeling that materialistic science could not carry the full weight of the human experience, reached back to a time when mind or meaning rather than mechanical necessity held the universe together. Interestingly, he tells us "[i]t was Einstein who first started me off thinking about a possible relativity of time as well as space, and their psychic conditionality. More than thirty years later this stimulus led to my relation with the physicist Professor W. Pauli and to my thesis of psychic synchronicity."[30]

Einstein and Jung became acquainted in Zurich shortly after the former had published his first papers on the special theory of relativity. Wolfgang Pauli, formulator of the Pauli exclusion principle in atomic physics, collaborated with Jung in drawing out the possible significance of synchronicity to science. Jung also took an interest in Niels Bohr's principle of complementarity, which proposes that something may possess two contradictory aspects, neither of which is more fundamental than the other and both of which are essential to a "complete," albeit necessarily somewhat paradoxical, understanding of the object. A stock example here is light, which under some circumstances appears as a particle and under other circumstances as a wave. Jung posited similar complementarity relationships between the conscious and the unconscious, and between psychic experience and external reality. These relationships (particularly the latter) blur the line between mind and matter. Since neither is more fundamental than the other, neither can be explained independently of the other. In effect, Jung proposed that physics and psychology lean on each other: no comprehensive theory of reality is possible until the two disciplines begin to merge in a complementary fashion.

To Jung (and many others), it seemed that recent revolutionary developments in physics had already cleared a path for such a merger. Reinterpreting the fundamental processes of nature in probabilistic and acausal terms, quantum physics offered space for Jung's belief that psychic interconnections are enabled by something other than mechanical causality. Classical (pre-1900) physics had seen the world as a ceaseless flow of lifeless atoms, all locked into

MAGIC, MYSTERY, AND SCIENCE

the mechanical requirements of Newton's laws of motion. Now physics was challenging philosophical premises it had once held dear. Particles were not hard-edged little entities reacting deterministically to other particles; they had a wave aspect that made their behavior uncertain, at least to a small degree. Furthermore, this uncertainty was ontological rather than epistemological; that is, it resided in nature itself rather than in our inability to clearly observe or measure nature. Physicists were not just reaching the limits of their technology but were in fact venturing into a radically new vision of physical reality.

Because it is ontological in origin, quantum uncertainty allows certain events to occur uncaused. When, for example, a radioactive particle decays, nothing causes or compels it to decay at that moment. It could have decayed at a different moment. The particle, originating out of a probabilistic wave, simply inclines one way or the other, and nothing whatsoever forces or requires the inclination. Put differently, the decay event occurs spontaneously within a range of possibilities, none of which is determined in an ironclad way by prior circumstances.

The import of this new outlook can hardly be overstated. Since the eighteenth century, physicists had assumed that events followed deterministically from prior events; there was, consequently, no "free play" or spontaneity in nature. And because the story of nature amounted to a mechanical unfolding of events, it was possible, in principle, to work out that story from beginning to end. With quantum physics, however, this conceptually tidy, sharply detailed picture goes out of focus. Not only does it become impossible to make precise predictions about individual particles, but the very idea of an individual, self-contained particle becomes problematic. That idea presupposes a well-defined location in space and time, but, because of their wave properties, particles do not always show up as distinct, particle-like entities. To some extent they are "smeared" across space-time regions in ways that invalidate the classical definition of a particle.

While some lamented these striking developments, Jung found them provocative. If the fundamental constituents of the world—subatomic particles—are not confined to precise space-time limits, then it would seem probable that human beings, in subtle ways, are similarly unconstrained. Given the right circumstances, our thoughts might overleap space and time intervals instantaneously. This possibility gained plausibility as quantum physicists began to talk about non-locality, non-separability, and quantum entanglement. These terms, roughly equivalent, refer to the incredible discovery that two distantly separated particles interact non-locally; that is, as if they were conjoined.[31] They appear blithely indifferent to the separating modalities of space and time.

All this pointed toward what Jung called *unus mundus* (one world): the recognition that mind and matter interpenetrate to the point of unity. The

ESP AND PSI PHENOMENA

mind is not separate from outer reality; it does not somehow double or reflect outer reality from across the Cartesian divide of ontological duality. In other words, the living, active mind is not the categorical opposite of inert, passive matter. Rather, it may be said to draw its capacity for sense experience and thought from a living, knowing universe. And the physical brain may be likened to a tuning fork that vibrates sympathetically with the larger intelligence of the cosmos.

This outlook makes psi phenomena normal rather than paranormal or anomalous. As long as physical nature is deemed inert and mechanical, psi effects shape up as inexplicable instances of mind extending beyond its scientifically assigned residence in the brain. But if the universe were bound together by its own innate intelligence, then those effects would fall fully within the realm of expectation. The universe, naturally mindful of its mind-saturated contents, could facilitate the meaningful transfer of thought, image, or feeling across vast reaches of space and time.

Turning to psychology, Jung adduced evidence for the existence of a communal mind experience that all humans freely share in. Science springs from our conscious experience of the world, but we habitually exit consciousness and drift into unconsciousness. The two states, although opposite, stand in complementary relation to each other. Whereas consciousness is individuated and sharply demarcated by space-time intervals, unconsciousness is collective and unbounded by space and time. During dreams, people freely intermingle: the dead return, faraway friends or long-forgotten acquaintances appear, two individuals merge into one, and one person morphs into another. It is as if space-time barriers, so ubiquitous and absolute during consciousness, no longer hold sway.

The skeptic may object that unconsciousness is merely "down time" for the waking mind and therefore counts for nothing in our attempt to understand the world. Jung's response is that this is easy to say but impossible to put into practice, for unconsciousness counts for much in everyday life. We are amphibians who maintain overall health and balance by tacking back and forth between both realms. As the Greeks realized long ago, neglecting the unconscious—the irrational—short-circuits our power to reason about the world.[32] We cannot cut ourselves off from the madness of our nightly dreams, for instance, without having that madness invade waking reality. (Try going several days without sleep.) To launch a sustained attack on the unconscious, to insist on its triviality, therefore, one must regularly give oneself up to its wild contents.

Bolstering his argument, Jung further elaborated the similarity between wave-particle duality and the conscious-unconscious complementarity relation. As a rule, conscious experience is filled with distinct (particle-like) entities precisely located in space and time. These we have no difficulty observing; in fact, observation is a defining feature of waking reality. Unconscious experience, however, is impossible to observe directly—we are unconscious of it—and hard to observe indirectly. We may recall our dreams (generally in vague details) but these occur during periods of light sleep when the mind is surfacing toward consciousness. Dreamless sleep is completely inaccessible in a direct, immediate way, but, as Socrates noted, it feels great afterward (so we know we experienced it). The crucial point is that what we do so instinctively during consciousness—observe, analyze, and so on—never occurs during unconsciousness. In a roughly similar way, waves in quantum physics do not lend themselves to direct observation: the moment researchers try to see or measure a wave, it becomes its complementary opposite—a particle.

Now consider what happens the moment a dreamer tries to step outside her dream to observe or analyze it rationally: she awakes from it and returns to the particle-like, individuated world of conscious experience. The narrowly focused objective gaze pops the delicate dream-bubble. It also pops waves, or, as physicists put it, observation "collapses the wave function." Before the pop (the "quiff," in quantum slang), however, both waves and dreams are sites of surreal complexity: they gather together what waking, rational reality (space and time) holds apart. The probabilistic wave teems with possibilities, all mutually exclusive from a rational point of view, and only collapses upon a single possibility when pricked from the outside by an objective gaze. Or, perhaps, the wave is perforated from the inside as the would-be observer opts for a third-person, outside perspective.

If this sounds strange, that is because it *is* strange. Richard Feynman, perhaps the most celebrated physicist of the last half of the twentieth century, regularly insisted that quantum physics "describes Nature as absurd from the point of view of common sense."[33] Still, there are metaphors that facilitate understanding, and one often invoked to describe the collective unconscious relies on our familiar experience with waves. Consider a sine wave intersected by a horizontal axis. Above the axis are peaks, each separate from all the others. These may be said to represent the individuated egos of conscious experience. When sleep occurs, the axis drops down so that individuality or differentiation is lost in the oceanic expansiveness of the unconscious state. As with water waves, the separate peaks are merely superficial projections of a single underlying unity.[34]

Putting the issue in broad perspective, James Jeans wrote that there "is no longer a dualism of mind and matter, but of waves and particles; these seem to be the direct, although almost unrecognizable descendents of the older mind and matter, the waves replacing mind and the particles matter."[35] In other words, upon close inspection (quantum experimentation), the older dualism

ESP AND PSI PHENOMENA

transmutes into the newer one. As mind scrutinizes matter, it finds wave-like traces of its own presence in the particulate phenomena. What is it doing "out there" when, according to the canons of materialistic science, it is only "in here"?

Most people, following Freud, think of the unconscious as a private, strictly "in here" affair. Jung, breaking with his erstwhile mentor, characterized it as collective and transpersonal. The meaning it mediates far eclipses anything we could summon up in our conscious, egocentric fantasies, and so our lives become personally meaningful in ways that are unspeakable, even sacred. In other words, thanks to our nightly passage into unconsciousness, personal meaning does not spiral in on itself but, rather, spirals outward toward truths that transcend individual anxiety. Jung called these truths archetypes. Since archetypes are sources of meaning, we can gain no explanatory advantage over them; motivating the explanatory impulse, they are thereby unthreatened by it. As Jung observed, "[T]he position of the archetype would be located beyond the psychic sphere, analogous to the position of the physiological instinct, which is immediately rooted in the stuff of the organism."[36] Elsewhere he stated that archetypes are "irrepresentable."[37]

Notwithstanding their immunity to representation and explanation, archetypes register their existence across cultures by organizing human experience in common ways. Jung inferred their existence from studying the content of dreams and myths. Others have insisted that archetypal images (not archetypes themselves but expressions thereof) show up in other ways. In fact, Jung was not the first to broach the idea. Behind every phenomenon, said Goethe, is an ur-phenomenon—"an ultimate which can not itself be explained, which is in fact not in need of explanation, but from which all that we observe can be made intelligible."[38] To illustrate his thesis, Goethe noted morphological similarities among many different plants and argued that these could be traced to an archetypal plant, which may be regarded as the template for all plants. To vary the metaphor, the plants we see are notes held together by a universal melody, the archetypal plant. Since this plant shows up nowhere in particular but everywhere as a general formative principle, it may be likened to Plato's forms, which structure the world by virtue of their transcendent reality.

We need not digress into Plato, other than to say that he, like Jung and Goethe, believed that human experience is conditioned by archetypal principles, although humans often fail to realize as much. These principles not only shape our experience; they also—as Goethe proposes above—light it up with intelligibility. For some, this is an unexpected but highly pleasing aspect of Jung's outlook. It takes us by surprise because we are used to viewing physical nature as an obstacle to understanding, not as the very occasion of understanding. Materialistic science, proceeding from the Cartesian premise that mind and matter are utterly dissimilar, seems to stare past the monumental difficulty that that premise engenders: How can mind make contact with (know) matter when each is real in a completely different way? According to Carl Friedrich von Weizsacker, a noted physicist who was sympathetic to Jung's views, this difficulty has been repressed so successfully that it no longer registers as a problem for most people; even philosophers often take the explanatory success of science in stride without bothering to ask how such is possible given science's commitment to mind-matter dualism. To follow Weizsacker: "Present-day philosophy of science has not only been unable to answer the question [of] why or how fundamental science is possible; it has not even been able to see what is the problem."[39]

If this intransigence is real, then we are brought back to William James's point that anomalies such as telepathy, if openly acknowledged, might "undo the uniformity of nature and all sorts of other things without which scientists cannot carry on their pursuits." James wrote this before quantum theory began to shock the physics community, and had he lived to experience that revolution, would certainly have mined it for philosophical implications. The physicists who brought it about could not help debating its metaphysical import, and, interestingly, some sought to reorient science toward the prospect of mind-matter unity.[40] "Yet, curiously," write Robert Jahn and Brenda Dunne, "the degree to which they and their students pondered and discussed these [quantum] dilemmas . . . seems substantially less appreciated by present practitioners and students of science than are their analytical formalisms and physical data."[41] B. Alan Wallace, arguing that inner reality—subjectivity or consciousness—is neither understood by science nor admitted into its forums (we can talk about it but only under the pretense of objectivity—as if we were outside looking in), makes the same point: "Given the startling conclusions of quantum mechanics, it is remarkable that its insights have had so little impact on science as a whole."[42] This lack of impact he attributes to the practical exigencies of World War II, which interrupted the philosophical conversation initiated by Bohr, Einstein, Schrödinger, and others, and to the successes of materialistic science in other quarters. These developments, Wallace believes, have made it easy for scientists to disregard the subtle but unanticipated ways mind seems to insert itself in physical matter at the quantum level. As a consequence, "we in the modern West are unknowingly living in a dark age."[43]

But it is fear of another dark age—the so-called dark ages of medieval Europe—that figures into the birth throes of modern science. Jung would reply that we need not let the pendulum swing that far back. Using its own discoveries, science can correct its own excesses without, as Freud speculated, being

ESP AND PSI PHENOMENA

swept away by the occult. For Jung, *unus mundus* brought mind and matter onto the same playing field and thereby sanctioned the reality of psi effects while affording a means of understanding them. More important, *unus mundus* promised to humanize science. With the universe suffused with meaning, personal meaning would no longer seem so out of place.

11 NAZISM AND ANCESTRAL GERMAN MEMORIES

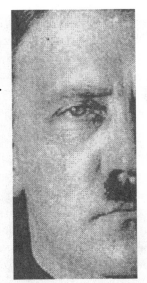

> I cannot be mistaken. What I do and
> say is historical.
>
> —*Adolf Hitler*[1]

> With childlike lack of sophistication
> [the Nazis] only wanted to be the
> greatest humans, the master race. . . .
> They were the *halbgebildeten*, drunk,
> as is the way with the half-educated,
> with the half-truth.
>
> —*Peter Padfield*[2]

Historians often make their mark by rehabilitating unpopular figures. Richard Nixon, for example, enjoyed a slight vogue of redemptive acknowledgment during his last years, thanks in part to his own efforts and to several mostly positive scholarly reassessments of his presidency. It did not hurt either that Watergate fell into place as a strictly historical event; because it has no mythic resonance, with each passing year it gets smaller and easier to deal with charitably. For all his faults, Nixon was still, after all, a relatively normal human being.

Opposite Nixon are rare individuals for whom it is hard to muster up any sympathy. Adolf Hitler is one of these. His crimes do more than repulse us;

Figure 41. Adolf Hitler

MAGIC, MYSTERY, AND SCIENCE

they stagger our ability to see him as a fellow human being. He therefore looms up as archetypally evil, a kind of demonic interloper on the stage of human affairs. Bearing this aspect, Hitler has invited a great deal of occult speculation, the assumption being that only one in league with the powers of darkness could wreak so much destruction. According to one author, Hitler was driven to megalomaniac madness by the holy "spear of destiny" (the spear that pierced Christ's side as he hung on the cross), whose spell he came under during his youthful, knockabout years in Vienna.[3] Other writers have developed links with Aleister Crowley (the English magician who proclaimed himself "the Great Beast"), Gurdjieff, UFOs, astrology, the Holy Grail, and a host of other occult possibilities.[4] The truth is that most of these were at best peripheral to Hitler's thinking. To be sure, Hitler and some of his paladins—Heinrich Himmler, in particular—were caught up in fantasies that fall easily under the occult rubric, but these stemmed principally from Germanic folklore which suggested that Germany and Austria, badly defeated in the Great War, were destined for ultimate victory and redemption. Mixed into this glorious prospect was a pseudo-evolutionary theory that exalted the Aryan race and impugned the principles of liberal democracy. In and of itself, this outlook was just one of any number of misinformed readings of the past and future. What made it danger-ous and darkly occultic was the blind and mystical fervor with which it was espoused.

"To 'learn' history," wrote Hitler, "means to seek and find the forces which are the causes leading to those effects which we subsequently perceive as his-torical events."[5] Historians may redress the injustices of the past in their books, but academic concern with historical fact signals an ignorance of the underlying forces that sweep peoples toward their destiny. Believing that he had sought and found those forces, Hitler felt himself fated to bring about a final reckoning consisting of much more than a retrospective reshuffling of historical facts. The world, he said with Germany's World War I defeat in mind, would be cut free from "the chaos of an historic past that has become an absurdity."[6]

GRANDIOSE SELF-DECEPTION

In our discussion of Renaissance magic (chapter 2), we noted that ego infla-tion often accompanies the practice of magic. Feeling himself aligned with cosmic powers, the magician trespasses on the divine, and since All is One, he may make no distinction between his own individual destiny and that of the world at large. Surely Hitler failed to make that distinction, although it was not Renaissance magic that precipitated his fantasies of world deliverance but the earthier and purely psychological magic of Teutonic myth, in some cases mingled into and magnified by Richard Wagner's music. "Teutonic" refers to the peoples of Northern Europe whose languages and ancestry have Germanic or Nordic-Aryan roots—Germans, of course, but also Scandinavians and Anglo-Saxons. The designation is imprecise because the so-called Teutonic tribes had never isolated themselves from other ethnicities. In the Early Middle Ages, for example, Vikings streamed down from Scandinavia to conquer England, Normandy, and parts of western Russia, in the process mixing in with indigenous populations. Such blurrings, which are the broad highway of history, erode the notion that humankind naturally breaks apart into a hierarchy of fixed racial categories. Nevertheless, Hitler advocated a triumphalist worldview that pitted Aryans against other, "inferior" peoples whom he felt were trying to "bastardize" the master race and thereby keep it from fulfilling its providential destiny. Chief among these was the Jewish people.

Where did Hitler get his warped view of the past? Part of it no doubt stemmed from personal insecurities and compulsions. In *Mein Kampf*, the autobiography he wrote in prison, he exaggerated his youthful accomplishments by portraying himself as a well-liked, high-minded natural leader and an able scholar. In fact, he had few boyhood friends and struck his peers as remote and somewhat odd. And, instead of excelling at his studies, he failed some of his classes and did badly in others. Eventually he dropped out of school and lived off his parents (or a small inheritance when they died and an orphan's pension) without attempting to find regular employment. Most acquaintances during these early years recall that he was lazy or at least too caught up in his fantasies to apply himself to steady work. Inclined to extended periods of grandiose thought, he worked up a heroic self-image that contrasted sharply with the impression he made on others. Many found him banal, although in his own mind he was anything but.

This tendency to distort his own past spilt over into Hitler's sense of human history. Picking up on ideas already flourishing in some quarters, he determined that Aryans alone are capable of kindling the light of human understanding. Other peoples may benefit from and perpetuate that light, but they cannot strike it into existence. Aryans, then, are the creators and guardians of civilization, and this is a fact decreed by nature. The rub was that, in recent centuries, "the Eternal Jew" had "poisoned" Aryan bloodlines through marriage and rape, thereby threatening to drive the master race into extinction and throw the world into darkness. Or, to invoke another of Hitler's revolting metaphors, the weaker but more insidious race was winning the struggle for existence much as a parasite destroys a healthy body by infecting it with disease.

To reverse the enemy advantage, Hitler advocated taking up arms against liberal democracy, on the one hand, and Marxism, on the other. With the first ideology stressing human equality and the second international brotherhood, both threatened to level nature's racial hierarchy. And both—particularly

Marxism—were being masterminded by Jews. Given this and Germany's defeat in the Great War, another world war was, for Hitler, inevitable. The second war was necessary to roll back the progress of the Jews, who had engineered Germany's defeat and who now sought to extinguish the last spark of Aryan consciousness.

Believing that success is more likely when endeavors are charged with cosmic significance, Hitler characterized the conflict between Jews and Aryans as a death struggle whose outcome would either ratify or violate the will of heaven. "What we must fight for," he wrote, "is to safeguard the existence and reproduction of our race and our people, the sustenance of our children and the purity of our blood, the freedom and independence of the fatherland, so that our people may mature for the fulfillment of the mission allotted to it by the creator of the universe."[7]

Such language strikes deep emotional chords (whether it enthralls or offends), and Hitler understood that nothing motivates more effectively than simple concepts bathed in larger-than-life imagery and raised to a feverish, mystical pitch. No matter that the concepts lack empirical support so long as their metaphysical scope and import dramatizes one's worldview. Thus, Hitler subscribed to Hans Hörbiger's Cosmic Ice theory, wherein the universe cataclysmically rocks to and fro as fire battles with ice for ascendancy.[8] Similarly, Wagner's operas, starkly contrasting the glorious Teutonic past with the enfeebled present, enraptured the young Hitler into believing that cosmic disaster—*Götterdämmerung*, or twilight of the Teutonic gods—would ensue (or would remain in force) should he fail to keep his appointment with destiny. A boyhood friend, August Kubizek, recalled that, after one performance, he and Hitler retired in darkness to a hillside where Hitler vented his passion: "Words burst from him like a backed-up flood breaking through crumbling dams. In grandiose, compelling images, he sketched for me his future and that of his people."[9]

In all this there was, it seems, a sense of being seized upon by an outside power, not unlike that experienced by soothsayers and shamans when delivering knowledge from beyond. Hitler reports that when he first tried his hand at public speaking in obscure political venues in Munich, his audiences were "electrified" and "astonished." Not only that, but he himself realized that "the thing that I had always presumed from pure feeling without knowing it was now corroborated: I could 'speak.' "[10] Subsequently, his public addresses became command performances resonating sexual, mystical, and mediumistic overtones. They were, writes Joachim Fest, "curious couplings of delirium and rationality" ending in "frenzy, more climaxes, and then the ecstasies released by the finally unblocked oratorical orgasms."[11] Many recalled that Hitler appeared to slip into a trance and even ectoplasm, or something like it, seemed to enlarge

NAZISM AND ANCESTRAL GERMAN MEMORIES

his presence;[12] it was as if he were communing with higher (or lower) powers. Otto Strasser, writing after he had turned against Hitler, said this: "Adolf Hitler enters a hall. He snuffs the air. For a minute he gropes, feels his way, senses the atmosphere. Suddenly he bursts forth. . . . His words go like an arrow to their target, he touches each private wound on the raw, liberating the mass unconscious, expressing its innermost aspirations, telling it what it most wants to hear."[13] Hence, "[a]n exchange of pathologies took place."[14]

Whereas Joseph Goebbels, the other great orator of the Nazi regime, always prepared his addresses beforehand, Hitler extemporaneously spoke "as the spirit move[d] him" upon clairvoyantly sensing his listeners' wants.[15] At such moments, said Strasser, he acted with the self-assurance of a "sleepwalker," actually a "dream-walker" (*Traumwandler*).[16] And adding to the drama were the splendid stage effects, all carefully prepared in advance with the aim of reproducing the mysterious, magical atmosphere that attended Wagner's operas.[17] Particularly memorable were the Nuremberg rallies of the 1930s. One witness, a patron of Russian ballet, wrote that "for grandiose beauty," no ballet could compare with the mass gatherings.[18] Alan Bullock offers this description:

> To see the films of the Nuremberg rallies even today is to be recaptured by the hypnotic effect of thousands of men marching in perfect order, the music of the massed bands, the forest of standards and flags, the vast perspectives of the stadium, the smoking torches, the dome of searchlights. The sense of power, of force and unity was irresistible, and all converged with a mounting crescendo of excitement on the supreme moment when the Führer himself made his entry. Paradoxically, the man who was most affected by such spectacles was their originator, Hitler himself, and, as Rosenberg remarks in his memoirs, they played an indispensable part in the process of self-intoxication.[19]

Only gradually did the tide of everyday events begin to disabuse Hitler of his megalomania. After 1942, he ceased speaking in public, perhaps sensing that with the war going badly, he could no longer draw positive energy from large audiences.[20] Still, until the end of his life, he managed to find brief respite from waking reality by retreating into visions of world mastery.[21] Shoved away, the ugly present—the Red Army advancing from the East, the Allied bombings of German cities, and the D-Day invasion—momentarily yielded to the bright but illusory future of the thousand-year Reich.

In science, there is an old adage that beautiful theories are forever being pummeled by ugly facts of nature. By and large, Hitler and his deputies had little use for facts that did not conform to their preconceived views of reality. It was as if sheer will to power could decide the course of history. Since, however,

MAGIC, MYSTERY, AND SCIENCE

they believed that they were privy to the larger narrative of creation, it followed that history was on their side. This is the grand self-deception that often accompanies occult thinking: because my mind has been dilated to seemingly cosmic limits, I really do see things clearly. So deceived, Hitler spoke against "obscure mystical elements" and "cult rituals" because these insinuated murky, half-formed concepts. He laid claim instead to "clear knowledge" and "open avowal" which is "natural and hence willed by God."[22] He was so misled by miasmatic fantasies that he thought he was transcending them altogether.

THE MIASMA

Hitler's belief that he was "historical"—that he bestrode the stage of history like a colossus—kept him aloof from some of the more prosaic occult aspects of Nazism. While reports circulated that he consulted astrologers on political and military matters, evidence indicates that he disparaged astrology, despite horoscopes published by the German press favoring his rise to power. Around 1934, the press quit publishing horoscopes on all Nazi leaders, apparently because Hitler did not want the movement tainted by astrological obscurity or, even worse, inauspicious horoscopes. To some degree, however, Nazism was already infected by "obscure mystical elements," the like of which repelled Hitler. Astrology fascinated Rudolf Hess, a high-ranking deputy who flew solo to Scotland in 1941 to initiate peace talks with the British. He purportedly relied on astrological data as he planned the flight—but apparently to no avail: he was immediately locked up and spent the rest of his life (until the age of ninety-two) in prison.

Other Nazi officials, notably Joseph Goebbels and Heinrich Himmler, flirted with the notion that they had lived through earlier incarnations: Goebbels as an associate of Hitler in a bygone era, and Himmler as King Heinrich, a medieval king whose consolidation of German power prepared the way for the Holy Roman Empire. Of course, reincarnation *per se* does not betoken a predisposition to the occult, even in the West where a theosophical redolence still clings to it. (While General George Patton is generally not regarded as having occult sympathies, he yet explained his uncanny familiarity with European battle terrain as the residual memory of his earlier life as a Roman military commander.) Because, however, Himmler and Goebbels felt themselves spiritually connected to the prehistoric Aryan utopia that they were trying to reconstitute, they were vulnerable to a whole host of related deceptions.

For his part, Hitler had little romantic attachment to the distant past, except perhaps as it was mediated through Wagner's musical dramas. His interest was more current and he once stated that he had no forerunners except for Wagner.[23] Nevertheless, while living in Vienna, he may have come into contact with

NAZISM AND ANCESTRAL GERMAN MEMORIES

a particularly virulent strain of anti-Semitism—one based in theosophical pseudo-evolutionary thinking. We do know that he helped himself to the Jewish hate-literature that was readily available in Vienna and that, when he left the city in 1913 (at the age of twenty-four), his anti-Semitism had fully crystallized. Relative latecomers to the Industrial Revolution, Austria and Germany were changing rapidly, and Vienna's traditional German character and bucolic charm was threatened as Czechs, Hungarians, Poles, and other non-German peoples streamed into the city. Many of these were Jews, and Hitler felt that inferior races had conspired to erode the racial purity of Austrian Germans: "I was repelled by the conglomeration of races which the capital showed me, repelled by this whole mixture of Czechs, Poles, Hungarians, Ruthenians, Serbs, and Croats, and everywhere, the eternal mushroom of humanity—Jews and more Jews. To me the giant city seemed the embodiment of racial desecration."[24]

Hitler was not the only German Austrian who felt this way. Others also resisted the transforming, dislocating, mixing effects of modernization, particularly as those effects were held up against the mirror of a halcyon past. Guido von List, a native Viennese who died in 1919 after researching the German past for more than forty years, argued that Aryan masters once ruled the "slave races" of Europe.[25] This thesis he supported by his own idiosyncratic reading of history and Germanic mythology, along with the decipherment of various runes or hieroglyphs. In the latter part of his career, he studied Blavatsky's *The Secret Doctrine* and incorporated her concept of "root races" into an evolutionary scheme that identified "Ario-Germans" as the fifth root race—the next step in humanity's upward ascent. List also drew upon Cabala, Rosicrucianism, and Free Masonry while laying out the elements of a primordial Aryan religion. These included an elite priesthood, seasonal festivals, the supplication of Teutonic gods and nature deities, and the identification of sacred woods and hilltops. According to List, these all figured into a once-universal faith subsequently subverted and suppressed by Christianity.

List's writings struck a chord among many Germans disenchanted by modernization and the prospect of ethnic disintegration. Among these was Jörg Lanz von Liebenfels, another German Austrian with a predilection for fanciful history culled from many different sources. Lanz interpreted the Bible as a record of the Aryan race unsuccessfully resisting the sexual enticements of inferior races. The Fall came about when early Aryans compromised their purity in this way, and their descendents committed similar perversions.[26] From such arose a small, ape-like hybrid species sometimes raised for "deviant sexual pleasure."[27] These "love-pygmies,"[28] said Lanz, were the bane of Aryan civilization.

Mindful of scientific terminology, Lanz invented the word "theozoology" to

MAGIC, MYSTERY, AND SCIENCE

denote his theory of the corruption of ancient Aryans by inferior races. He saw these Aryans as being innately endowed with the ability to send and receive electric signals: they were, hence, telepathic and widely cognizant of their surroundings. (This characterization, notes Nicholas Goodrick-Clarke, was a response to turn-of-the-century progress in radio technology and the discovery of N-rays, X-rays, and radioactivity.[29]) Although lost through sexual (interbreeding) sins, these powers would come back, according to Lanz, as Germans practiced a program of segregation and eugenics. Partners selected for their racial purity were to procreate future generations of increasingly Aryan children. Eventually Aryans like those of old would appear to usher in a millennial era of peace and prosperity. In the meantime, the slave races could be shipped to Madagascar, turned into pack animals, or sacrificed to God as a burnt offering.[30]

Lanz published his views in *Ostara,* a periodical that circulated in Vienna during the time the young, impressionable Hitler was residing in the city. It is altogether possible that Hitler soaked up Lanz's bile, although it is hard to say for sure because in his reminiscences Hitler liked to present himself as his own man, impervious to the influence of others. In any event, Lanz became well known throughout Germany and figured into the ideological milieu that spawned the Nazi Party. As in Austria, esoteric groups and lodge organizations in Germany (notably the Germanenorden and the Thule Society) aspired to remedy contemporary ills by ushering in an era of Aryan supremacy. The subculture that embraced the thinking of Lanz and List soon became, under Hitler's leadership, the reigning political force in Germany. And, as Hitler made clear, Nazi politics were driven by the biological objective of creating a super race.[31]

DARKNESS ALL THE WAY UP

Very likely the Nazi official most drawn to the elitist, arcane side of the occult was Heinrich Himmler.[32] Before he turned to politics, Himmler tried farming, hoping to get close to the earth and back to the pre-industrial past. Like Hitler, he nurtured a *völkish* (rabidly nationalistic) worldview that exalted Aryans. This mythology, which appealed to many Germans at the time, emerged from a compulsive (mis)reading of people such as Charles Darwin, Francis Galton, Friedrich Nietzsche, H. S. Chamberlain, and Alfred Rosenberg—to indicate just a few of the better-known figures. Insofar as it spoke of "the struggle for existence" leading to "the survival of the fittest," Darwin's theory of evolution was taken by some to enshrine conflict among races as natural and inevitable. (Never mind that "race" has no biological meaning; the word was freely substituted for "species.") Galton, who was Darwin's cousin, developed the "science" of eugenics so as to upgrade the human gene pool through selective mating. Those deemed genetically inferior were to be barred or discouraged from reproducing. This was necessary, said Galton, to offset recent medical advances that allowed the "unfit" to live long enough to threaten future generations with defective genes.

Nietzsche's contribution to Western culture is variously interpreted, not least because of his richly imaginative prose. (He once stated that "[e]very profound thinker is more afraid of being understood than of being misunderstood."[33]) Nonetheless, he spoke of the coming of a Superman (*Übermensch*) who would transcend and destroy old "slave morality" values. These he seems to have identified with European civilization and more directly with Christian ideology that allowed inferior peoples to gain ascendancy over their natural masters. By propagating a gospel of meekness, the meek had turned their innate weaknesses into an ideal template for all humanity—in spite of the fact that some races do not share those weaknesses. Now shamed into "good" behavior, those whose right it is to conquer stifle their natural instincts and, psychologically crippled, blend innocuously into the democratic masses. This at least was one way of understanding Nietzsche.

Chamberlain and Rosenberg were not scholars of international renown, but their books sold well in Germany and Austria and helped stoke the inferno that eventually consumed much of Europe. Chamberlain was English by birth but settled down in Switzerland and then Germany. A passionate admirer of German culture in general and Richard Wagner's music in particular, he argued that Germans alone possess the creative spark that drives human progress. The Jewish race, however, having an innate need for darkness and destruction, stands athwart this thrust toward enlightenment and thereby represents a threat to all of humanity. Chamberlain's second marriage was to Wagner's daughter, and in 1924 the transplanted Englishman (by then a German citizen) was paid a personal visit by Adolf Hitler. No doubt the two men had little difficulty settling on a topic of conversation.

Chamberlain's books exercised a decisive influence on Rosenberg, who came to Germany in 1918 after fleeing the Bolshevik Revolution in Russia. No friend of Marxism, Rosenberg joined the Nazi Party in the early 1920s and used his position as editor of the party newspaper to develop a theoretical justification for Aryan supremacy. His reading of history convinced him that each individual possesses a "racial soul" and that great civilizations fall into decay once racial mixing occurs. Rejecting Marx's view that class struggle drives history, Rosenberg emphasized race and blood, insisting that the lowest race—Jews—compensate for their inferiority by mingling their seed into other races. Atop the racial pyramid, Aryans stand to lose the most—even their own soul—from this steady desecration of racial purity.

For those so inclined, a full-blown racist worldview was on hand, and the forebodings were clear. "All who are not of good race in this world are chaff," wrote Hitler in 1924.[34] Such thinking appealed to Himmler, who read more widely than Hitler, but frequently from books that excited the prejudices he held on race, blood, and soil. Interested in agronomy, Himmler applied the concept of selective breeding to humanity, all the while imagining himself as a scientifically informed benefactor of humankind. This would qualify him as one of Hitler's most effective henchmen: Himmler headed up the nefarious SS Corps (the *Schutzenstaffel* or protection squadron) that took primary responsibility for exterminating Jews and other "undesirable" peoples.

Predictably, Himmler's prejudices warped his scientific impulses. For him, as for Hitler, deep-seated feelings took priority over logical argument and concrete evidence, so science was simply a way of substantiating one's beliefs. According to Michael Kater, Himmler imagined the universe as a great mosaic filled with "hundreds of thousands of pebbles depicting the true image of the origin of the world and its history"; the task, then, of a scientist was to pick out just those pebbles that confirmed one's hypothesis. Should the hypothesis be challenged or modified through other considerations, there was no choice in Himmler's mind but to regard the research as wasted effort.[35] Everything had to point in one way or another to the primacy of the Aryan race.

Moreover, as Hitler often stressed, great causes are not advanced by faint-hearted half-measures and armchair reflection. To be effective, theories had to be invested with passion and translated into decisive action. Himmler took action on his racist views by implementing standards that would allow SS men and their families to regenerate the master race. Candidates for service had to submit genealogical proof—going back several generations—of their Aryan heritage. Wives and fiancées were similarly scrutinized. Physical features were much emphasized, although few men could fully measure up. Ideally, an SS man would be tall, blond, blue-eyed, have little body hair and a long, narrow head. (Wide heads were thought to suggest Slavic or Asiatic origins.) Himmler had brown hair and his head was wide, an imperfection he tried to mute by having his hair cut very close to the scalp on the sides and back.

The goal, said Himmler, was to create a "seedbed" from which about two hundred million pure Aryans would spring to save the world from Russian Bolshevism.[36] To achieve this, Himmler encouraged his men to marry early and have large families.[37] Not only that, he worked up an SS wedding ceremony along with other rituals and festivities meant to re-invoke the Aryan past (as he imagined it) and awaken within the SS a sense of kinship with their heroic forebears. The greatest of all holidays was Hitler's birthday (April 20), but springtime and the solstices were to be much celebrated as well. The winter solstice was set aside for reverencing Aryan ancestors, while a spring festival

NAZISM AND ANCESTRAL GERMAN MEMORIES

and the summer solstice were to be marked by dance, songs, and sporting competitions among the youth. Far from idle amusement, the competitions determined which boys and girls were best improving the Aryan race by winning the struggle for existence.

Himmler anticipated that these activities would satisfy the deep spiritual longings of Germans everywhere and thereby render Christianity alien and obsolete. Germanic paganism—the old true Aryan religion—would once more prevail, resurrected from centuries-long obscurity. Hoping to hasten progress toward this end, Himmler brought Otto Rahn into the SS. Rahn was a noted scholar of the Holy Grail and felt that it yet existed in southern France. The quest for the Holy Grail (the chalice used at the Last Supper and receptacle of the blood of Christ as he hung on the cross) was the stuff of medieval legend, notably *Parsifal,* a story put to music by Wagner. Although a Christian relic, the Grail was said to endow its possessors with rare spiritual powers. Furthermore, it could be understood as a Christian gloss on an older Aryan truth: the real Holy Grail was a "stone bearing the sacred inscriptions of Primordial Knowledge given by the gods."[38] Those gods supposedly dwelled far to the north in the land of Thule where they were preparing to rise again in destructive fury and reclaim their former dominions.

As a harbinger of things to come, Himmler promoted the SS as a "knightly Order, from which one cannot withdraw, to which one is recruited by blood and within which one remains with body and soul so long as one lives on this earth."[39] To facilitate this throwback to the medieval past, he restored an old castle to serve as SS headquarters. According to Peter Padfield, the castle, located at Wewelsburg and not far from where Hermann the Cherusker led his Germanic army to victory against the Roman legions of Varus in A.D. 9, functioned as "a mystical seat hidden from the gaze of the uninitiated, the towered sanctum of the higher orders of SS chivalry."[40] From this site the flower of Aryan civilization would emerge, pure-blooded men and women selflessly devoted to the cause of racial truth. The preservation of race, after all, took priority over individual interests.

Unfortunately, this was a zero-sum game, because the unchecked exaltation of one race implied the absolute negation of others. The storied Aryan past and the bright Aryan future necessitated the systematic destruction of millions of non-Aryans. And millions did die as they found themselves caught in the dreary present between the two radiant vistas dreamed up by Hitler and his minions.

MAGIC, MYSTERY, AND SCIENCE

12

UFOs AND
ALIEN
ABDUCTIONS

Be not forgetful to entertain strangers,
for thereby some have entertained angels unawares.

—*Hebrews 13:2*

Since the end of World War II, UFOs (unidentified flying objects) have become high drama for thousands, perhaps millions, of people worldwide. Normally associated with "flying saucers" from outer space, they have triggered an
evolving series of responses. Often in the early years, they were the craft of
Martians and Venusians who were coming to earth as "Space Brothers" to keep
earthlings from destroying themselves and contaminating the solar system with
nuclear weapons. This picture gradually gave way to darker possibilities: space
aliens wanted to take over the planet, either by invasion or through the surrep-
titious infiltration of human society. Then, when people began to report alien
abductions, the UFO experience took on yet another aspect. Now the extraterrestrials are said to be "harvesting" humans, perhaps with the goal of creating a
hybrid species that combines the best traits of both races. Furthermore, they
may already be integrating with us in everyday life. Whatever is happening, for
many human abductees, the experience is highly traumatizing and consequently difficult to summon up as a conscious memory; for others, it becomes
a source of love and expanded understanding once the initial fright and pain
have worn off. Perhaps the human race is not being mishandled and exploited
by aliens; rather, it is being gently trained or "tamed" into larger, more fulfilling
possibilities.

Along the way to alien abductions, the approach to understanding UFOs and space aliens also changed. Initially the "nuts and bolts" attitude held sway. If extraterrestrials existed, they could, in principle, be discovered in the light of everyday reality. They and their craft were physical entities amenable to scientific detection and testing. Now the sense is that aliens make their entry psychically or paranormally (even if they have physical bodies) and personal contact—often far too personal—is replacing night-sky sightings as the UFO norm. The U.S. Air Force, once assigned to monitor UFO activity, no longer seems a likely agency to track down trans-dimensional aliens whose powers of intelligence or intuition are more impressive than their technological wizardry. In the late 1940s and early 1950s, aliens could crash their spacecraft and allegedly leave behind physical wreckage. Such a notion now seems quaint, for aliens, once otherworldly in a planetary sense, have become otherworldly in a metaphysical, paranormal sense. Having migrated into other dimensions and realms of being, they leave little evidence save searing, often subconscious memories in the minds of their abductees.

THE BEGINNINGS

Strange objects in the sky have a very long history. The Romans reported flying shields, people in the Middle Ages saw Jesus and saints, and, as recently as the nineteenth century, reports circulated of "mystery airships."[1] But the modern wave of UFO sightings began just after World War II with Kenneth Arnold.[2] In 1947, Arnold, a civilian pilot, was flying over the Cascade Mountains in western Washington State, searching for a downed C-46 transport plane. As he looked toward distant Mount Rainier, he saw nine shiny flying objects in a chain-like configuration, as if in formation. The first object was crescent-shaped with a dome on top; the rest looked like flat pie pans. Arnold said that each object "flew like a saucer would if you skipped it across the water." Picking up on this description, the media coined the term "flying saucer."

The public was ready for the phenomenon. World War II had introduced the world to the marvels and terrors of jet aircraft, V-2 rockets, and the atomic bomb. Soon Americans reported hundreds of sightings and many speculated that visitors from outer space had landed. Others insisted that either the Russians or the U.S. government was testing a new kind of aircraft but denying responsibility. In any event, the government knew more than it was willing to admit: it was "covering up" information, either of space aliens or of an incredible new aeronautical breakthrough.

Two early incidents stand out, one giving birth to the rumor of crashed aliens and the other involving the fatal crash of an Air Force pilot. Just months after Kenneth Arnold's UFO sighting, a rancher near Roswell, New Mexico, found

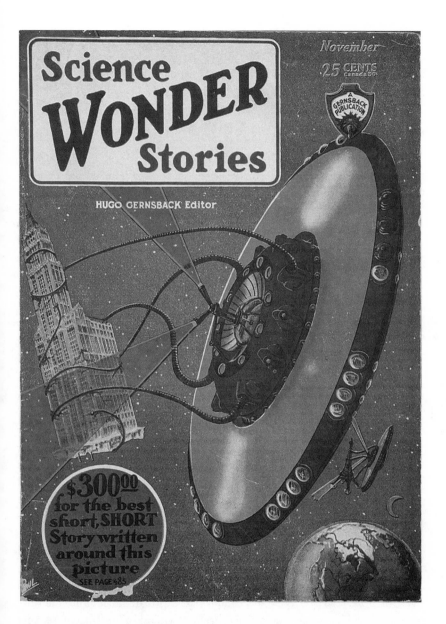

Figure 42. A 1929 drawing of a spacecraft. The term "flying saucer" would not be coined for another twenty years.

UFOs AND ALIEN ABDUCTIONS

a scattered heap of strange technological paraphernalia on his property and notified local law enforcement authorities. The next day, the Air Force issued a press release announcing the crash of a "flying disc." This was soon followed by an amended release identifying the equipment as a crashed weather balloon. The incident remained mostly a matter of local speculation until the 1970s, at which time it was widely publicized as an example of government cover-up. Witnesses alleged having seen the bodies of aliens at the crash site; these, along with other crash remnants, were whisked away by military authorities.

The bodies, if some facsimile thereof was actually present, may have been parachute dummies. According to those who dismiss the crashed alien theory, the equipment was classified by the government for Cold War purposes and the Air Force gathered it up so as not to compromise its existence. Information declassified since the incident confirms this judgment, although that has not stopped the city of Roswell from capitalizing on the event. In recent years, UFO advocates and those wishing to know more have flocked to the city during the summer to commemorate the flying saucer disaster. For those who believe, most if not all of counter-evidence is part of the government's continuing attempt to conceal the truth. For others less concerned with historical fact, the summer celebration is a pleasant diversion from everyday routine and belief in UFOs is not a prerequisite to the fun. As one resident noted, "you don't have to believe in a six-foot mouse to enjoy Disney World."[3]

The other, more tragic, incident occurred in 1948. Observers reported a UFO shaped like an ice-cream cone and topped in red flying over Godman Air Force Base in Kentucky. Four National Guard F-51s were scrambled to investigate. The voice of the flight leader, Captain Thomas Mantell, crackled over the radio: "I'm closing in now. . . . It's directly ahead of me and still moving at about half my speed. . . . The thing looks metallic and of tremendous size. . . . It's going up now and forward as fast as I am . . . that's 360 miles per hour. I'm going up to 20,000 feet, and if I'm no closer, I'll abandon chase."[4] The transmission then broke off as Mantell evidently lost control of his craft.

The other planes returned safely to base. The next day, Captain Mantell's decapitated body was found in the wreckage of his plane. He had apparently blacked out from lack of oxygen. What had he seen? Air Force investigators were baffled. They suggested Venus, but that explanation did not fit the circumstances. Closure on the incident was not achieved until three years later when the Navy disclosed that it had launched a top-secret balloon—codenamed "Skyhook" and designed to measure cosmic rays—in the vicinity of the sighting. Evidently, Mantell had chased the balloon to his death. In the meantime, however, the American public grew suspicious of the Air Force and its failure to offer credible accounts of its own encounters with UFOs.

With public interest in UFOs mounting and at times bordering on paranoia,

Figure 43. A devastating attack. Science fiction and actual sights share two classic motifs about visitors from outer space: (1) aliens are here to help us; and (2) aliens are here to harm us, as depicted in this very early illustration.

federal authorities decided to investigate the sightings, hoping to determine their causes. Responsibility for the investigation fell to the Air Force, both because it had the resources to carry off the inquiry and because it had a military obligation to protect America in the event space aliens or Russians really were preparing to launch an air attack. Unfortunately, for many interested citizens, the Air Force was already tainted by its failure to forthrightly clarify the Mantell incident. Furthermore, the Air Force, being an arm of the government, could not inspire public confidence as an independent research organization. It did not help matters when the Air Force opted to classify most of its UFO files.

The investigation, lasting until 1969 and best known by its last title, Project Blue Book, was headquartered at Wright-Patterson Air Force Base in Ohio. (It is no coincidence that Wright-Patterson stores the bodies of alien crash victims, according to rumor.) Realizing that many UFO sightings might be astronomical phenomena, the Air Force called in J. Allen Hynek, a professor of astronomy at Northwestern University. Hynek would become a leading investigator of UFOs, respected by most as a level-headed researcher. Neither a debunker nor a rabid enthusiast, he followed up on thousands of sightings and concluded that 90 percent of them were attributable to natural phenomena; the remaining 10 percent, however, warranted further investigation. Hynek insisted that the testimony of only one witness, although reliable, generally did not justify in-depth inquiry. If, however, a single testimony were augmented by others or by physical evidence, then a case should be opened. Moreover, it was Hynek who came up with the now-standard system for classifying UFO sightings.[5]

Steven Spielberg introduced the public to "close encounters of the third kind" in his movie of the same name. These encounters involve seeing UFOs and their occupants from a distance of less than two hundred yards; possibly communication with the occupants occurs as well. Close encounters of the second kind entail seeing a craft (but no occupants) and experiencing physical effects such as car ignition interference, burnt vegetation, or ground markings. Those of the first kind are simply sightings without physical effects. Distant encounters beyond two hundred yards may involve nocturnal lights, daylight disks, and anomalous radar objects that are also visually witnessed.

THE CONDON REPORT

In 1966, to allay charges by the public of covering up information (and to unburden itself of unwanted responsibility), the Air Force turned to an outside institution to independently study and solve the problem of UFOs. Receiving a half-million dollars for its services, the University of Colorado designated

Dr. Edward Condon to head a staff of thirty-six investigators and analysts. It was a comfortable agreement for both parties: the Air Force wanted someone to professionally dismiss UFOs and Condon was a skeptic from the beginning. After two years of study, his team published its findings—the Condon Report[6]—and concluded that further study was not warranted.[7]

Many people, including Hynek, deemed the Condon Report biased and poorly researched. One commentator described it as a "fine piece of scientific recklessness."[8] According to Hynek, it sometimes dismissed plausible or promising UFO reports without even interviewing witnesses. One case in particular was the Kirtland Air Force Base incident, which Hynek felt was bungled by both Condon's staff and Blue Book personnel.[9] At the New Mexico base on November 4, 1957, at 10:45 P.M., two air-traffic controllers alone in a tower saw a white light flying east at about two hundred miles per hour. They asked the base's radar station to identify the object, and the radar operator gave them the vector. Concerned that an unknown plane might be confused by the runway lights, the controllers vainly tried to establish radio contact. Through binoculars, they saw an egg-shaped object about twenty feet long stand on end and then cross the runways, hover about a minute, and then shoot up almost vertically. Again the controllers called for radar confirmation. Radar tracked the object as it moved in various directions before moving off the screen. To the consternation of many, both Blue Book and Condon officials decided against an in-depth investigation. The Condon Report's conclusion: The confused pilot of a "small, powerful private aircraft" accidentally tried to land at the base, and then flew off.[10]

FROM DISTANT TO CLOSE ENCOUNTERS

Like a plot that requires an accelerating infusion of dramatic novelty to sustain reader interest, UFO experiences have become increasingly more intense and participatory. As a result, Hynek's classification system both describes what may happen when UFOs are sighted *and* reflects an upward frequency shift over time from distant encounters through the various levels of close encounters. Each kind of encounter has in turn given way to the next level: distant encounters, once fully remarkable, have yielded to close encounters involving stalled cars, UFO landings, and aliens caught off guard outside their spaceships. Now even these are somewhat passé as abductions have achieved a new threshold of interaction and emotional intensity.

In the 1950s, many UFOs were spotted but hardly anyone actually went aboard one. A major exception was Professor George Adamski (the "Professor" was honorary, a title given Adamski by his followers), who became a minor celebrity upon claiming that his "space friends" from various planets had taken

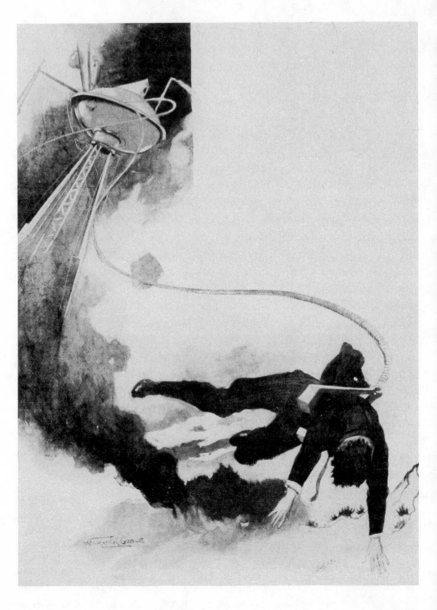

Figure 44. Perhaps the first illustration of a fictional alien abduction. Drawn for H. G. Wells's War of the Worlds *(1897).*

MAGIC, MYSTERY, AND SCIENCE

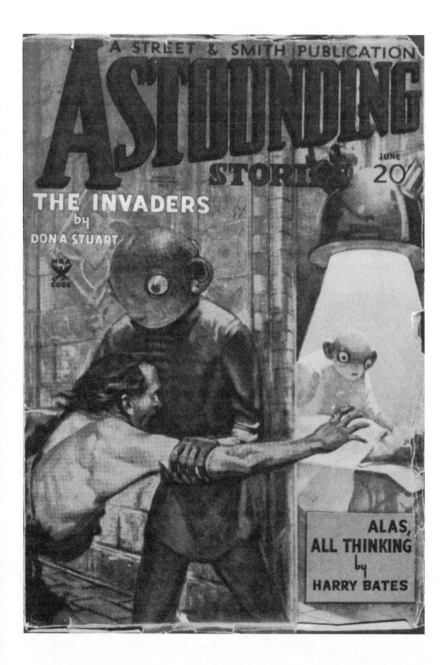

Figure 45. Alien examination. In this sketch for the cover of a 1927 science fiction magazine, an abducted woman lies on a table as she is about to be examined by inquisitive, large-eyed aliens.

UFOs AND ALIEN ABDUCTIONS

him aboard their ship many times for (joy) rides.[11] On one such excursion, Adamski was fortunate enough to see the backside of the moon and described it as having trees and snow-capped mountains. He further stated that his space friends were concerned about nuclear testing and had contacted him to persuade humankind to obey the laws of the "Creator of all." Adamski's aliens seem benign though, like his description of the moon, rather implausible. Some, he said, came from Venus, a planet far too hot to support life as we know it.

As Adamski told it, his experiences were thrilling and mind-expanding but not particularly frightening. The next people claiming to be taken aboard a UFO returned with a more sinister account.[12] The incident occurred in the White Mountains of New Hampshire in September 1961. Barney and Betty Hill had just vacationed in Montreal and were driving home at night when Betty observed two bright objects near the moon. Thinking it strange that one of the objects seemed to be following them, she excitedly asked Barney to stop the car and look at it through binoculars. He reluctantly did so, objecting to her conjecture that it might be a flying saucer. As he studied it, however, he thought he saw lighted windows in a craft and aliens within pulling levers. The apparent leader was dressed in black, like a "Nazi," as Barney later described it. Horrified, he jumped back into the car and the couple drove off, taking back roads to escape from the craft. Betty reported that Barney "began laughing or crying in a hysterical manner and repeating, 'They're going to capture us.' "[13]

The Hills got home two hours later than expected, reporting afterward that they could not account for the two hours. (The term "missing time" has since been coined to refer to periods of alleged amnesia during which an individual might have been taken hostage by aliens.) The next day, Betty, still agitated, told her sister about the incident. A few days later she reported it to a UFO interest group called the National Investigative Committee of Aerial Phenomena, but said nothing about being abducted. Then, several days later she *dreamed* that she and Barney had been abducted and taken aboard a flying saucer. Remarkably, the dream kept returning—five nights in a row—and after telling it many times to friends, family, and coworkers, Betty decided to write it down.

Before long, Betty was relating the incident-cum-dream to local groups. In the meantime, Barney underwent treatment for ulcers and high blood pressure, and his physician advised him to see Dr. Benjamin Simon, a prominent Boston psychiatrist. Inasmuch as Barney was black and his wife was white, his medical condition, which was apparently stress-related, could have stemmed from their unusual—at the time—marriage circumstance. Betty accompanied Barney to the psychiatrist, who put them both under regressive hypnosis and invited them to talk about their problems and UFO experiences. Separately each recounted

MAGIC, MYSTERY, AND SCIENCE

an abduction story. Both described being removed to a ramp leading up into a spacecraft. Barney was first taken aboard, physically examined, and brought back; then, Betty was treated the same way. (The craft was too small for both to be examined at once.) Betty's account was much more detailed than her husband's. During her examination, the beings prodded much of her body and took scrapings of her skin. They also stuck a large needle into her abdomen to see if she was pregnant. It was all very painful.

The story was not released to the public until 1965, about four years after the initial incident. The delay might have aroused more suspicion, but, because the full account was revealed under later hypnosis, it seemed legitimate to many. There is no question that hypnosis can elicit buried or forgotten memories. It can also, however, encourage patients to mix fact with dream and fantasy. Dr. Simon's opinion was that the Hills' abduction story was probably a fantasy, a re-telling of Betty's dream woven into other imaginative elements. She had told the story so often that it became the template for Barney's account as his mind dramatized the experience under hypnosis.

None of this seemed to matter, however, once the national wire services and other media outlets picked up the story. It became widely known through John Fuller's book *The Interrupted Journey* (1966), a series of *Look* magazine articles, and *The UFO Incident*, a made-for-TV movie starring James Earl Jones. Along with the public interest it generated, the story also appears to have cleared a space for a new kind of UFO experience: after its release, other abduction reports began to trickle in. When Travis Walton's reported abduction in November 1975 was widely publicized, the event seemed to confirm Barney and Betty Hill's story. Walton's experience has since been reenacted in the movie *Fire in the Sky* (1993). The experience itself occurred just two weeks after the Hills' abduction movie aired on TV.

MISSING TIME, INTRUDERS, AND COMMUNION

As alien abductions became more common, the rules of evidence changed and those who wished to keep UFOs within the realm of normal experience were gradually pushed to the sidelines. Jerome Clark details the tension, implicit from the first sightings, between matter-of-fact researchers, such as Hynek, and "saucerians," such as Adamski, whose approach to UFOs was religious and intuitive. Adamski's implausible accounts exasperated and angered the scientists (or those relying on scientific methodology) who sought to bring ufology alongside biology and chemistry as a legitimate research pursuit.[14] That this aim has yet to be realized represents a victory of sorts for Adamski and his crowd. It is worth noting as well that today the UFO researcher with professional credentials is more likely to be a social scientist than a physical scientist.[15]

To a substantial degree, psychology, sociology, and ethnography have replaced astronomy and physics as the disciplines best equipped to deal with UFOs and their elusive occupants.

Among those contributing to this shift is Budd Hopkins, whose book *Missing Time* appeared in 1981. A New York artist, Hopkins independently interviewed people troubled by unusual experiences, recurring dreams, and the vague but lingering sense that something was amiss in their lives. In the course of his work, Hopkins determined that alien abductions were occurring at an alarming rate; abductees could not, however, always consciously recall their experiences because aliens somehow blocked them out. Apparently, the Hills had been given this sort of amnesia treatment and that is why their memories had to be recovered through hypnotic regression. What's more, the night they saw the flying saucers, two hours slipped by that they could not account for later. Hopkins dubbed this "missing time" and proposed that an increasing number of people are suffering from it. At the end of his book, he included his postal address so that readers could write him if they, too, had experienced missing time or any of the other troubling symptoms associated with alien abductions. Hundreds wrote him, and the best cases were detailed in his next book, *Intruders* (1987).

What Hopkins calls his most convincing scenario involves a woman, given the pseudonym of Kathie Davis, from the Indianapolis area.[16] Already an anxious, unemployed divorcee with two children, Kathie became increasingly distressed when she began to have a recurrent dream of being abducted, examined, and released by aliens. Under hypnosis, Kathie recalled the entire, multi-abduction experience, which included being impregnated by an alien and then having the fetus transplanted to an extraterrestrial female. Later she was allowed to visit the baby (and other children developed from ova removed from her body). The purpose of the visit entailed more than gratitude on the part of the aliens: they were trying to learn how to be motherly and emotional and consequently wanted to observe Kathie as she interacted with the babies.

Hopkins uses this account to support his thesis that extraterrestrials are breeding with humans on a large scale. Kathie, however, still believes it is all a dream—or a sequence of dreams—and Hopkins agrees to call it that to soften the trauma. Aside from Kathie's memories, there is also, he points out, physical evidence that something strange is going on. Kathy has unusual, scoop-like scars on her legs that she cannot explain; her mother has one as well, and the scars show up on the bodies of other abductees. Evidently they are connected with the often-painful physical examination that is now a standard aspect of the abduction experience. The aliens are learning about our bodies, perhaps envious of them and wanting to evolve in the direction of human intimacy and love.

Since Kathie's true identity has been protected from the public, we have her story secondhand through Hopkins. Not so Whitley Strieber, another of the many people who contacted Hopkins. Strieber has since written two books on his abductions, *Communion* (1987) and *Transformation* (1988). According to Hopkins, Strieber was "very, very distraught" about his experiences.[17] He was, in fact, referred by Hopkins to a professional psychotherapist.

By profession, Strieber is a writer, and before he decided to relate his abduction experiences, he wrote horror fiction. At least two of his early novels are about vampires; others are about invaders from outer space. Moreover, fear seems to be Strieber's native element. Interviewing Strieber *before* he turned to alien abductions, Douglas Winter wrote that

> Whitley Strieber is one horror writer who doesn't have to work hard to find fear: "All I have to do is take my next breath." No other writer of horror fiction lives in fear as obviously or as intensely. He shudders visibly at the very mention of his childhood bogeyman, Mr. Peanut; he walks away from puppets and ventriloquist dummies; and he whispers with such fervor about conspiracies and secret government machinations that the unwashed might find him the quintessential paranoid. "Fear is the basis of existence," he says.[18]

Strieber says he has been a Roman Catholic, a white witch, a student of Meister Eckhart, a Zen disciple, and a devotee of Gurdjieff's teachings.[19] He also claims that he was almost killed in 1966 by Charles Whitman, a deranged sniper who gunned down many people from atop a tower at the University of Texas, and Strieber's memory of the event is filled with gruesome details.[20] In his book *Communion*, however, he states, "I wasn't there," and hypothesizes that his recollection of the shooting might be a "screen memory" manufactured by aliens to blot out an abduction experience.[21] But not long after writing this, Strieber told a conference that he was there when Whitman opened fire.[22]

Because of their emotional instability, Whitley Strieber and Kathie Davis are easy to dismiss as unfortunate victims of an over-heated imagination. (Although Strieber, whose *Communion* and *Transformation* became best-sellers, may not be so unfortunate.) Defenders argue, however, that this analysis reverses cause and effect: fear and anxiety stem from multiple abductions, not vice versa. In recent decades, society has learned to listen to privately abused women and children, even when their stories are "truths" almost too hard to bear. Now, alien abductions are another hard truth that is steadfastly resisted by many, and so blame or stigma comes to rest on the abductees.

Part of the difficulty is that definitive proof one way or another is hard to come by, particularly now that UFO experiences have become more mental than metal, more inward than outward. Strieber capitalizes on this shift by relating highly subjective experiences. What's more, he seems to assume that the reality of an experience is confirmed by its emotional intensity: if it's real to *me*, it's real. Thus, Strieber may be said to be playing his own game on his own turf, not on the public turf of science. Unchecked by the normal criteria that separate fact and fiction, he tells a richly ambiguous story in which he is both victim and truth-bearer.

In December 1985, Strieber and his wife and young son were spending time in their second home, a secluded cabin in upstate New York.[23] Despite the peaceful surroundings, he installed a sophisticated alarm system and each night checked all the rooms, closets, and crannies (even under the guest bed) for intruders, especially small ones. This, he says, was his routine even before extraterrestrials came into his life, which they did on the night of December 26. Hours after he had checked the house and gone to bed, he heard a "whooshing, swirling noise" in the living room and went downstairs to investigate. Looking around, he suddenly saw a compact figure about three and a half feet tall. Astonished, Strieber did nothing. Then the small creature rushed toward him and all was blackness. The next thing he recalled was being transported into the woods and then into a circular room with beings about five feet tall with slanting black eyes. These beings temporarily inserted a device into Strieber's brain.

Throughout the book—*Communion*—in which he tells this story, Strieber unpeels layer after layer of the abduction experience. (Evidently the full memory was too intense to be retrieved all at once.) Part of the experience involved a painful medical procedure with invasive needles; another part resembled horrible sexual nightmares. Then, finally, he was returned to his house. Later, Strieber realized that he had been abducted many times—that night was not his first experience. The beings allegedly continue to abduct him.

Strieber admits that all this sounds quite bizarre but adds that his book had to remain faithful to the "high strangeness content" of his "visitor experiences."[24] In *Communion* he is concerned for his sanity, sometimes repeating, "Am I sane? Am I sane?" But he says he feels and acts sane, and others confirm this judgment. On TV shows, he comes across as a reasonable, articulate person; furthermore, he has included in his books the professional opinions of several experts, all of which attest to his sanity. One testimony is from Donald Klein, the psychotherapist who guided Strieber through his hypnotic sessions. According to Klein, Strieber is "not hallucinating in a manner characteristic of psychosis. I also see no evidence of an anxiety state, mood disorder, or personality disorder. He is an excellent hypnotic subject, who appeared to make an honest attempt while under hypnosis to describe what he remembered."[25] That said, one still wonders if Strieber has not expanded the boundaries of everyday reality beyond their normal limits. After all, UFO experiences have evolved into a true twilight zone where physical reality and psychological reality are all but indistinguishable. Bill Ellis suggests that Strieber is a "fantasy-prone personality sincerely describing what he believes he remembers."[26]

In *Transformation*, Strieber writes that the aliens have informed him that he is a "chosen one" who is to warn our planet of coming dangers. The ozone layer, for instance, is becoming depleted over the poles and this will promote disease by weakening our immune systems. He also sees the aliens as our teachers and concludes from his experiences that we have souls; furthermore, these souls may well undergo reincarnation upon physical death. Many of his ideas, which allegedly originate with his alien teachers, echo New Age themes.

QUESTIONS AND POSSIBILITIES

Several years ago, one of the present authors heard that a local man who called himself "John the Revelator" was going to call down UFOs as a public demonstration of their existence. About one thousand people gathered to watch the spectacle but, much to their disappointment, storm clouds kept the UFOs from making an appearance. Later, when the author related this story to Ray Keller, a well-known figure in UFO circles, Keller remarked on the irony of UFOs being thwarted by a few storm clouds after traveling millions of miles to reach the earth. This comment captures much that is incongruous about the claim that we are being visited by beings from outer space. Before alien abductions became common, J. Allen Hynek ventured that "it seems ridiculous that super intelligence would travel great distances to do relatively stupid things like stop cars, collect soil samples, and frighten people."[27] Jacques Vallee, an astrophysicist, computer scientist, and noted ufologist, extended this judgment to abduction accounts by saying that "among the list of stupid things a superior extraterrestrial civilization with any knowledge of biology would not need to do would be to scoop up skin samples and remove embryos of millions of terrified Americans."[28] Others have proposed that if extraterrestrials were intelligent enough to overcome all the technical difficulties of interplanetary or intergalactic space travel, they would hardly be so clumsy or intrusive in their dealings with humans; in fact, they could probably study us without revealing their existence.[29]

Although these observations cast doubt on the reality of UFOs, one need not suppose that the issue necessarily reduces to just two contradictory possibilities. That is, UFOs may be real in more than one way. We have already seen that they have become more dream-like and inner-worldly since they were first spotted in 1947, and this suggests that they fulfill some sort of modern psychological need. As early as 1958, Carl Jung proposed that UFOs are mythic expressions of the collective unconscious that satisfy our yearning for salvation, albeit without compromising too severely the naturalistic faith we invest in science.

> The present world situation is calculated as never before to arouse expectations of a redeeming, supernatural event. If these expectations have not dared to show themselves in the open, this is simply because no one is deeply rooted enough in the tradition of earlier centuries to consider an intervention from heaven as a matter of course. We have indeed strayed far from the metaphysical certainties of the Middle Ages, but not so far that our historical and psychological background is empty of all metaphysical hope. Consciously, however, rationalistic enlightenment predominates, and this abhors all leanings toward the "occult." Desperate efforts are made for a "repristination" of our Christian faith, but we cannot get back to that limited world view which in former times left room for metaphysical intervention.[30]

Jung also remarks that the circularity of UFOs connotes God (who is "round, complete, perfect") as well as "order, deliverance, salvation, and wholeness." Moreover, "anything that is technological goes down without difficulty with modern man."[31] In this vein, one recalls Arthur C. Clarke's statement that "[a]ny sufficiently advanced technology is indistinguishable from magic."[32] But, along with good or white magic, there is also black magic, and UFOs straddle the divide between the two. By some accounts, they have come to save us from our own destructive tendencies; by others, they are here to subjugate us to their own selfish ends. UFOs may thus be seen as psychic projections of our ambivalence toward modern technology with its dual capacity to bless and blight human experience.

This is not to say, however, that UFOs are *just* mental artifacts. Feeling that mind and matter are mutually implicated, Jung warned against "one-sided" hypotheses that reenact the Cartesian split.[33] Similarly, Vallee has proposed that, while imagination surely figures into UFO phenomena, those phenomena are more than mental fabrications. Vallee, who has studied UFOs for several decades, argued in the late 1960s that the so-called space aliens are of this world and have been interacting with humans for millennia. In earlier centuries, when *terra incognita* took in large regions of the earth (as well as the atmosphere and the subterranean realm), all sorts of unusual beings made their appearance. Angels, fairies, demons, leprechauns, elves, and giants (just to name the more familiar types) have been widely reported in many cultures, and, while it is reflexive to dismiss these as fanciful, folklore indicates that they interact with humans in ways that parallel contemporary UFO encounters. Speaking of "fairy abductions," for example, Vallee quotes this statement from Edwin Hartland's 1891 *The Science of Fairy Tales: An Inquiry into Fairy My-*

MAGIC, MYSTERY, AND SCIENCE

thology: "The motive assigned to fairies in northern stories is that of preserving and improving their race, on the one hand by carrying off human children to be brought up among the elves and to become united with them, and on the other hand by obtaining the milk and fostering care of human mothers for their own offspring."[34]

Historically speaking, Vallee's approach is wide-angle and, although trained as a scientist, he insists that "[m]odern science rules over a narrow universe, one particular variation on an infinite theme."[35] He hence tries to dissolve the boundary between the modern scientific worldview—replete with images of technology—and earlier, more pastoral visions of reality. And, since "[e]ven science, which claims its methods are rationally developed, is really shaped by emotion and fancy, or by fear,"[36] it cannot isolate us from our non-scientific past or grant us immunity to inexplicable happenings. Indeed, one of the hallmarks of our modern scientific age, says Vallee, is the proliferation of "mythical material almost unparalleled in quantity and quality in the rich records of the human imagination."[37]

Fresh detail and argument notwithstanding, Vallee declines to offer a complete or unambiguous characterization of the beings with whom the human race is still interacting. He is not sure if UFOs are physically real, suggesting that they might be "windows" rather than "objects" while also proposing that their occupants are "biologically compatible with us."[38] More recently, in a darker vein, he has ventured that a small group of humans (perhaps pretending to be aliens) with superior technology may be controlling and deceiving the general public for unknown reasons.[39] Possibly they are trying to establish a new world order by eroding faith in government, science, or corporate business. Or perhaps the cabal is deeply immersed in one of these domains where key individuals are adjusting the levers of power through widespread social manipulation. Reverting back to the alien thesis, it may be as well that terrestrial non-humans with similar motives switch in and out of our reality by means of space-time wormholes to which we have no access.[40] Although Vallee's uncertainty gives him a long tether for the development of alternative hypotheses, he is confident that more is at issue than human imagination: something is really going on and that something is homegrown rather than extraterrestrial in origin.

Also inclined to the wide-angle, interdisciplinary approach is John Mack, Pulitzer Prize winner and professor of psychiatry at the Harvard Medical School. Mack's emphasis, however, is on consciousness expansion and spiritual transformation. He garners stories and insights from Wallace Black Elk and other "indigenous people" who affirm the earth's sacred nature and its ability to refract the "many faces of the spirit."[41] Thus, even if UFOs and alien abductions are not directly or publicly witnessed, they fit into a larger, evolutionary

UFOs AND ALIEN ABDUCTIONS

pattern of things and should not be thought outlandish. Mack also draws inspiration from thinkers such as Ludwig Wittgenstein, A. N. Whitehead, Paul Feyerabend, and Rupert Sheldrake, all of whom understood science but sought to "humanize" it by revealing its very human limitations.

Mack was introduced to abduction accounts by Budd Hopkins, who invited him to investigate further. Although skeptical, Mack agreed, and over the next four years conducted some ninety clinical case studies of alleged abductions. He is now convinced that many of the accounts are real experiences that cannot be explained away by other means. He does not ascribe to the aliens an extra-terrestrial origin; he more modestly states that they "have come to the abduc-tees from a source that remains unknown to us" and thus leaves the door of possibility wide open.[42] Like Vallee, Mack is certain that something is going on, although, as usual, physical evidence is sparse and, when available, highly ambiguous. Proof inheres in the remembered experience, not in its physical trappings, and the experience may be so intensely real that it becomes a yard-stick for revealing the inadequacy of the scientific worldview.

> The richly detailed narratives they [the abductees] provide, the appro-priate surprise, the convincing incredulity, and above all the genuine distress or other feelings they report, together with the observable emotion and intense bodily reactions they exhibit when their experi-ences are recalled—all these elements can give any witness the sense that something powerful has happened to these individuals, however impossible this may seem from the standpoint of our traditional world view.[43]

Elsewhere, Mack cites with approval William Crookes's response to skeptics on the subject of séance phenomena: "I never said it was possible. I said it was true."[44] Mack characterizes abductions as "crossover phenomena" from another reality or dimension, together with "near-death and out-of-body experi-ences . . . , strange animal mutilations, the complex crop formations that ap-pear mysteriously in a few seconds in fields of rape and other grains, apparitions of the Virgin Mary, and spontaneous shamanic experiences."[45] All of these occurrences, he asserts, are "strange hybrids of mind and matter" belonging to a " 'third zone of being' that does not conform to the inside/outside duality by which we conventionally polarize reality."[46] In short, he, like many who study psi effects, refuses to honor Descartes's mind-matter dichotomy, a standard conceptual fixture since the seventeenth century. By thus redefining the world, or at least his relationship to the world, Mack positions himself to discover entities closed off by traditional science. The question that lingers, however, is whether those entities, being partially made of mind's airy substance, may be seized upon by our own minds in any sort of satisfactory or conclusive way.

MAGIC, MYSTERY, AND SCIENCE

Once when UFOs were generally seen at a distance, people assumed that face-to-face contact with their occupants would dispel all uncertainty. Now that such contact has become the reported norm, uncertainty still prevails. Closing in on the aliens has produced virtually no answers and many questions.

13 GNOSTICISM, OLD AND NEW

I read like mad, and worked with feverish interest through a mountain of
mythological material, then through the
Gnostic writers, and ended in total confusion. I found myself in a state of perplexity similar to the one I had experienced at the clinic when I tried to
understand the meaning of psychotic
states of mind.

—Carl Jung[1]

Gnosis, a Greek word, means knowledge. For many in the ancient Near East,
it connoted precious or privileged knowledge, inner enlightenment vis-à-vis
the uncertain, borrowed understandings of the masses. The Christian Gnostics, with whom the early Christian Fathers did battle, elevated *gnosis* above
pistis or faith as the ultimate saving virtue. Faith might set one on the path to
heaven but no person could be saved in ignorance; that is, without knowledge
of God's involvement in the cosmos and, by extension, of one's own origin and
present situation. According to Theodotus, to possess *gnosis* is to know "who
we were, and what we have become; where we were . . . whither we are hastening; from what we are being released; what birth is, and what is rebirth."[2]
Equipped with such redemptive knowledge, Gnostics felt they could outmaneuver the powers of darkness. Others were enfeebled if not deceived by their
lack of understanding; in fact, zeal without knowledge could be dangerously
counterproductive. *Gnosis* alone allows one to penetrate the veils of ignorance
that shroud mortal experience.

In time, the more egalitarian doctrine of faith prevailed against *gnosis*. Anyone, even children, can exercise faith, but *gnosis,* like alchemy with which it

was often identified, was a call to spiritual and physical hardship. Furthermore, part of that hardship entailed enduring the scorn of the unenlightened majority. Thus, persecution, instead of driving Gnostics out of existence, might serve only to strengthen their resolve and drive them deeper underground. They thrive on the age-old disjunction between appearance and reality: what seems real is often only a comfortable, cocoon-like illusion very hard to dispel. The illusion in fact may be so mesmerizing as to pull all but a few—the Gnostics— into its orbit. By nature, then, gnosticism is an elitist outlook that runs against the tide of majority opinion and official thinking. Is truth, the rarest of all possessions, to be found in a lowest-common-denominator catechism? Does it offer itself like a common dandelion to the masses moving along a broad path? Or is that path to truth "straight and narrow" so that few find it? Those who affirm the latter may opt to embark on a personal quest for *gnosis*—that reve-latory spark of truth that cannot be packaged for public distribution.

EARLY CHRISTIAN GNOSTICISM

Gnosticism has flourished in many settings, always with the intent of intro-ducing its devotees to ultimate understanding. In the early Christian era it posed a threat to normative Christianity, not just because it devalued faith at the expense of *gnosis* but also because it offered a radically different vision of God and the universe. According to Christian doctrine, God lovingly created the world and its creatures so that they might share, to a limited degree, in his existence. With the Fall of Adam and Eve, however, humanity became es-tranged from God and only divine intervention could bring about reconcilia-tion. This occurred when Jesus, the Son of God, came to earth and allowed himself to be crucified for the sins of all humankind. With this act, everyone becomes eligible for everlasting life, or life with God, on condition of faith and obedience.

This salvation story is optimistic because a benevolent God stays fully in control of his creation from beginning to end. Even after the Fall, he did not abandon his children but implemented a plan to redeem them from their fallen state. Christian Gnostics, however, saw things differently. For them, the Fall was an unexpected catastrophe leading to the entrapment of God and human-kind in a depraved, nightmarish world. Gnostic texts speak of an accidental rupture in God's Fullness (*pleroma*) caused by Sophia, a lesser aspect of that Fullness which overstepped her lawful station. (Again, a female, or female principle, is at fault.) This led to the creation of a flawed being, the Demiurge, who, along with the divine spillage, tumbled from heaven into a dark and alien material world. Seizing the moment and wishing to create his own cosmos, the Demiurge incarcerated the scattered drops or sparks of God in physical matter, thereby preventing their return to heaven. Now dispersed throughout the cosmos as myriad sparks, God seeks to rescue himself by collecting the sparks back together. What is more, his attempt at self-rescue is identical with our own, for within each of us (or, at least within many people—some Gnostics did not include everyone) is a spark of God radiating inner light.

Put differently, a spark trapped and shrouded in physical matter is a person with the capacity to know that she is a part of God. The trouble is that physical matter smothers our spiritual sensibilities so that we forget our high origins. Still, fleeting thoughts and wispish memories sometimes beset us, and when these are taken to heart *gnostalgia* may lead to *gnosis*. By responding to the divine spark within, we recover our true nature, shed our physical trappings, and eventually make our way back home to heaven. The grand moment of salvation, says Hans Jonas, occurs when one is reunited with a "divided-off aspect" of oneself, something that is both other and same.[3] The reunion of the scattered sparks, the shattered pieces of God, is a heavenly homecoming that defies rational comprehension.

This outlook departs from traditional Christianity in at least three ways. First, the creator god is deemed evil and the physical cosmos—God's incarceration therein—a tragic accident. Second, Gnostics insisted that Adam and Eve were wise to listen to the serpent, for he heroically sought to liberate them from the Demiurge's tyranny. Indeed, Gnostics turned many of the stories of the Old Testament on their head by reading that text as a record of Israel's ongoing attempt to throw off the yoke of a god-monster. The moment of truth came with Jesus, who arrived, however, not as the son of the creator god but in direct opposition to him. Jesus brought saving knowledge or *gnosis,* the only virtue strong enough to rescue us from our calamitous predicament. Most other virtues, by engendering a positive or at least patient attitude toward the world, perpetuate the rule of darkness.

The third point of departure for Gnostics lay in their perception of God, whose being (they believed) was not distinct from their own: indeed, they were God, and self-knowledge amounted to knowledge of God. This followed from the fact that God—the scattered parts of God—literally constituted their being. Monoimus advised his disciples to:

> Abandon the search for God and the creation and other matters of a similar sort. Look for him by taking yourself as the starting point. Learn who it is within you who makes everything his own and says, "My God, my mind, my thought, my soul, my body." Learn the sources of sorrow, joy, love, hate. . . . If you carefully investigate these matters you will find him in yourself.[4]

MAGIC, MYSTERY, AND SCIENCE

Hence, God already indwells you and *is* you. This for many Gnostics was the great secret and the very essence of *gnosis.*

This outlook, by collapsing orthodox Christianity's God-human distinction, engenders the kind of self-intoxication that often marks the practice of magic. Thus, ancient Gnosticism and Hermeticism—teachings traced back to Hermes Trismegistus—are frequently mentioned in the same breath, along with Neoplatonism and Cabala. What all these systems conduce is a sense of closing in on the mysteries of creation and the possibility of god-like exaltation. Gnosticism, however, tends toward a more negative view of the physical cosmos. Nature does not mirror the Divine; it does not reproduce, however imperfectly, the beauty and harmony of a higher world. While the Demiurge may have sought to achieve this upon trapping the sparks of God, he instead created a nightmare of cosmic proportions. Later Gnostics did not always take this dim view of the universe, but they did hold to the even more defining belief that only *gnosis* can liberate one from the traumas of mortal existence.

MEDIEVAL GNOSTICS

As we noted earlier, opposition to gnosticism may prompt its growth and enhance its staying power, simply because *gnosis* implies personal, intuitive knowledge beyond the reach of public affirmation or authoritative judgment. In fact, it might seem that only firsthand knowledge qualifies as true knowledge; anything else would be merely borrowed opinion in which one may invest faith. And even if that opinion were right or true, it would be a truth without saving efficacy, for, having trickled down from elsewhere, it could not inspire the conviction to weather the storms of life.

To veer away from the monolithic authority of the Catholic Church in the Middle Ages required the kind of conviction that comes with *gnosis,* and chief among those who did veer away were the Cathars, a heretical sect that flourished in France and Italy during the twelfth and thirteenth centuries. The Cathars sought for purity (Cathar stems from *katharos,* a Greek word meaning pure or clean) in a world that seemed wrong to its very core. That is to say the problem of evil loomed so large for the Cathars that they (unlike Catholics) saw the world as beyond repair. Not only was it fallen and perverted; it had *never* been in a pristine, pre-fallen state because an evil god—Satan—had created it. Having lured angelic beings out of heaven, he then trapped them in physical matter. Meanwhile, the true God seeks to rescue us—for we are the angelic souls—by sending down radiant knowledge to dispel the gloom that enshrouds us. Supporting this view were biblical texts that hinted at a rebellion in heaven which resulted in the expulsion of Satan and his followers. While most Christians assumed this expulsion was unrelated to the presence of human beings in the physical world, the Cathars conflated the two. For them, as for the early Gnostics, the Fall shapes up as a cosmic and heavenly catastrophe.

The Catholic Church, by insisting that creation was good, had cast its lot with Satan and consequently grown large and powerful, according to the Cathars. It epitomized the false splendor and pomposity that physical matter offers. Not only that, but the Church's idolatrous commitment to physical matter had resulted in the erroneous doctrine of the Incarnation: God (or the Son of God) had come to earth in a physical body. Because matter was totally alien to God and innately evil, he would never descend into its imperfection.

This attitude—that matter is irredeemably evil—set the tone for Catharist doctrine. God and all that came from God was spirit, while matter had a separate origin as a vastly inferior substance. The Catharist aim, then, was to give oneself over to spiritual propensities and this allegedly entailed, among other things, abstaining from cheese, meat, and eggs. These, said one Catholic observer, were "begotten of coition" and therefore were felt to be spiritually debasing.[5] Fasting also promoted release from unrighteous bodily pleasures. To a great extent, similar practices with similar aims could be found in the Catholic Church, but the Cathars had no tolerance for physical matter and consequently differed with Catholics on the question of the resurrection of Jesus. Scriptural accounts indicated a physical resurrection,[6] but by Catharist lights this reading vulgarized the true event: Christ, who never came to earth in a body and who consequently never underwent crucifixion, also never regained a body after experiencing physical death. After delivering his *gnosis*, he simply returned to heaven as a spirit being.

In normative Christianity, physical death marks the point at which believers and unbelievers alike depart their mortal probation. Resurrection further underscores that departure by securing the body (if one opts to believe in the resurrection of the body) against physical degeneration. Because, however, Cathars saw the body as the depraved material cosmos writ small, it followed that by itself physical death served no redemptive purpose. Unless one had already escaped the retarding drag of the cosmos through spiritual enlightenment, at death one's divine spark simply fell back into matter to again suffer entrapment. Hence, the view arose among certain Cathars that the soul or divine spark migrates from one body to the next, sometimes even taking up residence within animal bodies. This process might go on interminably, or it might end after a soul had achieved sufficient spiritual clarity to be reincarnated as a Cathar priest.[7]

Cathar priests were called *perfecti* (singular, *perfectus*), and, as the name suggests, they were felt to be on the verge of escaping the material world. For the Cathar laity, *perfecti* were models of piety, but Catholics often cast them in

MAGIC, MYSTERY, AND SCIENCE

dark, hypocritical colors. (Of course, Cathars returned the compliment.) Among the points at issue was the *consolamentum,* a sacrament or rite whereby persons were admitted to the ranks of the *perfecti.* In principle, such persons were so pure that they deserved the title of *perfecti* and the *consolamentum* merely acknowledged that fact. In practice, however, *perfecti* sometimes fell short of their saintly office, and this made their moral failings stand out all the more. It seemed to many Catholics that *perfecti* merely feigned goodness to attract converts, all the while performing unseen works of darkness. Moreover, lay Cathars looked forward to receiving the *consolamentum* shortly before death, as a kind of rite of last unction. This they hoped would liberate the divine spark so that their souls could travel freely back to heaven. Catholics, however, countered that the rite itself could not ensure salvation: sins, even those committed before the *consolamentum,* had to be worked off through penance.

When Catholic authorities discovered they could not reconvert Cathars through debate and preaching, they sanctioned more extreme measures. Inquisitors sought to root out the heresy by questioning suspects and demanding that they abjure false beliefs, if any, and declare their allegiance to the Catholic Church. Some Cathars freely confessed but others resisted so that full-scale conflict erupted in many communities as Catholic Crusaders came against them. In the end, Catharism was stamped out, but at the cost of thousands of lives. Today, tourists flock to see castles and battlements, now dilapidated, where Cathars once mingled and practiced their faith. At least one modern writer, moreover, has celebrated their otherworldly virtue vis-à-vis the mundane materiality and totalitarian ethic of the medieval Catholic Church.[8]

SECRET SOCIETIES

Are the Cathars merely an interesting history lesson or a light now dimmed by centuries of folly and ignorance? Beyond the details of their historical existence, do they offer timeless wisdom to those not distracted by the soap opera of the here and now? Some writers, searching for a key with which to unlock both the past *and* the present, have connected the Cathars with the Knights Templar, another medieval organization that provoked the wrath of the Catholic Church. The Knights Templar was organized in 1118 shortly after Christian Crusaders wrested the Holy Land (Jerusalem and its environs) from Islamic suzerainty. Not far from the ruins of Solomon's Temple, nine men founded a military order committed to the defense of Christianity. Besides taking a vow of poverty, they covenanted to protect Christian pilgrims traveling to Jerusalem and to steadfastly resist any threat to Christian interests. In effect, the Templars were warrior-monks, defenders of the faith both spiritually and physically.

The Templars grew rapidly, partly because they won the pope's favor and were granted concessions not enjoyed by other, non-military, monastic orders. Furthermore, once Muslim forces retook Jerusalem, many crusaders entered Templar ranks, seeking to blend military heroism with saintly aspiration. Single-minded in their devotion, the Templars fought with distinction. They also grew wealthy throughout Europe and the Near East, both because of their business acumen and gifts received from benefactors. Some outsiders felt this was inconsistent with their humble beginnings and vow of poverty, but the Templars were not the first religious order to achieve material prosperity. Eventually, however, their wealth and semi-independence from regional or national governments, along with reports of secret initiation rites, sparked doubt regarding their commitment to Church interests. To some it seemed they had veered off on their own self-serving trajectory, and rumors circulated that they committed acts of sodomy, spit on the cross, and worshipped a strange idol called Baphomet.

Tensions climaxed in the early 1300s when King Philip IV, impressing his will upon Pope Clement V, obtained permission to disband the order. Templars were arrested and tortured until they confessed crimes invented for the occasion. Thereafter, many were publicly burned or otherwise executed, and their property was turned over to the Knights Hospitaller, a rival military order that had long coveted Templar possessions. Thus ended the brief but illustrious history of the Knights Templar.

Or did it? Notwithstanding the uncontested facts of their political and ecclesiastical demise, the Templars almost seemed too savvy, perhaps too well informed by some great secret or treasure, to just fade away completely. One popular (unscholarly) theory is that they found the Holy Grail, the chalice used to hold the wine at the Last Supper and to catch the blood of Jesus as he hung on the cross. For people in the Middle Ages, this was the most sacred of all relics and consequently the one with the most potential to spiritually transfigure its possessors. There is also the belief that the Templars, while campaigning in the Holy Land, found (prefiguring Indiana Jones) the Israelite Ark of the Covenant, a wooden receptacle containing the tablets of the law, a pot of manna, Aaron's rod that budded, and other holy objects. Finally, a third possibility is that the Templars were literal descendents of Jesus; that is, guardians of a royal and sacred bloodline that ran back to Jesus and Mary Magdalene.[9]

If indeed the Templars possessed some great treasure or *gnosis*—so this line of thought runs—then it is probable they went underground when Church and State combined to dissolve the order. The sacred possession would then be passed on furtively, or, when a more hospitable climate allowed, under the cover of another organization having no ostensive ties with the Templars. The Freemasons are sometimes mentioned in this regard, particularly by those who wish to extend Masonic provenance into the remote and hoary past. Evidence indicates that Freemasonry is only about three hundred years old, having begun in the British Isles as part of a changing social order that valued reason and the free (unfettered by ecclesiastical or political authority) pursuit of knowledge. That evidence also demonstrates, however, that early Masons felt that they were tapping ancient sources of wisdom as they anticipated a brighter, more enlightened future. Like nearly everyone of the time, they were especially impressed, even awed, by Sir Isaac Newton. But while many others sought to learn the new physics, Freemasons paid particular attention to Newton's study of Solomon's Temple, believing, like Newton himself, that even modern science issues up from older, larger understandings.

According to Steven Bullock, Newton "drank deeply from the mysteries of alchemy and biblical prophecy even as he forged many of the concepts that underlay the later mechanistic science that ultimately denied these occult connections."[10] In Newton's mind, the Temple modeled and mirrored the cosmos, having been constructed according to the plan of creation. The stonemasons building the Temple supposedly were heirs of a long tradition of divine knowledge dating back to the Old Testament patriarchs, who, of course, had communed with God when the world was still fresh and relatively untouched by sin and error. Thus, the practical aspects of stoneworking intimated sublime principles, at least to those initiated into the craft.

Although sometimes overshadowed by other, more secular considerations, this antiquarian outlook was seminal to Freemasonry. It is also reflected in the Masonic symbols that show up on the U.S. one-dollar bill (the truncated pyramid, the all-seeing eye, and a Latin inscription announcing a "new secular order"), there because many of the American founding fathers were members of the Masonic fraternity. Not averse to drawing inspiration from all ages, Freemasons also developed a Knights Templar ceremony that, like the medieval vow, committed candidates to the defense of Christianity.[11] All this and more, Bullock argues, represented "an extraordinary conflation" of ideas and ideals drawn from many quarters.[12] Organized into a hierarchy of degrees and made available in local lodges, Masonic wisdom constituted a remarkable political force in the decades before and after the Revolutionary War. Many took it as a bulwark against moral degradation and the collapse of civilization.

Originating about a century before Freemasonry but sometimes merging with it, Rosicrucianism aimed to collect all human knowledge—sacred and secular—into one great synthesis. Although the fraternity began in Germany in the early 1600s, its founders claimed to be following in the footsteps of a previously unknown (and probably mythical) figure named Christian Rosenkreuz (Rosy-Cross). Rosenkreuz allegedly lived about two centuries earlier and had made life-clarifying discoveries while searching for wisdom in Egypt, Pal-

GNOSTICISM, OLD AND NEW

estine, Syria, Arabia, Spain, and elsewhere. These discoveries and the adventures that attended them were written up anonymously by one of the order's founders, evidently to promote interest in the order and to confer upon it an aura of mystical longevity. Whatever the motivation, the books detailing Rosenkreuz's life attracted attention and became the seed crystal for a new source of occult wisdom in the West.

With Rosenkreuz as an intermediary link, the Rosicrucian genealogy of knowledge reaches back to the ancient Egyptians, perhaps further. And if there is an explanatory motif to Rosicrucian wisdom, it is that everything resonates or chimes in with everything else: no note is so discordant that it cannot be assimilated into the large, universal harmony of things. Certain esoteric principles, for instance, inform all sacred edifices, including the Temple of Solomon, Egyptian temples and pyramids, the Mosaic tabernacle, Gothic cathedrals, and the temple of the human body in all its physiological complexity; so any one of these structures points to all the others.[13] This syncretic approach, characteristic of many occult systems, rests on the Renaissance assumption that the birth of modern science was a rebirth of ancient knowledge. In the words of one exponent, Rosicrucianism is "wisdom that is primeval, yet ever new, expressed in a form suitable for the present age."[14]

For all its emphasis on arcane insights, Rosicrucianism (like Freemasonry) is not meant to be a self-centered brotherhood. Upon bringing things into larger relation, it purportedly catalyzes humanitarian impulses and thereby projects its devotees into the realm of mundane affairs where their wisdom can serve practical ends. Thus, the fraternity may be understood as a small bit of spiritual leaven hidden in the loaf of humanity. This metaphor assumes the Hermetic-Gnostic view that truth has to fight its way into the world by subtle means. Or, to go further: those who know—agents of light—often travel incognito until a moment of opportunity arises. They are in the everyday world discretely conveying tidings of another, higher world that has yet to materialize—or perhaps better said, "spiritualize"—in our midst. "The most striking aspect of the Rosicrucian movement," wrote Frances Yates, is "its insistence on a coming Enlightenment. The world, nearing its end, is to receive a new illumination in which the advances in knowledge made in the preceding age of the Renaissance will be immensely expanded. New discoveries are at hand, a new age is dawning. And this illumination shines inward as well as outward."[15]

Over the last century or so, the movement that capitalized most notoriously on these esoteric sentiments was the Hermetic Order of the Golden Dawn. Established in England in 1888, the order based its claim to ancient authority on an enciphered manuscript found by W. Wynn Westcott. Already a Rosicrucian and a Mason, Westcott was able to break the cipher, which consisted largely of alchemical symbols. In the process he discovered a reference to

MAGIC, MYSTERY, AND SCIENCE

Figure 46. Christian Rosenkreuz, the alleged founder of Rosicrucianism

Figure 47. Depiction of a Rosicrucian society ardently searching for wisdom

"Sapiens Dominabitur Astris," which he recognized as an occult code name for someone who might be able to tell him more about the manuscript.[16] This turned out to be Anna Sprengel, a woman allegedly living in Nuremberg who responded to Westcott's inquiries. Exchanging letters, Westcott learned that Sprengel headed up a Rosicrucian temple known as *Die Goldene Dämmerung* in Germany. She henceforth commissioned him to establish a similar temple in London and conferred upon him the rank of "Adeptus Exemptus."[17] Thereafter she died, and, except for the letters in Westcott's possession, no proof that she ever lived could be located. Nonetheless, Westcott was now master of a new Rosicrucian order whose putative ancestry ran back through its older German counterpart (also unconfirmed) to ancient sources of magical wisdom.

Within a couple of years, the order numbered about eighty members of both sexes, most of whom had previously affiliated with Freemasonry, theosophy, Spiritualism, or other Rosicrucian groups deemed bogus or inferior by Westcott and his associates. One of those associates, MacGregor Mathers, undertook the construction of the ceremonies to be enacted as candidates advanced from one level or grade of knowledge to the next, using the manuscript deciphered by Westcott. Mathers—who had an extraordinary grasp of arcane lore, a fertile imagination, and felt himself in touch with "Secret Chiefs" (Mahatmas in theosophical parlance)—was able to invest these rites with a great deal of esoteric breadth and splendor. One ceremony, for example, entailed "the spectacle of Mathers in glittering Egyptian robes rising from the tomb of Christian Rosenkreuz."[18] Additionally, elements of alchemy, Cabala, Tarot, Pythagoreanism, theosophy, and other occult systems were worked into the ritual.

Thanks in part to Mathers's contribution, the Golden Dawn attracted enough applicants throughout Britain to justify the organization of new temples. Two of the most noted members or adepts of the order were W. B. Yeats, the Irish poet, and Aleister Crowley, magician *par excellence*. (Arthur Conan Doyle was invited to join but declined.) Yeats had had previous ties with theosophy but preferred a Western orientation that promised to satisfy his curiosity about fairies, witches, and ghosts. Under the tutelage of Mathers, he saw, or thought he saw, strange figures that seemed to move under their own power.[19] When Crowley entered the order, he was already well practiced in the magical arts and so felt underwhelmed by the initial indoctrination. Afterward he remarked, rather facetiously, that the "priceless secrets" imparted to him consisted merely "of the Hebrew alphabet, the names of the planets with their attribution to the days of the week, and the ten Sephiroth of the Cabala. I had known it all for months; and obviously, any schoolboy in the lower fourth could memorize the whole lecture in twenty-four hours."[20]

Crowley repelled many people because he struck them as personifying evil or black magic. In addition to experimenting with personal attire, sex, and drugs, he insinuated an alliance with Satan by identifying himself as "the Great Beast." His notoriety extended beyond the Golden Dawn because by 1904 the order had collapsed from internal dissension. Among other things, Mathers contributed to Westcott's demise by questioning the reality of Anna Sprengel and, by implication, Westcott's claim to authority. Mathers was in turn unseated by other adepts. However short-lived, the Golden Dawn continues to evoke disparate responses. Some see it as a momentary flare-up of truth resulting from an extraordinary confluence of personalities and ideas; others, as occult folly gone amuck; still others, as an episode demanding further study.

THE MODERN TURN

In about 1950, Hans Jonas, a noted Gnostic scholar, observed a parallel between early Christian Gnosticism and contemporary Western culture: both posit an uncaring cosmos. Consider the stars, for example. Do they bespeak transcendence—a world or worlds higher and better than our own? By deeming them lifeless products of a blind cosmic process, modern science disputes the venerable view that stars signify the handiwork and purpose of divinity, even if they are not gods themselves. To be sure, people today may marvel at the beauty of the night sky but, with its meaning-free cosmogony, science stifles (although does not fully choke) the reverential impulse. Good and evil do not figure into astrophysics, and so the stars shape up as metaphysical blanks disconnected from human cares and concerns.

Jonas pointed out that in ancient Gnosticism, the stars—indeed, the whole cosmos—bore a similar aspect, albeit not quite as terrifying. In the Gnostic universe, the stars were minor deities subordinate to the Demiurge; thus "they stared man in the face with the fixed glare of alien power and necessity."[21] Like prison guards, they blocked off possible escape routes. But at least, says Jonas, they were aware of humankind and valued its incarceration. Furthermore, although displaced in a hellish universe, humankind yet had a heavenly home (origin) and destiny. In the universe of modern science, by contrast, no space exists for heaven or hell; there are no metaphysical highs and lows, just flat indifference. To follow the biologist Richard Dawkins: "The universe we observe has precisely the properties we should expect if there is, at bottom, no design, no purpose, no evil and no good, nothing but blind, pitiless indifference."[22]

Far from regretting nature's blank unconcern, Dawkins insists that such is simply one of the hard truths of science. For Blaise Pascal, however, the idea of a cold, impersonal universe was too severe. As he contemplated the Newtonian model of the cosmos three hundred years ago, he wrote: "[E]ngulfed in

MAGIC, MYSTERY, AND SCIENCE

the infinite immensity of spaces of which I am ignorant, and which know me not, I am frightened."[23] In addition to the fact that Pascal could not center or locate himself in infinite space and that he felt dwarfed to nothingness by its unending vastness, there was the more distressing realization that the cosmos *did not know him*. Even if he were to fully grasp Newton's theory of the cosmos, that knowledge would not elicit an affirmatory nod of recognition from the cosmos. Since he, an organism, was not cognate with the mechanical world, knowledge thereof merely amounted to one-way facts or information—not the mutual knowing that grows out of kinship and sometimes opens out onto unexpected vistas of love and beauty. This latter outlook had informed Dante's cosmology; for him, as for many others, the world's intelligibility was a function of its living intelligence. But modern science short-circuits the notion of a responsive, caring, intelligent cosmos by removing the spiritual qualities that were once said to animate nature.

Jonas credits the birth of modern nihilism and existentialism to the scientific worldview that first distressed Pascal. Forlornness, homelessness, angst, dread, and cosmic silence are now familiar terms expressing the modern predicament of living in a universe that is not congenial to our spiritual aspirations. Many people, of course, customize the universe to their own spiritual ends and thus believe in spite of science. Others find room for God in the vagaries and unanswered questions of science. A few, finally, have confronted science directly, arguing that, in its modern formulation, it constitutes a kind of anti-*gnosis* by misportraying the living, caring world as blind mechanism. *Gnosis* therefore involves awaking from our self-inflicted, premeditated ignorance of nature's all-enveloping revelation of life. Both William Blake and Johann Wolfgang Goethe took this stance, hoping to bring back into focus the obvious truths that they felt science had iterated out of sight.

NATURE AS A "HOLY OPEN SECRET"

Living in the wake of the Scientific Revolution, Blake (1757–1827) and Goethe (1749–1832) reacted against the adoration of reason that Newton's physics had in large measure inspired. Although notoriously difficult to categorize as thinker, Blake subscribed to some of the most radical elements of ancient Gnosticism and these set the tone for his attitude toward rational science. He rejected the God of the Old Testament as a tyrant, believing that divinity resides not in rule and commandment but in liberation of the spirit. His famous drawing of God the Father using a compass to create the world depicts an autocrat selfishly wishing to circumscribe humankind's innate faculties—to delimit and constrain what by nature is free and unbounded. Party to this unrighteous dominion were religious creeds and scientific theories that

GNOSTICISM, OLD AND NEW

constrained the mind and blocked the imagination, which said, in effect, the universe is finite. And, while Blake conceded the limitations of physical matter, he did not take them to be absolute and insisted that our dull material organs of perception need not dull the spiritual imagination. For, he wrote, "[i]f the doors of perception were cleansed, everything would appear to man as it is, infinite."

Put differently, where matter and sense experience leave off, imagination and eternity begin. Blake stated that:

> I assert for My Self that I do not behold the outward Creation & that to me it is hindrance & not Action; it is as the Dirt upon my feet, No part of me. "What," it will be Question'd, "When the Sun rises, do you not see a round disk of fire somewhat 'like a Guinea?' " O no, no, I see an Innumerable company of the Heavenly host crying, "Holy, Holy, Holy is the Lord Almighty." I question not my Corporeal or Vegetative Eye any more than I would question a Window concerning a Sight. I look thro' it & not with it.[24]

The "outward Creation" was for Blake the imprisoning cosmos of God the Father. When Jesus came, he rebelled against his father by replacing the tyrannical legal code of the Old Testament with truths that drive home the realization that the kingdom of God is *within*. The unbounded spiritual imagination, then, is where divinity resides, and given this, Blake let the traditional God-human barrier fall: "God is a Man & exists in us & we in him."[25] This, of course, is a sentiment dear to many occult outlooks.

Because Newtonian science kept the imagination within materialistic bounds, Blake found it unpalatable. His best-known indictment is: "May God us keep, From Single vision and Newton's sleep!"[26] Science's steady gaze at physical matter, motivated by the assumption that nothing else exists, numbed and contracted the mind. The result was that "[t]he Visions of Eternity, by reason of narrowed perceptions, Are become weak Visions of Time & Space, fix'd into furrows of death."[27] Without imagination to expand experience beyond empirical sense data, the "Atoms of Democritus" and "Newton's Particles of light" remained inert and lusterless; with imagination, however, they became "Gem[s] Reflected in the beams divine" and "sands upon the Red sea shore, Where Israel's tents do shine so bright."[28]

Although Goethe's critique of science was more measured than Blake's, it hit at similar issues. To be specific, Goethe disputed science's monopolistic claim to absolute knowledge and total explanation. Not only was this wrong, he said, but it faltered on the mistaken assumption that understanding climaxes in the abstract modeling of nature rather than in the immediate experience thereof. His view was that "[t]hinking is more interesting than knowing but

Figure 48. William Blake's autocratic God the Father delimiting humankind's poetic faculties

less interesting than looking."[29] That is, nature is best comprehended in its native sensorial splendor. At that point, it is "its own theory," its own story and the radiant telling thereof. It speaks for itself, and much is lost, argued Goethe, when we endeavor to reduce its colorful self-narrative to abstract symbolism.

Goethe did not just say this from a romantic or wishful impulse. He observed what invariably gets lost or garbled in secondhand communication: "We never sufficiently reflect that a language, strictly speaking, can only be symbolical and figurative, that it can never express things directly, but only, as it were, reflectedly."[30] Human language, whether verbal or mathematical, does not present natural phenomena in their full vigor but only re-presents them in a weakened, indirect, and secondhand way. Of course if we suppose that phenomena are mute—that they are lifeless and impersonal—then we have little choice but to try to speak for them. Goethe, however, granted to nature powers that most scientists of the day arrogated only to themselves, and this pushed him toward the older occult view of a knowing, sentient world.

What Goethe had in mind was that, in the very process of piquing our curiosity, all natural phenomena perform spiritual or metaphysical work. At the very least, they keep us from spiraling inward egocentrically by alerting us to the outside world. This expansive awakening is life-giving, and it would never occur, said Goethe, if the outside world had no stake in the life experience. That is, by the time we begin to interpret the world and resolve it into putatively lifeless objects, it has already arrived in a life-expanding, mind-stretching way. To assume, therefore, that nature is inanimate at bottom is to stare past the tremendous service it renders by opening us up to the largeness of being we know as life. In brief, nature is not just there in an idle, indifferent way—if it were, it would never draw us out; it is there in a living, intelligent, revelatory way that is not distinct from our own living intelligence.

It is obvious that Goethe sought to bring human beings into a more egalitarian relationship with nature than that dictated by Newtonian science. By his lights, we learn most when we converse with nature and let its living essence instruct us. But this assumption of an animate, knowing universe is fundamental to the occult worldview. Nevertheless, for Goethe, nature's appeal to the mind and senses was so primal that it could not be divorced from life itself. And, given the prevailing contrary opinion of materialistic science, he came to see nature—the living revelation thereof—as a "holy open secret."[31] The *gnosis* was out in the open, freely apprehensible, but separated from most by their own self-imposed veil of ignorance.

Alchemists had once described the Philosopher's Stone the same way: too elemental for ordinary apprehension, the grasping of it presupposed the development of latent spiritual powers. And this in turn implied "Easter in Ordinary," a sacred immanence to nature that, like a window, one looked *through*

MAGIC, MYSTERY, AND SCIENCE

rather than *at*. It followed that scientific knowledge, constructed as it was of outwardly public and purely material sense data, could never fully satisfy humankind's deepest yearnings because it deliberately stopped short of some larger vision of things. This is the note on which Goethe's *Faust* begins:

I've studied now Philosophy
And jurisprudence, Medicine,—
And even, alas! Theology,—
From end to end, with labor keen;
And here, poor fool! with all my lore
I stand, no wiser than before. . . .[32]

In earlier versions of the Faust legend, the learned doctor bartered away his soul to the Devil for a full complement of worldly fame, knowledge, and pleasure. But, in Goethe's version, Faust escapes hell because the glories of the material world fail to offer full satisfaction. The material world, in other words, is not sharply discontinuous with hell (as it is in normative Christianity), and so the Devil cannot, even temporarily, sate Faust with fleeting pleasures and the sense of absolute knowledge. The human soul holds out for something more than a materialistic metaphysics.

CONTEMPORARY GNOSTICISM

The following questions tempt some people more than others: Might folly be the norm and clear vision the surprising exception? Might madness be a social contagion that takes over whole cultures? Might *I* be privileged with extraordinary insight into the problems and possible solutions of the current era? Answering yes to any of these questions suggests an inclination to steer away from consensus thinking in order to find "the pearl of great price" or "the story behind the story." That is, the *gnosis*. In contemporary Western culture this inclination has resulted in

[d]isinterest in the goods of a consumer society, withdrawal into communes of the like-minded away from the bustle and clutter of big-city distraction, non-involvement in the compromises of the political process, sharing an in-group's knowledge both of the disaster-course of the culture and of an ideal, radical alternative not commonly known.[33]

All this, of course, is part and parcel with New Age thinking, to be treated in the next chapter. But aside from its broad counter-cultural appeal, Gnosticism has been mined for understanding in specific ways. When early Christian Gnostic texts were discovered in Egypt in 1945, Carl Jung was among the few professional outsiders who took an avid interest in them and who in fact overcame some of the bureaucratic obstacles that attended their public dissemination.[34] From the outset, he anticipated that the texts would reveal much about the human psyche and help elucidate contemporary culture. He compared ancient Gnostics to medieval alchemists: both sought to spiritually transfigure the soul so that it could escape the prison of mortality. In the mid-twentieth century, Jung continued, an increasing number of individuals were similarly afflicted by a need to escape the narrow confines of the conscious ego and merge into the collective unconscious. While Gnostics had looked outward for salvation, people now, with their more highly individuated egos, intuitively looked inward with the hope of re-capturing and re-integrating lost (or scientifically devalued) aspects of their psychic lives. These might include dreams, myths, and meaningful coincidences.

Jung stated that Gnosticism and alchemy "gave substance to my psychology."[35] In other words, they ensured that his theory was not just an intellectual quirk of the twentieth century and therefore unrepresentative of other eras and non-Western cultures. He aspired to see human experience from a wide-angle vantage point and felt that the Gnostics offered important insights if only because they "tackled the problem of evil on a broader basis than the [Christian] Church Fathers."[36] Curiously, however, as Jung developed his ideas on good and evil, he veered away from certain Gnostic understandings. To be sure, he appreciated their recognition that evil is a pervasive feature of the world, but he did not see it as something to escape from. Instead, he embraced the Taoist formula that polar opposites compose a single, indissoluble unity. Light, for example, is light only because it plays off darkness and is therefore mutually involved in darkness: the two opposites lean on each other and ultimately lean into each other. Put another way, connection to only one terminal, whether positive or negative, fails to produce life's electricity. Current flows when one is caught between the oppositional tension of good and evil, light and darkness, male and female. Or, as Jung has it, "Everything requires for its existence its own opposite, or else it fades into nothingness."[37]

This approach finds truth in tensions, relations, or syntheses rather than in parts that seem (but only seem) to be distinct and independent. In the end, however, it collapses the stark Christian tension between good and evil by assimilating one into the other. In taking this stance, Jung drew inspiration from the East, although he was less enamored of Hinduism and Buddhism than Blavatsky. In 1938, he visited India and wrote later that he was impressed by the Eastern view that "good and evil are meaningfully contained in nature, and are merely varying degrees of the same thing. I saw that Indian spirituality contains as much of evil as of good."[38] To acknowledge the evil within, rather than projecting it outward or dismissing it as mere convention, was for Jung insurance against psychic disaster: "Whenever we give up, leave behind, and

MAGIC, MYSTERY, AND SCIENCE

forget too much, there is always the danger that the things we have neglected will return with added force."[39]

Consistent with his penchant for collapsing dichotomies, Jung also blurred the distinction between outer and inner reality. Believing that inner microcosm or mind mirrored the contents of the macrocosmic universe and vice versa ("As above, so below"), he ventured that creation stories rehearse stages of personality development. For example, the unconscious equates to the *pleroma* or, variously, to the primordial waters of creation upon which the Holy Spirit shimmers—unbroken equilibrium. From this divine matrix emerges conscious egos, or if physical terms are preferred, living material organisms cut off from their native element. As the separation process continues, the heightening sense of individuality segues into forgetfulness of one's origins. For the Gnostics, this was overcome by messages from beyond the physical cosmos, delivered by Jesus and other denizens of the divine realm. For Jung, liberation occurred as unconscious glimmers of truth broke through one's sense of individuality, calling the person back home to the collective unconscious whence all individuals originate. In either case, joyful reunion followed a painful sojourn into separation and individuality.

Jung's account corresponds closely to that of the Gnostics and he went so far as to say that "it is clear beyond a doubt that many of the Gnostics were nothing other than psychologists."[40] Be that as it may, Robert Segal points out that Jung modified Gnosticism to his own occult and/or psychotherapeutic purposes.[41] As noted above, Jung did not believe that physical matter absolutely instantiates evil. This, writes Segal, was because he put Gnosticism within an alchemical context that posited the elaboration of good—the Philosopher's Stone—from mundane physical substances. Precious minerals, after all, lie hidden in the earth and in their ores, awaiting extraction and purification, and these processes bespeak comparable spiritual processes for alchemists. Similarly, Jung felt, truth reposes in the collective unconscious but goes unnoticed by those focused solely on the physical objects that dominate waking reality. One must occasionally go underground; one must accept the reality of the unconscious and embrace its ethereal (mythic, dream-like, irrational) offerings. Thus, in Jung's system, liberation is not an absolute leave-taking of consciousness but a return to a time when neither consciousness nor unconsciousness eclipsed the other. For Gnostics, however, salvation amounted to a complete leave-taking of the material cosmos.

Despite such differences, Gnostics of all eras embrace knowledge as the key to enlightenment. Mere belief is not good enough: better to know and to know that you know. But is it possible to completely bid adieu to belief while ascending to the realm of absolute knowledge? Many people would say no—when beliefs harden, they become knowledge and so uncertainty lingers but at an

GNOSTICISM, OLD AND NEW

unacknowledged level. Moreover, even the most dedicated Gnostic ironically clings to the *belief* that knowledge is stronger than belief. This belief-knowledge intimacy seems to render all human understanding fallible and incomplete. What about *divine* understanding, however? That, after all, is the Gnostic polestar.

14

NDEs, NEW AGE, AND NEW PHYSICS

Treasures that have long been buried and hidden away from the sight of those that were neither able to realize nor to appreciate their value are now brought to light; pearls of ancient wisdom are brought from the East; fountains of knowledge that have been for centuries closed up are again opened, and a flood of light is thrown over things that appeared impossible, mysterious, and occult.

—*Franz Hartmann*[1]

What happens after death? The question is indestructible. Taking their cues from the round of the seasons, ancient Egyptians prepared themselves for resurrection and endless life in the Kingdom of Osiris. In a much different age, nineteenth-century Spiritualists felt that, under the right circumstances, departed souls could reunite with the living. When Spiritualism lost momentum, other beliefs emerged to assert the reality of life after death. Reincarnation, for instance, turns this life into one of many, all regulated by the principle of karma or cosmic justice. Past lives may be glimpsed via yoga, hypnotic regression, or spirit-channeling, and future lives continue the karmic drama. So, as final as death may seem to be, it is swallowed up by the larger principle of life, according to reincarnationists.

Occult beliefs and practices posit a hidden side of reality to which ordinary consciousness has little or no access. The theme is an old one: everyday reality—

the daily grind—is not the full story. There is magic in the offing, a story behind the story where wrongs are righted, afflictions are healed, the vigor of youth is restored, and death is trumped by life. Whether this is really so is, of course, much contested. Be that as it may, in recent decades near-death experiences (NDEs) have been proffered as evidence for the soul's immortality. But while they seem distinctly new (they did not receive widespread public attention until the 1970s), NDEs have been around for millennia. They cannot, therefore, be said to constitute *new* evidence for life after death. Recall that séances once also seemed new and marvelous, but they share many characteristics with the age-old practice of necromancy. Will NDEs, like séances, eventually fade from public interest and be blended back into the great stream of human experience that resists consensual understanding? Or will they be lifted out of that stream to achieve a measure of scientific respectability and confirmation? A lot depends on how much the tenor of science has changed since the late nineteenth century.

PRE-MODERN ACCOUNTS

Reports of near-death or apparent-death experiences stretch back into antiquity. Among the best-known accounts is Plato's "Myth of Er" (as it is now called), a story of reincarnation detailing how recently deceased souls move on to new bodies in wise or foolish ways.[2] (Although Plato talks of Er as if he were a real person, the story, like Plato's thinking in general, possesses an otherworldly or mythic quality.) Er was a brave man killed in battle. Ten days later, those collecting the bodies of the dead were surprised that Er's body had not decayed. When it was placed on the funeral pyre to be burned, Er sprang to life and told of his (his soul's) post-mortem journey into another sphere. He further explained how and why he had returned to his body.

Er related that soon after his death, he saw souls from both heaven and earth mingling together and trading stories of woe and happiness. But whatever their tales, the souls received a tenfold reward or punishment for deeds done in previous lives. Particularly hateful characters (like tyrants) were flayed alive and thrown repeatedly into thorns. Furthermore, they were not allowed to move on to subsequent lives. All others, however, made an arduous trek to a meadow where they chose their new bodies and mortal situations. Since, however, there were a limited number of choices, some more eye-catching than others, souls were randomly assigned numbers to determine who would choose first, and so on. Even when they were lucky in their number assignments, bad souls generally made foolish choices by opting for wealth and power rather than situations that might lead to wisdom or spiritual development. Those choosing later

Figure 49. The soul hovering over the body. William Blake's drawing is reminiscent of the out-of-body experiences narrated by many recent NDE subjects.

would have slimmer pickings, but this might protect them from their own vanity. Some souls chose to be dictators; others, humans in ordinary circumstances; and still others, animals like eagles or swans.

Although Plato did not talk explicitly of karma, the process he (or Er) describes has a karmic feel to it. Some souls, it seems, never learn from their mortal experiences and so keep on repeating their mistakes. This is partly because, upon making their choices, they are allowed to drink from Lethe, the river of forgetfulness. Extremely thirsty after trekking across a barren plain to reach the meadow, many souls drink to their heart's content and consequently lose all memory of their past lives and the interim times spent choosing new situations. Others, however, sensing the need to carry memories—even dim ones—into the next life, just sip from the river. They then come to earth with a besetting nostalgia for a larger, fuller world, and, by acting on that nostalgia, they recover forgotten truths. For Plato, understanding occurred through the recollection of pre-mortal memories.

Not required to drink from Lethe, Er was returned to his body with full

NDEs, NEW AGE, AND NEW PHYSICS

memory of his post-mortem experience. His story addresses not only human-kind's perennial hope of life after death but also the less familiar motif of life before birth. William Wordsworth, for instance, wrote:

> Our birth is but a sleep and a forgetting:
> The Soul that rises with us, our life's Star,
> Hath had elsewhere its setting,
> And cometh from afar:
> Not in entire forgetfulness,
> And not in utter nakedness,
> But trailing clouds of glory do we come
> From God, who is our home.[3]

Some one thousand years after Plato recounted Er's experience, Salvius, a sixth-century Christian monk, rose from his funeral bier to tell a story that matches, in some respects, modern NDEs. After his apparent death from a fever, Salvius awoke to the amazement of those preparing his funeral. At first reluctant to say much (lest he reveal an unspeakable mystery), he merely expressed disappointment at having to come back to earth: "Merciful God, why has Thou allowed me to return to this gloomy place of life."[4] But, four days later, after being begged to reveal what he knew, Salvius told his story:

> I was seized by two angels and carried up to the high heavens [above the stars]. . . . Then I was taken through a door brighter than this light into that dwelling in which all the pavement was like shining gold and silver, a brightness and spaciousness beyond description, and such a multitude of both sexes were there that the length and breadth of the throng could not be seen.[5]

Whereupon Salvius was taken before a marvelously bright cloud which

> gleamed more brightly than the light of nature, and a voice came out of the cloud like a voice of many waters. . . . I stood where I was bidden and a very sweet odor enveloped me so that I was refreshed by this sweetness and up to the present have wanted no food or drink. And I heard a voice saying: "Let him return to the world since he is necessary to our churches." And I threw myself on the pavement and said with loud weeping: "Alas, alas, Lord, why didst Thou show me this if I was to be deprived of it." [The voice said,] "Go in peace, for I am your keeper until I bring you back to this place."[6]

The sublimity of the experience, the bright cloud or personage, and the profound regret at having to return to earth—these are all aspects of contemporary NDEs.

MAGIC, MYSTERY, AND SCIENCE

MODERN NEAR-DEATH EXPERIENCES

In 1975, Raymond Moody published *Life after Life,* a book that sparked both popular and scholarly interest in NDEs. Moody, who included the topic of death in his university philosophy courses, became intrigued as students came up after class to share their NDEs. He soon began to collect and corroborate these stories, and after having interviewed some fifty subjects, published his conclusions. Moody did not announce his findings as definitive; rather, he saw them as anecdotal and preliminary—a seed crystal to further research.[7] Nevertheless, he identified certain very common elements in NDE narratives. Although no single NDE would be expected to embrace every element, all elements do show up consistently when accounts are multiplied:[8]

1. The subject is very close to death, perhaps in deep pain and/or already pronounced dead by an attending physician.
2. The NDE occurs in an emergency or operating room during surgery.
3. The subject is at peace and senses no pain even though her body may be subjected to things that normally cause great pain.
4. The subject finds himself moving very rapidly through a dark tunnel and suddenly being outside his own physical body, perhaps looking down on his body or the people trying to revive it.
5. The subject may see deceased friends, relatives, and other light-filled beings, apparently guiding her to a destination. She feels a warm spirit of happiness.
6. The subject meets a being of light, apparently a Supreme Being, who directs him to review and evaluate his life.
7. When the subject realizes that she must return to her physical body, she resists, for she longs to stay in this wonderful place of peace, warmth, and happiness.
8. When the subject awakes, he is reluctant to share the experience with others because it is difficult to articulate, very unusual, and extraordinarily poignant.
9. The experience profoundly alters the subject's attitudes and lifestyle, often moving her toward service and learning opportunities.

Since Moody sketched this composite experience, others have conducted their own research. Some who were skeptical at first were impressed by how regularly certain elements—such as the tunnel and the radiant being—recur. They also were surprised that the elements seem to be universal rather than particular to Western culture. Not all NDE accounts, however, fit the above model. Some subjects experience not peace and warmth but terror brought on by hideous images or a sense of self-dissolution in an eternal void. Also, some researchers have found that one need not be near death to have a typical NDE.[9] That is, NDEs, as described by Moody, may occur when death is far away.

The issue is complicated by the fact that life and death do not always respect our best medical definitions of life and death. A flat EEG normally indicates "brain death," the shutting down of the central nervous system and, by implication, the imminent and irreversible termination of all life processes. But occasionally a clinically dead subject—one pronounced dead by medical authorities—"returns" to life.[10] The quotation marks register the difficulty in establishing an exact moment of death, and that moment may differ from person to person or from situation to situation. So, what some may regard as a miracle others will see as the breakdown of a conventional definition, and there is still no consensus on whether the subject actually died. This is why "near-death experience" is a cautious expression—if it errs, it does so on the side of the scientific proposition that actual death is irreversible.

Given this, skeptics argue that NDEs tell us nothing about the possibility of life *after* death: they are responses of bodies still alive. It may be that in moments of extreme crisis the brain sometimes adapts or escapes by producing soothing experiences. Perhaps it calls forth exceedingly poignant memories of birth and early infancy. These explanations, of course, are not decisive, and believers often counter that some NDEs include factual information unavailable to the supposedly hallucinating or unconscious mind. Details of surgery or of an accident scene, witnessed by a subject under anesthesia or in shock who feels himself viewing things from an out-of-body perspective, may match actual events.

One cardiac arrest victim was brought to the emergency ward, close to death and in a deep coma. As the medical team took action, the man's dentures were removed and whisked away with other effects. A week later after the man had regained consciousness and spent several days recuperating, he described the emergency room scene in accurate detail, surprising the physician who had been in charge that night. More amazingly, he told what had happened to his dentures so that the hospital staff were able to retrieve them. The man insisted that he had seen everything from an out-of-body perspective.[11]

If NDEs are fully self-contained productions of the brain, how is it that "outside" events are incorporated into the production, particularly when the subject is presumably unconscious; furthermore, how is it that subjects accurately see things from extraordinary angles of vision? Often the subject sees her body lying on the ground or operating table. Is this traceable to the brain's almost frightening capacity to conjure up realistic scenarios from a mere handful of details, or has the mind or spirit momentarily left the body just as it

MAGIC, MYSTERY, AND SCIENCE

Figure 50. Tunnel of light. In this nineteenth-century illustration, Dante and Beatrice, in Dante's Divine Comedy, *stand before a "tunnel" of angels leading to the bright light of God.*

NDEs, NEW AGE, AND NEW PHYSICS

purportedly does (for an extended time) at death? The questions are easy to ask but hard to resolve.

NEW AGE MOVEMENT(S)

For many, NDEs and the conviction that humans possess immortal souls overlap into New Age thinking. We use the term "New Age" cautiously, recognizing that while it has been around for decades, the momentous changes it seems to promise have yet to materialize. Perhaps that is why many bookstores no longer use the label, having replaced it with "Metaphysics" just as they once replaced "Occult" with "New Age." But while the term may be passé, the concepts are not. Thanks to people like Blavatsky, increasing globalization, and the consequent sense in the West that other cultures have much to offer, what was once thought fringe or alien has now become mainstream. Corporate leaders and business schools, for example, now seem more open to seminars on "self-actualization," "guided visualization," and "The New Paradigm" where the accent is on "out-of-the-box" thinking and "non-linear" behavior.

This may seem vague, but New Age intentionally defies ready definition: it is a reaction against the taxonomic urge to label, organize, and pinpoint. "It kills in order to analyze" might be the New Age indictment of traditional thinking. Not surprisingly, this let-it-flow attitude militates against the establishment of a central organization headed up by widely acknowledged leaders. Nevertheless, three broadly shared beliefs inform most New Age movements:

1. Transcendence. One may break the frame of everyday reality through various tools, techniques, and teachings. Yoga may release some people from the mundane, while spirit channeling, crystals, or Tarot will work for others.

2. Unity. Despite appearances to the contrary and the scientific tendency to reduce nature to parts that are putatively separate and fundamental, the world hangs together as a whole. To invoke older occult terminology, each microcosm (part) recapitulates the macrocosm (whole).

3. New Age. The dawning of new light as the present era passes away. This very likely is part of a cosmic evolutionary process (recall Blavatsky and Steiner) having astrological overtones—thus, the dawning of the Age of Aquarius as Aquarius replaces Pisces on the eastern horizon at the vernal equinox. Added to this is the expectation of a New Age Master or Messiah (like Krishnamurti) to guide humankind toward a higher plateau of understanding.

Beyond these core elements, New Age is very individualistic. Indeed, it is marked by a kind of smorgasbord syndrome wherein devotees pick and choose ideas according to personal taste and (often) according to what's fashionable. And, as the menu of possibilities is always changing and growing through a free-for-all process of fragmentation and novel recombination, there are no towering figures like Blavatsky to wield widespread influence. Moreover, since the basic themes are well worn, newness comes from fresh variations thereon, and many of the new ideas enjoy brief heydays. Ten years from now, crystal power and the teachings of Ramtha (discussed later in this chapter) may go the way of pyramid power and biorhythms, but the New Age will remain.

Mixed into this mélange is a strong sense of tolerance for others' ideas, which may segue into a purely relativistic view of truth if taken too far. But, while New Agers tend toward the outlook that all truth claims are equal, most would not approve of the Ku Klux Klan and other hate groups. Furthermore, as suggested above, much New Age thinking is a reaction against orthodox patterns of thought, Western science and religion in particular. More palatable are the Western occult disciplines, Eastern and Native American religions, and marginal sciences such as parapsychology. To embrace these often entails embracing one or more of the following: reincarnation, karma, trance channeling, holistic health, vegetarianism, environmentalism, lost continents, ascended masters, and any number of other things already discussed in earlier chapters. Then, too, there is New Age music, which was originally designed to create a mood of therapeutic relaxation that might lead to transformational experiences or altered states of consciousness. Today the term applies to all sorts of "easy listening" music (like soft jazz) that come across as voguish and even musically groundbreaking to some but as cliché-ridden and derivative to others. Suffice it to say, New Age is a hope that has yet to wear out its marketing welcome.

TOWARD TRANSFORMATION, UNITY, AND THE COMING NEW AGE

Key to New Age thinking is the search for a transforming spiritual experience.[12] In other circles, such might be called a "religious experience," but most New Agers shy away from the word *religious* because it savors of orthodoxy and organization. All the same, the devotee aspires to a mystical watershed experience. This may come about through crystals, New Age healings, yoga, or imbibing the wisdom of a New Age master. And, as the newness or effectiveness of one technique wears off, another may take its place so that stagnancy never sets in. The aim of all this is, of course, growth and enlightenment, and, although individual paths may vary tremendously, they all lead to the same destination—truth.

Implicit in this search for truth are definitions of good and evil. Many New

Agers hold underlying moral, or "enlightened," beliefs that they claim are true for everyone. For instance, saving the environment (particularly rain forests, whales, and other threatened life forms) is not only good but also imperative for all people. Other New Agers, however, insist that ultimately there is no good or evil as these terms are normally understood. To take one example, J. Z. Knight's channeled entity Ramtha (an ancient Lemurian, presumably a being from Blavatsky's Lemurian root race) denies that actions like murder are wrong, asserting, "I do not abhor the act. I have reasoned it. I have understood it. I am beyond it."[13] Within an occult or New Age context, this attitude may be rationalized by the belief that karma ensures that all "evil" actions undergo rectification over the course of many incarnations. Going further, one may also invoke the higher-enlightenment principle of observer-created reality to eliminate conventional notions of good and evil. The world we see and affect is, at a primary level, one's own creation, and this because All is One. Separability or apartness is a fiction: I am the sweep of my experience, and that means I am you and anyone (or anything) else taken in thereby. My seamless apprehension of all integrates the cosmos, and so I am its creator, "I am God."[14] Thus, individual acts—even those thought evil—have a divine origin and are consequently immune to human standards of right and wrong that presuppose apartness.

This outlook is an integral aspect of the magical worldview, and many New Agers anticipate that it will become commonplace in the approaching era of peace and harmony.[15] Keeping pace with the cosmos as it spirals upward, humankind is felt to be growing into new understandings if not also acquiring new spiritual faculties. We are entering what astrologers have long called the Age of Aquarius, a time of universal brotherhood far removed from the conflict-ridden present era. As noted in chapter 4, this will occur—is already occurring—as Aquarius distills its native astrological qualities on the human race. Hence, the transformation is to some degree inevitable, a natural consequence of the universe's evolutionary ascent. Still, human free will also plays into the transition and there is no consensus as to how precisely the New Age will come about at the ground level, so to speak. Some emphasize public activism, participation in such activities as the various green movements and political lobbying. Others underscore personal enlightenment, insisting that once a critical mass of collective spiritual enlightenment is achieved, humanity will enter its next evolutionary phase. Put differently, a little leaven expands the loaf, and, in this case, just a few transformed individuals may function as leaven.

Other questions also elicit differing responses. There is disagreement as to whether the fateful transition will emerge peacefully or catastrophically. Furthermore, some New Agers, particularly those with theosophical leanings, claim that a teacher or messiah will appear at the critical moment, just as

MAGIC, MYSTERY, AND SCIENCE

Buddha and others appeared in the past. Even in the absence of such a teacher, most believers posit the creation of a universal religion drawn together from the teachings of all religions and amenable to local variations. (Very likely this would be a restoration or approximation of humankind's aboriginal wisdom, if Blavatsky may be trusted.) Added to this religion is the idea of universal power, which is variously called "prana, mana, odic force, orgone energy, holy spirit, the chi, mind, and the healing force."[16] This power, the primal energy of the cosmos, may be tapped and focused through meditation, crystals, and assorted other means for purposes of consciousness expansion and psychic healing. Shirley Maclaine's channeled spirit "John" gives it a pantheistic characterization: "God, or the God force, of which all things are a part . . . is the Divine Energy that created and holds it together harmoniously."[17] Another description, known to nearly everyone in the West, comes from George Lucas's famous *Star Wars* trilogy. Who can forget Master Yoda's instruction to the young Luke Skywalker: "My ally is the Force. And a powerful ally it is. Life creates it and makes it grow. Its energy surrounds us and binds us. Luminous beings we are, not crude matter. . . . Feel the flow. Feel the Force around you. Here . . . between you and me, and that tree and that rock."[18]

These ideas, as noted above, may seem cutting-edge, but many originate with Madame Blavatsky and the Theosophical Society, an organization now over a century old. Other sources of influence include the Cabala, astrology, and Anthroposophy, along with the popularization (or re-popularization) of Eastern thought since the end of World War II, particularly Zen Buddhism. Finally, there is the "direct revelation" to be had through spirit channeling.

CHANNELING

In New Age practice, a channel is a person who allows a spiritual being to take control of him or her in order to gain spiritual or paranormal insight. Often the spirit speaks in a different voice and manner than its human host. At other times, it may communicate through such means as automatic writing (recall Lady Conan Doyle's séance with Harry Houdini). Some of the most famous modern channels (with their channeled entities in parentheses) are Jane Roberts (Seth), J. Z. Knight (Ramtha), Pat Rodegast (Emmanuel), and Jack Pursel (Lazaris).

One may profitably compare channeling to the ancient Greek practice of consulting oracles and the spirit and demonic possessions of the Middle Ages. More important for our purposes, there is considerable continuity between modern channeling and the summoning of spirits in the nineteenth century. But, notwithstanding the obvious similarity—both practices reach for contact with the supernatural—there are also important differences. Whereas spiritualist mediums concentrated almost exclusively on communicating with deceased humans, channels rarely limit themselves in this way. They make contact with long-dead races (Lemurians and Atlanteans, for example), with dolphins, with extraterrestrials, with spirit masters who were never human, and even with the universal group-mind.[19] Then, too, not all channels claim such esoteric sources but, rather, say that so-called spirit guides are merely tools by which they tap into their own higher selves. Since All is One, precise distinctions are unnecessary.

Among many New Agers, the source is less important than the message. In this, New Age channeling differs sharply from nineteenth-century mediumship. Spiritualism thrived on the dead speaking—that was the miracle of it all—and only secondarily drew vigor from what they said. Often those who sat for a séance did so simply to gain the peace of mind of knowing their deceased loved ones had survived death. Also, many people took a scientific interest in Spiritualism, thinking that it might provide compelling proof for the immortality of the soul.

Modern channeling, however, offers little or no empirical data for scientific investigation. For one thing, the experience is highly personal and messages are caught in trance states or on a kind of intuitive rebound; hence, channels do not rely on outward effects to establish their bona fides. If anything, the message speaks for itself, sometimes hitting its recipient(s) with preternatural force and clarity. Another consideration: How does one scientifically verify the existence of a spirit master (or dolphin, or group-mind) for whom no birth or death certificate exists? One of the authors participated in a session in which the channel contacted an extraterrestrial between the orbits of Uranus and Neptune. Several questions were asked and one person felt she received important personal direction, but others wondered if anything remarkable had actually occurred. Perhaps we were expecting too much and failed to appreciate the intuitive subtlety of the experience. In any case, knowing historical facts about a deceased friend or relative afforded the possibility of scientific control during a séance: participants could question the spirit regarding facts to which only they and a few others were privy. No such record checking is possible with entities like Ramtha.

REINCARNATION

In brief, channeling does not offer, or even pretend to offer, empirical evidence for life after death. That evidence is now sought for in NDEs. But, thanks to the concept of reincarnation, the idea of the immortality of soul in New Age thinking stretches off in both directions—future and *past*—and some researchers have tried to verify our pre-birth existence through hypnotic regression. Recall that Plato proposed that some people have dim memories of previous incarnations and that the clarification and recovery of these memories puts them in touch with truth. In Hinduism and Buddhism, it is similarly felt that the remembrance of past lives facilitates entry into Nirvana.

For some individuals, the doctrine of recollection rings true: they are inexplicably drawn to a particular country, culture, or historical figure and only later hypothesize association during an earlier lifetime. One woman of our acquaintance, for instance, grew up in Wisconsin but, after graduating from high school, moved to San Diego. Living near the Pacific Ocean rekindled an old nostalgia for the sea, she said, and eventually she decided that she had once lived in a Mediterranean country. There are of course other ways to explain this sense of familiarity, but the reincarnation thesis appeals to many. Moreover, it has been subjected to scientific, or, as some claim, pseudo-scientific scrutiny.

Earlier in this book, we discussed how some UFO researchers use hypnosis to recover abduction memories of those purportedly taken hostage by aliens. Might the same approach work for recalling past lives? Hypnosis certainly offers some important medical benefits, but zealous or less-than-careful hypnotists can easily lead or coax their subjects into make-believe scenarios that seem perfectly real. Because hypnotic suggestion (whether deliberate or unwitting) readily catalyzes the imagination, extraordinary accounts given under hypnosis are, almost by definition, suspect. There is the additional challenge, moreover, of satisfying the historical record. Given an account of a past life, how well does it agree with known facts; furthermore, does it agree with them with enough exactitude to impress a scholar of the era in question? Most people can generate a superficial description of the American frontier during the late 1800s, say, but very few can go into precise and illuminating detail.

The real question, then, is not whether people can tell stories about their past lives but, rather, whether the stories they tell offer compelling evidence that they actually lived in the past. Affecting some semblance of scientific rigor, a few researchers have tried to hypnotically regress subjects back beyond the birth experience and into a previous life. One of the first and best-known cases involved Virginia Burns Tighe, a young woman living in Denver, Colorado, in the 1950s, who "remembered" under hypnosis her life as Bridey Murphy in nineteenth-century Ireland. Both believers and non-believers went to Ireland to investigate, but some skeptical reporters went to Chicago, Tighe's childhood home. Although there is no record that a Bridey Murphy lived in Ireland at the time, the hypnotized Tighe related Irish experiences—such as her courtship and marriage, and kissing the Blarney Stone—in an Irish brogue. Reporters for the *Chicago American*, however, found that, as a young girl, Tighe had memorized Irish monologues for school, and more importantly, that she had a long acquaintance with Mrs. Anthony Corkell, an Irish woman who lived across the street from Tighe's childhood home. Mrs. Corkell's maiden name was Bridey Murphy.[20] Skeptics do not say that Tighe was consciously lying, rather that this is a case of crypto-amnesia, a more plausible explanation than reincarnation—and good science values plausibility. Believers respond by saying (among other things) that skeptics need to cast a critical eye at their own skepticism, which is an ideological agenda rather than an attitude for seeing things clearly.

On the whole, the scientific hope of demonstrating reincarnation through hypnotic regression has foundered on dubious methodology and data. In the 1970s, the psychologist Helen Wambach approached the issue in a wide-angle way by regressing large numbers of people into their past lives, asking them questions, and then working up statistical profiles. Because statistics characterize much scientific discourse, her books appear to be works of scholarly substance. But, in this case, the number crunching fails to persuade because the compiled data can be construed in any number of ways and are therefore inconclusive. Wambach expresses surprise that only half of the 1,050 subjects, all Americans, who regressed to the early 1860s, situated themselves in the United States. She thought most would place themselves in the United States—if they were fabricating. But, given all the unknowns that plague this kind of study, how can any such inference be more than mere speculation? Another case in point: Mike Talbot, who sees the study as strong proof for reincarnation, is exuberant that only three subjects mentioned the Civil War in their recollections. If subjects were making up experiences, he reasons, the Civil War would have automatically come to mind. But how many people know the precise years of the Civil War, and, of those, how many reflexively link those years with the Civil War experience? Perhaps the minuscule percentage of individuals mentioning the Civil War reflects a modern ignorance of history rather than support for reincarnation.

Wambach's first book, *Reliving Past Lives* (1978), sold well enough to warrant the publication of her second, *Life before Life* (1979). Both books are fascinating reading for the already converted, but for someone on the fence it may seem that Wambach ends up proving only what she initially presupposes. How, after all, would a hypnotist regress a subject back before birth without first suggesting that he lived before birth? "I want you to go now to the time just before you were born into your current lifetime," Wambach instructed her subjects. "Are you choosing to be born?" Since only living beings are capable of choice, any response (whether "yes" or "no") pre-decides the issue in a manner favorable to reincarnation. Also, many of the questions Wambach asked her subjects have no way of being verified. "Did you choose your sex?" An interesting query perhaps, but can the responses given be checked against data from other, more reliable sources? Even Wambach admitted that she was operating in a scientific vacuum: "There was no way I could find any proof or verification for the answers reported by my subjects. I was running a kind of Gallup Poll of hypnotized subjects."[21]

Not surprisingly, Wambach's failure to tie her research to established scientific moorings allowed her free passage into New Age thinking. Asserting that some of her subjects were actually being projected into the future rather than the past, she and her colleague Chet Snow developed the technique of future life progression. They hypnotized hundreds of subjects and sent them forward into future incarnations. The study may be interesting but it cannot be considered scientific, because it is completely self-contained: there is nothing external to check it against. This is not to say that reincarnation is not true, just that as things stand, it cannot be made to fall under the analytic eye of science.

THE NEW PHYSICS

Of the momentous intellectual developments of the twentieth century, none is more provocative than the near-simultaneous elaboration of relativity theory and quantum physics. These two theories constitute modern physics—the "new physics"—and together challenge many longstanding assumptions about nature and our relationship to it. As throughout this book we have tried to discuss the occult while casting an eye toward modern science, it is time to drive home the point that science, like the occult, is neither static nor monolithic. It changes over time, and some thinkers now argue that science (or at least physics) is outgrowing its old materialism that was the bane of occult thinking. Consider the complex of interlocking attitudes that conditioned mainstream scientific thought during the eighteenth and nineteenth centuries:

1. Cartesian dualism. Mind and matter are separate and dissimilar entities. Mind is active, knowing, immaterial, and dimensionless; matter is passive, lifeless, material, and spatially extended. Despite their utter dissimilarity, somehow the two make contact so that understanding occurs.
2. Objectivity. Humans are distinct from nature and can thereby view it objectively; that is, dispassionately, neutrally, "as it really is." The reasoning mind interacts with nature (matter) without affecting or participating in it.
3. The clockwork universe or mechanical philosophy. Because material bodies are passive and lifeless, their motions are mere mechanical responses to outside forces. Thus, the material world is a vast mechanism, and while it may be complex, it is in principle fully knowable through the exercise of reason. Machines, after all, are

magical or miraculous only to the uninitiated. The technician feels no awe in their presence.

4. Reductionism. Like a child who takes a toy apart to understand its inner operation, we can grasp the mechanism of nature by working upward from its smallest parts through increasingly comprehensive levels of explanation. Ultimately, the complete toy—the universe— is understood in all its manifold aspects.

5. Locality. Every part in the system of nature has a specific location in space and time and therefore cannot affect other parts except through direct mechanical contact. Even when the moon tugs on the earth gravitationally, that action is mechanically propagated through an intervening substance (ether) or "field" so that there is no such thing as non-contact action at a distance. All impact is local impact.

None of these attitudes or assumptions escaped unscathed from the development of the new physics. It is now clear that scientists do affect the phenomena they observe, at least to a small degree that cannot be ignored when trying to reduce nature to its smallest parts. What's more, the unintended effect cannot be fully predicted or calculated; it is an uncontrollable disturbance that the researcher creates but cannot completely catch up with. So the hope of producing a comprehensive theory of the universe founders on the realization that we inevitably participate in nature: nature is a game that allows no spectators. We cannot sit in the audience and blithely take in the play; we are on the stage, deeply involved and unpredictably ratcheting up the world's complexity while attempting to understand it.

Moreover, our impact on the world may exceed the local limitations imposed by classical (nineteenth century) science and common sense. This is the most astonishing aspect of the new physics—the concept of non-locality or non-separability. Experiments indicate that two particles originating from a common subatomic event but flying off in opposite directions remain instantaneously connected or mutually involved regardless of the distance that separates them.[22] Thus, it would appear that the smallest parts of nature are capable of timelessly registering faraway changes. Space and time, the great separating modalities of classical science, no longer seem so absolute.

This loss of absoluteness also has invaded other scientific concepts that were once thought impregnable. What could be more foundational than atoms, or the subatomic particles that constitute atoms? In the latter half of the nineteenth century, Sir Lyon Playfair asserted that "[a]n established truth in science is like the constitution of an atom in matter—something so fixed in the order of things that it has become independent of further dangers in the struggle for existence."[23] But today subatomic particles are sometimes described as momentary events rather than distinct, unalterable bodies forever flying through space. A noted physicist comes close to describing them as verbs rather than nouns: "[T]he world is not made up of stuff, but of processes by which things happen. Elementary particles are not static objects just sitting there, but processes carrying little bits of information to new processes. They are much more like the elementary operations in a computer than the traditional picture of an eternal atom."[24] With the once-bedrock constituents of the world re-conceptualized as processes, the idea of "an established truth in science" begins to look like a relic from an earlier worldview.

Stated more broadly, the conceptually tidy, sharply detailed, every-part-in-its-place world picture of classical science no longer seems fully persuasive. Among other things, the mind-matter dichotomy, while yet deeply ingrained in Western thought, emerges as a gravely flawed assumption. At the atomic level, it is not clear where mind leaves off and matter begins, and if these two entities or "parts" cannot be clearly demarcated, then perhaps physicists should not be surprised when other parts—even those widely separated by space and time—also begin to blur together.

We hasten to add that these issues, albeit originating in the early decades of the twentieth century, are still hotly debated by physicists and philosophers of science, and no consensus universally prevails as to their interpretation. Nevertheless, the foregoing account faithfully rehearses the general themes and perplexities, the whole of which has inspired some people to declare that science is coming around to ideas that have long been current in religious and occult thought. As early as 1930, the astronomer James Jeans wrote that, because of recent startling advances in physics, the universe appears less like a "wholly mechanical world . . . [into which] life had stumbled by accident" and "more like a great thought" that governs "the realm of matter."[25] Since then, others have moved from a thought to a thinker, often by asserting that the new physics affirms the Eastern belief in a sentient, holistic universe.[26]

Once the cosmos is reinvested with intelligence or even life, then possibilities long precluded by materialistic science open up. Conceivably, the universe could be moving toward a goal of transcendent significance, or perhaps it connotes a mind-like design. It also may be inhabited by other beings normally hidden up in higher-dimensional realities. These possibilities follow from the rule of life that Jeans re-introduces, which gives us a universe in which life is the default state, in which (to modify slightly Arthur Schopenhauer's phrase) we could no more fall out of life than we could fall out of existence.[27]

Steadfastly resisting this view are those who foresee harmful consequences should science give itself over to a living, caring cosmos, or even a non-random "great thought" cosmos. Here is the response of the geneticist Richard Lewon-

NDEs, NEW AGE, AND NEW PHYSICS

tin, who frankly concedes the technical and conceptual shortfalls of materialistic science:

> We take the side of science *in spite* of the patent absurdity of some of its constructs, *in spite* of its failure to fulfill many of its extravagant promises of health and life, *in spite* of the tolerance of the scientific community for unsubstantiated just-so stories, because we have a prior commitment, a commitment to materialism. It is not that the methods and institutions of science somehow compel us to accept a material explanation of the phenomenal world, but, on the contrary, that we are forced by our *a priori* adherence to material causes to create an apparatus of investigation and a set of concepts that produce material explanations, no matter how counterintuitive, no matter how mystifying to the uninitiated. Moreover, that materialism is absolute, for we cannot allow a Divine Foot in the door.[28]

Lewontin realizes that leaps of faith and imagination play into the construction of all systems of thought. In the public arena, therefore, questions of ultimate import are decided on the basis of emotion-inflated "facts," and for the past three hundred years the austere materialistic thesis of an uncaring, accidental cosmos has been part of the success story of science. Lewontin obviously would like to keep it that way but, with the new physics challenging old assumptions, one wonders if his *a priori* commitment to materialism verges on a kind of blind faith or pre-meditated blindness. If, however, we single him out as a negative example, we do him a profound injustice: here is a first-rate scientist who clearly sees that, even in science, issues boil down to choices that cannot be fully rationalized. To characterize the occult (or religion, or the arts, etc.) as the sole preserve of human subjectivity is, then, grossly unfair. If that were the case, the world would be less fascinating and ambiguous than it invariably shapes up to be. The occult is one response to the world's phoenix-like capacity to rise from the ashes of explanation and refresh itself in mystery.

MAGIC, MYSTERY, AND SCIENCE

NOTES

INTRODUCTION

1. Jan Hilgevoord, ed., *Physics and Our View of the World* (Cambridge: Cambridge University Press, 1994), p. 13.

2. H. G. Wells, "The Rediscovery of the Unique," *The Fortnightly Review,* July 1891, p. 111.

3. Johann Wolfgang von Goethe, *Faust,* trans. George Madison Priest (Chicago: William Benton, 1952), Part 1, line 439 [p. 13].

4. John F. A. Taylor, quoted in Frank Webb, *Webb on Water Color* (Cincinnati, Ohio: North Light Books, 1990), p. 7.

5. Quoted in Laura Dassow Walls, *Seeing New Worlds: Henry David Thoreau and Nineteenth-Century Natural Science* (Madison: University of Wisconsin Press, 1995), p. 157.

6. Henry D. Thoreau, *Walden,* ed. J. Lyndon Shanley (Princeton, N.J.: Princeton University Press, 1971), p. 287.

7. Roelof van den Broek and Wouter J. Hanegraaff, eds., *Gnosis and Hermeticism: From Antiquity to Modern Times* (Albany: SUNY Press, 1998), pp. vii–x.

8. Bertrand Russell, "A Free Man's Worship," in *Mysticism and Logic* (Garden City, N.Y.: Doubleday & Co., 1918), p. 45.

9. Plato, "The Dialogues of Plato," [*The Republic*] in *Great Books of the Western World,* vol. 7, ed. Mortimer J. Adler (Chicago: Encyclopedia Britannica, 1952), p. 396.

10. Giorgio de Santillana and Hertha von Dechend, *Hamlet's Mill: An Essay on Myth and the Frame of Time* (Boston, Mass.: David R. Godine, 1977), p. 49.

1. EGYPTIANS AND THE OCCULT

1. George Berkeley, "Siris: A Chain of Philosophical Reflexions and Inquiries," in *The Works of George Berkeley, Bishop of Cloyne,* vol. 5 (London: Thomas Nelson and Sons, 1953), p. 139.

2. Loren Eiseley, *Darwin and the Mysterious Mr. X* (New York: E. P. Hutton, 1979), p. 2.

3. Otto Neugebauer states that the "heliacal rising [of Sirius] ideally begins the year." The implicit hedge refers to the fact that the flooding of the Nile and the heliacal return of Sirius slowly lost synchrony. For the Egyptians, this was one of several interrelated calendrical difficulties. *The Exact Sciences in Antiquity,* 2nd ed. (New York: Dover Publications, 1969), p. 87.

4. Steven Weinberg, *Dreams of a Final Theory* (New York: Vintage Books, 1992), p. 255.

5. Mircea Eliade, *The Sacred and the Profane: The Nature of Religion,* trans. Willard R. Trask (San Diego: Harcourt Brace & Co., 1959), p. 165.

6. Thomas Huxley, *Evolution and Ethics and Other Essays* (London: Macmillan, 1893–1894), p. 83.

7. Eliade, *The Sacred and the Profane,* p. 45.

8. H. Frankfort, H. A. Frankfort, John A. Wilson, Thorkild Jacobsen, and William A. Irwin, *The Intellectual Adventure of Ancient Man: An Essay on Speculative Thought in the Ancient Near East* (Chicago: University of Chicago Press, 1977), p. 24.

9. H. Frankfort, *Ancient Egyptian Religion: An Interpretation* (New York: Harper Torchbooks, 1948), p. 50.

10. Eliade, *The Sacred and the Profane,* p. 64.

11. Berkeley, "Siris," p. 138.

12. H. Frankfort writes that in the Egyptian mind "the survival of the dead belonged to the data of actual experience." *Ancient Egyptian Religion,* p. 89.

13. Shirley Case Jackson, *The Origins of Christian Supernaturalism* (Chicago: University of Chicago Press, 1946), p. 1.

14. Shirley Case Jackson, *Origins.*

15. Quoted by Arthur Zajonc, *Catching the Light: The Entwined History of Light and Mind* (New York: Oxford University Press, 1993), p. 206.

16. I. E. S. Edwards, *The Pyramids of Egypt* (Harmondsworth, U.K.: Penguin Books, 1952), pp. 27–28.

17. See Martin Buber, *I and Thou,* trans. Walter Kaufmann (New York: Charles Scribner's Sons, 1970).

18. Frankfort et al., *Intellectual Adventure of Ancient Man,* pp. 4–8.

19. Quoted in Zajonc, *Catching the Light,* p. 39.

20. Zajonc, *Catching the Light.*

21. John Wilson in Frankfort et al., *The Intellectual Adventure of Ancient Man,* p. 66.

22. For the mythic or revelatory reception of the cosmos, see Frankfort et al., *The Intellectual Adventure of Ancient Man,* pp. 8–9, and Eliade, *The Sacred and the Profane,* pp. 62–65.

23. Frankfort, *Egyptian Religion,* p. 96.

24. Frankfort, *Egyptian Religion,* p. 107.

25. Frankfort, *Egyptian Religion,* p. 93.

26. In discussing the Edwin Smith Surgical Papyrus, Marshall Clagett states that it

"says something of the brain as a control center for the nervous system." Clagett, *Greek Science in Antiquity* (New York: Collier Books, 1955), p. 19.

27. John 14:27.

28. Blaise Pascal, *The Thoughts of Blaise Pascal* (Garden City, N.Y.: Dolphin Books, 1960), p. 98.

29. R. T. Rundle Clark, *Myth and Symbol in Ancient Egypt* (London: Thames and Hudson, 1959), p. 122.

30. Quoted in James Hamilton-Paterson and Carol Andrews, *Mummies: Death and Life in Ancient Egypt* (New York: Viking Press, 1979), pp. 195–196. This is an excellent source of information for the "curse," and much of the discussion borrows from it.

31. Clark, *Myth and Symbol in Ancient Egypt*, p. 263.

2. MAGIC AND MIRACLES

1. Franz Hartmann, *The Life and the Doctrines of Paracelsus*, 4th ed. (New York: Macoy Publishing and Masonic Supply Co., 1932), p. xi.

2. Erwin Schrödinger, *What Is Life? The Physical Aspect of the Living Cell* (Cambridge: Cambridge University Press; New York: Macmillan, 1945), p. 88.

3. William Shakespeare, *Hamlet*, Act I, Scene V, lines 166–167.

4. Quoted in Hartmann, *The Life and the Doctrines of Paracelsus*, p. 199.

5. Hartmann, *The Life and the Doctrines of Paracelsus*.

6. Arthur C. Clarke, *Report on Planet Three and Other Speculations* (New York: Harper & Row, 1972), p. 139.

7. Bert Hansen, "The Complementarity of Science and Magic before the Scientific Revolution," *American Scientist* 74 (Mar.–Apr. 1986), p. 128.

8. Arthur E. Imhof, *Lost Worlds: How Our European Ancestors Coped with Everyday Life and Why Life Is so Hard Today*, trans. Thomas Robisheaux (Charlottesville: University Press of Virginia, 1996).

9. A. N. Whitehead, *Science and the Modern World: Lowell Lectures, 1925* (New York: New American Library of World Literature, 1964), p. 91.

10. J. T. Fraser, *Of Time, Passion, and Knowledge* (New York: George Braziller, 1975), p. 377.

11. Derek J. de Solla Price, "Clockwork before the Clock and Timekeepers before Timekeeping," in *The Study of Time*, vol. 2, ed. J. T. Fraser and N. Lawrence (New York: Springer-Verlag, 1975), p. 369.

12. See Lorraine Daston and Katherine Park, *Wonders and the Order of Nature, 1150–1750* (New York: Zone Books, 1998), particularly chap. 5, "Monsters: A Case Study," pp. 173–214.

13. Francesco Maria Guazzo, *Compendium Maleficarum* (New York: Dover, 1988), Book I, chap. 2, p. 5.

14. Richard Kieckhefer, *Magic in the Middle Ages* (Cambridge: Cambridge University Press, 1990).

15. Galileo's own theory of the tides entailed a sloshing of the oceans because of the double motion (rotational and orbital) of the earth. See Jerome J. Langford, *Science, Galileo, and the Church*, 3rd ed. (Ann Arbor: University of Michigan Press, 1992), pp. 125–126.

16. Newton to Richard Bentley, Feb. 25, 1693; *Corres 3*, 253–254. Quoted in

Richard S. Westfall, *Never at Rest: A Biography of Isaac Newton* (Cambridge: Cambridge University Press, 1980), p. 505. Spelling and punctuation modernized.

17. Quoted by Richard S. Westfall, *The Construction of Modern Science: Mechanisms and Mechanics* (New York: John Wiley & Sons, 1971), p. 158. Spelling modernized.

18. Valerie I. J. Flint, *The Rise of Magic in Early Medieval Europe* (Princeton, N.J.: Princeton University Press, 1991), p. 7.

19. Flint, *Rise of Magic,* p. 4.

20. William Shakespeare, *Macbeth,* Act II, Scene IV, lines 11–15.

21. Einhard, *Life of Charles the Great,* selected excerpts in Patrick J. Geary, ed., *Readings in Medieval History* (Peterborough, Ont.: Broadview Press, 1989), p. 310.

22. Quoted in Alfred W. Crosby, *The Measure of Reality: Quantification and Western Society, 1250–1600* (Cambridge: Cambridge University Press, 1997), p. 24.

23. Manilius, *Astronomica,* trans. G. P. Goold (Cambridge, Mass.: Harvard University Press, 1977), Book IV, pp. 293–295.

24. Walt Whitman, "Song of Myself," *The Complete Poetry and Prose of Walt Whitman* (Garden City, N.Y.: Garden City Books, 1948), pp. 113, 84.

25. Hartmann, *The Life and Doctrines of Paracelsus,* pp. 70–74.

26. Alexander Pope, *An Essay on Man,* ed. Frank Brady (Indianapolis: Bobbs-Merrill, 1965), Epistle 1, lines 237–241.

27. Francis Thompson, "Mistress of Vision" (1897), stanza 22, in D. H. S. Nicholson and A. H. E. Lee, eds., *The Oxford Book of English Mystical Verse* (Oxford: Clarendon Press, 1953), p. 416.

28. For an excellent treatment of magic, see Richard Cavendish's *The Black Arts* (New York: Putnam, 1983).

29. Cavendish, *The Black Arts,* pp. 231–246.

30. Cavendish, *The Black Arts,* p. 236.

31. Georg Luck, *Arcana Mundi: Magic and the Occult in the Greek and Roman Worlds* (Baltimore, Md.: Johns Hopkins University Press, 1985), p. 91.

32. Luck, *Arcana Mundi,* p. 98.

33. Albertus Magnus, *Egyptian Secrets; or, White and Black Art for Man and Beast* (Chicago: De Laurence, Scott & Co., 1910), pp. 75, 117.

34. The dream is described in Arthur Zajonc, *Catching the Light: The Entwined History of Light and Mind* (New York: Oxford University Press, 1993), pp. 88–91.

35. Odell Shepard, ed., *The Heart of Thoreau's Journals* (New York: Dover, 1961), p. 94.

36. Henry D. Thoreau, *Walden,* ed. J. Lyndon Shanley (Princeton, N.J.: Princeton University Press, 1971), p. 8.

37. See Fetscher's postscript in Hans Christoph Binswanger, *Money and Magic: A Critique of the Modern Economy in the Light of Goethe's Faust,* trans. J. E. Harrison (Chicago: University of Chicago Press, 1994), p. 119.

3. NUMEROLOGY, THE CABALA, AND ALCHEMY

1. Lynn Thorndike, *A History of Magic and Experimental Science,* vol. 1 (New York: Columbia University Press, 1923), p. 2.

2. Herbert Butterfield, *The Origins of Modern Science, 1300–1800* (London: G. Bell and Sons, 1949), p. 115.

3. George Steiner, *Real Presences* (Chicago: University of Chicago Press, 1989), pp. 93–94, 105.

4. Alfred W. Crosby, *The Measure of Reality: Quantification and Western Society, 1250–1600* (Cambridge: Cambridge University Press, 1997), p. 46.

5. Richard Cavendish, *The Black Arts* (New York: G. P. Putnam's Sons, 1967), p. 61.

6. Bertrand Russell, *A History of Western Philosophy: And Its Connection with Political and Social Circumstances from the Earliest Times to the Present Day* (New York: Simon & Schuster, 1964), p. 37.

7. See Eugene Wigner, "The Unreasonable Effectiveness of Mathematics in the Natural Sciences," in *Symmetries and Reflections: Scientific Essays of Eugene P. Wigner,* ed. Walter J. Moore and Michael Scriven (Bloomington: Indiana University Press, 1967), pp. 222–237.

8. Quoted in E. A. Burtt, *The Metaphysical Foundations of Modern Physical Science,* rev. ed. (Amherst, N.Y.: Humanity Books, 1999), p. 75.

9. Werner Heisenberg, *Physics and Philosophy: The Revolution in Modern Science* (Amherst, N.Y.: Prometheus Books, 1999), pp. 71–72.

10. See Banesh Hoffmann, *Albert Einstein: Creator and Rebel* (New York: Plume, 1972), pp. 122–124; see also Steven Weinberg, *Dreams of a Final Theory* (New York: Pantheon Books, 1992), pp. 132–165.

11. Exodus 3:13–14.

12. Cavendish, *Black Arts,* p. 118.

13. G. S. Kirk, J. E. Raven, and M. Schofield, *The Presocratic Philosophers: A Critical History with a Selection of Texts,* 2nd ed. (Cambridge: Cambridge University Press, 1983), pp. 286–294.

14. E. J. Holmyard, *Alchemy* (Harmondsworth, U.K.: Penguin Books, 1957), p. 170.

15. Sappho, *Sappho of Lesbos: Her Works Restored,* trans. Beram Saklatvala (London: Charles Skilton, 1968), p. 140.

16. Henry D. Thoreau, *Walden,* ed. J. Lyndon Shanley (Princeton, N.J.: Princeton University Press, 1971), pp. 254–255.

17. Mircea Eliade, *The Forge and the Crucible,* 2nd ed., trans. Stephen Corrin (Chicago: University of Chicago Press, 1978), p. 47.

18. Eliade, *The Forge and the Crucible,* p. 56.

19. Edward F. Edinger, *The Mystery of the Coniunctio: Alchemical Image of Individuation,* ed. Joan Dexter Blackmer (Toronto: Inner City Books, 1994), p. 18.

20. Quoted in Eliade, *The Forge and the Crucible,* pp. 163–164.

21. T. S. Eliot, "The Dry Salvages," *The Complete Poems and Plays: 1909–1950* (New York: Harcourt Brace, Jovanovich, 1952), p. 136.

22. Geoffrey Chaucer, "The Canon's Yeoman's Tale," in *The Canterbury Tales,* trans. into modern English by Nevill Coghill (Baltimore, Md.: Penguin Books, 1952), p. 496. The original lines read: "Philosophres speken so mistily / In this craft, that men can nat come therby," lines 1394–1395.

23. Quoted in Eliade, *The Forge and the Crucible,* p. 123.

24. J. B. Craven, *Count Michael Maier: Life and Writings* (Kirkwall: William Peace & Son, 1910), p. 19.

25. Chaucer, "The Canon Yeoman's Tale," p. 487.

26. Richard S. Westfall, "The Influence of Alchemy on Newton," in *Mapping the*

Cosmos, ed. Jane Chance and R. O. Wells (Houston: Rice University Press, 1985), pp. 98–117.

27. Chaucer, "The Canon Yeoman's Tale," p. 481.

28. When discovered near the beginning of the twentieth century, nuclear energy (here inclusive of radioactive energy) suggested to many the unlimited possibility traditionally associated with the Philosopher's Stone. Indeed, some felt that the age-old promise of the Stone was about to be realized through energy. After describing the Stone as one of humankind's "oldest and most universal beliefs," the chemist Frederick Soddy wrote: "If we can judge from what our engineers accomplish with their comparatively restricted supplies of energy, such a race could transform a desert continent, thaw the frozen poles, and make the whole world one smiling Garden of Eden." *The Interpretation of Radium: And the Structure of the Atom* (New York: G. P. Putnam's Sons, 1920), pp. 182–183. Ernest Rutherford's Nobel Prize citation read in part: "Rutherford's discoveries led to the highly surprising conclusion, that a chemical element . . . is capable of being transformed into other elements, and thus in a certain way it may be said that the progress of investigation is bringing us back to the transmutation theory propounded by the alchemists of old." K. B. Hasselberg, "The Nobel Chemistry Prize," in *Les Prix Noble en 1908* (Stockholm, 1909), p. 21. Rutherford himself makes the ancient-modern connection in his *The Newer Alchemy* (Cambridge: Cambridge University Press, 1937).

29. Eliade, *The Forge and the Crucible,* p. 172.

30. Eliade, *The Forge and the Crucible,* p. 174.

4. ASTROLOGY

1. Manilius, *Astronomica,* Book II, trans. G. P. Goold (Cambridge, Mass.: Harvard University Press, 1977), p. 93.

2. Laura Ackerman Smoller, *History, Prophecy, and the Stars: The Christian Astrology of Pierre D'Ailly, 1350–1420* (Princeton, N.J.: Princeton University Press, 1994), p. 3.

3. Anthony Grafton, "Starry Messengers: Recent Work in the History of Western Astrology," *Perspectives on Science* 8, no. 1 (2000): 72.

4. Plato, *Timaeus,* 47b–c; trans. Francis M. Cornford. In *Plato's Timaeus* (Indianapolis: Liberal Arts Press, 1959), p. 45.

5. Plato, *Timaeus,* 47a–b (p. 44).

6. Plato, *Timaeus,* 37d (p. 29).

7. See Jonathan Lear, *Aristotle: The Desire to Understand* (Cambridge: Cambridge University Press, 1988), pp. 7–10.

8. Lear, *Aristotle,* p. 10.

9. Manilius, *Astronomica,* Book I (p. 45).

10. Quoted as an introductory epigram by Liba Taub, *Ptolemy's Universe: The Natural and Ethical Foundations of Ptolemy's Astronomy* (Chicago: Open Court, 1993).

11. Macrobius, *Commentary on the Dream of Scipio,* trans. William Harris Stahl (New York: Columbia University Press, 1952), p. 72.

12. Macrobius, *Commentary on the Dream of Scipio,* pp. 133–137.

13. Tamsyn Barton, *Ancient Astronomy* (London: Routledge, 1994), pp. 109–111.

14. Quoted in Barton, *Ancient Astrology,* p. 105.

15. Ptolemy, *Tetrabiblos* (Chicago: Aries Press, 1936), p. 13.

16. Ptolemy, *Tetrabiblos.*

17. Quoted in Barton, *Ancient Astrology,* p. 103.

18. Keith Hutchinson, "Why Does Plato Urge Rulers to Study Astronomy," Victorian Centre for the History and Philosophy of Science, La Trobe University, preprint 2/94, p. 10.

19. Manilius, *Astronomica,* Book I (p. 25).

20. Manilius, *Astronomica,* Book II (p. 89).

21. George Berkeley, "Siris: A Chain of Philosophical Reflexions and Inquiries," in *The Works of George Berkeley, Bishop of Cloyne,* ed. A. A. Luce and T. E. Jessop, vol. 5 (London: Thomas Nelson and Sons, 1948–1957), p. 130.

22. Dante Alighieri, *The Divine Comedy,* trans. Carlyle-Wicksteed (New York: Modern Library, 1952), p. 406.

23. Manilius, *Astronomica,* Book IV (p. 279).

24. Quoted in Franz Hartmann, *The Life and the Doctrines of Paracelsus,* 4th ed. (New York: Macoy Publishing and Masonic Supply Co., 1932), p. 259.

25. Hartmann, *The Life and the Doctrines of Paracelsus,* p. 260.

26. Hartmann, *The Life and the Doctrines of Paracelsus,* p. 261.

27. Barton, *Ancient Astrology,* p. 106.

28. Quoted in Ann Geneva, *Astrology and the Seventeenth Century Mind: William Lilly and the Language of the Stars* (Manchester: Manchester University Press, 1995), p. 264.

29. See John D. North, "Celestial Influence: The Major Premiss of Astrology," in *Stars, Mind, and Fate: Essays in Ancient and Medieval Cosmology* (London: Hambledon Press, 1989), pp. 243–298.

30. Ted Schultz, ed., *The Fringes of Reason* (New York: Harmony Books, 1989), p. 196.

31. Stephen Jay Gould, *Time's Arrow, Time's Cycle: Myth and Metaphor in the Discovery of Geological Time* (Cambridge, Mass.: Harvard University Press, 1987), p. 7.

32. See Grafton, "Starry Messengers."

33. See Manilius's Stoic plea in *Astronomica,* Book IV (pp. 223–297).

34. Manilius, *Astronomica,* Book IV (p. 245).

35. Manilius, *Astronomica,* Book IV.

36. Ptolemy, *Tetrabiblos,* pp. 5–7.

37. Manilius, *Astronomica,* Book IV (p. 253).

38. Anthony Grafton, *Cardon's Cosmos: The Worlds and Works of a Renaissance Astrologer* (Cambridge, Mass.: Harvard University Press, 1999), p. 199.

39. Grafton, *Cardon's Cosmos,* p. 202.

40. Ptolemy, *Tetrabiblos,* p. 9.

41. Michel Gauquelin, *The Scientific Basis of Astrology: Myth or Reality* (New York: Stein and Day, 1970), pp. 143–144.

42. Gauquelin, *The Scientific Basis of Astrology,* p. 145.

43. Andrew Pickering, *Constructing Quarks: A Sociological History of Particle Physics* (Edinburgh: Edinburgh University Press, 1984), p. 413.

44. Geneva, *Astrology and the Seventeenth Century Mind,* p. 163. See also Ptolemy, *Tetrabiblos,* pp. 72–73.

45. Quoted in Arthur Koestler, *The Act of Creation* (New York: Macmillan, 1964), pp. 375–376.

5. ANCIENT EVIL

1. From Henry E. Sigerist, *A History of Medicine*, vol. 1: *Primitive and Archaic Medicine* (New York: Oxford University Press, 1951), pp. 449–450.

2. Sophocles, Fragment 946, in Hugh Lloyd-Jones, ed. and trans, *Sophocles: Fragments*, vol. 3 of The Loeb Classical Library (Cambridge, Mass.: Harvard University Press, 1996), p. 407. Listed as Fragment 843 in earlier works.

3. Ruma Bose, "Psychiatry and the Popular Conception of Possession among the Bangladeshis in London," *International Journal of Social Psychiatry* 43, no. 1 (Spring 1997): 1–15.

4. What are popularly called "genies" in English.

5. Bose, "Psychiatry and the Popular Conception of Possession," pp. 4–6. For an orthodox Muslim girl, putting on lipstick could certainly be seen as anti-religious.

6. For this view of the Egyptian gods, see Erik Hornung's *Conceptions of God in Ancient Egypt: The One and the Many*, trans. John Baines (Ithaca, N.Y.: Cornell University Press, 1982), p. 213.

7. J. Worth Estes, *The Medical Skills of Ancient Egypt* (Canton, Mass.: Science History Publications/USA, 1989), p. 14. Estes notes these headache remedies are to be found in the Chester Beatty V Papyrus (written in the thirteenth century B.C.), and cites Alan H. Gardiner, ed., *Hieratic Papyri in the British Museum, Ser. 3, Chester Beatty Gift*, vol. 1, *Text* (London, 1935), pp. 50–51.

8. Will Durant and Ariel Durant, *The Story of Civilization*, vol. 1: *Our Oriental Heritage* (New York: Simon and Schuster, 1954), p. 204.

9. See James B. Pritchard, ed., *Ancient Near Eastern Texts: Relating to the Old Testament*, 3rd ed. with suppl. (Princeton, N.J.: Princeton University Press, 1969), p. 328.

10. Pritchard, *Ancient Near Eastern Texts*, p. 328. This incantation is also found in Sigerist, *A History of Medicine*, vol. 1, p. 275.

11. Sigerist, *A History of Medicine*, vol. 1, pp. 272–274.

12. Estes gives an excellent introduction to their activities in his *Medical Skills of Ancient Egypt*, pp. 13–26.

13. This worldview was shared by nearly all ancient, medieval, and early-modern cultures, and back-reading Elmer Gantry–like motives to these priests, physicians, and exorcists would be both counter-productive and incorrect.

14. Roy Porter, *The Greatest Benefit to Mankind: A Medical History of Humanity* (New York: W.W. Norton, 1997), p. 49.

15. Estes, *The Medical Skills of Ancient Egypt*, p. 16. This same technique of literally drinking magic words was used as recently as 1860 in Egypt, according to Lane, and is used by a modern healer in Sudan, except in both cases the text contains quotes from the Qurʾan, invokes the names of angels, and helps control jinn (who may be the cause of illness or may help in healing), cf. Estes, pp. 115–116. Edward William Lane, *Manners and Customs of the Modern Egyptians* (New York: E. P. Dutton, 1954, reprint of the 1908 edition), p. 260.

16. Pritchard, *Ancient Near Eastern Texts*, p. 328.

17. Sigerist, *A History of Medicine*, vol. 1, pp. 282–283.

18. Sigerist, *A History of Medicine*, vol. 1, p. 275. From the *Hearst Medical Papyrus* now housed at the University of California, Berkeley.

19. Roy Porter, *The Greatest Benefit to Mankind*, p. 46.

20. Sigerist, *A History of Medicine*, vol. 1, p. 283; cf. Pritchard, *Ancient Near Eastern Texts*, p. 328, and n. 5, where this is translated: "sweet for men, (but) bitter for those who are yonder [i.e., the dead]."

21. Estes has an excellent study of honey as an antibiotic in his *Medical Skills of Ancient Egypt*, pp. 68–71. He states that "honey inhibits bacterial growth chiefly because it is hypertonic and, therefore, kills micro-organisms by drawing water out of them along an osmotic gradient" (p. 69).

22. Estes, *The Medical Skills of Ancient Egypt*, p. 147.

23. Pritchard, *Ancient Near Eastern Texts*, pp. 328–329.

24. The dating of the story and its status as a pious forgery, along with a translation, are from Pritchard, *Ancient Near Eastern Texts*, pp. 29–31. The story is also recounted in Estes, *The Medical Skills of Ancient Egypt*, p. 15, but he describes the princess as a Hittite.

25. Georges Roux, *Ancient Iraq*, 2nd ed. (New York: Penguin Books, 1980), p. 100.

26. For one of the earliest accounts of this depressing after-life, see *The Epic of Gilgamesh*, trans. N. K. Sandars, rev. ed. (New York: Penguin Books, 1972), pp. 26–30, 92–93.

27. See Sabatino Moscati, *Ancient Semitic Civilizations* (New York: Capricorn Books, 1957), pp. 60–61. For the connection of sin and sickness, see Sigerist, *A History of Medicine*, vol. 1, p. 283.

28. D. J. Wiseman, *Nebuchadrezzar and Babylon* (Oxford and New York: Published for the British Academy by Oxford University Press, 1985), p. 99.

29. For Nebuchadnezzar's massive building programs, see Wiseman, *Nebuchadrezzar and Babylon*, pp. 64–80.

30. For depictions of Ashurbanipal, see Megan Cifarelli's "Gesture and Alterity in the Art of Ashurnasirpal II of Assyria," *Art Bulletin* 80 (June 1998): 210–239. For his ornamented garden, see "Garden of Evil," *Civilization* 4, no. 2 (Apr./May 1997): 37, and Jack Finegan's *Light from the Ancient Past: The Archeological Background of the Hebrew-Christian Religion* (Princeton, N.J.: Princeton University Press; Oxford: Oxford University Press, 1959, rpt. 1969), vol. 1, p. 216 and fig. 81.

31. H. W. F. Saggs, *Everyday Life in Babylonia and Assyria* (New York: Dorset Press, 1965, rpt. 1987), p. 185.

32. Moscati, *Ancient Semitic Civilizations*, p. 60; Saggs, *Everyday Life*, pp. 182–183.

33. Sigerist, *A History of Medicine*, vol. 1, pp. 442–446. The evil eye is one of the most ancient and persistent of human beliefs. For a five-thousand-year-old Sumerian incantation against the evil eye, see Stephen Langdon's translation of "An Incantation in the 'House of Light' against the Evil Eye," in Alan Dundes, *The Evil Eye: A Folklore Casebook* (New York: Garland Press, 1981), pp. 39–40, reprinted from Stephen Langdon, *Babylonian Liturgies* (Paris: Librarie Paul Geuthner, 1913), pp. 11–12.

34. Thorkild Jacobsen, *The Treasures of Darkness: A History of Mesopotamian Religion* (New Haven, Conn.: Yale University Press, 1976), pp. 12–13.

35. Jacobsen, *The Treasures of Darkness*, p. 12.

36. Sigerist, *A History of Medicine*, vol. 1, pp. 442–443; Moscati, *Ancient Semitic Civilizations*, p. 60.

37. On epilepsy, see Porter, *The Greatest Benefit to Mankind*, p. 46, and Georges Roux, *Ancient Iraq*, 2nd ed. (New York: Penguin Books, 1980), p. 340; concerning pregnancy, see Saggs, *Everyday Life*, p. 182.

38. Durant, *Our Oriental Heritage*, p. 243.

39. See A. Leo Oppenheim's *Ancient Mesopotamia: Portrait of a Dead Civilization* (Chicago: University of Chicago Press, 1977), pp. 199–200; for more on "luck," cf. Jacobsen, *The Treasures of Darkness*, p. 12.

40. See Oppenheim, *Ancient Mesopotamia*, pp. 223–224, 272; Sigerist, *A History of Medicine*, vol. 1, pp. 419–420, 483–484; Roux, *Ancient Iraq*, pp. 339–340; Georges Contenau, *Everyday Life in Babylon and Assyria* (London: Edward Arnold, 1954), pp. 282–283.

41. Saggs, *Everyday Life*, pp. 185–187.

42. *Vendidad*, chap. 22.

43. This, at least, is the late Zoroastrian view.

44. The term *devas* refers to good deities in polytheistic Hinduism (from the Sanskrit *deva* for god), but in anti-polytheistic Zoroastrianism the same designation *daevas* comes to mean exactly the opposite: demons. From the Sanskrit *deva* comes the Greek *theos*, the Latin *deus*, the French *Dieu*, and the English "divine."

45. See the introduction of *Textual Sources for the Study of Zoroastrianism*, ed. and trans. Mary Boyce (Totowa, N.J.: Barnes & Noble Books, 1984), pp. 20–21.

46. See the *Greater Bundahishn*, chap. 4, verses 1–11, and chap. 5, verses 1–2, in Boyce, *Textual Sources for the Study of Zoroastrianism*, pp. 50–51, and in R. C. Zaehner, *The Teachings of the Magi: A Compendium of Zoroastrian Beliefs* (London: Allen & Unwin; New York: Macmillan, 1956), pp. 45–48.

47. See the *Greater Bundahishn*, chap. 4, verse 1, in Zaehner, *The Teachings of the Magi*, pp. 43–46.

48. See the *Greater Bundahishn*, chap. 4, verse 11, in Zaehner, *The Teachings of the Magi*, p. 48. For the millions, see Durant, *Our Oriental Heritage*, p. 368.

49. In S. Shaked, "The Notions of *menog* and *getig* in the Pahlavi Texts and Their Relation to Eschatology," *Acta Orientalia* 33 (1971): 83, as cited in M. Yamauchi, *Persia and the Bible* (Grand Rapids, Mich.: Baker Books, 1996), p. 443.

50. Yamauchi, *Persia and the Bible*, p. 408.

51. Job 1:6–12; 2:1–6.

52. 1 Chronicles 21:1.

53. Zechariah 3:1–2.

54. Genesis 3:1.

55. Deuteronomy 32:17; "They sacrificed their sons and their daughters to demons." Psalms 106:37 (New International Version [hereafter NIV]).

56. See Francis Brown's *The New Brown-Driver-Briggs-Gesenius Hebrew and English Lexicon, with an Appendix Containing the Biblical Aramaic* (Lafayette, Ind.: Associated Publishers and Authors, 1978), p. 993.

57. It is uncertain whether the children, ranging from premature infants to ages three or four, were killed before being burned or by being burned. "Baal," which means "lord" or "master," was more a title of a god than a specific name, hence Baal Melqart of the Tyrians and Baal Hammon of the Carthaginians. Serge Lancel, *Carthage: A History*, trans. Antonia Nevill (Oxford: Blackwell, 1995), pp. 193–194; Michael Brett, "Carthage: The God in the Stone," *History Today* 47, no. 2 (Feb. 1997): 44–51.

58. 2 Kings 16:3; the parallel passage, 2 Chronicles 28:3, says they sacrificed several sons.

59. 1 Kings 11:1–11.

60. See Jeremiah 7:31–32, cf. also 2 Kings 23:10. The valley later came to be used as a trash dump for the city, a place "for burning corpses of criminals and animals. . . .

Hence the name came to be used as a synonym for hell, the Hebrew phrase *gê* ('valley of') *hinnōm* becoming *geena* in Greek, whence *Gehenna* in Latin and English. Jewish tradition at one time held that the mouth of hell was in the valley." D. F. Payne, "Hinnom, Valley of," in J. D. Douglas et al., *New Bible Dictionary*, 2nd ed. (Leicester, U.K.: Intervarsity-Press; Wheaton, Ill.: Tyndale House, 1982), p. 484.

61. 1 Samuel 16:14–23. The first-century historian Josephus adds that, "as for Saul, some strange and demoniacal disorders came upon him, and brought upon him such suffocations as were ready to choke him." Josephus, *The Antiquities of the Jews*, 6.8.2, in *The Works of Flavius Josephus*, trans. William Whiston (Grand Rapids, Mich.: Baker Book House, 1974), vol. 2, p. 375.

62. In early usage, the Hebrew word for "prophesying" could mean one went into a religious ecstasy—exactly the form seen elsewhere in the ancient world, for example, at the Delphic Oracle. Of course in Saul's case, the religious delirium must have been brought on by evil, not good. For the Hebrew definition of "prophesying," see Brown's *The New Brown-Driver-Briggs-Gesenius Hebrew and English Lexicon*, p. 612.

63. 1 Samuel 18:6–13.

64. See Michael Wise et al., *The Dead Sea Scrolls: A New Translation* (San Francisco: HarperSanFrancisco, 1996), 4Q510–4Q511, pp. 414–417, and 11Q11, pp. 453–454.

65. Pseudo-Philo, *Biblical Antiquities*, 60:1–3, in James H. Charlesworth, ed., *The Old Testament Pseudepigrapha* (Garden City, N.Y.: Doubleday, 1985), vol. 2, p. 373 [hereafter *Pseudepigrapha*].

66. The books of the *Pseudepigrapha* date anywhere from the third century B.C. to the third century A.D. and beyond, so some were influenced by Christian writers and vice versa. According to Samuel Sandmel, relatively little of the Pseudepigrapha was transmitted directly into rabbinic traditions. Cf. Sandmel's "Foreword for Jews," in *Pseudepigrapha*, vol. 1, pp. xi–xiii. However, it comes as no surprise that there are many parallels between them, as these variant works were part of the formative milieu. Also, given such a widely varying array of material (from strict monotheistic to proto-gnostic and dualist literature), the *Pseudepigrapha* display a cornucopia of demonological perspectives.

67. An abbreviated version of Proverbs 16:18: "Pride goeth before destruction, and an haughty spirit before a fall" (King James Version [hereafter KJV]).

68. These are the angels (described in the Hebrew book of Ezekiel, chap. 1) who each have six wings and four faces, the face of a man, a lion, an ox, and an eagle.

69. *Apocalypse of Abraham*, 18:8–12, in *Pseudepigrapha*, vol. 1, p. 698.

70. See J. Z. Smith's introduction in the *Prayer of Joseph*, in *Pseudepigrapha*, vol. 1, p. 703, which cites Solomon Buber, ed., *Midrash Tanhuma* (Vilna: Romm, 1885), Bereshit [i.e., Genesis], 1.10.

71. *The Prayer of Joseph*, Fragment A, verse 5, in *Pseudepigrapha*, vol. 1, p. 703. Of course, the account in Genesis 32:22–32 mentions none of this.

72. *Martyrdom and Ascension of Isaiah*, chap. 10:29–31, in *Pseudepigrapha*, vol. 2, p. 174. This was an explicitly Christian work dated from the second to fourth century A.D.

73. The exception is *II Enoch*. One of the archangels named Satain [Satan], thought "that he might place his throne higher than the clouds . . . and that he might become equal to my [God's] power." So he and the others who followed him were hurled down into the air, where they flew, ceaselessly. *II Enoch*, version [J], chap. 29:3–5, in *Pseudepigrapha*, vol. 1, p. 148 (late first century A.D.; Slavonic). The late date of this text keeps

it from anticipating the Christian doctrine of Satan's fall, which was already well developed at the time.

74. *Life of Adam and Eve [Vita]*, 12:1–16:3, in *Pseudepigrapha*, vol. 2, p. 262. The translator, M. D. Johnson, has a very useful introduction and notes to this work.

75. A reference to Genesis 1:26.

76. Genesis 6:2 (NIV); Genesis 6:4 (KJV). The Hebrew word translated as "Giants" by the King James is the word "Nephilim." In Numbers 13:31–33, the term "Nephilim" is clearly associated with people of "giant" size and strength. Moses sent spies into the Promised Land, and when they reported back, all but Joshua and Caleb said that the people were giants, "We saw the Nephilim . . . and we seemed like grasshoppers in our own eyes" (NIV).

77. *I Enoch* (i.e., The Ethiopic Apocalypse of Enoch), chaps. 6–7, in *Pseudepigrapha*, vol. 1, pp. 15–16. The Ethiopic version is dated between the second century B.C. and the first century A.D.

78. *I Enoch*, chaps. 54–56, in *Pseudepigrapha*, vol. 1, pp. 38–39.

79. *I Enoch*, chap. 15:8–12, in *Pseudepigrapha*, vol. 1, pp. 21–22.

80. Matthew 8:14.

81. Matthew 4:24 (NIV).

82. Matthew 8:28–34; Mark 5:1–20; Luke 8:26–40.

83. A. Scott Moreau, "Demon," in *Baker's Evangelical Dictionary of Biblical Theology* (Grand Rapids, Mich.: Baker, 1996).

84. Joseph Henry Thayer, *The New Thayer's Greek-English Lexicon of the New Testament, Being Grimm's Wilke's Clavis Novi Testamenti, Translated and Revised and Enlarged by Joseph Henry Thayer* (Lafayette, Ind.: AP&A, 1979), pp. 192–193.

85. Luke 17:21.

86. Matthew 17:14–21.

87. Moreau, "Demon."

88. All the accounts are found in the Acts of the Apostles fairly soon after the resurrection; exorcisms are done by Peter, Paul, and Philip, and there is an attempt by the non-Christian sons of Sceva. Acts 5:16; 8:7; 16:16–18; 19:13–16.

89. Matthew 4:1–11.

90. Luke 10:18 (NIV).

91. Isaiah 14:12–14 (NIV). A statement also found in the mouth of Satan in some of the *Pseudepigrapha*.

92. See Brown's *The New Brown-Driver-Briggs-Gesenius Hebrew and English Lexicon*, p. 237; *A Lexicon Abridged from Liddell and Scott's Greek-English Lexicon* (Oxford: Clarendon Press, 1966), p. 237; E. A. Andrews, *A Copious and Critical Latin-English Lexicon Founded on the Larger Latin-German Lexicon of Dr. William Freund* (New York: Harper & Bros., 1858), p. 898; Davis, *New Bible Dictionary*, p. 713.

93. Revelation 12:3–4 (NIV).

94. Revelation 12:7–10.

95. Revelation 20:10.

6. SATAN, DEMONS, AND JINN

1. Homer, *Iliad*, III, 395–399. See Homer, *The Iliad*, with trans. by A. T. Murray; Loeb Classical Library, 170 (London: William Henemann; New York: G. P. Putnam's Sons, 1930), vol. 1, pp. 146–147.

2. Aeschylus, *Persians,* 619–622, in *Aeschylus;* vol. 1: *Suppliant Maidens, Persians, Prometheus, Seven against Thebes,* with an English trans. Herbert Weir Smyth; Loeb Classical Library, 145 (Cambridge, Mass.: Harvard University Press, 1956), vol. 1, pp. 160–161. Euripides, *Alcestis,* 995–1005, in *Euripides;* vol. 1: *Cyclops, Alcestis, Medea,* with an English trans. by David Kovacs; Loeb Classical Library, no. 9 (Cambridge, Mass.: Harvard University Press, 1994–), vol. 1.

3. Homer, *Iliad,* VI, 405–407, 484–487.

4. *Hullin,* 105b. Epstein, *Babylonian Talmud,* vol. 24, 105b.

5. Albert Einstein and Leopold Infeld, *The Evolution of Physics* (New York: Simon & Schuster, 1961), p. 31.

6. William Wordsworth, "Lines Composed a Few Miles above Tintern Abbey," lines 92–101, in *The Complete Poetical Works* (London: Macmillan and Co., 1888). Available online at <http://www.bartleby.com/145/>. Accessed Sept. 16, 2002.

7. As told by Diogenes Laertius, *Thales,* I, 27, in Diogenes Laertius, *Lives of Eminent Philosophers,* with an English trans. R. D. Hicks; Loeb Classical Library, no. 184 (Cambridge, Mass.: Harvard University Press; London: William Heinemann, 1959), vol. 1, pp. 26–27.

8. Plato, in *Symposium,* 202d–203a, places this speech in the mouth of Diotima; so, as always, it is difficult to know whether it is Plato's view or not. See Plato, *Lysis; Symposium; Gorgias,* trans. W. R. M. Lamb; Loeb Classical Library, no. 166, Plato in Twelve Volumes, vol. 3 (Cambridge, Mass.: Harvard University Press; London: Heinemann, 1975), vol. 3, pp. 176–179.

9. R. H. Barrow, *Plutarch and His Times* (Bloomington: Indiana University Press, 1967), p. 87.

10. Plato, *Timaeus,* 90a–90b. Plato, *Timaeus; Critias; Cleitophon; Menexenus; Epistles,* with an English trans. by R. G. Bury; Loeb Classical Library; Plato in Twelve Volumes (Cambridge, Mass.: Harvard University Press; London: William Heinemann, 1981, 1929), vol. 9, pp. 244–247. See also Plato's *Phaedo,* 107d, in Plato, *Euthyphro; Apology; Crito; Phaedo; Phaedrus,* trans. Harold North Fowler, The Loeb Classical Series (Cambridge, Mass.: Harvard University Press, 1982), vol. 1, pp. 370–371.

11. Socrates' "divine sign" is frequently mentioned in his works, such as Plato's *Phaedrus,* 242b–242e, and *Euthydemus,* 272d–272e and 273a. See Plato, *Euthyphro; Apology; Crito; Phaedo; Phaedrus,* trans. Fowler, vol. 1, pp. 458–461; and Plato, *Laches; Protagoras; Meno; Euthydemus,* with an English trans. W. R. M. Lamb; Loeb Classical Library, no. 165; Plato in Twelve Volumes, vol. 2 (London: W. Heinemann; New York: G. P. Putnam's Sons, 1924), vol. 2.

12. For example, see Plato, *Theages,* 128d, in Plato, *Charmides; Alcibiades I and II; Hipparchus; The Lovers; Theages; Minos; Epinomis,* with an English trans. by W. R. M. Lamb; Loeb Classical Library, no. 201; Plato in Twelve Volumes, vol. 12 (London: W. Heinemann; New York: G. P. Putnam's Sons, 1927), vol. 12.

13. See Plato, *Euthydemus,* 272d–e and 273a; Plato, *Phaedrus,* 242b–e, and Plato's *Apology,* 40b, in *Euthyphro; Apology; Crito; Phaedo; Phaedrus,* trans. Fowler, vol. 1, pp. 138–141.

14. Plato, *Theages,* 128d–129e.

15. Xenophon, in his *Memorabilia,* 1.1.1, stated the indictment against Socrates was for rejecting the gods, introducing "strange deities" (*kaina daimonia*), and corrupting the youth of Athens. See Xenophon, *Memorabilia, and Oeconomicus,* trans. E. C. Marchant; and *Symposium, and Apology,* trans. O. J. Todd; Loeb Classical Library, no. 168;

Xenophon in Seven Volumes, vol. 4 (Cambridge, Mass.: Harvard University Press; London: William Heinemann, 1968), vol. 4. See also Plato, *Apology*, 31c–e, in *Euthyphro; Apology; Crito; Phaedo; Phaedrus*, trans. Fowler; vol. 1, pp. 112–115, and Barrow, *Plutarch and His Times*, pp. 86–87.

16. Plato, *Apology*, 40a, 40c–d; Xenophon, *Memorabilia*, 1.1.4–8, and his *Apology of Socrates*, 3–7, in Xenophon, *Memorabilia, et al.*, vol. 4.

17. Plato, *Phaedrus*, 242d–e.

18. "Daimon," in *The Oxford Classical Dictionary*, ed. Simon Hornblower and Antony Spawforth, 3rd ed. (Oxford and New York: Oxford University Press, 1996), p. 426; Valerie Flint, "The Demonisation of Magic and Sorcery in Late Antiquity: Christian Redefinitions of Pagan Religions," in Bengt Ankarloo and Stuart Clark, eds., *Witchcraft and Magic in Europe: Ancient Greece and Rome* (Philadelphia: University of Pennsylvania Press, 1999), pp. 281–292.

19. Barrow, *Plutarch and His Times*, pp. 87–91.

20. J. Rives, "Human Sacrifice among Pagans and Christians," *Journal of Roman Studies* 85 (1995): 77–82.

21. Rives, "Human Sacrifice," pp. 74–77, 80–85.

22. Christopher A. Faraone, "The Agonistic Context of Early Greek Binding Spells," in *Magica Hiera: Ancient Greek Magic and Religion*, ed. Christopher A. Faraone and Dirk Obbink (New York and Oxford: Oxford University Press, 1991), pp. 3–6.

23. Faraone emphasizes that these tablets were not normally intended to kill the victim, but to inhibit them in some way. Faraone, "Agonistic Context," *Magica Hiera*, p. 8.

24. See, for example, the first-century B.C. spell in John J. Winkler's "The Constraints of Eros," in *Magica Hiera*, pp. 224–225.

25. Faraone, "Agonistic Context," *Magica Hiera*, pp. 11–13.

26. Plato, *Republic*, 364b. Plato, *The Republic*, with an English trans. by Paul Shorey, Loeb Classical Library (Cambridge, Mass.: Harvard University Press; London: W. Heinemann, 1980–1982), vol. 1. See also Faraone, "Agonistic Context," *Magica Hiera*, p. 4.

27. Faraone, "Agonistic Context," *Magica Hiera*, p. 4.

28. Roy Kotansky, "Incantations and Prayers for Salvation on Inscribed Greek Amulets," *Magica Hiera*, p. 117.

29. J. H. M. Strubbe, "Cursed Be He That Moves My Bones," *Magica Hiera*, p. 42.

30. Hans Dieter Betz, "Magic and Mystery in the Greek Magical Papyri," *Magica Hiera*, pp. 251–252, citing *Papyri Graecae Magicae*, vol. 1, pp. 42–195. See Hans Dieter Betz, ed. and trans., *The Greek Magical Papyri in Translation, including the Demotic Spells* (Chicago: University of Chicago Press, 1986–), vol. 1.

31. *Brachot* 6a (sometimes called *Berakoth*). The *Babylonian Talmud* was begun in the third and completed in the fifth century. The Standard English translation runs to thirty-five volumes. Isidore Epstein, ed., *Babylonian Talmud*, 35 vols. in 18 (London: Soncino Press, 1978; reprint of the 1935–1952 edition), *Berakoth*, 6a, vol. 1.

32. For their preference for ruins (and roofs), see *Brachot*, 3a–3b, *Taanit*, 20b, *Pesachim*, 111b. Both palms and sorb trees seemed to be favored haunts, *Pesachim*, 111b. Epstein, *Babylonian Talmud*, vol. 1, *Berakoth*, 3a–3b; vol. 5, *Pesachim*, 111b; vol. 9, *Ta'anith*, 20b.

33. *Brachot*, 43b; *Pesachim*, 112a. One should never sleep in the house alone,

Shabbat, 151b. Epstein, *Babylonian Talmud*, vol. 1, *Berakoth*, 43b; vol. 3, *Shabbath*, 151b; vol. 5, *Pesachim*, 112a.

34. These toilet tales are found in *Brachot*, 62a. An incantation to protect against a toilet demon is in *Shabbat*, 67a. Epstein, *Babylonian Talmud*, vol. 1, *Berakoth*, 62a; vol. 3, *Shabbath*, 67a.

35. *Pesachim*, 112a. Epstein, *Babylonian Talmud*, vol. 5, *Pesachim*, 112a.

36. *Pesachim*, 111b. Epstein, *Babylonian Talmud*, vol. 5, *Pesachim*, 111b.

37. *Pesachim*, 112a. Epstein, *Babylonian Talmud*, vol. 5, *Pesachim*, 112a.

38. *Brachot*, 51a. Epstein, *Babylonian Talmud*, vol. 1, *Berakoth*, 51a.

39. *Pesachim*, 112a. Epstein, *Babylonian Talmud*, vol. 5, *Pesachim*, 112a.

40. *Erubin*, 41b. From this description, rabbinic demons were very similar to the jinn described later in the Qurʾan. Muhammad, of course, had come into frequent contact with Jews in Arabia and elsewhere. For jinn, see below in the text. Epstein, *Babylonian Talmud*, vol. 4, *Erubin*, 41b.

41. Raphael Patai, *On Jewish Folklore* (Detroit: Wayne State University Press, 1983), pp. 300–301. There are obvious similarities between this demonic marriage and Muslim beliefs in the marriage of jinn.

42. *Pesachim*, 111b. Epstein, *Babylonian Talmud*, vol. 5, *Pesachim*, 111b.

43. *Brachot*, 6a. Epstein, *Babylonian Talmud*, vol. 1, *Berakoth*, 6a.

44. *Baba Kama*, 16a (sometimes spelled *Babha Qamma*, etc.). Epstein, *Babylonian Talmud*, vol. 16, *Baba Kamma*, 16a.

45. See Alan Humm's creation (<http://ccat.sas.upenn.edu/humm/Topics/Lilith/>, accessed June 25, 2002), for an excellent website on Lilith, which not only contains almost every English translation of texts relating to her but also is an active meeting place for scholars to debate the meaning of Lilith.

46. Concerning Lilith's possible Sumerian/Akkadian relationship to the goddess Inanna, see Anne Baring and Jules Cashford, *The Myth of the Goddess: Evolution of an Image* (London: Arkana, Penguin Books, 1993), pp. 216–218.

47. *Zohar*, 3:76b. Sperling, *The Zohar*, vol. 1. Cf. Raphael Patai, *Gates to the Old City: A Book of Jewish Legends* (Northvale, N.J.: J. Aronson, 1988), pp. 456–466; Graves, *Hebrew Myths*, pp. 66–67.

48. *Zohar*, 1:19b. Sperling, *The Zohar*, vol. 1.

49. Patai, *On Jewish Folklore*, p. 406. In the seventeenth and eighteenth centuries, some East European Jews placed the foreskin of a recently circumcised child into the mouth of a newborn while reading part of the mezuzah in its ear—the babe would then be safe from Lilith.

50. See, for example, the collection of essays, edited by Enid Dame et al., *Which Lilith? Feminist Writers Re-create the World's First Woman* (Northvale, N.J.: Jason Aronson Publishers, 1998).

51. The Lilith Fair summer festivals were designed as a venue for female songwriters and musicians. *Lilith: The Independent Jewish Women's Magazine* is now in its third decade. See the article "Lilith" in the *American Jewish Desk Reference* (New York: Random House, 1999), p. 509.

52. For a sampling in fantasy and science fiction, see George MacDonald's *Lilith*; C. L. Moore's *Fruit of Knowledge*; Octavia E. Butler's trilogy *Lilith's Brood*, beginning with *Dawn*; and the French vampire novel by Alina Reyes, *Lilith*. The recent opera is simply titled *Lilith*. "*Lilith* (Opera)," review in *Opera News* 66, no. 9 (Mar. 2002): 74.

53. Anti-Lilith amulets can still be purchased according to Susan Weidman Schneider, editor of the journal *Lilith*. Jake Tapper, "And Just Who Was Lilith, Anyway?" *The Washington Post*, July 27, 1997.

54. Charles Norris Cochrane, *Christianity and Classical Culture: A Study of Thought and Action from Augustus to Augustine* (London: Oxford University Press, 1972, reprint of the rev. 1944 ed.), p. 268.

55. St. Augustine, *The City of God*, trans. Marcus Dods (New York: Modern Library, 1950), Book VIII, chaps. 12–22, pp. 257–269, and all of Book IX, pp. 280–302.

56. St. Augustine, *The City of God*, Book VIII, chap. 14, pp. 259–260.

57. St. Augustine, *The City of God*, Book XXII, chap. 8, p. 825.

58. Jacobus de Voragine, "St. Lupus, September 1," *The Golden Legend*, trans. Granger Ryan and Helmut Ripperger (New York: Longmans, Green, & Co., 1941), p. 516. Rabbinic legends also told of slamming lids down on demons.

59. Dudden, *Gregory the Great*, vol. II, p. 353, citing *Dialogues*, vol. I, 4. This story had staying power, for it was still being repeated in the thirteenth century by Jacobus de Voragine, "Exaltation of the Cross, September 14," *The Golden Legend*, p. 549.

60. Guibert of Nogent, *Self and Society in France: The Memoirs of Abbot Guibert of Nogent (1064?–c. 1125)*, ed. John F. Benton, trans. C. C. Swinton Bland (New York: Harper Torchbooks, 1970), Book III, chap. 19, pp. 222–223.

61. In Jeffrey Burton Russell's excellent series on the history of Satan and evil, see his *Lucifer: The Devil in the Middle Ages* (Ithaca, N.Y.: Cornell University Press, 1984), chap. 8, "Lucifer in High Medieval Art and Literature," pp. 209–244, and chap. 9, "Lucifer on Stage," pp. 245–273.

62. Cf. Philip Schaff's *History of the Christian Church*, vol. 5, pt. 1, *The Middle Ages*, by David S. Schaff (New York: Charles Scribner's Sons, 1907), pp. 880–885.

63. Pauline Aiken, "Vincent of Beauvais and the Green Yeoman's Lecture on Demonology," *Studies in Philology* 35 (Jan. 1938): 3, citing the *Speculum Historiale Vincentii Belvacensis*, XXIX, chap. VI, "De Novicio Cisterciensi Temptato a Dyabolo."

64. The Devil appeared as a black lentil. This story is cited in Schaff, *History of the Christian Church*, vol. 5, pt. 1, p. 882, and n. 2, *Vita Norberti*, XIII. *The Life of St. Norbert (versions A & B)* can be found on the Web in their original Latin and in English at the Premonstratensians website (the order was founded by St. Norbert). This possession story is located in version A, chap. 14 (<http://www.premontre.org/subpages/vitae/tocvitae.htm>, accessed July 21, 2002).

65. Aquinas simply split attacks into two major categories, temptation and physical assault. Thomas Aquinas, *Summa Theologica*, Part 1, Quarto 114, art. 1. For the English, see Aquinas, *The Summa Theologica*, trans. Fathers of the English Dominican Province, rev. by Daniel J. Sullivan, Great Books of the Western World (Chicago: Encyclopaedia Britannica, 1952), vol. 1, pp. 581–582.

66. Some Christians believed that to be possessed, one had to leave oneself open to it—leaving the cockpit door ajar, to continue the analogy.

67. For "obsession," see Vincent of Beauvais, in Aiken, "Vincent of Beauvais," p. 5.

68. And demons could take on the form of apparitions. Cf. Aiken, "Vincent of Beauvais," p. 4.

69. Norman Cohn, *Europe's Inner Demons: The Demonization of Christians in Medieval Christendom*, rev. ed. (Chicago: University of Chicago Press, 2000), pp. 26–27, who cites Caesarius of Heisterbach, *Dialogus miraculorum*, Book XII, chap. 4.

70. Harley's examples come from Calvinist and other non-conformist theologians,

but apparently this differentiation was common. David Harley, "Explaining Salem: Calvinist Psychology and the Diagnosis of Possession," *American Historical Review* 101 (Apr. 1996): 311–313.

71. Harley, "Explaining Salem," p. 311.

72. The quote is from a paraphrase of Father Amorth's words. See "Giving Satan a Chance: An Exorcist's Complaint (Vatican)," *Catholic Insight* 10, no. 5 (June 2002): 24.

73. Taken from the article "Exorcism," in Rossell Hope Robbins's *The Encyclopedia of Witchcraft and Demonology* (New York: Crown Publishers, 1959), pp. 186–187. For the updated 1952 version (translated into English in 1964) see Part XIII, chap. 2, "Exorcisms," in *The Roman Ritual, Complete Edition* [= *Rituale Romanum,* or officially, *Pontificale Romanum*] trans. Philip T. Weller (Chicago: Bruce Publishing, 1964). The complete English version is on the Web at <http://choccult.8m.com/ritrom.htm>, accessed July 10, 2002. The modern Latin version is at <http://members.aol.com/liturgialatina/pontificale/150.htm>, accessed July 10, 2002.

74. These exorcisms are mentioned throughout the Rituale Romanum; see especially Part II on the Rites of Baptism; Part XI on Blessings and Other Sacramentals, and Part XIII on Exorcisms.

75. *The Roman Ritual,* ed. Weller, Part XI, chap. 4, no. 7.

76. Michael Goodich, ed., *Other Middle Ages: Witnesses at the Margins of Medieval Society* (Philadelphia: University of Pennsylvania Press, 1998), p. 151.

77. *The Roman Ritual,* ed. Weller, Part II, chap. 2, nos. 3, 7, 12; for the omission of exorcisms "according to the 'Instruction' of September 26, 1964," see Part II, chaps. 5 and 6.

78. *The Roman Ritual,* ed. Weller, Part II, chap. 4, nos. 18–24, 25–31, 32–40.

79. *The Roman Ritual,* ed. Weller, Part XIII, chap. 3.

80. *Congregation for the Doctrine of Faith: Instruction on Prayers for Healing—Ardens Felicitatis (Instructio de orationibus ad obtinendam a Deo sanationem),* Sept. 14, 2000. Part II. Disciplinary Forms, Article 8, sects. 1–3. This can be found in the Doctrinal Documents at the Papal Curia's website: <http://www.vatican.va/roman_curia/congregations/cfaith/>, accessed July 12, 2002.

81. Papal Curia, Congregation for Divine Worship, "De Exorcismus et Supplicationibus Quibusdam," Jan. 26, 1999. This instruction can be found (in Italian) on the Vatican's website: <http://www.vatican.va/roman_curia/congregations/ccdds/documents/rc_con_ccdds_doc_20000630_il-rito-degli-esorcismi_it.html>, accessed July 12, 2002.

82. According to Henry Charles Lea, although legends of incubi were current throughout the Middle Ages, it was not until the twelfth century that they became a reality for the medieval mind. Henry Charles Lea, *Materials toward a History of Witchcraft,* ed. Arthur C. Howland (Philadelphia: University of Pennsylvania Press, 1939; reprint, New York: Thomas Yoseloff, 1957), vol. 1, p. 147.

83. Thomas Aquinas, *Summa Theologica,* Part 1, Q. 52, article 3, reply to objection 6. For the English, see Aquinas, *The Summa Theologica,* Great Books of the Western World, vol. 1, p. 278.

84. For Merlin, see the grand storyteller Geoffrey of Monmouth, *The History of the Kings of Britain* (New York: Penguin Books, 1966), Part VI, sect. 18, pp. 167–168. Concerning the birth of Eleanor, see Schaff, *History of the Christian Church,* vol. 5, pt. 1, p. 886, and n. 5. Schaff's citation is unclear, but appears to be to Caesarius of Heisterbach's *Dialogues,* vol. II, p. 80.

85. For a full description of these "long-lived" beings, see C. S. Lewis's *The Discarded Image: An Introduction to Medieval and Renaissance Literature* (Cambridge: Cambridge University Press, 1964), chap. 6, "The Longaevi" [i.e., "long-living ones"], pp. 122–138.

86. The earliest account is in Moses Pitt's letter of 1696, but a nineteenth-century retelling of this legend of Cornwall by Robert Hunt gives the amorous details. It is difficult to know whether these are later accretions or might have been oral traditions that would not have been written in a proper seventeenth-century book. (Cf. *Paranormal Phenomena: Opposing Viewpoints*, ed. Terry O'Neill [San Diego: Greenhaven Press, 1991], pp. 63–64.) Moses Pitt, *An account of one Ann Jefferies, now living in the county of Cornwall, who was fed for six months by a small sort of airy people call'd fairies, and of the strange and wonderful cures she performed with salves and medicines she received from them, for which she never took one penny of her patients. In a letter from Moses Pitt to the Right Reverand Father in God, Dr. Edward Fowler, Lord Bishop of Glocester* (London: Richard Cumberland, 1696; microfilm reprint, Ann Arbor, Mich.: University Microfilms, 1974 [Early English books, 1641–1700; 505:14]). The entire text is available online at <http://www.gandolf.com/cornwall/fairies/AnnJeffries.shtml>, accessed July 12, 2002.

87. Brian P. Levack, *The Witch-Hunt in Early Modern Europe* (New York: Longmans, 1987), p. 229; Angela Bourke, *The Burning of Bridget Cleary: A True Story* (New York: Penguin, 2001).

88. There are many variant spellings in English. Here, the fairly standard *jinn* will be used for the plural, and *jinni* for the singular. *Jinnia* will be used for a (temporarily) female *jinni*. *Jinn* comes from the Arabic *janna* for cover, conceal, hidden, as *jinn* are invisible.

89. Qurʾan, 15:27; 51:56; 55:15. Angels, according to the Hadith, were created from light, while humans from clay or dust (and from thence a blood clot) and/or from water. On angels, see Cyril Glassé, ed., *The Concise Encyclopedia of Islam* (San Francisco: Harper & Row, 1989), p. 43; and see the Hadith of *Sahih Muslim*, Book 42, chap. 12, no. 7134:

> Aʾisha reported that Allah's Messenger (may peace be upon him) said: The Angels were born out of light and the Jinns were born out of the spark of fire and Adam was born as he has been defined (in the *Qurʾan*) for you (i.e., he is fashioned out of clay).

See Muslim ibn al-Hajjaj al-Qushayri, *Sahih Muslim: Being Traditions of the Sayings and Doings of the Prophet Muhammad as Narrated by His Companions and Compiled Under the Title al-Jami'-us-sahih*, trans. 'Abdul Hamid Siddiqui (Lahore: Muhammad Ashraf, 1976–1981), Book 42, chap. 12, no. 7134 (cited as *Sahih Muslim* below).

On humans, see Qurʾan, 6:2; 15:26; 22:5; 40:67 (from clay/dust/bloodclot), 25:54 (from water). When pondering the difference between angels and jinn, Al-Ghazzali framed the question in Aristotelian terms: they were either different in substance or accident—if substance, they were different species, if in accidents (such as the difference between a "complete" and "incomplete man") then they were of the same species. He did not resolve the problem. The ambiguity is prominent in the identity of Iblis/Satan discussed below. See Duncan Black Macdonald, *The Religious Attitude and Life in Islam: Being the Haskell Lectures on Comparative Religion Delivered before the University of Chicago in 1906* (Beirut: Khayats, 1965), p. 292.

90. In one of the Hadith, Muhammad prays to Allah, saying in effect, "O Allah, you are ever-living, but the Jinn and mankind die." The Hadith are the sayings and deeds of Muhammad as reported by his companions (most were not collected until about 250 years after Muhammad's death). They are second in authority only to the Qur'an for many Muslims. See *Sahih Muslim*, Book 35, chap. 17, no. 6561.

91. Excepting, perhaps, the ambiguous Iblis/Shaytan.

92. See the Hadith, *Sahih al-Bukhari*, vol. 1, Book 4, no. 144, in Muhammad ibn Ismail Bukhari, *Sahih al-Bukhari = The Translation of the Meanings of Sahih al-Bukhari, Arabic-English*, trans. Muhammad Muhsin Khan, 4th rev. ed. (Chicago: Kazi Publications, 1976–). See also *Sahih Muslim*, Book 3, chap. 31, no. 729–730.

93. Apparently, human dung made other dung inedible. The Hadith rather than the Qur'an mention this curious exchange between the jinn and Muhammad. See *Sunan Abu Dawud*, Book 1, no. 39.

94. Edward William Lane, *Manners and Customs of the Modern Egyptians* (New York: E. P. Dutton, 1954, reprint of the 1908 ed.), pp. 233–234; Edward Westermarck, "The Nature of the Arab Ğinn, Illustrated by the Present Beliefs of the People of Morocco," *Journal of the Anthropological Institute of Great Britain and Ireland* 29, no. 3/4 (1899): 259.

95. Concerning the non-existence of ghouls, see *Sahih Muslim*, Book 26, chap. 31, no. 5514–5516; and *Sunan Abu Dawud*, Book 29, no. 3904.

96. Porter, *The Greatest Benefit to Mankind: A Medical History of Humanity*, p. 93; Westermarck, "The Nature of the Arab Ğinn," pp. 254–255.

97. Westermarck, "The Nature of the Arab Ğinn," pp. 255–258; Lane, *Manners and Customs of the Modern Egyptians*, pp. 231–260. Muhammad advised a particular ritual prayer to be said before sexual intercourse to protect the (possible) child against Satan. See the Hadith, *Sahih al-Bukhari*, vol. 4, Book 54, nos. 493 and 503, in Bukhari, Muhammad ibn Ismail, *Sahih al-Bukhari*.

98. This approach is called the *diafa* in Morocco; see Westermarck, "The Nature of the Arab Ğinn," pp. 256–257; see also Porter, *The Greatest Benefit to Mankind*, p. 93.

99. An "Islamic Psychology" website reproduces a portion of Dr. Abu Ameenah Bilal Philips's book *The Exorcist Tradition in Islaam* (Sharajh: Dar Al Fatah, 1997), which includes interviews with modern Islamic exorcists. One can even listen to "authentic" incantations and exorcism rituals there. See <http://www.angelfire.com/al/islamicpsychology/exorcism.html>, accessed July 2002.

100. Lane, *Manners and Customs of the Modern Egyptians*, p. 229.

101. *Sunan Abu Dawud*, Book 41, nos. 5236 and 5240; and Malik's *Muwatta*, Book 54, sect. 12, no. 33, see Malik ibn Anas [Muwatta. English], *Al-Muwatta of Imam Malik ibn Anas: The First Formulation of Islamic Law*, trans. Aisha Abdurrahman Bewley (London and New York: Kegan Paul; distributed by Routledge, Chapman, and Hall, 1989 [cited later in the notes as Malik's *Muwatta*]).

102. Angels in the Qur'an are portrayed as sexless (or at least *not* females), see the Qur'an, 43:19, 53:27.

103. The Qur'an, 55:70–73, Dawood's translation, *The Koran*, p. 533.

104. Macdonald, *The Religious Attitude and Life in Islam*, p. 144.

105. *Sunan Abu-Dawud*, Book 41, no. 5088. Aisha was the third wife of Muhammad: she was married at six, the marriage was consummated at age nine, and she was widowed at age eighteen. She was a wealth of information concerning the last years of Muhammad in the Hadith. Sadly, after Muhammad's death, her life was a tragedy; after

losing the civil war against Muhammad's cousin Ali, she spent most of her life under virtual house arrest. Cf. the Hadith, *Sahih al-Bukhari*, vol. 7, Book 62, no. 88; vol. 5, Book 58, nos. 234, 236; vol. 8, Book 73, no. 171, in Bukhari, Muhammad ibn Ismail, *Sahih al-Bukhari* and *Sahih Muslim*, Book 8, chap. 10, no. 3311.

106. See Jacob Lassner's *Demonizing the Queen of Sheba: Boundaries of Gender and Culture in Postbiblical Judaism and Medieval Islam* (Chicago: University of Chicago Press, 1993).

107. Macdonald, *The Religious Attitude and Life in Islam*, pp. 17–20; Tor Andrae, *Mohammed: The Man and His Faith*, trans. Theophil Menzel (Salem, N.H.: Ayer Co., reprint of 1936 ed.), pp. 36–38; Karen Armstrong, *Muhammad: A Biography of the Prophet* (San Francisco: HarperSanFrancisco, 1992), pp. 84–86.

108. Poets possessed by jinn must have been a common view of pre-Islamic Arabs, for the polytheists accused Muhammad of being just such in the Qurʾan, 37:36: "And [they] say: 'What! Shall we give up our gods for the sake of a Poet possessed?' " *The Holy Qurʾan*, trans. Abdullah Yusuf Ali (Jeddah, Saudi Arabia: Islamic Education Centre, 1946), p. 1196.

109. The standard version of these events, as reported by Muhammad's wife Aisha, is recorded at the beginning of *Sahih al-Bukhari*, vol. 1, Book 1, no. 3. Ibn Ishaq, Muhammad's early biographer, however, reports that Muhammad was asleep (at home?). The events that followed are roughly the same in both accounts, except that Ishaq has Gabriel pressing Muhammad down with a brocade so hard that he thought he was dying. Ibn Ishaq, Muhammad [*Sirat Rasul Allah*. English], *The Life of Mohammad: A translation of Ishaq's Sirat rasul Allah*, trans. A. Guillaume, Jubilee ed. (New York: Oxford University Press, 1997; first published 1955), pp. 106–107.

110. W. Montgomery Watt, *Muhammad: Prophet and Statesman* (Oxford: Oxford University Press, 1961), p. 15; Armstrong, *Muhammad*, p. 84. Cf. Tabari [Tarikh al-Rusul Wa-al-Muluk. English. Selections], *Muhammad at Mecca*, trans. W. Montgomery Watt and M. V. McDonald; *The History of al-Tabari*, vol. 6 (Albany: SUNY Press, 1988).

111. In the Hadith, Muhammad runs into his wife crying, "Cover me! Cover me!" See *Sahih al-Bukhari*, vol. 1, Book 1, no. 3, and Ibn Ishaq, *The Life of Mohammad*, pp. 106–107. See also F. E. Peters, *Muhammad and the Origins of Islam* (Albany: SUNY Press, 1994), pp. 150–151.

112. The Qurʾan, 81:22. For more on this, see Peters, *Muhammad and the Origins of Islam*, p. 143.

113. The name "Iblis" probably derives from the Greek *diabolos*—"devil." See Jeffrey Burton Russell's chapter on the Muslim Devil in his *Lucifer: The Devil in the Middle Ages* (Ithaca, N.Y.: Cornell University Press, 1984), pp. 52–61; "Iblis," in Glassé, *The Concise Encyclopedia of Islam*, pp. 165–167; and Andrew Rippin's "Devil," in *Encyclopaedia of the Qurʾān*, ed. Jane Dammen McAuliffe (Leiden and Boston: Brill, 2001–), vol. 1, pp. 524–527.

114. The Qurʾan, 7:11–13, Dawood's translation, *The Koran*, pp. 150–151.

115. This switch in name, from Iblis to Shaytan (Satan), seems the best inference from the narratives, as the fall of Iblis is immediately followed by the temptation of Adam and Eve in the Garden by Shaytan.

116. The Qurʾan, 2:34, 7:11, 15:30, 17:61, 18:50, 20:116, and 38:74.

117. The Qurʾan, 18:50.

118. But if Iblis was not an angel, why was he required to obey God's command to the angels? One can see the quandary.

119. Tabari [Tarikh al-Rusul Wa-al-Muluk. English. Selections], *General introduction, and, From the Creation to the Flood,* trans. Franz Rosenthal; *The History of al-Tabari,* vol. 1 (Albany: SUNY Press, 1988), pp. 250–254.

120. That is, "Satan and the satans" (plural, *shayatin*). Cf. Rippin, "Devil," in *Encyclopaedia of the Qurʾan,* vol. 1, 524.

121. The Qurʾan, 2:36, 20:117–121.

122. The Qurʾan, 15:36, 17:62, 18:52, 38:82.

123. The Qurʾan, 4:60, 4:119, 7:20, 7:27, etc.

124. *Sahih al-Bukhari,* vol. 4, Book 54, no. 509; vol. 8, Book 73, nos. 242 and 245; and *Sahih Muslim,* Book 42, chap. 11, nos. 7129–7132. Fortunately for humanity, whenever the call to prayer begins, Shaytan "breaks wind with noise" and takes to his heels! *Sahih al-Bukhari,* vol. 4, Book 54, no. 505.

125. For the upper nose, see *Sahih al-Bukhari,* vol. 4, Book 54, no. 516. For the dangers of the call of nature, see *Sahih al-Bukhari,* vol. 1, Book 4, no. 144; and *Sahih Muslim,* Book 3, chap. 31, nos. 729–730. For Satan's infiltration during intercourse, see *Sahih al-Bukhari,* vol. 4, Book 54, nos. 493 and 503.

126. We can only hope this last comment was a bit of humor from Muhammad, but from his concern about Satan and bodily orifices it does not seem so. *Sahih al-Bukhari,* vol. 2, Book 21, no. 245, and vol. 4, Book 54, no. 492.

127. The Qurʾan, 21:82, 34:12.

128. The Qurʾan, 34:12–14.

129. The Qurʾan, 34:14.

130. To be sure, some Muslims questioned the existence of jinn, just as educated people today question the existence of quarks and other science-sanctioned objects that elude direct observation. For most Muslims, however, doubting the existence of jinn impugned the veracity of the Qurʾan. Thus, few believers, even among the philosophers, expressed reservations, if indeed they had any. Al-Ghazzali, author of *The Incoherence of the Philosophers,* was so convinced of the jinn's existence that he undertook training to see and talk with them. His frank report, however, is that all he ever saw were silent shadows (Macdonald, p. 145). An exception to this rule of belief may be Ibn Sina (Avicenna), the famous eleventh-century philosopher and physician, who defined jinn as airy animals that could change their form. Then he added: "This is an explanation of the name (or noun)," suggesting that they had no objective existence (Macdonald, p. 152). Ibn Khaldun, though an orthodox Muslim, classed all references to both jinn and angels in the Qurʾan as "obscure verses," about which our knowledge is uncertain. He certainly believed in magic, however, having seen a magician split a sheep in half merely by making a slashing motion toward it (Macdonald, pp. 62, 114).

131. Ignaz Goldziher, *Introduction to Islamic Theology and Law,* trans. Andras and Ruth Hamori (Princeton, N.J.: Princeton University Press, 1981), pp. 63–64; Samuel M. Zwemer, *The Influence of Animism on Islam* (New York: Macmillan, 1920), chap. 7: "Jinn."

132. See Macdonald, *The Religious Attitude and Life in Islam,* pp. 149–150, who cites Ibn Askar's *The Shaikhs of Morocco in the XVIth Century,* trans. T. H. Weir (Edinburgh: Morton, 1904), p. 121.

133. Goldziher, *Introduction to Islamic Theology and Law,* p. 64.

134. Goldziher, *Introduction to Islamic Theology and Law*, pp. 64–65.

135. Goldziher, *Introduction to Islamic Theology and Law*, pp. 64–65, and n. 88.

136. Macdonald, *The Religious Attitude and Life in Islam*, pp. 143, 153. One other legal question concerned abolition—slavery had been a problem for many jinn for centuries. Walter Skeat reported in 1900 "that Genii (it is to be hoped orthodox ones) may be sometimes *bought* at Mecca from the 'Sheikh Jin' (headman of Genii) at prices varying from $90 to $100 a piece" (Skeat's emphasis; Walter W. Skeat, *Malay Magic: An Introduction to the Folklore and Popular Religion of the Malay Peninsula* [New York: Macmillan, 1900; reprint, New York: Barnes & Noble, 1966], p. 96 and note.) A Saudi royal decree abolished human slavery in 1962, but jinn were not mentioned in the edict.

137. Macdonald, *The Religious Attitude and Life in Islam*, p. 143.

138. Many thanks to Fatih Kucuk and his enlightening discussions about some modern Turkish views on jinn.

139. Westermarck, "The Nature of the Arab Ǧinn," pp. 252–253.

140. Well known in Turkey, he is little known in the United States, although articles about him have appeared occasionally in the *New York Times* and elsewhere.

141. As of this writing, Gülen is elderly, very ill, and awaiting trial in Turkey for mixing religion and politics. He has played a major role in the opposition Virtue Party that wished to bridge the ethnic gap of Turks and Kurds, as well as the gap between secularists and religionists of various stripes. Apparently, he is seen as a threat to secularists and nationalist separatists alike, since he wants to bring together all sides, whatever their ethnicity or religion.

142. The title of his brief article on the Web, "Can We Employ E.T.s (Jinns) in Different Jobs?" hints at a way to make the jinn more palatable to skeptical Westerners—equate them with alien beings. Available at <http://www.pearls.org/et/can_we_employe_jinns.htm>, accessed July 8, 2002. The homepage for information on Gülen is "The Pearls of Wisdom: 'Windows to Spirituality,' " available online at <http://www.pearls.org>, accessed July 8, 2002.

143. This is the title of Stuart Clark's monumental *Thinking with Demons: The Idea of Witchcraft in Early Modern Europe* (Oxford: Oxford University Press, 1999).

7. WITCHES AND WITCH-HUNTS IN THE WEST

1. Jean-Paul Sartre, "No Exit," in *No Exit and Three Other Plays* (New York: Vintage Books, 1949), p. 47.

2. This, of course, is President Reagan's characterization, delivered in the 1980s.

3. The twelve-volume Garland series is simply titled *Articles on Witchcraft, Magic, and Demonology: A Twelve Volume Anthology of Scholarly Articles*, ed. Brian P. Levack (New York: Garland Publishing, 1992). The more recent six-volume Routledge series is *New Perspectives on Witchcraft, Magic and Demonology*, ed. Brian P. Levack (New York: Routledge, 2001).

4. For a hint at the huge number of books on the subject by the mid-1970s alone, see *Witchcraft: Catalogue of the Witchcraft Collection in Cornell University Library*, ed. Martha J. Crowe (Millwood, N.Y.: KTO Press, 1977).

5. Homer, *Odyssey*, XI. For a Roman instance of necromancy, see Virgil, *Aeneid*, VI.

6. Lucan, *Pharsalia,* trans. Jane Wilson Joyce (Ithaca, N.Y.: Cornell University Press, 1993), VI, 413–830.

7. Cicero, *Against Vatinius,* 14.

8. Valerie I. J. Flint, *The Rise of Magic in Early Medieval Europe* (Princeton, N.J.: Princeton University Press, 1991), p. 13, citing Pliny the Elder, *Natural History,* XXX, iv–v; ed. and trans. W. H. S. Jones, *Pliny Natural History,* vol. 8 (Loeb Classical Library, 1963), pp. 286–289.

9. Tacitus, *Annales,* II, 32. Tiberius, however, who was adept at astrology himself, continued to employ an astrologer for guidance.

10. Apuleius, *Apologia,* 47; trans. H. E. Butler, *The Apologia and Florida of Apuleius of Madaura* (1909; reprint, Westport, Conn.: Greenwood Press, 1970), p. 84.

11. *Lex XII Tabularum,* table VIII, 1a–b. The penalty sounds harsh, but the penalty for merely singing a *slanderous* song against someone was being clubbed to death. See Hans Julius Wolff, *Roman Law: An Historical Introduction* (Norman: University of Oklahoma Press, 1951), pp. 53, 59.

12. One wonders whether the destruction of tombs was merely desecration or a hidden link to necromancy as well. Judith Evans Grubbs, "Constantine and Imperial Legislation on the Family," in *The Theodosian Code,* ed. Jill Harries and Ian Wood (Ithaca, N.Y.: Cornell University Press, 1993), p. 128.

13. Flint, *Rise of Magic,* pp. 16–17, citing the *Theodosian Code,* 9, 16, 4; *The Theodosian Code and Novels, and the Sirmondian Constitutions,* trans. Clyde Pharr (1952; reprint, New York: Greenwood Press, 1969), p. 237.

14. Didorus Siculus, *Bibliotheca Historica,* xxii, 5, 1. See J. Rives, "Human Sacrifice among Pagans and Christians," *Journal of Roman Studies* 85 (1995): 72–73.

15. Rives, "Human Sacrifice among Pagans and Christians," pp. 72–73.

16. The earliest account of this fantasy appears to go back to the Stoic Posidonius (135–51 B.C.), who relates that, when Antiochus IV Epiphanes sacked the Jewish Temple in 168 B.C., he found a Greek in chains within who related the tale. See Gavin I. Langmuir, *Toward a Definition of Antisemitism* (Berkeley: University of California Press, 1990), p. 212.

17. Josephus, *Against Apion,* II, 52–113. According to Rives, the story was expunged from all remaining Greek copies of Josephus and is only found in a Latin translation. See Rives, "Human Sacrifice among Pagans and Christians," pp. 70–71, and n. 30.

18. Norman Cohn, *Europe's Inner Demons: The Demonization of Christians in Medieval Christendom,* rev. ed. (Chicago: University of Chicago Press, 1993), p. 12.

19. Tacitus, *Annals,* 15.44, in *The Complete Works of Tacitus* (New York: Modern Library, 1942), pp. 380–381.

20. Pliny the Younger, *Letters of Pliny,* X (to Trajan), 96–97, in Henry Bettenson, ed., *Documents of the Christian Church,* 2nd ed. (Oxford: Oxford University Press, 1967), p. 4; cf. Rives, "Human Sacrifice among Pagans and Christians," p. 65.

21. That is, an "Agape Feast" of Christian or brotherly love; the original term is related to other terms for love and affection in Greek. See Jude, vol. 12, and 1 Corinthians 11:17–33.

22. Cohn, *Europe's Inner Demons,* pp. 5–12. Weirdly enough, for a number of years, Karl Marx himself was convinced that early Christians performed ritual murder and cannibalism! Cf. Cohn, pp. 14–15.

23. Rives, "Human Sacrifice among Pagans and Christians," p. 65, and n. 2.

24. Cohn, *Europe's Inner Demons*, p. 3.

25. Eusebius, *The History of the Church from Christ to Constantine*, trans. G. A. Williamson (New York: New York University Press, 1966), Book 5, sect. 1, pp. 201–202.

26. "Wergeld," literally "man-money," is the amount required of a defendant (and his extended family) if found guilty of murder. The earliest manuscripts of the *Lex Salica* date from the fifth or sixth century A.D. and are already partially Christianized. "Pactus Legis Salicae," XIX, 1, in *The Laws of the Salian Franks*, trans. Katherine Fischer Drew (Philadelphia: University of Pennsylvania Press, 1991), p. 83.

27. "Pactus Legis Salicae," LXIV, 3, in *The Laws of the Salian Franks*, p. 125. The Germanic belief that witches were cannibals who should be punished by being eaten was mentioned in Carolingian law as well.

28. "Pactus Legis Salicae," XIX, 2–4, in *The Laws of the Salian Franks*, p. 84.

29. "Pactus Legis Salicae," LXIV, 1, in *The Laws of the Salian Franks*, p. 125.

30. "Pactus Legis Salicae," LXIV, 2, in *The Laws of the Salian Franks*, p. 125. Merely calling someone a "prostitute" (and not proving it) cost 45 solidi, and calling someone "fox," "rabbit," or "covered in dung" cost three. "Pactus Legis Salicae," XXX, 2–5, p. 94.

31. *Leges Langobardorum*, 376; cited in Cohn, *Europe's Inner Demons*, p. 164.

32. "Canons of a Synod of Patrick, Auxilius, and Iserninus," 16, in John T. McNeill and Helena M. Gamer, ed., *Medieval Handbooks of Penance: A Translation of the Principal* Libri poenitentiales *and Selections from Related Documents* (New York: Columbia University Press, 1990), p. 78.

33. "Selections from the Penitential of Silos," sect. XI, 107, in McNeill, *Medieval Handbooks of Penance*, p. 289.

34. "The Burgundian Penitential," 20, in McNeill, *Medieval Handbooks of Penance*, p. 276. Similar penance was required for soothsayers and diviners; see no. 25, pp. 275–276.

35. "The Burgundian Penitential," 36, in McNeill, *Medieval Handbooks of Penance*, p. 277.

36. Flint, *Rise of Magic*, p. 67, citing Giovanni Domenico Mansi, ed., *Sacrorum Conciliorum Nova et Amplissima Collectio*, vol. X, p. 611.

37. Charlemagne's *Capitularies* at Paderborn (A.D. 785), nos. 4, 7; in Patrick J. Geary, ed., *Readings in Medieval History* (Lewiston, N.Y.: Broadview Press, 1989), p. 316.

38. Charlemagne, *Capitularies* at Paderborn (A.D. 785), no. 6; in Geary, *Readings in Medieval History*, p. 316.

39. Agobard, *Liber contra insulsam vulgi opinionem de grandine*, found in J. P. Migne's *Patrologia Latina* (Paris, 1844–1864), 104, as cited by Pierre Riché, *Daily Life in the World of Charlemagne*, trans. Jo Ann McNamara (Philadelphia: University of Pennsylvania Press, 1983), p. 320, n. 7.

40. Riché, *Daily Life in the World of Charlemagne*, p. 183.

41. Riché, *Daily Life in the World of Charlemagne*.

42. Flint, *Rise of Magic*, p. 63, citing Paschasius Radbertus, *Vita Walae*; G. H. Pertz, ed., *Monumenta Germaniae Historica*, vol. 2, Scriptores rerum Sangallensium: annales, chronica et historiae aevi Carolini (Stuttgart: Hierseman; New York: Kraus Reprint Corp., 1963; reprint of Hannoverae, 1829), pp. 553–554.

43. Jeffrey Burton Russell, *Witchcraft in the Middle Ages* (Ithaca, N.Y.: Cornell University Press, 1972), pp. 75–76.

44. An English translation is found in Charles Henry Lea, *Materials toward a History of Witchcraft*, vol. 1, pp. 178–180; which is reprinted in Alan C. Kors and Edward Peters, *Witchcraft in Europe, 1100–1700: A Documentary History* (Philadelphia: University of Philadelphia Press, 1972), pp. 28–31.

45. Lea, *Materials toward a History of Witchcraft*, vol. 1, p. 178; a twelfth-century English penitential goes further: such women should be beaten with birch twigs, as well as driven from the parish. See Bartholomew Iscanus, Bishop of Exeter, *Poenitentiale*, quoted in G. C. Coulton, *Life in the Middle Ages*, vol. 1, p. 35.

46. Guillaume de Lorris and Jean de Meun, *The Romance of the Rose*, trans. Harry W. Robbins, ed. Charles W. Dunn (New York: Dutton, 1962), chap. 85, pp. 391–392, lines 93–120. Robbins gives the Old French line numbers for the chapter as 18299–18606.

47. Philip Schaff, *History of the Christian Church*, vol. V, pt. 1, p. 884.

48. Schaff, *History of the Christian Church*, vol. V, pt. 1, p. 887.

49. M. D. Lambert, *Medieval Heresy: Popular Movements from Bogomil to Hus* (London: Edward Arnold, 1977), pp. 67–91, 151–164; David Christie-Murray, *A History of Heresy* (Oxford: Oxford University Press, 1989), pp. 102–104. In 1254, Reinarius Saccho, a former Cathar leader turned Dominican inquisitor, drew up a convenient list of the Waldensian "heresies" in his *Of the Sects of the Modern Heretics*. Moore, *Birth of Popular Heresy*, pp. 132, 144–145, 153–154.

50. Cohn, *Europe's Inner Demons*, pp. 48–50; Pope Gregory IX, "Vox in Rama" (excerpts), in Kors, *Witchcraft in Europe*, no. 6, pp. 48–49.

51. The ice-cold devil, particularly in sexual liaisons, is much discussed in the witch trials. Toads were often associated with heretics; the thirteenth-century Bishop Luke of Tuy related that, during the burning of one set of heretics, a giant toad leapt into the flames and ripped the tongue of the leader out. The next day, the ashes of the heretic had turned to toads. See Lucae Tudensis Episcopi, *De Altera Vita*, Book III, chap. 15, in James Harvey Robinson, ed., *The Pre-Reformation Period*, in Translations and Reprints from the Original Sources of European History, vol. 3, no. 6 (Philadelphia: University of Pennsylvania Press, 1896), pp. 7–9.

52. Piers Paul Read, *The Templars* (New York: St. Martin's Press, 2000), pp. 266–270; Malcolm Barber, *The New Knighthood: A History of the Order of the Temple* (Cambridge: Cambridge University Press, 1994), pp. 301–310; Cohn, *Europe's Inner Demons*, pp. 88–101.

53. Robert E. Butts, *Witches, Scientists, Philosophers: Essays and Lectures* (Dordrecht: Kluwer Academic Publishers, 2000), p. 22.

54. Pope Alexander IV, *Quod super nonullis* (1258), in Kors, *Witchcraft in Europe*, no. 11, pp. 77–79.

55. Franco Mormando, "Bernardino of Siena, Popular Preacher and Witch-Hunter: A 1426 Witch Trial in Rome," *Fifteenth-Century Studies* 24 (1998): 84–85; also in Levack, ed., *New Perspectives on Witchcraft, Magic and Demonology*, vol. 1: *Demonology, Religion, and Witchcraft*, pp. 130–131.

56. Mormando, "Bernardino of Siena," p. 87.

57. Mormando, "Bernardino of Siena," pp. 93–94, 98–99.

58. Joan was burned at the stake on May 30, 1431, five years after Bernardino's preaching in Rome.

59. Johannes Nider, *Formicarius* (*The Ant Hill*), quoted in G. C. Coulton, *Life in the Middle Ages*, vol. 1, p. 212.

60. The Vulgate calls it the sin "ariolandi" (hariolandi), that is, of soothsayers and fortunetellers.

61. Johannes Nider, *Formicarius*, Book 5, chap. 3; selection trans. George L. Burr, *The Witch-Persecutions*, in *Translations and Reprints from the Original Sources of European History*, vol. 3, no. 4 (Philadelphia: University of Pennsylvania Press, 1897), pp. 6–7. This selection is also reprinted in Kors, *Witchcraft in Europe*, no. 17, pp. 102–104.

62. Nider, *Formicarius*, Book 5, chap. 3; Burr trans., *The Witch-Persecutions*, p. 7.

63. For a detailed analysis of this confrontation, see Eric Wilson, "Institoris at Innsbruck: Heinrich Institoris, the *Summis Desiderantes* and the Brixen Witch-Trial of 1485," in *Popular Religion in Germany and Central Europe, 1400–1800*, ed. Bob Scribner and Trevor Johnson (New York: St. Martin's Press, 1996), 87–100.

64. Burr, trans., *The Witch-Persecutions*, pp. 7–10; also in Kors, *Witchcraft in Europe*, no. 18, pp. 107–112.

65. Burr, *The Witch-Persecutions*, pp. 8–9.

66. Burr, *The Witch-Persecutions*, pp. 8–9.

67. Wilson, "Institoris at Innsbruck," p. 93.

68. Wilson, "Institoris at Innsbruck," p. 95.

69. This was a conditional release; the women could still be brought back in on charges of witchcraft later.

70. Wilson, "Institoris at Innsbruck," p. 98.

71. Wolfgang Behringer, "Witchcraft Studies in Austria, Germany and Switzerland," in *Witchcraft in Early Modern Europe: Studies in Culture and Belief*, ed. Jonathan Barry et al. (Cambridge: Cambridge University Press, 1998), p. 83.

72. Wilson, "Institoris at Innsbruck," p. 100.

73. There were a number of Latin editions published and there has been an English translation since the 1920s that has been reprinted by Dover since the 1970s. Heinrich Kramer and James [*sic*] Sprenger, *The Malleus Maleficarum*, trans. Rev. Montague Summers (New York: Dover Publications, 1971).

74. Kramer, *Malleus Maleficarum*, trans. Montague Summers, pp. xliii–xlv. Behringer, "Witchcraft Studies in Austria, Germany and Switzerland," pp. 82–83.

75. Brian P. Levack, *The Witch-Hunt in Early Modern Europe*, 2nd ed. (New York: Longman, 1995), pp. 54–55.

76. Kramer, *Malleus Maleficarum*, Part II, Q. 1, chap. 12; trans. Summers, p. 139.

77. To disbelieve in the possibility of night-flight was manifest heresy; Kramer, *Malleus Maleficarum*, Part II, Q. 1, chap. 3; trans. Summers, p. 104. For sex with the Devil, see Kramer, *Malleus Maleficarum*, Part II, Q. 4; trans. Summers, pp. 109–114.

78. Kramer, *Malleus Maleficarum*, Part I, Q. 1; trans. Summers, pp. 1–11.

79. Kramer, *Malleus Maleficarum*, Part I, Q. 1; trans. Summers, p. 3.

80. Kramer, *Malleus Maleficarum*, Part III, "General and Introductory," trans. Summers, pp. 192–205.

81. On using technicalities, see Kramer, *Malleus Maleficarum*, Part III, Q. 10, trans. Summers, p. 218; on keeping the names of accusers secret, see Part III, Qs. 9–10, trans. Summers, pp. 216–218.

82. Kramer, *Malleus Maleficarum*, Part III, Q. 10, trans. Summers, p. 218.

83. Christina Larner, *Witchcraft and Religion: The Politics of Popular Belief* (Oxford: Blackwell, 1984), chap. 3, pp. 35–67.

84. Kramer, *Malleus Maleficarum*, Part II, Q. 1, chap. 13; trans. Summers, p. 141.

85. Kramer, *Malleus Maleficarum*, Part I, Q. 6; trans. Summers, pp. 41–48.

86. Kramer, *Malleus Maleficarum*, Part I, Q. 6; trans. Summers, p. 43.

87. Kramer, *Malleus Maleficarum*, Part II, Q. 1, chap. 7, trans. Summers, pp. 121–122. For a powerful article on this subject, see Walter Stephens, "Witches Who Steal Penises: Impotence and Illusion in *Malleus maleficarum*," *Journal of Medieval and Early Modern Studies* 28 (Fall 1998): 495–529. For its context in world folklore, see Moira Smith, "The Flying Phallus and the Laughing Inquisitor: Penis Theft in the *Malleus Maleficarum*," *Journal of Folklore Research* 39 (Jan.–Apr. 2002): 85–119.

88. Kramer, *Malleus Maleficarum*, Part II, Q. 1, chap. 7, trans. Summers, p. 121.

89. For example, see Francesco Maria Guazzo, *Compendium Maleficarum, the Montague Summers Edition*, trans. E. A. Ashwin (London: John Rodker, 1929; reprinted, slightly altered ed., New York: Dover, 1988), Book II, chap. 8, pp. 105–111.

90. In the Matthew Hopkins trials in England, for example, Anne West was said to have drowned a boy through witchcraft, and others were accused of much the same. Jim Sharpe, "The Devil in East Anglia: The Matthew Hopkins Trials Reconsidered," in Barry et al., ed. *Witchcraft in Early Modern Europe: Studies in Culture and Belief,* p. 241.

91. Sharpe, "The Devil in East Anglia: The Matthew Hopkins Trials Reconsidered," p. 242.

92. Kramer spills much ink on this; for some samples, see *Malleus Maleficarum,* Part I, Qs. 8 and 11; Part II, Q. 1, chaps. 6, 7, 11–14, etc.

93. The 1.8 million estimate comes from Henri Boguet, *An Examen of Witches,* pp. xxii, xxiv, as cited in Levack, *The Witch-Hunt in Early Modern Europe,* 2nd ed., p. 26, n. 53. For King James's dire concerns, see the Preface of his *Daemonologie,* in *Daemonologie (1597); Newes from Scotland: Declaring the Damnable Life and Death of 'Doctor' Fian, a Notable Sorcerer Who Was Burned at Edenbrough in Ianuary Last (1591),* ed. G. B. Harrison (London: Bodley Head, btwn. 1922–1926; reprint, New York: Barnes & Noble, 1966), p. [xi].

94. Guazzo, *Compendium Maleficarum, the Montague Summers Edition,* Book I, chap. 12, p. 36.

95. Kramer, *Malleus Maleficarum*, Part II, Q. 1, chap. 3, trans. Summers, pp. 104–109. Guazzo, *Compendium Maleficarum, the Montague Summers Edition,* Book I, chap. 12, pp. 33–50.

96. Guazzo, *Compendium Maleficarum, the Montague Summers Edition,* Book II, chap. 15, p. 135.

97. Nicolas Remy, *Demonolatry,* Book I, chap. 14, trans. E. A. Ashwin; ed. Montague Summers (London: J. Rodker, 1930).

98. Guazzo, *Compendium Maleficarum, the Montague Summers Edition,* Book I, chap. 6, pp. 13–19.

99. Guazzo, *Compendium Maleficarum,* Book I, chap. 6, p. 15.

100. Reminiscent of the famous staircase scene in the movie *The Exorcist.* Guazzo, *Compendium Maleficarum, the Montague Summers Edition,* Book I, chap. 12, p. 35.

101. Guazzo, *Compendium Maleficarum, the Montague Summers Edition,* Book I, chap. 12, pp. 37–39.

102. It was said to be as painful as childbirth. For the coldness, see Guazzo, *Compendium Maleficarum, the Montague Summers Edition,* Book II, chap. 15, p. 136; also

Sharpe, "The Devil in East Anglia: The Matthew Hopkins Trials Reconsidered," pp. 246–247.

103. In the twentieth century, the bizarre Montague Summers believed that there was a giant, conspiratorial group of devil worshippers known as witches; that is, the demonologists were correct. The equally curious Egyptologist, Margaret Murray, believed that a pan-European pagan fertility cult had been misidentified as a diabolical witch cult by early modern judges. Although there is no historical evidence for Murray's position, it is still espoused by some in the neo-pagan and Wiccan communities. See Levack, *The Witch-Hunt in Early Modern Europe*, 2nd ed., pp. 18–20.

104. C. R. Unsworth, "Witchcraft Beliefs and Criminal Procedure in Early Modern England," in *Legal Record and Historical Reality*, ed. Thomas Watkin (London: Hambledon, 1989), pp. 80–81.

105. Unsworth, "Witchcraft Beliefs and Criminal Procedure in Early Modern England," p. 82; Levack, *New Perspectives*, vol. 3, p. 12; Briggs, *Witches and Neighbors*, pp. 29–31.

106. Sharpe, "The Devil in East Anglia: The Matthew Hopkins Trials Reconsidered," p. 249.

107. Aldous Huxley, *The Devils of Loudon* (New York: Harper & Row, 1952).

108. Few may have realized that there are Notary Publics in Hell. For a copy of this pact, see Rossell Hope Robbins, *The Encyclopedia of Witchcraft and Demonology* (New York: Crown Publishers, 1974), pp. 375–379.

109. Note that the "Devil's mark" and "pricking" were later developments of the witchcraft trials and only became common to the trials after 1560. The *Malleus* (1486) did not mention them. Levack, *The Witch-Hunt in Early Modern Europe*, 2nd ed., pp. 51, 54.

110. Martin Del Rio, *Disquisitionum Magicarum*, Book. 5, sect. 4, no. 28, quoted in *The Occult in Early Modern Europe: A Documentary History*, ed. and trans. P. G. Maxwell-Stuart (New York: St. Martin's Press, 1999), no. 57, p. 187. Eight years later, Guazzo uses almost these exact words to describe the shape of these Devil's marks and the places on their body. Guazzo, *Compendium Maleficarum, the Montague Summers Edition*, Book I, chap. 6, p. 15, which does not mention Del Rio, but does cite earlier works on the Devil's mark, including Lambert Daneau (*Les sorciers*, 1574), Jean Bodin (*De la démonomanie des sorciers*, 1587), and John George Gödelmann (*Tractatus de magis, veneficis et lamiis*, circa 1590).

111. David Harley, "Historians as Demonologists: The Myth of the Midwife-Witch," *Social History of Medicine* 3, no. 1 (Apr. 1990): 24–26; Linda A. Pollock, "Childbearing and Female Bonding in Early Modern England," *Social History* 22 (Oct. 1997): 301.

112. Henry Charles Lea noted long ago that insensitivity to pain is common in some mental disorders. And, by all accounts, the twentieth-century Dutchman and "fakir," Mirin Dajo, could have a rapier-like blade thrust completely through his torso with little ill effect or loss of blood. He was closely studied by Swiss physicians who took X-rays of him while impaled. Unfortunately he died after swallowing a fourteen-inch sharpened rod. Believe it, or not. See Milbourne Christopher, *Mediums, Mystics, and the Occult* (New York: Thomas Y. Crowell, 1975), pp. 150–153. For Lea's note, see *Materials toward a History of Witchcraft*, vol. 3, p. 1043.

113. King James, for example, argued that the mark is always present and always

insensitive to pain. King James I of England, *Daemonologie,* Book II, chaps. 2 and 3, in *Daemonologie (1597),* ed. G. B. Harrison, pp. 33, 36.

114. Levack, *The Witch-Hunt in Early Modern Europe,* 2nd ed., pp. 180–181.

115. Brian P. Levack, "The Great Scottish Witch-Hunt of 1661–1662," *Journal of British Studies* 20, no. 1 (Autumn 1980): 90.

116. Levack, "The Great Scottish Witch-hunt of 1661–1662," pp. 99–108.

117. Trials by ordeal were quite ancient, stretching back to Anglo-Saxon and Germanic times. They were outlawed in England by Henry III, because they were seen to tempt God. For an example of the Anglo-Saxon use of the ordeal, see *Athelstan's Ordinance,* 6–6.1, in Dorothy Whitelock, ed., *English Historical Documents, c. 500–1042,* 2nd ed. (New York: Oxford University Press, 1979), pp. 417–418; Robbins, *The Encyclopedia of Witchcraft and Demonology,* pp. 492–494.

118. King James I, *Daemonologie,* Book III, chap. 6, in *Daemonologie (1597),* ed. G. B. Harrison, pp. 80–81.

119. Kramer, *Malleus Maleficarum,* Part III, Second Head, Q. 15; trans. Summers, p. 227.

120. Larner, *Witchcraft and Religion: The Politics of Popular Belief,* chap. 3, pp. 35–67.

121. Alfred Soman, "The Parlement of Paris and the Great Witch Hunt (1565–1640)," *Sixteenth Century Journal* 9, no. 2 (1978): 40–42.

122. Robin Briggs, *Witches and Neighbors: The Social and Cultural Context of European Witchcraft* (New York: Penguin Books, 1996), p. 360.

123. Briggs, *Witches and Neighbors,* p. 361.

124. Briggs, *Witches and Neighbors,* p. 362.

125. Andrea Dworkin, "Gynocide: The Witches," chap. 7 in *Women Hating* (New York: Dutton, 1974); Mary Daly, *Gyn/Ecology: The Metaethics of Radical Feminism* (Boston: Beacon Press, 1978); earlier, Daly stated that the witch-hunts were "the selective total destruction of a large number of women," in her *Beyond God the Father: Toward a Philosophy of Women's Liberation* (1973; Boston: Beacon Press, 1985), p. 63. Carolyn Merchant, *The Death of Nature: Women, Ecology, and the Scientific Revolution—A Feminist Reappraisal of the Scientific Revolution* (San Francisco: Harper & Row, 1980). In a recent article, Marianne Hester states that "the witch-hunts were part of, and one example of, the ongoing mechanisms for social control of women within a general context of social change and the reconstruction of a patriarchal society." Marianne Hester, "Patriarchal Reconstruction and Witch-Hunting," in Barry et al., ed., *Witchcraft in Early Modern Europe: Studies in Culture and Belief,* pp. 288–289. The website of "Gendercide Watch" uses the witch-hunts as a case study; see <http://www.gendercide.org/case_witchhunts.html>, accessed July 14, 2002.

126. Levack, *New Perspectives on Witchcraft, Magic and Demonology,* vol. 4: *Gender and Witchcraft,* introduction, p. vii; and Larner, *Witchcraft and Religion,* p. 87.

127. See Richard M. Golden, "Satan in Europe: The Geography of the Witch-Hunts," in *Changing Identities in Early Modern France,* ed. Michael Wolfe (Durham, N.C.: Duke University Press, 1997), pp. 229–230; also in Levack, ed., *New Perspectives on Witchcraft, Magic and Demonology,* vol. 2: *Witchcraft in Continental Europe,* pp. 15–16.

128. Larner, *Witchcraft and Religion,* p. 87.

129. Robin Briggs, "Women as Victims? Witches, Judges and the Community,"

French History 5 (1991): 442; Golden, *Satan in Europe,* pp. 229, 232–235. The total number of executed witches in Russia was relatively small—at least in official trials—probably no more than a few hundred. Golden, "Satan in Europe," pp. 234–235.

130. Marko Nenonen, " 'Envious Are All the People, Witches Watch at Every Gate': Finnish Witches and Witch Trials in the 17th Century," *Scandinavian Journal of History* 18 (1993): 85; also in Levack, *New Perspectives on Witchcraft, Magic and Demonology,* vol. 2: *Witchcraft in Continental Europe,* p. 84.

131. Assuming the number executed was ten thousand and the population in 1600, one million, stayed roughly the same. Golden, *Satan in Europe,* pp. 222, 234.

132. Golden calculates that in the Pays de Vaud region, 34 percent were male, while in the Jura region, 40 percent were male. Golden, *Satan in Europe,* p. 222.

133. William Monter, "Toads and Eucharists: The Male Witches of Normandy, 1564–1660," *French Historical Studies* 20 (Autumn 1997): 563–564.

134. Monter, "Toads and Eucharists," pp. 563–564.

135. Stuart Clark, "The 'Gendering' of Witchcraft in French Demonology: Misogyny or Polarity?" *French History* 5 (1991): 426–437; also in Levack, *New Perspectives on Witchcraft, Magic and Demonology,* vol. 4: *Gender and Witchcraft,* pp. 54–65.

136. Stuart Clark, *Thinking with Demons: The Idea of Witchcraft in Early Modern Europe* (Oxford: Oxford University Press, 1997), pp. 130–133.

137. In the United States in 1999, women accounted for about 14 percent of all incarcerated violent offenders; thus, men for 86 percent. See Lawrence A. Greenfield and Tracy L. Snell, *Women Offenders: Bureau of Justice Statistics, Special Report,* NCJ 175688 (U.S. Department of Justice, Office of Justice Programs, Dec. 1999), p. 1.

138. Over half of those accused were older than fifty, according to Levack, *The Witch-Hunt in Early Modern Europe,* 2nd ed., pp. 141–142.

139. In England, only about 10 percent of the population in the 1690s was over sixty years old. J. A. Sharpe, *Early Modern England: A Social History, 1550–1760,* 2nd ed. (London: Arnold, 1997), p. 41.

140. Jonathan Barry, "Introduction: Keith Thomas and the Problem of Witchcraft," in Barry et al., eds., *Witchcraft in Early Modern Europe: Studies in Culture and Belief,* p. 37; Briggs, *Witches and Neighbors,* pp. 143–157.

141. Levack, *The Witch-Hunt in Early Modern Europe,* 2nd ed., pp. 145–146.

142. Barry, introduction, in Barry et al., eds., *Witchcraft in Early Modern Europe,* pp. 1–12.

143. Kramer, *Malleus Maleficarum,* Part I, Q. 11, and Part II, Q. 1, chap. 13; trans. Summers, pp. 66, 140–144.

144. E. A. Wrigley, *Population and History* (New York: World University Library, 1969), p. 125.

145. See especially, David Harley, "Historians as Demonologists: The Myth of the Midwife-Witch," *Social History of Medicine* 3 (1990): 1–26; also in Levack, *New Perspectives on Witchcraft, Magic and Demonology,* vol. 5: *Witchcraft, Healing, and Popular Diseases,* pp. 49–74. See also Briggs, *Witches and Neighbors,* pp. 76–78.

146. Briggs, *Witches and Neighbors,* pp. 121–125; Robin Briggs, "Women as Victims? Witches, Judges, and the Community," *French History* 5 (1991): 442–443; also in Levack, *New Perspectives on Witchcraft, Magic and Demonology,* vol. 4: *Gender and Witchcraft,* pp. 44–45; Willem de Blécourt, "Witch Doctors, Soothsayers and Priests: On Cunning Folk in European Historiography and Tradition," *Social History* 19, no. 3 (1994): 285–

303; also in Levack, *New Perspectives on Witchcraft, Magic and Demonology*, vol. 5: *Witchcraft, Healing, and Popular Diseases*, pp. 75–93.

147. Willem de Blécourt, "Witch Doctors, Soothsayers and Priests," p. 291, also in Levack, *New Perspectives on Witchcraft, Magic and Demonology*, vol. 5: *Witchcraft, Healing, and Popular Diseases*, p. 81. Blécourt cites Alan Macfarlane, *Witchcraft in Tudor and Stuart England: A Regional and Comparative Study* (London: Routledge & Kegan Paul, 1970), p. 128.

148. Much later, the boy admitted he had made the whole thing up because he wanted to avoid a beating—he had been playing when he was supposed to bring the cows home. See J. T. Swain, "The Lancashire Witch Trials of 1612 and 1634 and the Economics of Witchcraft," *Northern History* 30 (1994): 68–69; also in Levack, *New Perspectives on Witchcraft, Magic and Demonology*, vol. 3: *Witchcraft in the British Isles and New England*, pp. 80–81.

149. Holmes, "Women: Witnesses and Witches," in Levack, vol. 4: *Gender and Witchcraft*, pp. 140–141; Robbins, *The Encyclopedia of Witchcraft and Demonology*, pp. 381–382; Wallace Notestein, *A History of Witchcraft in England from 1558 to 1718* (New York: Thomas Y. Crowell, 1968), pp. 151–154.

150. Clive Holmes, "Women: Witnesses and Witches," *Past and Present* 140 (1993): 47–48; also in Levack, *New Perspectives on Witchcraft, Magic and Demonology*, vol. 4: *Gender and Witchcraft*, pp. 121–122.

151. Holmes, "Women: Witnesses and Witches," in Levack, vol. 4, *Gender and Witchcraft*, pp. 123–124.

152. Larner, *Witchcraft and Religion*, p. 86. See also Julian Goodare, "Women and the Witch-Hunt in Scotland," *Social History* 23 (Oct. 1998): 288–290.

153. Louise Jackson, "Witches, Wives, and Mothers: Witchcraft Persecutions and Women's Confessions in Seventeenth-Century England," *Women's History Review* 4 (1995): 63–83; also in Levack, *New Perspectives on Witchcraft, Magic and Demonology*, vol. 4: *Gender and Witchcraft*, pp. 257–277.

154. Golden, *Satan in Europe*, pp. 230–231; Bengt Ankarloo, "Sweden: The Mass Burnings (1668–1676)," in *Early Modern European Witchcraft*, ed. Bengt Ankarloo and Gustav Henningsen (Oxford: Oxford University Press, 1990), pp. 285–317; also in Levack, *New Perspectives on Witchcraft, Magic and Demonology*, vol. 2: *Witchcraft in Continental Europe*, pp. 35–68.

155. Behringer, "Witchcraft Studies in Austria, Germany and Switzerland," p. 84; P. G. Maxwell-Stuart, *Witchcraft in Europe and the New World, 1400–1800* (New York: Palgrave, 2001), p. 58.

156. H. R. Trevor-Roper, *The European Witch-Craze of the Sixteenth and Seventeenth Centuries, and Other Essays* (New York: Harper & Row, 1967), p. 152. Guazzo also believed witchcraft ran in families. Guazzo, *Compendium Maleficarum, the Montague Summers Edition*, Book II, chap. 6, pp. 96–98.

157. Guazzo, *Compendium Maleficarum, the Montague Summers Edition*, Book I, chap. VII, p. 20. Guazzo claims to have gotten the story from Rémy.

158. Wolfgang Behringer, *Witchcraft Persecutions in Bavaria: Popular Magic, Religious Zealotry and Reason of State in Early Modern Europe* (Cambridge: Cambridge University Press, 1997), pp. 336–337.

159. In a later, but smaller, case in the Prince-Bishopric of Freising (1720–1722), the numbers are even more bizarre. There, three middle-aged women and eight young

men were burned as witches, but all the old women were set free! By this time, the local witch stereotype had apparently shifted toward boy-sorcerer beggars. Behringer, *Witchcraft Persecutions in Bavaria*, pp. 337–338.

160. Behringer, *Witchcraft Persecutions in Bavaria*, p. 337, n. 53.

161. Letter from the Chancellor of the Prince-Bishop of Würzburg to a friend, August of 1629. *The Witch-Persecution at Würzburg*, From *Codex german. 1254* of the Munich library, as printed by Leitschuh, *Beiträge zur Geschichte des Hexenwesens in Franken*, selection trans. George L. Burr, *The Witch-Persecutions*, in *Translations and Reprints from the Original Sources of European History*, vol. 3, no. 4 (Philadelphia: University of Pennsylvania Press, 1897), pp. 28–29. This selection is also reprinted in Kors, *Witchcraft in Europe*, no. 29, pp. 251–252.

162. Robert S. Walinski-Kiehl, "The Devil's Children: Child Witch-Trials in Early Modern Germany," *Continuity and Change* 11, no. 2 (1996): 173–174; Behringer, *Witchcraft Persecutions in Bavaria*, p. 165.

163. Michael Kunze's *Highroad to the Stake* is a meticulous, yet movingly written, account of the Pappenheimer family. The following pages give the specifics mentioned here. Michael Kunze, *Highroad to the Stake: A Tale of Witchcraft*, trans. William E. Yuill (Chicago: University of Chicago Press, 1987), pp. 181–183, 219, 406–415.

164. For the significance of infant hands and "thieves' candles," see Butts, *Witches, Scientists, Philosophers*, p. 13.

165. "It is computed from historical records that nine millions of persons were put to death for witchcraft," she states, but she gives no hint as to who calculated this figure. Gage's work is an entertaining compilation of nearly every anti-clerical legend ever concocted; she tells poignant stories (some true) of the witch burnings, mixed with wild, unsubstantiated tales—all presented as fact. Her reading on the witch trials sounds surprisingly modern: "When for 'witches' we read 'women,' we gain fuller comprehension of the cruelties inflicted by the church" (p. 291). Matilda Joslyn Gage, *Woman, Church and State: A Historical Account of the Status of Woman through the Christian Ages, with Reminiscences of the Matriarchate*, 2nd ed. (New York: Truth Seeker Co., 1893; reprinted, Salem, N.H.: Ayer Co., 1985), p. 247.

166. Gerald B. Gardner, *The Meaning of Witchcraft* (Lakemont, Ga.: Copple House Books, 1959), p. 263; Starhawk, *The Spiral Dance: A Rebirth of the Ancient Religion of the Goddess* (New York: Harper & Row, 1979), p. 5.

167. Andrea Dworkin, "What Were Those Witches Really Brewing?" *MS* 2 (1974): 52, as cited in Golden, "Satan in Europe," p. 220, table 1.

168. Levack, *The Witch-Hunt in Early Modern Europe*, 2nd ed., pp. 21–25; Golden, "Satan in Europe," pp. 220–221.

169. A woman in England, for example, was at least one thousand times *more* likely to die in childbirth and twenty times more likely to accidentally drown than to be burned as a witch. It is estimated that, in seventeenth-century England, for every one thousand births, fourteen to eighteen mothers died during or after childbirth. That is, fourteen thousand deaths per million pregnancies. And, in pre-industrial Europe, the average woman would have had five to six births to look forward to over her lifetime. For maternal mortality, see E. A. Wrigley and R. S. Schofield, "English Population History from Family Reconstitution: Summary Results 1600–1799," *Population Studies* 37, no. 2 (July 1983): 181–183. For the average number of births, see Flinn, *The European Demographic System, 1500–1820*, p. 33. In London in the 1630s, the likelihood of accidentally drowning was 143 per million per year. P. E. H. Hair, "Deaths from Violence

in Britain: A Tentative Secular Survey," *Population Studies* 25 (1971): 13, n. 50. The probability of witch execution was much lower, as the following note suggests.

170. Here we assume the population of Europe to be ninety million (a low estimate) in 1600 and a 50:50 gender ratio. If one hundred thousand people (the high figure for most scholars) were executed and 80 percent of these were women, then the probability of a European woman being executed between 1450 and 1750 was about six in one million (one in 166,666). Allowing for intense periods of persecution increases the odds in particular localities, but for the *average woman* (a bloodless concept, to be sure), the prospect of being burned as a witch was not great.

171. According to the FBI, the chance of being murdered in the United States during the year 2000 was fifty-five in one million. Assuming roughly half the victims were female, this is nearly five times the figure given above (six in one million) for witch-hunts. See Federal Bureau of Investigation and U.S. Department of Justice, *Crime in the United States, 2000: Uniform Crime Reports*, Printed Annually (Washington, D.C.: U.S. Government Printing Office, 2001), p. 14.

172. Anne Llewellyn Barstow, "On Studying Witchcraft as Women's History: A Historiography of the European Witch Persecutions," *Journal of Feminist Studies in Religion* 4 (1988): 7, n. 1; also in Levack, *New Perspectives on Witchcraft, Magic and Demonology*, vol. 4: *Gender and Witchcraft*, p. 1, n. 1.

173. Over a 130-year period in Cheshire, for example, thirty-three women were hanged for infanticide, compared to eleven people (men and women) for witchcraft. J. A. Sharpe, *Crime in Early Modern England, 1550–1750* (London: Longman, 1984), p. 61. Briggs takes up this question in his article " 'Many Reasons Why': Witchcraft and the Problem of Multiple Explanation," in Barry et al., *Witchcraft in Early Modern Europe*, p. 55.

174. Timothy Curtis and J. A. Sharpe, "The Criminal Past: Crime in Tudor and Stuart England," *History Today* 38, no. 2 (Feb. 1988): 28.

175. Rossell Hope Robbins notes that there were 82 known witch executions and 535 indictments during Elizabeth's rule, *The Encyclopedia of Witchcraft and Demonology*, p. 158.

176. J. A. Sharpe, "Witches and Persecuting Societies," *Journal of Historical Sociology* 3, no. 1 (Mar. 1990), pp. 82–83. As Levack notes, over the last century "the witch-hunt has been attributed, in whole or in large part, to the Reformation, the Counter-Reformation, the Inquisition, the use of judicial torture, the wars of religion, the religious zeal of the clergy, the rise of the modern state, the development of capitalism, the widespread use of narcotics, changes in medical thought, social and cultural conflict, an attempt to wipe out paganism, the need of the ruling class to distract the masses, opposition to birth control, the spread of syphilis, and the hatred of women." Levack, *The Witch-Hunt in Early Modern Europe*, 2nd ed., pp. 2–3.

177. Barry, introduction, in Barry et al., *Witchcraft in Early Modern Europe*, p. 13.

178. Barry, "Introduction: Keith Thomas and the Problem of Witchcraft," pp. 11–13; J. A. Sharpe, *Crime in Early Modern England, 1550–1750* (London; New York: Longman, 1984), p. 53.

179. Barry, "Introduction: Keith Thomas and the Problem of Witchcraft," pp. 13–14; Briggs, *Witches and Neighbors*, pp. 137–168.

180. Letter from the Chancellor of the Prince-Bishop of Würzburg to a friend, August of 1629, in Burr, *The Witch-Persecutions*, pp. 28–29.

181. Golden, "Satan in Europe," pp. 217, 236–237.

182. Golden, "Satan in Europe," p. 221.

183. See Golden, "Satan in Europe," table 2, p. 234.

184. Behringer, "Witchcraft Studies in Austria, Germany and Switzerland," pp. 85–86.

185. Two Prince-Bishops of Bamberg, fifteen hundred; Two Prince-Bishops of Würzburg, twelve hundred; Three Prince-Bishops of Mainz, eighteen hundred. Behringer, "Witchcraft Studies in Austria, Germany and Switzerland," pp. 85–86.

186. This is reflected in Ankarloo and Henningsen, eds., *Early Modern Witchcraft: Centres and Peripheries;* see also Golden, "Satan in Europe," p. 234.

187. Frederick C. Drake, "Witchcraft in the American Colonies, 1647–62," *American Quarterly* 20 (1968): 694–725. These were almost entirely individual cases.

188. The New England population in 1690 was approximately 86,000, and that of the American colonies as a whole was 196,000, which increased to 240,000 by 1700. See Michael R. Haines and Richard H. Steckel, eds., *A Population History of North America* (Cambridge: Cambridge University Press, 2000), table 5.1, p. 151. Iceland, which executed a total of at least 22 witches, had a population in 1600 of 50,000. Thus, Iceland was executing witches at about four times the rate of the Colonies. See Golden, "Satan in Europe," pp. 229, 234.

189. Nenonen, " 'Envious Are All the People, Witches Watch at Every Gate,' " p. 85; also in Levack, ed., *New Perspectives on Witchcraft, Magic and Demonology*, vol. 2: *Witchcraft in Continental Europe*, p. 77.

190. This response is best exemplified by the caustically anti-religious work of Andrew Dickson White. In 1896, White completed his work on the warfare of science and religion; chapter subheadings such as "The Invasion of Skepticism" and "Theological Efforts at Compromise: The Final Victory of Science," reveal his stance. For one of the major sections on witchcraft and demonology, see White, *A History of the Warfare of Science and Theology in Christendom*, abridged (New York: Free Press, 1965), pp. 240–281.

191. For the compatibility of science, demonology, and witchcraft in the Scientific Revolution, see Clark, *Thinking with Demons*, sect. II, "Science," and especially chap. 19, "Witchcraft and the Scientific Revolution," pp. 294–311. For the encouragement of the belief in witchcraft by Robert Boyle and Joseph Glanvill (a central figure in the Royal Society) see Clark, *Thinking with Demons*, pp. 296–298, and Richard Olson, "Spirits, Witches, and Science: Why the Rise of Science Encouraged Belief in the Supernatural in 17th-Century England," *Skeptic* 1, no. 4 (Winter 1992): 34–43. See also Clark, "The Scientific Status of Demonology," in *Occult and Scientific Mentalities in the Renaissance*, ed. Brian Vickers (Cambridge: Cambridge University Press, 1984), pp. 351–374; also in Levack, *Articles on Witchcraft, Magic and Demonology*, vol. 4: *The Literature of Witchcraft* (New York: Garland, 1992), pp. 313–336.

192. Clark, *Thinking with Demons*, pp. 296–298.

193. Cited by Clark, *Thinking with Demons*, p. 297, n. 8, to be found in J[oseph] G[lanvill], *A Blow at Modern Sadducism in Philosophical Considerations about Witchcraft* (London, 1668), p. 93. Clear parallels can be drawn with the scientific investigation of Spiritualism in the nineteenth and twentieth centuries, and of psi phenomena, UFOs, and near-death experiences in the twentieth and twenty-first centuries.

194. Clark, *Thinking with Demons*, pp. 304–305.

195. For the English Civil War, see Diane Purkiss, "Desire and Its Deformities: Fantasies of Witchcraft in the English Civil War," *Journal of Medieval and Early Modern*

Studies 27 (1997): 103–106. See also Peter Elmer, " 'Saints or Sorcerers': Quakerism, Demonology and the Decline of Witchcraft in Seventeenth-Century England," p. 166, and Ian Bostridge's "Witchcraft Repealed," pp. 309–334, both in Barry et al., eds., *Witchcraft in Early Modern Europe: Studies in Culture and Belief.*

196. Briggs, *Witches and Neighbors,* pp. 388–389. Jonathan L. Pearl, *The Crime of Crimes: Demonology and Politics in France, 1560–1620* (Waterloo, Ont.: Wilfrid Laurier University Press, 1999), chap. 3: "Politics and Demon Possession," pp. 41–58; Clark, *Thinking with Demons,* pp. 390–397; Anita M. Walker and Edmund H. Dickerman's " 'A Woman under the Influence': A Case of Alleged Possession in Sixteenth-Century France," *Sixteenth Century Journal* 22 (1991): 535–554; D. P. Walker, *Unclean Spirit: Possession and Exorcism in France and England in the Late Sixteenth and Early Seventeenth Centuries* (Philadelphia: University of Pennsylvania Press, 1981), pp. 33–42; Briggs, *Witches and Neighbors,* pp. 202–204.

197. Michel Montaigne, *Essais,* Book 3, Essay 11 [On cripples], quoted in Maxwell-Stuart, ed., *The Occult in Early Modern Europe: A Documentary History,* no. 56, pp. 186–187. See also Pearl, *The Crime of Crimes,* pp. 104–106.

198. Ian Bostridge, *Witchcraft and Its Transformations, c.1650–c.1750* (Oxford and New York: Clarendon Press, 1997), p. 158.

199. Emphasis added. John Wesley, *The Works of John Wesley,* ed. Albert C. Outler [et al.], vol. 22: *Journal and Diaries V, 1765–1775* (Nashville: Abingdon Press, 1984–), [after] June 28, 1770, p. 238.

200. John Wesley, *The Works of John Wesley,* ed. Albert C. Outler [et al.], vol. 22, *Journal and Diaries V, 1765–1775* (Nashville: Abingdon Press, 1984–), May 25, 1768 [and the two following days], p. 135.

201. D. P. Walker, *Unclean Spirits: Possession and Exorcism in France and England in the Late Sixteenth and Early Seventeenth Centuries* (Philadelphia: University of Pennsylvania Press, 1981), pp. 66–73; Benjamin Kaplan, "Possessed by the Devil? A Very Public Dispute in Utrecht," *Renaissance Quarterly* 49 (Winter, 1996): 740–741. D. P. Walker, "The Cessation of Miracles," in *Hermeticism and the Renaissance: Intellectual History and the Occult in Early Modern Europe,* ed. Ingrid Merkel and Allen G. Debus (Washington, D.C.: Folger Shakespeare Library; Associated University Presses, 1988), pp. 110–124. See also Reginald Scot's discussion of the cessation of miracles in his *The Discoverie of Witchcraft* first published in 1584. Reginald Scot, *The Discoverie of Witchcraft* (1886; reprint, Totowa, N.J.: Rowman and Littlefield, 1973), Book 8, chaps. 1–6, pp. 125–134.

202. It is not clear that, for Calvin, the cessation of God's miraculous "sign gifts" to Christians would have implied that Satan's "miraculous" activities would have also ceased. In the early modern view, these "miracles" of Satan would be the manipulation of natural laws, and therefore more akin to high technology than biblical miracles. See Calvin's commentary on Mark 16:17, in John Calvin, *Calvin's Commentaries,* vol. 9: *A Harmony of the Gospels* (Lafayette, Ind.: Calvin Publications, [1978?]), p. 590. Walker, *Unclean Spirits,* pp. 72–73. Walker, "The Cessation of Miracles," pp. 116–117.

8. SPIRITS, SCIENCE, AND PSEUDO-SCIENCE IN THE NINETEENTH CENTURY

1. William James, "Review of Human Personality and Its Survival of Bodily Death by F. W. H. Myers," *Proceedings of the Society for Psychical Research* 18 (1903): 23.

2. For the concept of scientism, see Nicholas Rescher, *The Limits of Science* (Berkeley: University of California Press, 1984).

3. William James, *The Varieties of Religious Experience* (New York: Vintage, 1990), p. 440.

4. Plato, *The Republic*, in *The Dialogues of Plato*, trans. Benjamin Jowett, vol. 7 of *Great Books of the Western World* (Chicago: William Benton, 1952), p. 434.

5. Robert Darnton, *Mesmerism and the End of the Enlightenment in France* (Cambridge, Mass.: Harvard University Press, 1968), p. 23. Much of the discussion of Mesmerism is based on Darnton's delightful book and two others: Frank Podmore, *From Mesmer to Christian Science: A Short History of Mental Healing* (New Hyde Park, N.Y.: University Books, 1963), and the introduction to Adam Crabtree, *Animal Magnetism, Early Hypnotism, and Psychical Research, 1766–1925: An Annotated Bibliography* (White Plains, N.Y.: Krause International Publications, 1988).

6. Frank Podmore, *From Mesmer to Christian Science*, pp. 135–137.

7. Podmore, *From Mesmer to Christian Science*, pp. 137–140.

8. Thomas Huxley, *Science and the Hebrew Tradition* (New York: D. Appleton, 1903), p. 10.

9. As quoted in Marion Mainwaring's " 'Phys/Phre'—Why not to Take Each Other at Face Value," *Smithsonian* 11 (Nov. 1980): 202.

10. David de Giustino, *Conquest of Mind: Phrenology and Victorian Social Thought* (London: Croom Helm, 1975), pp. 219–222.

11. De Giustino, *Conquest of Mind*, p. 25.

12. Arthur Conan Doyle, "The Psychic Question As I See It," in Trevor H. Hall, *Sherlock Holmes and His Creator* (London: Duckworth, 1978), p. 95.

13. Quoted in Reuben Briggs Davenport, *The Death-Blow to Spiritualism: Being the True Story of the Fox Sisters, as Revealed by Authority of Margaret Fox Kane and Catherine Fox Jencken* (New York: Dillingham, 1888; reprint, New York: Amo Press, 1976), p. 57.

14. Cited in E. E. Fournier, *The Life of Sir William Crookes* (New York: D. Appleton and Co., 1924), pp. 191–193.

15. See Mary Farrell Bednarowski, "Women in Occult America," in *The Occult in America*, pp. 177–195.

16. Trevor Hall, *Sherlock Holmes and His Creator* (London: Duckworth, 1978), p. 114.

17. Hall, *Sherlock Holmes and His Creator*, p. 114.

18. For Houdini's side of the story, see his *Magician among the Spirits* (New York: Harper and Bros., 1924), pp. 150–158. For Doyle's side, see his *Our American Adventure* (London: Hodder and Stoughton, n.d.).

19. Doyle, *Our American Adventure*, pp. 130–131.

20. Quoted in Christopher Milbourne, *Mediums, Mystics and the Occult* (New York: Thomas Y. Crowell, 1975), p. 207.

21. Milbourne, *Mediums, Mystics and the Occult*, p. 221.

22. J. B. Rhine, "One Evening's Observation on the Margery Mediumship," *Journal of Abnormal and Social Psychology* 21 (1927): 401–421.

23. Quoted in an interview with Rhine, Sept. 24, 1970, according to Denis Brian in his *Enchanted Voyager: The Life of J. B. Rhine* (Englewood Cliffs, N.J.: Prentice Hall, 1982), p. 42. Also mentioned in *Spirit Summonings* (Alexandria, Va.: Time-Life, 1989), p. 116. See also the article in the *Boston Herald:* "Conan Doyle Backs Crandons. Famous

English Author in Letter to *Herald* Defends Medium. Answers Attack by Dr. Rhine."
Boston Herald, Mar. 5, 1927, p. 212.

24. Most of the information concerning Lenora Piper is drawn from C. E. M. Hansel, *ESP: A Scientific Evaluation* (New York: Scribner, 1966), pp. 224–227.

9. NEW AGE PRELUDES

1. Quoted in Jerome J. Langford, *Galileo, Science and the Church,* 3rd ed. (Ann Arbor: University of Michigan Press, Ann Arbor Paperbacks, 1992), p. 132.

2. Quoted in Ronald W. Clark, *Einstein: The Life and Times* (New York: World Publishing Co., 1971), pp. 98–99.

3. Marion Meade, *Madame Blavatsky* (New York: Putnam's Sons, 1980), p. 73.

4. Gertrude Marvin Williams, *Priestess of the Occult: Madame Blavatsky* (New York: Alfred A. Knopf, 1946), p. 30.

5. Anne Taylor, *Annie Besant: A Biography* (Oxford: Oxford University Press, 1992), p. 227.

6. Bruce F. Campbell, *Ancient Wisdom Revived: A History of the Theosophical Movement* (Berkeley: University of California Press, 1980), pp. 35–37.

7. Taylor, *Annie Besant,* p. 230.

8. H. P. Blavatsky, *The Secret Doctrine: The Synthesis of Science, Religion, and Philosophy,* vol. 1: *Cosmogenesis* (Pasadena, Calif.: Theosophical University Press, 1970), p. viii.

9. Quoted in Campbell, *Ancient Wisdom Revived,* p. 93.

10. Quoted in Taylor, *Annie Besant,* p. 249.

11. H. P. Blavatsky, *The Secret Doctrine,* vol. 1, pp. 604–605.

12. Shirley Nicholson, *Ancient Wisdom-Modern Insight* (Wheaton, Ill.: Theosophical Publishing House, 1985), p. 5. Following Michel Montaigne, Blavatsky wrote: "I have here made only a nosegay of culled flowers, and have brought nothing of my own but the string that ties them." *The Secret Doctrine,* vol. 1, p. xlvi.

13. Most of the second volume of Blavatsky's *The Secret Doctrine* details the evolution of these seven root races.

14. Blavatsky, *The Secret Doctrine,* vol. 2, p. 266.

15. Blavatsky, *The Secret Doctrine,* vol. 2, pp. 164–165 and 138.

16. Blavatsky, *The Secret Doctrine,* vol. 2, p. 350.

17. H. P. Blavatsky, *An Abridgement of the Secret Doctrine,* ed. Elizabeth Preston and Christmas Humphreys (Wheaton, Ill.: Theosophical Publishing House, 1992), p. 250.

18. But even if you live a good and blameless life, that may not be enough to break out of the karmic cycle. According to some views of karma, one must cease all activity. See the article on "Karma" in *The Encyclopedia of Philosophy,* ed. Paul Edwards (New York: Macmillan, 1967), vol. 4, pp. 325–326.

19. Ray Billington, *Understanding Eastern Philosophy* (London: Routledge, 1997), p. 31.

20. "Castes Conflict in India; Affirmative Action Ignites Protest, Suicides," *The Washington Post,* Oct. 18, 1990, pp. A1, A36–A37.

21. Quoted in Colin Wilson, *Rudolf Steiner: The Man and His Vision* (Wellingborough, Northamptonshire: Aquarian Press, 1985), p. 28.

22. John Keats, "Lamia," in *Complete Poems and Selected Letters*, ed. Clarence Dewitt Thorpe (New York: Odyssey Press, 1935), p. 373.

23. A. N. Whitehead, *Science and the Modern World: Lowell Lectures, 1925* (New York: Mentor Books, 1954), pp. 80, 55.

24. Johann Wolfgang von Goethe, *Theory of Colours*, trans. Charles Lock Eastlake (Cambridge, Mass.: MIT Press, 1970), p. 301.

25. Rudolf Steiner, *The Spiritual Hierarchies and the Physical World: Reality and Illusion* (Hudson, N.Y.: Anthroposophic Press, 1996), p. 38.

26. Steiner, *Spiritual Hierarchies*, p. 175.

27. See Christopher Bamford's Introduction in Steiner's *Spiritual Hierarchies*, pp. 7–14.

28. Steiner, *Spiritual Hierarchies*, p. 96.

29. Rudolf Steiner, *An Outline of Occult Science* (Spring Valley, N.Y.: Anthroposophic Press, 1979), p. 309.

30. Quoted in Steiner, *Spiritual Hierarchies*, pp. 34–35.

31. G. I. Gurdjieff, *Meetings with Remarkable Men* (London: Arcana, 1985), pp. 164–176.

32. G. I. Gurdjieff, *Life Is Real Only Then, When "I Am"* (New York: Triangle Editions, 1975), pp. 8–12.

33. James Webb, *The Harmonious Circle: The Lives and Work of G. I. Gurdjieff, P. D. Ouspensky, and Their Followers* (London: Thames and Hudson, 1980), p. 36. This work informs much of the discussion of Gurdjieff.

34. G. I. Gurdjieff, *Life Is Real Only Then, When "I Am,"* p. 20.

35. Gurdjieff, *Life Is Real Only Then, When "I Am,"* pp. 22–23.

36. Gurdjieff, *Life Is Real Only Then, When "I Am,"* p. 24.

37. Quoted in Webb, *The Harmonious Circle*, p. 241.

38. Quoted in Webb, *The Harmonious Circle*, p. 241.

39. G. I. Gurdjieff, *Life Is Real Only Then, When "I Am,"* p. 44.

40. Quoted in Kathleen Riordan Speeth and Ira Friedlander, *Gurdjieff: Seeker of the Truth* (New York: Harper Colophon Books, 1980), p. 10.

41. Webb, *The Harmonious Circle*, p. 235.

42. Quoted in Webb, *The Harmonious Circle*, p. 235.

43. Sophia Ouspensky as quoted in Kathleen Riordan Speeth, *The Gurdjieff Work* (New York: Pocket Books, 1976), p. 92.

44. Taliesin as quoted in Speeth, *The Gurdjieff Work*, p. 95.

45. Gurdjieff as quoted in P. D. Ouspensky, *In Search of the Miraculous: Fragments of an Unknown Teaching* (New York: Harcourt, Brace & World, 1949), p. 88.

46. Webb, *The Harmonious Circle*, p. 89.

47. P. D. Ouspensky, *The Fourth Way: A Record of Talks and Answers to Questions Based on the Teachings of G. I. Gurdjieff* (London: Routledge and Kegan Paul, 1957), p. 193.

48. Webb, *The Harmonious Circle*, p. 518.

49. Edwyn Bevan as quoted in Webb, *The Harmonious Circle*, p. 256.

50. The book was *Tertium Organum: The Third Canon of Thought* (1912). He felt it extended and advanced in a revolutionary way Francis Bacon's *Novum Organum*, which had done the same to Aristotle's *Organon*.

51. Title page of P. D. Ouspensky, *Tertium Organum: The Third Canon of Thought*, 2nd ed. (London: Kegan Paul, Trench Trubner & Co., 1937).

52. J. H. Reyner, *Ouspensky: The Unsung Genius* (London: George Allen & Unwin, 1981), pp. 34–35.

53. Webb, *The Harmonious Circle*, p. 127.

54. Webb, *The Harmonious Circle*, p. 128.

55. Ouspensky, *In Search of the Miraculous*, p. 4.

56. Ouspensky, *In Search of the Miraculous*, p. 11.

57. Quoted in Webb, *The Harmonious Circle*, p. 99.

58. Linda Henderson, *The Fourth Dimension and Non-Euclidean Geometry in Modern Art* (Princeton, N.J.: Princeton University Press, 1983), p. 29.

59. Henderson, *The Fourth Dimension*, p. 114.

60. Ouspensky, *Tertium Organum*, p. 42.

61. Ouspensky, *Tertium Organum*, p. 231.

62. Ouspensky, *Tertium Organum*, p. 335.

63. Ouspensky, *Tertium Organum*, p. 197.

64. Quoted in Banesh Hoffmann, *Albert Einstein: Creator and Rebel* (New York: A Plume Book, 1972), pp. 257–258.

10. ESP AND PSI PHENOMENA

1. Quoted in Franz Hartmann, *The Life and the Doctrines of Paracelsus*, 4th ed. (New York: Macoy Publishing and Masonic Supply Co., 1932), p. 348.

2. William James, *The Varieties of Religious Experience* (New York: Vintage Books, 1990), p. 349.

3. Arthur S. Berger and Joyce Berger, *The Encyclopedia of Parapsychology and Psychical Research* (New York: Paragon House, 1991), p. 338.

4. Eric Carlton, *The Paranormal: Research and the Quest for Meaning* (Aldershot: Ashgate, 2000), pp. 170–171.

5. William James, "The Will to Believe," in *William James, Writings 1878–1899* (New York: Library of America, 1992), p. 463.

6. David Ray Griffin, "Why Critical Reflection on the Paranormal Is So Important—And So Difficult," in *Critical Reflections on the Paranormal*, ed. Michael Stoeber and Hugo Meynell (Albany: SUNY Press, 1996), p. 91.

7. C. G. Jung, *Memories, Dreams, Reflections* (New York: Pantheon Books, 1963), p. 150. Jung goes on to state that "[w]hat Freud seemed to mean by 'occultism' was virtually everything that philosophy and religion, including the rising contemporary science of parapsychology, had learned about the psyche."

8. Denis Brian, *The Enchanted Voyager: The Life of J. B. Rhine* (Englewood Cliffs, N.J.: Prentice-Hall, 1982), pp. 220, 243, 310, 321–325.

9. J. B. Rhine, *New Frontiers of the Mind: The Story of the Duke Experiments* (New York: Farrar & Rinehart, 1937), p. 79.

10. The most rigorous critic has been C. E. M. Hansel, who worked in Rhine's laboratory at Duke University. See his *ESP: A Scientific Evaluation* (New York: Charles Scribner's Sons, 1956).

11. Susan Blackmore, "Confessions of a Parapsychologist," in *The Fringes of Reason: A Whole Earth Catalog* (New York: Harmony Books, 1989), pp. 70–74.

12. Michael Crichton, "Spoon Bending," in *Travels* (New York: Knopf, 1988), pp. 318–321. The last chapter of this book, "Postscript: Skeptics at Cal Tech," is a stirring defense for the study of paranormal phenomena.

13. James, *The Varieties of Religious Experience,* p. 191.

14. James, *The Varieties of Religious Experience,* p. 224.

15. Griffin, "Why Critical Reflection on the Paranormal Is So Important—and So Difficult," pp. 90, 109.

16. See Fred M. Frohock, *Lives of the Psychics: The Shared Worlds of Science and Mysticism* (Chicago: University of Chicago Press, 2000), p. 69; Dean I. Radin, *The Conscious Universe: The Scientific Truth of Psychic Phenomena* (New York: HarperEdge, 1997), pp. 157–174.

17. Eric Carlton writes, "The key problem is that paranormal phenomena rarely conform to regular patterns. They are often spontaneous, and occur without prior planning or preparation for observational control. Even experimentation is of doubtful use in many cases because repeatability and predictability are by no means certain." *The Paranormal: Research and the Quest for Meaning* (Aldershot, England: Ashgate, 2000), p. 2.

18. Radin, *The Conscious Universe,* pp. 177–178.

19. Carlton, *The Paranormal,* p. 2.

20. Radin, *The Conscious Universe,* p. 134.

21. "Marginal" is the word preferred by Robert G. Jahn and Brenda J. Dunne in their *Margins of Reality: The Role of Consciousness in the Physical World* (San Diego: Harcourt Brace & Co., 1987), pp. x, 48, 79, 102, 301, 324, 337.

22. Frohock, *Lives of the Psychics,* p. 9.

23. William James, "The Last Report: The Final Impressions of a Psychical Researcher," in *William James on Psychical Research,* ed. Gardner Murphy and Robert O. Ballou (New York: Viking Press, 1960), p. 310.

24. Niels Bohr, "Light and Life," *Nature* 131 (1933): 458.

25. William James, "Human Immortality," in *William James, Writings 1878–1899* (New York: Library of America, 1992), p. 1113.

26. James, "Human Immortality," p. 1118.

27. C. G. Jung, *Synchronicity: An Acausal Connecting Principle,* trans. R. F. C. Hull (Princeton, N.J.: Princeton University Press, 1973).

28. C. G. Jung, *The Essential Jung* (Princeton, N.J.: Princeton University Press, 1983), pp. 339–341.

29. James, *The Varieties of Religious Experience,* p. 298.

30. Jung to Carl Seelig, Feb. 25, 1953, in *C. G. Jung Letters,* vol. 2, trans. R. F. C. Hull (Princeton, N.J.: Princeton University Press, 1975), p. 9.

31. See Raymond Y. Chiao, Paul G. Kwiat, and Aephraim M. Steinberg, "Faster than Light?" in *Scientific American* 269, no. 2 (1993): 52–60.

32. See E. R. Dodds, *The Greeks and the Irrational* (Berkeley: University of California Press, 1951).

33. Richard P. Feynman, *QED: The Strange Theory of Light and Matter* (Princeton, N.J.: Princeton University Press, 1985), p. 10.

34. Gustav Fechner, *Elemente der Psychophysik,* vol. 2 (1860), pp. 526–530. Quoted by William James, *William James, Writings, 1878–1899,* pp. 1116–1117.

35. James Jeans, *Physics and Philosophy* (Cambridge: Cambridge University Press, 1943), p. 204.

36. Jung, *Collected Works,* vol. 8, para. 420.

37. Jung, *Collected Works,* para. 417.

38. Quoted in David Seamon and Arthur Zajonc, eds., *Goethe's Way of Science: A Phenomenology of Nature* (Albany: SUNY Press, 1998), p. 4.

39. Quoted by Charles R. Card, "The Emergence of Archetypes in Present-Day Science and Its Significance for a Contemporary Philosophy of Nature," *Dynamical Psychology*, 1996. Available online at <http://www.goertzel.org/dynapsyc/1996/natphil.html>, accessed Oct. 10, 2001.

40. For statements by Max Planck, Niels Bohr, Erwin Schrödinger, Louis de Broglie, Werner Heisenberg, James Jeans, Wolfgang Pauli, and Arthur Eddington, see Jahn and Dunne, *Margins of Reality.*

41. Jahn and Dunne, *Margins of Reality,* p. 58.

42. B. Alan Wallace, *The Taboo of Subjectivity: Toward a New Science of Consciousness* (Oxford: Oxford University Press, 2000), p. 143.

43. Wallace, *The Taboo of Subjectivity,* p. 4.

11. NAZISM AND ANCESTRAL GERMAN MEMORIES

1. Quoted by Otto Strasser, *Hitler and I,* trans. Gwenda David and Eric Mosbacher (Boston: Houghton Mifflin Co., 1940), p. 67.

2. Peter Padfield, *Himmler: Reichsführer-SS* (New York: Henry Holt and Co., 1990), p. 19.

3. Trevor Ravenscroft, *The Spear of Destiny: The Occult Power behind the Spear which Pierced the Side of Christ* (New York: G. P. Putnam's Sons, 1973).

4. Some of the possibilities do not figure into Nazism except in an incidental way. During Ronald Reagan's presidency his wife consulted an astrologer, but that had no conceivable bearing on his politics (even if one critic did accuse him of "voodoo economics").

5. Adolf Hitler, *Mein Kampf,* trans. Ralph Mannheim (Boston: Houghton Mifflin Co., 1971), p. 14.

6. Hermann Rauschning, *The Voice of Destruction* (New York: G. P. Putnam's Sons, 1940), p. 232 (Rauschning's record of his conversations with Hitler during the early 1930s).

7. Hitler, *Mein Kampf,* p. 214.

8. Joachim C. Fest, *Hitler,* trans. Richard and Clara Winston (New York: Harcourt Brace Jovanovich, 1973), p. 207.

9. August Kubizek, *Adolf Hitler, mein Jugendfreund* (Graz and Göttingen, 1953), pp. 140ff. Quoted in Fest, *Hitler,* pp. 22–23. The opera was *Rienzi,* the story of a man who sought to re-establish the Roman Empire, a non-Teutonic realm. Interestingly, Hitler identified Northern Europeans as the master race while drawing much of his inspiration from the southern latitudes. Michael H. Kater writes: "It remains one of the curiosities of the Third Reich that Adolf Hitler, a former applicant to the Building Academy [*Bauakademie*] and freelance architect, could never muster much enthusiasm for the [ancient] Germans because they . . . grubbed out their existence in the boggy North in unimpressive huts. The Greeks and Romans in the sunny South, by contrast, founded their imperialistic culture on buildings heroically constructed out of stone." *Das "Ahnenerbe" der SS: 1935–1945* (Stuttgart: Deutsche Verlags-Anstalt, 1974), pp. 23–24. (This is the personal translation of the authors.) In *Mein Kampf,* Hitler insists that the ancient Germans were not barbarians. However, "[o]nly the harshness of their northern

homeland forced them into circumstances which thwarted the development of their creative forces. If . . . they had come to the more favorable regions of the south, and if the material provided by lower peoples had given them their first technical implements, the culture-creating ability slumbering within them would have grown into radiant bloom just as happened, for example, with the Greeks" (p. 393).

10. Hitler, *Mein Kampf,* pp. 215–216, 219, 255.

11. Fest, *Hitler,* p. 324.

12. For references to ectoplasm or "magnetic fluid," see Louis Pauwels and Jacques Bergier, *Morning of the Magicians,* trans. Rollo Myers (New York: Stein and Day, 1983), p. 194; "Office of Strategic Service: Hitler Source Book: Hitler's Wonderland by Michael Fry," *The Nizkor Project,* p. 1, <http://www.nizkor.org/hweb/people/h/hitler-adolf/oss-papers/text/oss-sb-fry.html>, accessed Feb. 14, 2002.

13. Strasser, *Hitler and I,* p. 65.

14. Fest, *Hitler,* 327.

15. Strasser, *Hitler and I,* pp. 62–66.

16. Strasser, *Hitler and I,* p. 64, and Otto Strasser, *Mein Kampf: Eine Politische Autobiografie* (Frankfurt am Main: Streit-Zeit Bücher, 1969), p. 35.

17. Fest, *Hitler,* p. 325.

18. Nevile Henderson, *Failure of a Mission: Berlin 1937–1939* (New York: G. P. Putnam's Sons, 1940), pp. 66–67.

19. Alan Bullock, *Hitler: A Study in Tyranny,* rev. ed. (New York: Harper Torchbooks, 1962), p. 379. See also Fest, *Hitler,* pp. 422–423.

20. After noting that as early as the late 1920s Hitler reduced the number of his speaking engagements, Fest writes: "There are indications that at this period he began to see the advantages of living in semidivine remoteness" (*Hitler,* p. 254).

21. Fest writes: "In March, 1945, when the Red Army was at the gates of Berlin, he had the plans for the rebuilding of Linz [an Austrian city where he spent much of his youth] brought to him in the bunker under the chancellory and for a long time stood dreamily over them" (*Hitler,* p. 23). This was no more than two months before his suicide.

22. Quoted in Ken Anderson, *Hitler and the Occult* (Amherst, N.Y.: Prometheus Books, 1995), p. 138.

23. Fest, *Hitler,* p. 49.

24. Hitler, *Mein Kampf,* p. 123.

25. The material on List and Lanz is taken primarily from Nicholas Goodrick-Clarke, *The Occult Roots of Nazism: The Ariosophists of Austria and Germany, 1890–1935* (Wellingborough, U.K.: Aquarian Press, 1985).

26. According to Hitler, "Blood sin and desecration of the race are the original sin in this world." *Mein Kampf,* p. 249.

27. Goodrick-Clarke, *The Occult Roots of Nazism,* p. 94.

28. Goodrick-Clarke, *The Occult Roots of Nazism,* pp. 94–95.

29. Goodrick-Clarke, *The Occult Roots of Nazism,* p. 95.

30. Goodrick-Clarke, *The Occult Roots of Nazism,* p. 97.

31. Hermann Rauschning, *The Voice of Destruction,* pp. 246–247.

32. Much of the material on Himmler is taken from Peter Padfield, *Himmler: Reichsführer-SS.*

33. Friedrich Nietzsche, *Beyond Good and Evil,* trans. Walter Kaufmann (New York: Vintage Books, 1966), p. 229.

34. Hitler, *Mein Kampf*, p. 296.
35. Kater, *Das "Ahnenerbe" der SS*, p. 19.
36. Padfield, *Himmler*, p. 101.
37. He also envisioned breeding facilities where men and women would be paired according to physical characteristics for no other purpose than procreating racially ideal children. See Goodrick-Clarke, *The Occult Roots of Nazism*, p. 97.
38. Jean-Michel Angebert, *The Occult and the Third Reich: The Mystical Origins of Nazism and the Search for the Holy Grail*, trans. Lewis A. M. Sumberg (New York: Macmillan, 1974), p. xi.
39. Quoted in Padfield, *Himmler*, p. 139.
40. Padfield, *Himmler*.

12. UFOs AND ALIEN ABDUCTIONS

1. For the late nineteenth century, see Daniel Cohen, *The Great Airship Mystery: A UFO of the 1890s* (East Rutherford, N.J.: Putnam Publishers, 1981).
2. For an excellent source on pre-1980s UFOs, see Ronald Story, *The Encyclopedia of UFOs* (Garden City, N.Y.: Double Day, 1980). The Arnold story is rehearsed on pages 25–26.
3. Julie Shuster, "Roswell Gears Up for 2001 UFO Festival," *Albuquerque Journal*, July 4, 2001. Available online at <http://www.abqjournal.com/roswell/pmufo07-04-01.htm>, accessed Dec. 11, 2001.
4. Story, *The Encyclopedia of UFOs*, pp. 220–221.
5. See J. Allen Hynek, *The UFO Experience: A Scientific Enquiry* (New York: Ballantine, 1972), pp. 37–186.
6. Edward U. Condon, dir., and Daniel S. Glymour, ed., *Final Report of the Scientific Study of Unidentified Flying Objects: Conducted by the University of Colorado under Contract to the United States Air Force* (New York: E. P. Dutton & Co., 1969).
7. See Hynek, *The UFO Experience*, pp. 217–241.
8. Jacques Vallee, *Passport to Magonia: From Folklore to Flying Saucers* (Chicago: Henry Regnery Co., 1969), p. 154.
9. Hynek, *The UFO Experience*, pp. 87–90.
10. Condon and Glymour, *Final Report*, pp. 141–143.
11. Story, *The Encyclopedia of UFOs*, pp. 2–4.
12. For the most complete account of this case, see John Fuller, *The Interrupted Journey: Two Lost Hours "Aboard a Flying Saucer"* (New York: Dial Press, 1966). Abbreviated accounts may be found in Hynek, *The UFO Experience*, pp. 178–184; John Rimmer, "Evaluating the Abductee Experience," in *Phenomenon: Forty Years of Flying Saucers* (New York: Avon, 1988), pp. 157–159; and Philip Klass, *UFOs—Identified* (New York: Random House, 1968), pp. 226–248.
13. Story, *The Encyclopedia of UFOs*, p. 174.
14. Jerome Clark, "The Extraterrestrial Hypothesis in the Early UFO Age," in *UFOs and Abductions: Challenging the Borders of Knowledge*, ed. David M. Jacobs (Lawrence: University Press of Kansas, 2000), pp. 122–140.
15. Of the ten contributors to *UFOs and Abductions: Challenging the Borders of Knowledge* (2000), a volume affirming the existence of UFOs and aliens, six are professors of psychology (or psychiatry), sociology, or folklore, one is an artist, one is a historian, one is a "UFO researcher and writer," and one is a professor of "natural science."

This cross section, of course, is not random but it does seem to reflect the growing emphasis on the social sciences in UFO and alien abduction studies.

16. Budd Hopkins, *Intruders: The Incredible Visitations at Copley Woods* (New York: Random House, 1987), pp. 1–175. Davis's case constitutes more than half the book.

17. Philip Klass, *UFO Abductions: A Dangerous Game* (Buffalo, N.Y.: Prometheus Books, 1988), p. 127.

18. Douglas E. Winter, *Faces of Fear: Encounters with the Creators of Modern Horror* (New York: Berkeley Books, 1985), p. 193.

19. Winter, *Faces of Fear*, pp. 201–202; John E. Mack, *Passport to the Cosmos: Human Transformation and Alien Encounters* (New York: Crown Publishers, 1999), p. 17.

20. Winter, *Faces of Fear*, pp. 192–193; Klass, *UFO Abductions*, p. 128.

21. Whitley Strieber, *Communion: A True Story* (New York: Beech Tree Books, 1987), p. 21. Strieber's screen memories are odd, for normally screen memories replace horrible events with more routine, less traumatic recollections.

22. Philip Klass, *UFO Abductions*, pp. 128–129. Incredibly, the freelance journalist Ed Conroy believes that since Strieber called his own account into question, his obvious contradiction should not be seen as important in evaluating his testimony concerning his alleged abductions. But if we cannot trust his stories when we can check his facts, should we trust him when we cannot check his facts? See Conroy's highly sympathetic treatment of Strieber in *Report on Communion: An Independent Investigation of and Commentary on Whitley Strieber's Communion* (New York: William Morrow and Co., 1989), pp. 70–77.

23. Details of the story that follows in the text are culled from *Communion*.

24. Conroy, *Report on Communion*, p. 150.

25. In Strieber, *Communion*, p. 296.

26. Bill Ellis, "UFOs Are Hallucinations," in *Paranormal Phenomena*, ed. Terry O'Neill (San Diego: Greenhaven Press, 1991), p. 63.

27. Quoted in Jacques Vallee, *Revelations: Alien Contact and Human Deception*, rev. ed. (New York: Ballantine Books, 1992), p. 290.

28. Vallee, *Revelations*, pp. 290, 272–273.

29. Arthur C. Clarke suggests this possibility, along with others, in *Report on Planet Three and Other Speculations* (New York: Harper & Row, 1972), pp. 93–107.

30. C. G. Jung, "Flying Saucers: A Modern Myth of Things Seen in the Skies," in *Civilization in Transition*, trans. R. F. C. Hull (Princeton, N.J.: Princeton University Press, 1964), p. 328.

31. Jung, "Flying Saucers: A Modern Myth," pp. 327–328.

32. Arthur C. Clarke, *Report on Planet Three and Other Speculations* (New York: Harper & Row, 1972), p. 139.

33. C. G. Jung, "Flying Saucers: A Modern Myth," pp. 347, 411–412.

34. Jacques Vallee, *Passport to Magonia*, p. 105.

35. Vallee, *Passport to Magonia*, p. 22.

36. Vallee, *Passport to Magonia*, p. 150.

37. Vallee, *Passport to Magonia*, p. vii.

38. Vallee, *Passport to Magonia*, pp. 57, 153, 129.

39. Jacques Vallee, *Messengers of Deception: UFO Contacts and Cults* (New York: Bantam Books, 1980).

40. Vallee, *Revelations*, pp. 246–278.

41. See Mack, *Passport to the Cosmos*, p. 202.

42. John E. Mack, *Abduction: Human Encounters with Aliens* (New York: Scribner's, 1994), p. 422.

43. Mack, *Passport to the Cosmos*, pp. 50–51.

44. Mack, *Passport to the Cosmos*, p. 8.

45. Mack, *Passport to the Cosmos*, p. 9.

46. Mack, *Passport to the Cosmos*, p. 54. Here Mack is relying in part on the work of Michael Grosso.

13. GNOSTICISM, OLD AND NEW

1. C. G. Jung, *Memories, Dreams, Reflections*, ed. Aniela Jaffé, trans. Richard and Clara Winston (New York: Vintage Books, 1963), p. 162.

2. Quoted in Elaine Pagels, *The Gnostic Gospels* (New York: Random House, 1979), p. xix.

3. Hans Jonas, *The Gnostic Religion: The Message of the Alien God and the Beginnings of Christianity*, 2nd ed. revised (Boston: Beacon Press, 1963), p. 122.

4. Quoted in Pagels, *The Gnostic Gospels*, pp. xix–xx.

5. Malcolm Barber, *The Cathars: Dualist Heretics in Languedoc in the High Middle Ages* (Harlow, England: Longman, 2000), p. 95.

6. See, e.g., Luke 24:36–39.

7. These beliefs were not necessarily subscribed to by all Cathars. See Barber, *The Cathars*, pp. 90–91.

8. The writer is Simone Weil. See Barber, *The Cathars*, pp. 203–225.

9. All of these theories, but particularly the last, are favorably discussed in Marilyn Hopkins, Graham Simmans, and Tim Wallace-Murphy, *Rex Deus: The True Mystery of Rennes-le-Château and the Dynasty of Jesus* (Shaftesbury, Dorsey: Element, 2000). See also Michael Baigent, Richard Leigh, and Henry Lincoln, *Holy Blood, Holy Grail* (New York: Delacorte Press, 1982).

10. Steven C. Bullock, *Revolutionary Brotherhood: Freemasonry and the Transformation of the American Social Order, 1730–1840* (Chapel Hill: University of North Carolina Press, 1996), p. 10. Bullock's book informs much of our discussion of Freemasonry.

11. Bullock, *Revolutionary Brotherhood*, p. 254.

12. Bullock, *Revolutionary Brotherhood*.

13. See, for example, Khei X, *Rosicrucian Fundamentals: An Exposition of the Rosicrucian Synthesis of Religion, Science and Philosophy* (New York: Flame Press at the Sign of the Rose Bush, 1920), pp. 317–350.

14. Rudolf Steiner, *The Theosophy of the Rosicrucians* (London: Rudolf Steiner Publishing Co., 1953), p. 7.

15. Frances Yates, *The Rosicrucian Enlightenment* (Routledge & Kegan Paul, 1972), p. 232.

16. R. A. Gilbert, *The Golden Dawn: Twilight of the Magicians* (Wellingborough, U.K.: Aquarian Press, 1983), p. 28.

17. Gilbert, *The Golden Dawn*, p. 28.

18. Gilbert, *The Golden Dawn*, p. 38.

19. Gilbert, *The Golden Dawn*, pp. 46–47.

20. Quoted in Gilbert, *The Golden Dawn*, p. 59.

21. Jonas, *The Gnostic Religion*, p. 328.

22. Richard Dawkins, *River Out of Eden* (New York: Basic Books, 1995), p. 133.

23. Blaise Pascal, *The Thoughts of Blaise Pascal* (Garden City, N.Y.: Dolphin Books, n.d.), p. 77.

24. Quoted in Jos Van Meurs, "William Blake and His Gnostic Myths," *Gnosis and Hermeticism: From Antiquity to Modern Times,* eds. Roelof van den Broek and Wouter J. Hanegraaff (Albany: SUNY Press, 1998), pp. 275–276.

25. Quoted in Meurs, "William Blake and His Gnostic Myths," p. 282.

26. William Blake, *The Letters of William Blake,* ed. Geoffrey Keynes (Cambridge, Mass.: Harvard University Press, 1968), p. 62. Spelling normalized.

27. Alfred Kazin, ed., *The Portable Blake* (New York: Viking Press, 1968), p. 475.

28. Kazin, *The Portable Blake,* p. 142.

29. Quoted in Clifford A. Pickover, *Computers and the Imagination: Visual Adventures Beyond the Edge* (New York: St. Martin's Press, 1991), frontispiece.

30. Johann Wolfgang von Goethe, *Theory of Colours,* trans. Charles Lock Eastlake (London: Frank Cass & Co., 1967), p. 300.

31. Goethe quoted in Walter Heitler, "Goethean Science," *Goethe's Way of Science: A Phenomenology of Nature,* eds. David Seamon and Arthur Zajonc (Albany: SUNY Press, 1998), p. 59.

32. Johann Wolfgang von Goethe, *Faust,* Part 1, Scene 1, trans. Bayard Taylor (New York: Modern Library, 1912), p. 15.

33. James M. Robinson, *The Nag Hammadi Library in English* (New York: Harper & Row, 1977), p. 1. The volume is a compilation of early Christian Gnostic texts.

34. Gilles Quispel, "Gnosis and Psychology," in Robert A. Segal, June Singer, and Murray Stein, eds., *The Allure of Gnosticism: The Gnostic Experience in Jungian Psychology and Contemporary Culture* (Chicago: Open Court, 1995), pp. 11–12.

35. Jung, *Memories, Dreams, Reflections,* p. 205.

36. Carl Jung, *Aion, Collected Works,* vol. 9, 2 (Princeton, N.J.: Princeton University Press, 1959), p. 41.

37. Carl Jung, *Psychology and the East,* trans. R. F. C. Hull (Princeton, N.J.: Princeton University Press, 1978), p. 184.

38. Jung, *Memories, Dreams, Reflections,* p. 276.

39. Jung, *Memories, Dreams, Reflections,* p. 277.

40. Carl Jung, "The Structure and Dynamics of the Self," *Collected Works* 9.2:222.

41. Robert A. Segal, "Jung's Fascination with Gnosticism," in Segal, Singer, and Stein, eds., *The Allure of Gnosticism,* pp. 26–38.

14. NDEs, NEW AGE, AND NEW PHYSICS

1. Franz Hartmann, *The Life and the Doctrines of Paracelsus,* 4th ed. (New York: Macoy Publishing and Masonic Supply Co., 1945), pp. x–xi.

2. Plato, *The Republic,* Book 10. (Trans. Benjamin Jowett [New York: Vintage Books, 1991], pp. 388–397.)

3. William Wordsworth, "Intimations of Immortality from Recollections of Early Childhood," *The Poetical Works of Wordsworth* (Boston: Houghton Mifflin, 1982), p. 354.

4. Quoted in Gregory, Bishop of Tours, *History of the Franks,* trans. Ernest Brehaut (New York: Norton, 1979), Book 7, pp. 170–171. For an excellent, insightful work on both medieval and modern NDEs, see Carol Zaleski, *Otherworld Journeys: Accounts of*

Near-Death Experience in Medieval and Modern Times (New York: Oxford University Press, 1987).

5. Gregory, *History of the Franks*, pp. 170–171.

6. Gregory, *History of the Franks*, pp. 170–171.

7. In view of the anecdotal nature of his research, Moody has recommended the following books as treating the subject more rigorously: Kenneth Ring, *Life at Death: A Scientific Investigation of the Near-Death Experience* (New York: Coward, McCann, and Geoghegan, 1980), and Michael B. Sabom, *Recollections of Death: A Medical Investigation* (New York: Harper & Row, 1982).

8. See Raymond Moody, *Life after Life: The Investigation of a Phenomenon—Survival of Bodily Death* (New York: Walker, 1975), chap. 2.

9. See Bruce Greyson and Nancy Evans Bush, "Distressing Near-Death Experiences," *Psychiatry: Interpersonal and Biological Processes*, vol. 55 (Feb. 1992), pp. 95–111.

10. See Dina Ingber, "Visions of an Afterlife," *Science Digest* (Jan./Feb. 1981), pp. 96–97.

11. Pim van Lommel, Ruud van Wees, Vincent Meyers, and Ingrid Elfferich, "Near-Death Experience in Survivors of Cardiac Arrest: A Prospective Study in the Netherlands," *The Lancet*, vol. 358 (Dec. 15, 2001), pp. 2039–2045.

12. Much of this discussion is based on J. Gordon Melton, Jerome Clark, and Aidan Kelly, *New Age Almanac* (New York: Visible Ink Press, 1991), especially pages 301–306 and the beginnings of each of the other chapters. This is an exceptional source for understanding New Age views. Because the authors are refreshingly even-handed in their approach, readers may enjoy a brief respite from the polemics that characterize many other treatments.

13. As quoted in Ted Schultz, "Voices from Beyond: The Age-Old Mystery of Channeling," in *The Fringes of Reason: A Whole Earth Catalog* (New York: Harmony Books, 1989), p. 63.

14. "John," a channeled entity, told Shirley MacLaine, "*You* are God. *You* know you are Divine. But you must continually remember your Divinity and, most important, act accordingly." See *Out on a Limb* (New York: Bantam Books, 1983), p. 210.

15. For an important earlier work detailing New Age changes, see Marilyn Ferguson, *The Aquarian Conspiracy: Personal and Social Transformation in the 1980s* (Los Angeles: J.P. Tarcher, 1980).

16. Melton et al., *New Age Almanac*, p. 304.

17. MacLaine, *Out on a Limb*, p. 205.

18. Donald F. Glut [based on a story by George Lucas], *The Empire Strikes Back* (New York: Ballantine Books, 1980), p. 123.

19. See *Spirit Summonings* (Alexandria, Va.: Time-Life Books [n.d.]), pp. 130–153, and the *New Age Almanac*, pp. 37–101.

20. Martin Gardner, *Fads and Fallacies in the Name of Science (formerly published under the title "In the Name of Science")* (New York: Dover, 1957), pp. 315–320. The best-selling book by the hypnotist Morey Bernstein, who had originally regressed Tighe, did not, of course, mention anything about Mrs. Corkell. Even in a later edition it is brushed off as insignificant. Bernstein, *The Search for Bridey Murphy, with New Material by William J. Barker*, new ed. (New York: Doubleday, 1965). Like the earlier Spiritualists, the science fiction author Robert Heinlein had "predicted that before the year 2001 the survival of the soul after death would be demonstrated with 'scientific

rigor' by following the path broken by Bernstein." Gardner, *Fads and Fallacies,* p. 316, who cites *Amazing Stories* (April 1956).

21. Helen Wambach, *Life before Life* (New York: Bantam Books, 1979), p. 23.

22. Raymond Y. Chiao, Paul G. Kwiat, and Aephraim M. Steinberg, "Faster than Light?" *Scientific American* 269, no. 2 (1993): 52–60.

23. George Basalla, William Coleman, and Robert H. Kargon, eds., *Victorian Science: A Self-Portrait from the Presidential Addresses of the British Association for the Advancement of Science* (Garden City, N.Y.: Anchor Books, 1970), p. 83.

24. Lee Smolin, *Three Roads to Quantum Gravity* (New York: Basic Books, 2001), pp. 63–64.

25. James Jeans, *The Mysterious Universe* (New York: Macmillan Co., 1930), p. 158.

26. See, e.g., Fritjof Capra, *The Tao of Physics: An Exploration of the Parallels between Modern Physics and Eastern Mysticism* (London: Wildwood House, 1975).

27. Arthur Schopenhauer, *The World as Will and Idea,* trans. R. B. Haldane and J. Kemp, (London: Trüber & Co., 1886), vol. III, p. 283.

28. Richard Lewontin, "Billions and Billions of Demons," *The New York Review of Books,* Jan. 9, 1997, p. 31.

ILLUSTRATION CREDITS

Frontispiece. *The Alchemist in Search of the Philosopher's Stone* (1771–1775), by Joseph Wright. Courtesy the Derby Museum and Art Gallery.

1. From the standard version of *The Egyptian Book of the Dead* as found in the Ancient Studies Library, the Harold B. Lee Library at Brigham Young University.

2. From *The Book of the Dead: Facsimile of the Papyrus of Ani in the British Museum* (London: British Museum, 1890), plate 17. Lilly Library, Indiana University.

3. From *The Book of the Dead: Facsimile of the Papyrus of Ani in the British Museum* (London: British Museum, 1890), plate 3. Lilly Library, Indiana University.

4. Used by permission of the Griffith Institute, Ashmolean Museum, Oxford, England.

5. From Robert Fludd's *Utriusque cosmic maioris* (Oppenhemii: de Bry, 1617–1624), title page. Lilly Library, Indiana University.

6. From Daniel Defoe's *A Compleat System of Magick* (London: J. Clarke, 1729), frontispiece. Lilly Library, Indiana University.

7. From Jean Jacques Boissard's *Tractatus posthumus Jani Jacobi Boissardi Vesvuntini De Divinatione & Magicis Praestigiis* (Oppenhemii: Galleri [1611]), p. 140. Lilly Library, Indiana University.

8. From Petrarca's *Von der Artzney bayder Gluck*, leaf III verso. Lilly Library, Indiana University.

9. From the Weldon Mss., Lilly Library, Manuscripts Dept., Indiana University.

10. Public domain.

11. From Salomon Trissmosin's [pseudo.] *Aureum Vellus* (Rorschach am Bodensee, 1598–1604), p. 37. Lilly Library, Indiana University.

12. From Salomon Trissmosin's [pseudo.] *Aureum Vellus* (Rorschach am Bodensee, 1598–1604), p. 27. Lilly Library, Indiana University.

13. From Olaus Magnus's *Historia de Gentibus Septentrionales* (Rome, 1555), p. 114. Lilly Library, Indiana University.

14. From Joannes de Sacro Bosco's *Sphera volgare*... (Venetia: B. Zanetti, 1537), title page, verso. Lilly Library, Indiana University.

15. From Fludd's *Utriusque cosmic maioris* (Oppenhemii: de Bry, 1617–1624), p. 9. Lilly Library, Indiana University.

16. From Paul Carus's *The History of the Devil and the Idea of Evil* (Chicago: Open Court Publ., 1900), p. 158. Lilly Library, Indiana University.

17. From Paul Carus's *The History of the Devil and the Idea of Evil* (Chicago: Open Court Publ., 1900), pp. 462–463. Lilly Library, Indiana University.

18. From Olaus Magnus's *Historia de Gentibus Septentrionales* (Rome, 1555), p. 127. Lilly Library, Indiana University.

19. From Paul Carus's *The History of the Devil and the Idea of Evil* (Chicago: Open Court Publ., 1900), p. 141. Lilly Library, Indiana University.

20. From *Art Journal* (London, 1861), p. 325. Fine Arts Library, Indiana University.

21. From Gaspar Schott's *P. Gasparis Schotti . . . physica curiosa, sive mirabilia naturae et artis*, 3rd ed. (Herbipoli: J. Hertz, 1697), plate 17, opposite p. 614. Lilly Library, Indiana University.

22. From John Ashton's *The Devil in Britain and America* ([n.p.]: Ward & Downey, 1896), p. 169. Lilly Library, Indiana University.

23. From Olaus Magnus's *Historia de Gentibus Septentrionales* (Rome, 1555), p. 117. Lilly Library, Indiana University.

24. From Urich Molitor de Constantia's *De Laniis [i.e., lamiis] et phitonicis [i.e., pithonicis] mulieribus Teutonice unholden vel hexen* ([Reutlingen: Johan Otmar, not before 10 Jan. 1489]). Lilly Library, Indiana University.

25. From Paul Regnard's *Sorcellerie Magnétisme, Morphinisme Délire des Grandeurs* (Paris: E. Plon, Nourrit et Cie., 1887), p. 30. General Collections, Indiana University.

26. From Urich Molitor de Constantia's *De Laniis [i.e., lamiis] et phitonicis [i.e., pithonicis] mulieribus Teutonice unholden vel hexen* ([Reutlingen: Johan Otmar, not before 10 Jan. 1489]). Lilly Library, Indiana University.

27. From John Ashton's *The Devil in Britain and America* ([n.p.]: Ward & Downey, 1896), p. 161. Lilly Library, Indiana University.

28. From *[Austria. Laws] Constitutio Criminalis Theresiana* (Wien: J. T. Edlen von Trattnern, 1769), plates at end: XLV. Lilly Library, Indiana University.

29. From Paul Regnard's *Sorcellerie Magnétisme, Morphinisme Délire des Grandeurs* (Paris: E. Plon, Nourrit et Cie., 1887), p. 228. General Collections, Indiana University.

30. From William Windsor's *Loma: Citizen of Venus* (St. Paul, Minn.: Windsor & Lewis, 1897), p. 420. Lilly Library, Indiana University.

31. From Henry Ridgely Evans's *Hours with the Ghosts, or Nineteenth Century Witchcraft* (Chicago: Laird & Lee, circa 1897), pp. 158–159. University of Minnesota Library.

32. From Theodore Flournoy's *Spiritism and Psychology*, translated by Hereward Carrington (New York: Harper & Brothers, 1911), plate opposite p. 270. General Collections, Indiana University.

33. From Annie Besant's *Annie Besant: An Autobiography* (London: T. Fisher Unwin, 1893), p. 342. General Collections, Indiana University.

ILLUSTRATION CREDITS

34. Illustrated by H. R. Hammond, in *Amazing* (May 1940), back cover. Lilly Library, Indiana University.

35. From Besant's *Annie Besant: An Autobiography* (London: T. Fisher Unwin, 1893), frontispiece. General Collections, Indiana University.

36. © 2003, Marc-Charles Ingerson. For any future illustration usage, contact said illustrator at mci@byu.edu.

37. Courtesy Duke University Archives.

38. From the Sinclair Mss., under Mental Radio, Misc. Experiments and Photographs, #2. Manuscripts Department, Lilly Library, Indiana University.

39. Courtesy Duke University Archives.

40. Courtesy Duke University Archives.

41. Courtesy Bayerische StaatsBibliothek München.

42. From Frank R. Paul's cover illustration for *Science Wonder Stories*, Nov. 1929. Lilly Library, Indiana University.

43. Illustration of H. G. Wells's *War of the Worlds*. Frank R. Paul's cover illustration for *Amazing Stories* (Aug. 1927). Lilly Library, Indiana University.

44. From H. G. Wells's "War of the Worlds," *Pearson's Magazine* 3 (1897), p. 609. General Collections, Indiana University.

45. From Frank R. Paul's cover illustration for *Amazing Stories Annual* 1, no. 1 (1927). Lilly Library, Indiana University.

47. Theolophilus Schweighardt, Speculum Sophicum Rhodo-Stauroticum, Das ist: Weilauffige Entdeckung des Collegii und axiomatum von sondern erleuchten Fraternitet Christi-Rosen Creutz, 1618.

48. William Blake's *Europe, a Prophecy* (facsimile). Frontispiece: Ancient of Days. The Metropolitan Museum of Art, Rogers Fund, 1930.

49. Illustration by William Blake, in Robert Blair's *The Grave, A Poem* (London: R. Ackermann, 1813). Lilly Library, Indiana University.

50. From Dante Alighieri's *Purgatory and Paradise*, translated by Henry Francis Cary and illustrated by Gustave Doré (Philadelphia: Henry Altemus [before 1883?]), plate 59. General Collections, Indiana University.

ILLUSTRATION CREDITS

INDEX

Cleopatra, 84
Clock, 10, 55; mechanical, 38; as a model of the cosmos, 14
Cloning animals, 59
Cohn, Norman, 152, 153
Cold War, 149, 274
Columbus, Christopher, 185
Communism, 149, 181
Computer, 86, 327
Condon, Dr. Edward, 277
Copernicus, 54, 97, 225, 239
Corelli, Marie, 31
Cosmic energy, 6
Cosmic harmony, 5, 95–97
Cosmology, 78; diverse, 230
Cosmos, 3, 11, 30, 290, 294, 304, 327; evolving, 224; filled with purpose, 44; map of, 27; material, 309; mechanical, 222; modern, 14; Newtonian model of, 302, 303; physical, 309; uncaring, 251
Coulomb, Emma, 213, 214
Crandon, Margery, 200, 205, 206, 240
Crookes, Sir William, 198, 199, 200
Crowley, Aleister, 8, 54, 67, 69, 261, 301
Crusaders: Catholic, 295; Christian, 56, 295
Culture, 318; ancient, 208; German, 268; Greek, 55; modern, 9, 10, 11; non-Western, 308; popular, 42; pre-modern, 12; Roman, 55; scientifically conditioned, 3; Western, 268, 307, 315
Curse, ancient Roman, 53

Da Vinci, Leonardo, 54, 111
Daemon. *See* Demons
Dalton, John, 84
Dante, 96, 200, 303, *317*
Darwin, Charles, 199, 214, 267
De Medici, Cosimo, 56
De Voragine, Jacobus, 135
Dead Sea Scrolls, 121
Demiurge, 291–293, 302
Democritus, 304
Demonic possession, 116, 124, *124*, 136, 344n66; the account of the Gadarene, 123
Demon(s), *50, 134, 137, 142*, 150, 151, *164, 167, 168;* in ancient Judaism, 123; in ancient Mesopotamia, 117; defenses against, 117, 118; and Greeks, 127; as matter of inference, 128. *See also* Incubus; Rabbinic demons
Descartes, René, 14, 59, 85, 239, 254, 257, 288; naturalistic view of nature, 55; on truth, 2
Determinism, 227, 253
Devil, 126, 134, 135, 137, 140, 156, 158, 159, 161–163, 177, 307. *See also* Demon(s); Satan
Devil's mark, 169, 170, 175, 356n109, 356–357n113

Digital root, 62, 63
Disease, 59, 116, 189, 337n21; Alzheimer's, 45; cancer, 149, 157; as demonic possession, 117; germ theory of, 131. *See also* Illness(es)
Divination, 88, *89*, 129, 150; the aim of, 88
Divine Comedy (Dante), *317*
Doctor(s): ancient Egyptian, 116; French, 187; spiritual, 157
Doe, Baby Jane, the case of, 61
Dominicans, 158, 159
Doyle, Arthur Conan, 193, 194, 200, 203–206, 240, 301, 321
Dracula, 115
Dudley, E. E., 206
Dunne, Brenda, 257

Eckhart, Meister, 283
Edwards, I. E. S., 15
Egypt, 6, 17, 22, 27, 29, 31, 72, 90, 100, 145, 147, 211, 226, 232, 233, 307
Egyptians. *See* Ancient Egypt(ians)
The Egyptian History of the Pyramids, 31
Einstein, Albert, 67, 128, 208, 222, 235, 236, 252, 257
Eisley, Loren, 9
Eleanor of Aquitaine, 140
Electricity, 96, 186, 187, 308
Electromagnetism, 34, 39, 95, 248, 250
Elements: Aristotelian, 224; four earthly, 94; periodic table of, 74; three fundamental, 75
Eliade, Mircea, 10, 12, 77, 86
Ellis, Bill, 285
Emerson, Ralph Waldo, 14
Empedocles, 75
Emperor Constantine, 151
Emperor Julian the Apostate, 133
Emperor Marcus Aurelius, 153
Emperor Nero, 152
Emperor Tiberius, 151
Enlightenment, 1, 156, 229, 231, 290, 294, 298, 309, 319, 320
Enneagram, 230, *231*
Entropy, law of, 33
Equinox: Autumnal, 103; Vernal, 103, 109
ESP phenomena, 185, 200, 237, 243, 247, 248
Essay on Man (Pope), 48
Ethiopic Apocalypse of Enoch, 122
Ethnography, 282
Eugenics, 267, 268
Euripides, 127
Eusebius, 153
Evolutionary theory, 199, 209, 214, 224, 267
Existentialism, 303
Exorcism(s), 115, 116, 120, 123–126, 138, 139; cosmic, 14; Islamic, 144; music, 121

Fairies, 140, 141, 286, 301
Fall, the, 266, 291, 294

Faust, 1, 49, 307
Fest, Joachim, 263
Fetscher, Iring, 59
Feyerabend, Paul, 288
Feynman, Richard, 255
Ficino, Marscilio, 56
Flint, Valerie, 42
Flying saucer(s), 271, 272, *273, 275,* 280, 282.
    See also UFOs
Fortune-telling, 63
Fourth Dimension, the, 233, 234
Fox, Margaret, Catherine, and Leah, 194–
    196, 200
Franciscans, 158
Frankfort, Henry and H. A., 12
Franklin, Benjamin, 186, 187
Fraser, J. T., 39
Fravashis, 120
Free Masonry, 266, 301. *See also* Freemasons
Free will, 143, 146, 192, 193. *See also* Auton-
    omy
Freemasons, 296, 297, 298
Freud, Sigmund, 240, 256
Frohock, Fred, 249

Galileo, 14, 40, 97, 208, 331n15; on impor-
    tance of understanding mathematics, 67
Gall, Franz-Josef, 190, 192
Galton, Francis, 267, 268
Gandhi, Mohandes K., 221
Gauquelin, Michel and Françoise, 108, 111
Gene(s), 45, 59, 114, 268
Geneticists, 327–328
Genie(s), 143. *See also* Jinn
Geometry, 67, 235; Euclidean, 222, 234;
    Greeks' penchant for, 65
Germs: demons and, 132; as ghosts, 116
Glanvill, Joseph, 180, 181
Global warming, 95
Gnosis, 290–294, 303, 307; and the occult, 4
Gnostic(ism), 58, 156, 290–294, 298, 308–310;
    ancient, 302, 303; contemporary, 307; early
    Christian, 291; new, 290; old, 290
Goebbels, Joseph, 264, 265
Goethe, Johann Wolfgang, 222, 223, 256,
    303, 304, 306, 307
The Golden Legend (de Voragine), 134
Golden scarab, 251
Grafton, Anthony, 88, 106
Gravity, 40, 41, 44, 86, 88, 96, 186, 187, 245,
    250, 251, 326
Great Beyond, 201, 204
Great Flood, 122
Great Pyramid, 6, 31, 33, 34
Great War, 263
Great Year, 109
Greece, 55, 71
Greek astrology, 99
Greek astronomy, 90

Greek philosophy, 58, 67
Greek Pythagoreans, 64
Greek(s), 8, 17, 43, 56, 69, 70, 75, 95, 113,
    119, 128, 129, 133, 150, 152, 254; ancient,
    20, 95, 106, 321; democratized astrology, 99
Greeley, Horace, 193
Griffin, David Ray, 240
Grimoires, 51
Gurdjieff, G. I., 225–233, 261, 283

Hadith, 143–145
Halloween, 149
Hamlet, 36
Hansen, Bert, 37–42
Harley, David, 137
Harmonic balance, 66
Hartmann, Franz, 35, 311
Harvey, William, 175
Heart: purity of, 37; as seat of intelligence, 23.
    See also Heart formula; Heart number;
    Heart surgery; Weighing of the Heart
Heart formula, 30
Heart number, 63
Heart surgery, 13
Heaven, ancient Egyptian concept of, 14
Hebrew alphabet, 68; cabalistic view as code,
    69–71
Hebrew(s), 69–71, 113. *See also* Jews
Heidegger, Martin, 20
Heisenberg, Werner, 67
Hermetic Order of the Golden Dawn, 298,
    301
Hermeticism, 293, 298
Herodotus, 8
Hess, Rudolf, 265
Hill, Barney and Betty, 280, 281
Himmler, Heinrich, 261, 265, 267, 269, 270,
    371n37
Hindu(ism), 224, 235, 308, 323
Hindus, 211, 214
Hinton, C. H., 235
Hitler, Adolf, 71, 218, 259, *260,* 261–269, 369–
    370n9, 370nn20,21,26
Hodgson, Richard, 207, 213
Holy Ghost/Spirit, 138, 309
Holy Grail, 270, 296
Holy Land, 296
Home, Daniel Dunglas, 203, 211, 212
Homer, 127
Hopkins, Budd, 282, 283, 288
Hopkins, Matthew, *168*
Horatio, 36
Hörbiger, Hans, Cosmic Ice theory, 263
Horoscopes, 100, 102, 107; a summary of,
    105. *See also* Astrology; Zodiac
Horus, 17, 19, 22, 25, 28, 29, 99
Houdini, Harry, 200, 203–205, 240, 321
Hugo, Victor, 200
Humankind, as center of universe, 56

Huxley, Aldous, 169
Huxley, Thomas, 11, 192
Hynek, J. Allen, 276, 277, 281, 285
Hypnosis, 7, 188, 189, 280–282, 284, 323, 324

Iblis, 145, 348n115, 349n118
Ibn al-Nadim, Muhammad ibn Ishaq, 144
Ichthys, 70, 109
Illness(es),189; demonic, 113, 115; encoded in body, 45; mental, 143, 356n112. *See also* Disease
Imagination, 37, 39, 42, 59, 77, 111, 126, 143, 287, 304; modern, 9; over-heated, 283; spiritual, 225; Western, 216
Imhof, Arthur, 38
Incantation, 52. *See also* Spells
Incubus, 140, *141;* nighttime incubi, 136. *See also* Demons
India, 209, 212–214, 219, 221, 224, 226, 232
Infinite, hope in the, 2
Inquisition, 39; Italian, 158; Spanish, 158, 178
Iridologist, 45
Isis, 17, *18,* 19, 23, 212
Islam, 119, 141, 143, 146, 147

Jackson, Shirley Case, 14
Jahn, Robert, 257
James, William, 183, 207, 237, 239, 245, 249, 250, 252, 257
Jeans, James, 255, 327
Jeffries, Anne, 141
Jerusalem, 120, 132, 226
Jesus Christ, 8, 17, 24, 56, 70, 82, 84, 95, 109, 123, *124,* 125, 138, 153, 159, 200, 270, 272, 291, 294, 296, 309
Jews, 69, 121, 152, 163, 205, 262, 263, 266, 268; ancient, 127, 128
Jinn, 112, 127, 141, 143–147, 346n89, 349n130, 350n136. *See also* Genie(s)
Joan of Arc, 158, 159
Jonas, Hans, 292, 302
Joseph, the biblical story of, 99
Josephus, 152
Judaism, 67, 119, 120; ancient, 123
Julius Caesar, 151, 207
Jung, Carl, 41, 240, 252–254, 256–258, 285, 290, 307–309

Ka, 20, 21, 23, 24, 29, 31
Karma, 209, 217–219, 224, 311, 365n18
Kater, Michael, 269
Keats, John, 222
Keller, Ray, 285
Kepler, Johannes, 5, 14, 40, 67, 97, 144
Khadija, 144
Kieckhefer, Richard, 40–41
King Ahab, 120
King David of Israel, 8, 121

King James, 170
King Philip IV, 296
King Richard the Lionheart, 84
King Saul, 120, 121
King Solomon, 121, 145
King Tutankhamen, 31, *32,* 33
Klein, Donald, 284
Knight, J. Z., 321
Knights Templar, 156, 157, 295–297
Knowledge: categories of, 5; as power, 71; for power, 47
Koestler, Arthur, 41
Kramer, Heinrich, 159–162, 173, 175
Kubizek, August, 263

Language, as a part of the miracle of creation, 61
Lanz von Liebenfels, Jorg, 266, 267
Last Supper, 270
Late Roman Empire, 151
Lavoisier, Antoine, 84, 186
Leadbeater, Charles, 219, 221, 224
Lear, Jonathan, 90
Lebensraum, 177
Lemurians, 215, *216,* 320, 322
Levack, Brian P., 150
Levi, Eliphas, 67
Lewis, C. S., 125
Lewontin, Richard, 327, 328
Library of Alexandria, 72
Life of Adam and Eve, 122
Life of Charlemagne (Einhard), 43
Lilith, 132, 133, 343n49
Locke, John, 85
Lombroso, Cesare, 202
London Medical Society, 189
Lucifer, *125,* 126. *See also* Satan

Maat, 29; the feather of, 30
Macbeth (Shakespeare), 43
Mack, John, 287, 288
MacLaine, Shirley, 321, 375n14
Macrobius, 92
Macrocosm/microcosm, 45, *46,* 47, 48, 72, 78, 96, 225, 309, 318
Magic, 23, 28, 34, 55, 58, 175, 293, 312; as technology, 37; ancient Greek, 131; black, 151, 302; ceremony, 52; circle, *50,* 52; definition of, 36–37; demonic, 40; Egyptian, 24; everyday or low, 49, 51–53; and experimental science, 60; Great Work of, 42; high or ritual, 49; imitative, 54; "love magic," 130, 150; magical link in, 54; meaning of, 42; natural, 37; over reason, 39; reclassified, 39; Renaissance, 209, 261; ritual, 51, 52; sympathetic, 54, 116; three major stages to ritual, 51; two cardinal principles of, 54; two major ways to practice, 49; two views of, 36;

INDEX

Magic (*continued*)
unnatural, 38–39; white, 151. *See also* Magician(s)

Magician(s), 4, 8, 36, *50, 56,* 59, 151, 158, 202, 261, 301, 349n130; aim to reach unity, 49; disbelief in opposites, 49; as first to experiment, 60; objective of, 36; power as ultimate goal of, 49, *58. See also* Agrippa, Cornelius; Crowley, Aleister; Nimrod; Trismegistus, Hermes

Magnet(ism), 96, 102, 186, 187

Magnus, Albertus, 53, 97

Magus, 37, 58, *58*

Maier, Michael, 81, 82

Major Arcana, 72, *73*

Maleficia, 155, *164*, 166, 175

Malleus Maleficarum (Kramer and Sprenger), 159–162, 170, 173, 176

Manifest Destiny, 177

Manilius, 45, 87, 90, 95, 105, 106

Mansfield, Katherine, 227

Mantell, Captain Thomas, 274, 276

Marduk, 117

Marquis de Puysegur, 188

Marxism, 262, 263, 268

Materia medica, 115

Materialism, 181, 234, 328; scientific, 199

Mathematics, 34, 65, 90, 250; algebra, 65; as key to unlocking secrets of nature, 55; as ladder to eternity, 92; Pythagorean view of, 64–67; technique in, 98

Mathers, MacGregor, 52, 301, 302

Mecca, 226

Medicine, 79, 113, 114, 186, 207, 268, 307, 316, 323; ancient, 114, 228; ancient Egyptian, 115; ancient healers in, 115; Islamic healer, 112, 113; Medieval Catholic, 140; Medieval Christians and, 106; Medieval theologians and, 136; Oriental, 228; and prayer recitations, 115

Medina, 144

Meetings with Remarkable Men (Gurdjieff), 226

Mein Kampf (Hitler), 262

Merlin, 140

Mesmer, Franz Anton, 185, 186–189

Mesmerism, 186–189, 196; fluid hypothesis, 186; founder (*see* Mesmer, Franz Anton); and magnetized water, 187, *188;* Mesmerists, 185

Mesopotamia, 31, 115, 118, 143, 145; ancient, 98, 116; demons of, 143

Metallurgy, 77

Metamorphoses, or The Golden Ass (Apulius), 151

Metropolitan Museum of Art, 33

Michelangelo, 54

Middle Ages, 37, 40, 75, 81, 135, 147, 150, 153, 156, 272, 286, 293, 296, 321; Early,

154, 262; European, 133; High, 136, 157; Late, 138, 157, 249

Milky Way, 92

Milton, 122

Mind, 87; affinity with cosmos, 47

Mind and matter, 239, 254–257, 286, 288, 325, 327

Mining, 147

Minor Arcana, 72

Misogyny, 173, 176

Modern civilization, 9; "As above, so below," 98, 102; "first is best," 12; Judeo-Christian, 2, 116; Judeo-Christian ideals, 74; Latin, 56, 297; Middle East, 56, 225; Near East, 143, 147, 296; Ottoman Empire, 147; progress, 5; Western, 2, 147, 182

Modern science, 11, 16, 38, 41, 47, 59, 61, 67, 70, 74, 86, 94, 97, 111, 126, 185, 209, 212, 223, 225, 234, 236, 239, 240, 249, 257, 287, 297, 302, 303, 325; biology, 45; social constructivist view of, 98; view of humanity, 35

Molecules, 146, 190

Monism, 20, 49; "all is one," 261, 320, 322; doctrine of unity, 51; oneness, 95, 97

Monoimus, 292

Montaigne, Michael, 181

Moody, Raymond, 315

Moses, 8, 56, 69

Mount Sinai, 69

Mozart, 187

Muhammad, 119, 143, 144, 145, 348n108

Mummies and/or mummification, 23, 24, 26, 27, 29, 31, 33, 114

Munich, Germany, 263

Muslim(s), 143, 146, 147, 296, 336n5

Mysticism, 45

Myth, 9

Names: meaning of, 61, 62; naming, *168;* power of, 52, 60

Nature, 87, 222, 223, 303, 306, 308, 325; for alchemists, 77; alive with supernatural forces, 14; beauty of, 222; as calendar, 10; as continuum, 48; cycle of, 29; and Egyptians, 10; and free will, 192; geometric rendering of, 65; and God as one, 8; as "holy open secret," 306; laws of, 40, 41, 44, 99, 127, 128; materialistic conceptions of, 181; in mechanical terms, 55; Mother, *76,* 77; organic alchemical view of, 86; phenomena of, 128; physical, 254, 256; processes of, 85; round of, 10, 12, 22; understanding of, 55; uniformity of, 239

Nazi(sm), 71, 259, 265, 267, 268. *See also* Himmler, Heinrich; Hitler, Adolf

Nazi death-camp workers, 61

NDEs. *See* Near-death experience(s)

Near-death experience(s), 4, 7, 185, 240, 288,

Psi phenomena, 41, 42, 237–241, *241*, *242*, 243, *243*, *244*, 245, 247–250, 254, 258
Psychiatric disorder, 112
Psychiatrist(s), 251, 280
Psychiatry, 251
Psychokinesis, 41, 238, 246, 247
Psychologist(s), 202, 205, 207, 237, 239, 309, 324
Psychology, 129, 228, 252, 254, 282
Psychotherapist, 284
Ptolemy, Claudius, 90, 92, *93*, 94, 97, 100, 105–107, 110
Pursel, Jack, 321
Pythagoras, 64, 233
Pythagoreans, 65, 66, 69, 95, 209, 224, 301; view of God, 67

Quantum discontinuity, 239
Quantum mechanics, 67, 257
Quantum physics, 9, 106, 252, 253, 255, 325
Queen Cleopatra, 19
Queen Elizabeth, 178
Queen Jezebel, 120
Queen of Sheba, 144
Queen Victoria, 193
Qur'an, 113, 143–146

Rabbinic demons, 131, 342n32
Rabbinic literature, 132
Rabbinic tradition, 113
Radiation, 200
Radioactivity, 267
Rahn, Otto, 270
Ramses II, 116
Rationalism, 182; Greek, 2
Reality: as ethical system, 31; theories of, 2
Reason, 183, 184; Age of, 184; scientific, 185
Rebirth, 82, 208, 218. *See also* Reincarnation
Red Sea, 69
Reductionism, 326
Reflexologist, 45
Reincarnation, 4, 209, 217, 218, 224, 294, 311, 312, 324. *See also* Rebirth
Relativism, 109
Relativity theory, 208, 228, 239, 252, 325; General Theory of Relativity, 67
Religion, 4, 40, 211, 212, 221, 234, 236, 321, 328; Aryan, 270; Eastern, 209, 212, 319; Native American, 319. *See also* Ancient Egypt(ians); Buddha/Buddhism; Calvinism; Catholic Church; Christianity; Hindu(ism); Islam; Judaism
Remy, Nicholas, 163, 176, 179
Renaissance, 37, 42, 47, 51, 54–56, 58, 59, 67, 68, 74, 75, 106, 126, 174, 183; magic, 6
Rhine, J. B., 206, 240, *241*, 243, *244*, 245–248
Roberts, Jane, 321
Rodegast, Pat, 321
Romans, 43, 44, 55, 109, 113, 118, 130, 131,

150–153, 272; and ancient Egyptian wisdom, 8
Rosenberg, Alfred, 267, 268
Rosenkreuz, Christian, 297, 298, *299*
Rosicrucian(ism), 266, 297, 298, *299*, *300*, 301
Roswell, New Mexico, 272, 274
Royal Society, 84, 181
Rumpelstiltskin, 52
Russell, Bertrand, 3, 65, 222

Sacrifice: animal, 52, 120; child, 120, 151; human, 52, 130, 152; infant, 150
St. Augustine, 133, 134
St. Jerome, 126
St. Lupus, 134
St. Norbert, 136
St. Patrick, 154
Salve, on weapon, 54
Salvius, 314
Sappho, 76
Sartre, Jean-Paul, 149
Satan, 119, 120, 122, 123, *125*, 126, 127, 131, 135, 136, 139, 149, 155, 158, 160, 162, 169, 293, 294, 302, 339–340n73, 347n97, 363n202; medieval, 140; Sabbat of, 157
Schaff, Philip, 156
Schopenhauer, Arthur, 327
Schrodinger, Erwin, 35, 257
Science, 4, 87, 88, 97, 147, 181, 183, 185–187, 193, 194, 196, 199, 202, 209, 211, 222, 225, 228, 234, 236, 239, 240, 246, 248, 250, 254, 257, 258, 264, 268, 284, 286–288, 302, 312, 325, 327; age of invention, 187; and alchemy, 85, 86; ancient, 92; authoritative, 7; biases, 9; classical, 326; conditions our thinking, 10; contemporary, 214, 222; as court of last appeal, 109; early practitioners of, 55; early-twentieth-century, 251; excessive rationalism of, 42; goal of, 1; and God, 92; human side of, 1; and ignorance, 14; and intellectual humility, 239; materialistic, 222, 223, 239, 252, 256, 257, 306, 327, 328; mind-matter dualism, 257; vs. myth, 20; naturalistic, 217; and nature, 15; Newtonian, 304, 306; objective, 16; and occult thesis, 3; and the past, 5; physical, 192; rational, 303; and replication, 243; rise and reason of, 180; traditional, 288; as universal yardstick, 108; H. G. Wells's image of, 1; Western, 319; and witchcraft, 180
Scientific Revolution, 6, 38, 39, 98, 113, 148, 180, 184, 189, 303
Scientist, playing God, 59
The Screwtape Letters (Lewis), 125
Séance, 196, *197*, 198, 199, 201–207, 240, 245, 288, 312, 321
Second law of thermodynamics, 3
The Secret Doctrine (Blavatsky), 212, 214, 215, 226, 266

Vatican, 138
Vesalius, Andrus, 55
Vietnam War, 149
Vincent of Beauvais, 136, 156
Von List, Guido, 266
Von Weizsacker, Carl Friedrich, 257
Voodoo: doll, 54; West Indian, 54

Wagner, Richard, 261, 265, 268, 270
Waldensians, 156
Waldo, Peter, 156
Wallace, B. Alan, 257
Wambach, Helen, 324, 325
War of the Worlds (Wells), *278*
Watergate, 259
Watson, John, 240
Webb, James, 230
Weighing of the Heart ceremony, 26, 29, *30,* 31
Wells, H. G., 2, *278;* image of science, 1
Wesley, John, 182
Wessecker, Louisa, 240
Westcott, W. Wynn, 298, 301, 302
Westfall, Richard S., 85, 86
Whitehead, A. N., 38, 222, 228
Whitman, Charles, 283
Whitman, Walt, 45, 193
William of Canterbury, 44
Wilson, John, 19
Winter, Douglas, 283
Wisdom, 211, 312, 319; Aboriginal, 321; ancient, 212; Asian, 228; coyote, 228; Egyptian, 8; magical, 301; Masonic, 297; occult, 298; Rosicrucian, 298; sacred, 221
Witchcraft, 153, 155–157, 159, 161, 162, 171, 173, 177, 178, 182; genesis of, 158; history of, 150
Witch(es), 137, 138, 149, 150, 155, 156, 159, 160, 161, 163, *164, 165,* 166, *167,* 174, 176, 181, 301; burnings of, 154, 160, 360–361n169, 361n170; concept of, 154, 352n27; dunking of, 170; European concept of, 150; evil, 151, 153; Greek, 150; plagues and diseases, 162; pricking of, 169, 170; Roman,

150; Swiss, 159; torture of, 157, 171, 177; trials of, 171, 175, 176, 178–180; white, 283
Witches' Sabbat, 158, 159, 163, 166, *166,* 174, 175, 176, 179, 180
Witch-hunts, 149, 150, 158, 160, 169, 171, *172,* 173, 175, 177, 179, 180, 359–360n159, 361nn171,173,175,176, 362n188; Great Scottish, 170
Wittgenstein, Ludwig, 288
Words, 336n15; hidden meaning, 63; power of, 61; and the world, 61
Wordsworth, William, 2, 128, 129, 314
World: categories of phenomena, 38, 39, 42; as machine, 55; material, 65
World Age, 109, 110
World War I, 261
World War II, 71, 257, 271, 272
World-Soul, 129
Worldview(s), 3, 7, 36, 88, 108, 111, 146, 181, 184, 209, 225; Aristotelian, 98; astrological, 109; earlier, 327; Egyptian, 9; magic, 42, 43, 45, 47, 49; mechanical, 184; modern, 240; modern scientific, 14, 287; nationalistic, 267; occult, 306; older, 44; racist, 269; scientific, 288

Xenocrates, 129, 130
X-rays, 200, 267

Yahweh, 52
Yates, Frances, 298
Yeats, W. B., 301

Zarathustra, 119
Zen, 7, 79, 283
Zener cards, 241, *243, 244*
Zeus, 92, 130
Zodiac, 100–103, 224; cardinal quadruplicity, 103; decans, 104–105; fixed quadruplicity, 103; mutable quadruplicity, 103; triplicities, 104; twelve houses, 104
Zohar, 132, 133
Zoroaster, 119
Zoroastrianism, 118–120; founder of, 119; good vs. evil in, 119

INDEX

DAN BURTON
IS ASSISTANT PROFESSOR
OF HISTORY AND POLITICAL
SCIENCE AT THE UNIVERSITY
OF NORTH ALABAMA.

DAVID GRANDY
IS ASSOCIATE PROFESSOR
OF PHILOSOPHY AT BRIGHAM
YOUNG UNIVERSITY.